CAMBRIDGE COMMONWEALTH SERIES

General Editor: Professor E.T. Stokes

The Scramble for Southern Africa, 1877–1895

CAMBRIDGE COMMONWEALTH SERIES

These monographs are published by the Press Syndicate of the University of Cambridge in association with the Managers of the Cambridge University Smuts Memorial Fund for the advancement of Commonwealth Studies.

The Scramble for
Southern Africa, 1877–1895

The politics of partition reappraised

D. M. SCHREUDER

CAMBRIDGE UNIVERSITY PRESS

Cambridge
London New York New Rochelle
Melbourne Sydney

Published by the Press Syndicate of the University of Cambridge
The Pitt Building, Trumpington Street, Cambridge CB2 1RP
32 East 57th Street, New York, NY 10022, USA
296 Beaconsfield Parade, Middle Park, Melbourne 3206, Australia

© Cambridge University Press 1980

First published 1980

Photoset and printed in Malta by Interprint Limited

Library of Congress Cataloguing in Publication Data
Schreuder, Deryck Marshall.
The scramble for southern Africa, 1877–1895.
   (Cambridge Commonwealth series)
Bibliography: p.
Includes index.
1. Africa, Southern-Colonization. 2. Africa,
Southern – History. 3. South Africa – History—1836–1909.
I. Title.
DT745 S36   325'.30968   78-58800
ISBN 0 521 20279 5

To Paddy – for three very special reasons

'A distinctively colonial or South African expansion was the policy of the politicians, financiers, and adventurers up to the failure of the Jameson Raid; reluctantly they sought the co-operation of British imperialism to aid them their absorbing aim hereafter will be to relegate British imperialism to what they conceive to be its proper place, that of an *ultima ratio* to stand in the far background while colonial imperialism manages the business and takes the profits. A South African federation of self-governing States will demand a political career of its own, and will insist upon its own brand of empire, not that of the British Government, in the control of the lower races in South Africa.'

J. A. Hobson, 'Imperialism: a study' (1902)

Contents

Abbreviations of sources cited

AYB	*Archives Year Book*, South Africa.
Bower MSS	Private papers of Sir Graham Bower; unpublished 'Memoir'.
BM	British Museum.
Br. P.	Private papers of Charles Brownlee, KCL, Durban.
CAD	Cape Archival Deposit, Cape Town.
CHBE	*Cambridge History of the British Empire.*
Ch. P.	Private papers of Joseph Chamberlain, Birmingham University.
Co. P.	Private papers of Bishop Colenso, KCL, Durban.
CO	Colonial Office official records, PRO, London.
DP	Private papers of 15th Earl of Derby, Knowsley Hall, Lancs.
Devon. P.	Private papers of the 8th Duke of Devonshire, (Lord Hartington), Chatsworth.
Dilke P.	Private papers and diaries of Sir Charles Dilke, BM, London.
DSAB	*Dictionary of South African Biography.*
FO	Foreign Office official papers, PRO, London.
GP	Private papers of William Ewart Gladstone, BM, London.
Gr. P.	Private papers of 2nd Earl Granville, PRO, London.
Grosse Politik	*Die Grosse Politik der Europäischen Kabinette, 1871–1914.*
HD	The private diaries of Sir Edward Hamilton, BM, London.
HP	Private papers of Jan Hofmeyr, SAL, Cape Town.
KCL	Killie Campbell Library, University of Natal, at Durban.
Lob. P.	Private papers of King Lobengula, NAR, Salisbury.
LQV	G. E. Buckle, (ed.), *The Letters of Queen Victoria*, 2nd ser. (London, 1928), vol. iii (1862–85).
Mack. P.	Private papers of Rev. John Mackenzie, Witwatersrand University Library, Johannesburg.
Ma. P.	Private papers of Edward Maund, Witwatersrand.

Mo. P.   Private papers of Rev. John Moffat, NAR, Salisbury.

MP   Private papers of John X. Merriman, SAL, Cape Town.

NAD   Natal Archival Deposit, Pietermaritzburg.

NAR   National Archives of Rhodesia, Salisbury.

NCMH   *New Cambridge Modern History.*

OHSA, II,   *Oxford History of South Africa*, (eds) M. Wilson and
                L. M. Thompson, vol. ii (Oxford, 1971).

PRO   Public Records Office, Chancery Lane, London.

Ramm   Agatha Ramm, (ed.), *The political correspondence of Mr
                Gladstone and Lord Granville, 1876–86*, 2 vols. (Oxford,
                1962).

RHL   Rhodes House Library, Oxford; Afr. MSS Collection.

Ri. P.   Private papers of Lord Ripon, BM, London.

RP   Private papers of Cecil John Rhodes, RHL, Oxford; and
                NAR, Salisbury.

SAL   South African Library, Cape Town.

Sh. P.   Private papers of Sir Theophilus Shepstone, NAD,
                Pietermaritzburg.

St. P.   Private papers of Sir Walter Stanford, University of
                Cape Town, Jagger Library.

SP   Private papers of the 3rd Marquis of Salisbury, Christ
                Church College, Oxford.

'Vindex'   (psued. of Rev. F. Verschoyle, ed.) *Cecil Rhodes, his political
                life and speeches, 1881–1900*, (London, 1900).

Preface

'I am tired of this mapping out of Africa at Berlin; without occupation, without development ... the gist of the South African Question lies in the extension of the Cape Colony to the Zambesi.'

Cecil John Rhodes in the Cape Assembly,
23 July 1888

The book offers a concise history of the Scramble for Southern Africa in the era of the New Imperialism. It is concerned with the two levels at which Rhodes discerned the politics of Partition to have operated, and of the ways in which they interacted: empire as a product of the international politics of Great Power rivalry; and expansion growing out of the local ambitions of white agencies already deeply involved in the conquest and exploitation of Africa south of the Zambesi. The work is a natural extension of my earlier investigation into the role of the Imperial Factor on the highveld in the early 1880s. Even more than that study in 'colonial home rule', his narrative trenches on the internal history of the societies of southern Africa. Yet it remains, in my mind at least, essentially an essay in 'empire and expansion', an exploration of the political phenomenon of 'imperialism' in the later nineteenth-century world.

The book covers the broad period from the annexation of the Transvaal in 1877 to the closing of the last strategic frontier by the British in 1895. Despite the apparent complexity of the narrative, reflecting the many factors and forces involved in the actual process of expansion, this work is still largely an 'overview', an attempt at synthesis and reappraisal. Regional and thematic studies are still much needed within certain aspects of the period of the Scramble for Southern Africa; I shall be content if this quintessential narrative, and its critical commentary, leads others to further investigations and closer analysis. I have been encouraged to sketch this general perspective by the vitality of the continuing debate on the New Imperialism, where the Southern African case has not always been canvassed or well developed, and also by the interested and often acute questions of my students.

I have tried hard not to moralise about either imperialism in general or about the pattern of conquest in South Africa in particular. Yet it is also hard to deny the truth of Joseph Conrad's remark, in *The heart of darkness*, that the expansion of Europe is really 'not a pretty picture when you look into it too closely'. Not only did the New Imperialism have the effect of a 'fatal impact' on the traditional African societies of Southern Africa, but it also acted in a manner corrosive of the best in European culture. 'Whenever settlers from a people in an advanced stage of civilisation come into contact with the aborigines of a barbarous country,' as a young William Gladstone put it in 1838, 'the result is always prejudicial to both parties, and most dishonourable to the superior.'

The centenary year of the Transvaal annexation of 1877, the very beginning of the Scramble in earnest for Southern Africa, is perhaps an appropriate moment at which to stand and review the coming of the New Imperialism to this vast region, and its complex legacy to the peoples of the veld.

Attempting an essay of reappraisal – 'something of a pastiche of other peoples' ideas cemented and varnished by the authors' idiosyncrasies', as Michael Craton modestly yet sharply puts it in introducing his short history of British slavery, *Sinews of Empire* (London, 1975) – necessarily means developing very considerable debts to other scholars of empire and Africa. I am all too conscious of how heavily I have relied on pioneer work other than my own. I have most conscientiously tried to declare those debts, and my sincere thanks, in the full notes to each chapter which have been placed at the end of this book. I trust that scholars recognising their findings in my text will take it as a compliment and feel that my acknowledgements have been adequate.

I have also taken the opportunity of re-examining, or examining for the first time, all the primary manuscript collections which bear on the Scramble for Southern Africa, whether private or official. I am most grateful to their owners and custodians for permission to use these deposits, often extensively by way of quotation. A list of manuscript sources consulted can be found in a table at the front of this volume.

Examining these primary resources involved archival work in both Britain and Africa; and I am deeply indebted to a research grant from the Canada Council, and to research funds from Trent University, for supporting my travels and publication.

The final draft of this work was written in the perfect conditions of the Research School of Social Sciences, Australian National University, where Professor Oliver MacDonagh did so much to improve the lucidity of the argument and generally to inspirit the author. I am also indebted to

Barry Smith, John Eddy, Allan Martin, Ken Inglis, Cameron Hazlehurst, John Cookson and Ged Martin (all then at R.S.S.S., A.N.U.), as well as Brian Heeney, Freddy Hagar, David Cameron and John Stubbs (all of Ontario) who were more supportive as friends than they could ever have known.

Professor John Gallagher, Trinity College, Cambridge, first interested me in this subject and his pioneer work pointed out the new frontiers to explore. He is the real *Voortrekker*.

Only Carol Sherman could have typed so impeccable a working-text from my initial literary draft, while May McKenzie and Lois Simms performed wonders in producing so polished a final manuscript. Eldean Wills kindly assisted with the proofs.

I owe a very special debt of gratitude to Professor Eric Stokes, who has been more than mere editor of this series. It was he who constantly encouraged me to write for the 'plain reader', and not merely the specialist, and who acted as a most trenchant but always friendly critic of the work. Robert Seal, then of Cambridge University Press, was kind enough to goad me gently into producing the final text within a most reasonable deadline;

Lastly, I place here the name of Paddy. She made the writing of this book possible – and so much more.

DMS

Dingane's Day, 1977

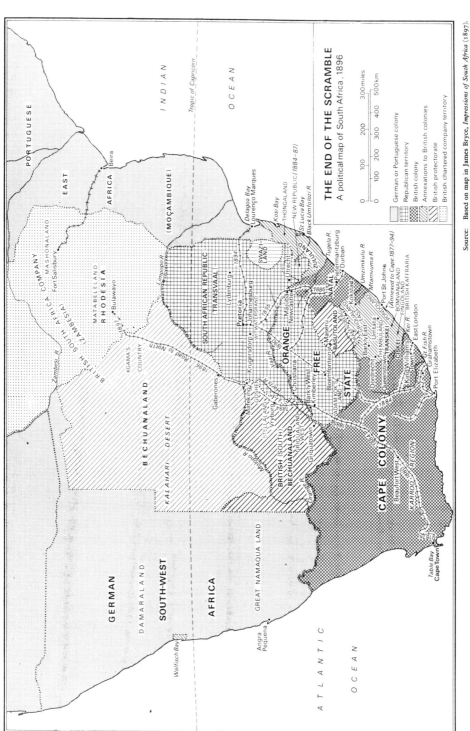

THE END OF THE SCRAMBLE
A political map of South Africa, 1896

	German or Portuguese colony
	Republican territory
	British colony
	Annexations to British colonies
	British protectorate
	British chartered company territory

0 100 200 300 miles
0 100 200 300 400 500 km

Source: Based on map in James Bryce, *Impressions of South Africa* (1897).

PORTUGUESE EAST AFRICA (MOÇAMBIQUE)

INDIAN OCEAN

Tropic of Capricorn

Beira

BRITISH SOUTH AFRICA COMPANY

MASHONALAND
Fort Salisbury

MATABELELAND RHODESIA
1891 Bulawayo

BRITISH SOUTH AFRICA (ZAMBESIA)

Zambesi R.

KGAMA'S COUNTRY

1896 Road to North

BECHUANALAND

KALAHARI DESERT

Gaberones

Delagoa Bay
Lourenço Marques

Kosi Bay
THONGALAND

NEW REPUBLIC (1884–87)
St Lucia Bay
Black Umfolozi R.

SOUTH AFRICAN REPUBLIC (TRANSVAAL)
1894
Lydenburg
Pretoria
Johannesburg
WITWATERSRAND
1896
Krugersdorp
WATERSRAND

SWAZI LAND

ZULULAND

Tugela R.
Pietermaritzburg
Utrecht
Majuba
Newcastle 1886
Durban

NATAL

Umzimkulu R.

Mtamvuma R.

Port St Johns
Kokstad

Annexed to Cape 1877–94

Umtata
THEMBULAND
EMIGRANT
TEMBULAND
BOMVANALAND
GRIQUALAND
EAST
Kei R.
BRITISH KAFFRARIA

East London

ORANGE FREE STATE
Bloemfontein
BASUTOLAND
Maseru

GERMAN SOUTH-WEST AFRICA

DAMARALAND

Walfisch Bay

GREAT NAMAQUA LAND

Angra Pequena

ATLANTIC OCEAN

Limpopo R.

BRITISH (SOUTH) BECHUANALAND
Vryburg
GOSHEN
STELLALAND
1895
1884

Mafeking
Christiana
Barkly West
Kimberley
GRIQUALAND WEST
Griquatown

Vaal R.
Modder R.
Orange R.

CAPE COLONY

Beaufort West

KARROO REGION

Dordrecht
Barkly East
Aliwal North
Queenstown
TRANSKEI
1884
King Williams Town
Great Fish R.
Grahamstown
Port Elizabeth

Table Bay
Cape Town

Introduction and argument

'Once embarked on the fatal policy of establishing a frontier in South Africa and defending that frontier by force, there seems to be neither rest nor peace till we follow our flying enemies across the Congo and plant the British standard on the walls of Timbuctoo. To subdue one tribe is only to come in contact with another equally fierce, impracticable, and barbarous . . . The theory of war is that it should be the mother of peace, but in South Africa we merely seem to carry on war in order to make it a stepping stone to another.'

Editorial in *The Times*, 28 February 1853.

South Africa was one of the great 'Questions' which strained the ingenuity and conscience of the makers of British external policy throughout most of the nineteenth century.[1] Like the enduring 'Eastern Question', or the emerging 'Indian Problem', it proved resistant to any enduring or just 'solution'. Not only was the South African Question bound up with the defence of vital British interests in international politics, but it was also increasingly and intimately concerned with the internal history of the peoples and societies of this vast 'frontier world'. Indeed, so intractable did the Question appear to be by the 1880s – the centre of our period of concern here – that Gladstone, as the British premier, could speak despairingly of the issue as the 'one unsolved, and perhaps unsolvable problem of our colonial system', and depict policy towards the region and its inhabitants as 'a history of difficulties, continual and unthought of.[2]

This book is about one critical phase in that 'history of difficulties'. Its focus is the period of the great European Scramble for Africa 1877–95, years which witnessed a massive struggle for final hegemony and resources on the veld. These crucial events represented the South African version of the more general Partition of Africa by the agencies of Western expansion. And that African Scramble was, of course, part of an even larger assault by the geo-political forces of the New Imperialism on the undeveloped world beyond Europe.[3]

In his pioneer history, *The Partition of Africa* (London, 1895), J. S. Keltie wrote – a little breathlessly in the aftermath of the event – that during 'the last ten years there has been a mad rush and nearly the whole Continent has been gobbled up'.[4] The late-Victorians were pre-eminent in that 'mad rush' for Africa. Between 1882 and 1898 over 70 million Africans were politically incorporated into systems of British rule and over-rule, at a cost of some 15p each.[5] By 1895 Southern Africa (including 'Zambesia') had contributed over a million square miles to that sequence of conquest, and perhaps as many as 5 million inhabitants (including half a million settlers) – as well as a unique mixture of economic resources, administrative problems and dilemmas in power politics.[6]

The origins of this particular upheaval in African politics were less easy to define than its manifestations. Since Keltie's initial 'history' the Partition has certainly not lacked either critics or analysts – the two roles sometimes coming together, as in J. A. Hobson's famous polemic *Imperialism* (1902) written after personal experience in South Africa. Yet if the debate on the Scramble has grown ever more complex and sophisticated, reflecting both the complexity of the politics of the Partition and the differing perspectives on imperialism in an age of 'decolonisation', we are not necessarily any closer to a generally accepted and unequivocal explanation or thesis for the events.[7] Few scholars would admit to sharing Lord Salisbury's laconic view, 'I do not know the cause of it'. But few again would now suggest anything less than a pluralistic thesis – embracing European developments, African politics and the inter-relationship between them – as an ultimately satisfying historical explanation of a geo-political sequence of change in Africa embracing international forces and an entire continent over the course of nearly two decades of world history.

In this extended essay I have worked from two modest presumptions about that historiographical debate; namely, that if we are to make any sense of the tangle of the Partition we shall have to examine it in reasonably manageable regional components; and that we shall probably have to study with care the humdrum piece-meal process of expansion itself before we can advance larger claims for the relative potency of particular expansive forces or ideological factors. The result, in this instance, is a close regional case-study of narrative and analysis, with what might be termed a largely 'extra-European' focus of attention. I have not consciously neglected the play of high politics in the cabinets and chancelleries of Europe. But I have thought it vitally important to examine also the immediate effects of these interplays when translated into immediate action in Southern Africa itself. The interaction of forces and societies within the geographical environment of Africa south of the Zambesi is revealing of the degree to which European expansion in the age of the New Imperialism was not merely a function of continental politics but also of the 'frontier world' itself.

The reasons for this emphasis in the analysis are simple yet important. They go beyond a search for mere novelty of interpretation in what is, after all, an old intellectual argument about motivation and origins; or even an attempt directly to provide a modern Southern African variant of the increasingly respected scholarly view that it is in the 'periphery' that we shall run the elusive New Imperialism to ground.[8] Rather, in a more matter of fact way, it appeared to me as I re-examined the documentation on the Scramble for South Africa 1877–95 – something not really attempted in any singular way since R. I. Lovell's work in the 1930s[9] – that a concern with the metropolis alone was simply insufficient to explain the massive and final Partition after 1877. My researches suggested rather that the 'politics of the periphery' were crucial in shaping the events under study. Indeed, it seemed that the local agencies of Western expansion, increasingly interacting and clashing with the trans-frontier communities of Africans and Boers, had provided the first impetus for a general Scramble in Africa south of the Zambesi.[10] It was only in the 1880s that the 'New Imperialism' of European rivalry had drawn the region into a world pattern of geo-political 'Partition', and had thereby given a new life and a new ferocity to the Scrambles for Southern Africa *already* in progress there.

As a thesis this is a much less original interpretation than it might appear. It is to be found, even if not fully explored there, in the pioneer works of Professors Walker and de Kiewiet, completed in the inter-war years. There has also, of course, been a growing recognition by recent writers on British imperialism, that the 'frontier' and 'local crisis' generally, played very important roles in the expansion of the empire in the later nineteenth century.[11] Above all, in the major writings of the authors of *Africa and the Victorians* (1961), there is to be found a highly sophisticated revisionist theory for the New Imperialism as applied to the African Partition which derives not least from basic suppositions akin to an extra-European, or 'peripheral' explanation.[12] First, Professors Robinson and Gallagher have argued that an economy of effort was the hall-mark of British expansion in Africa; and secondly, that it was the eruption of 'local crises' – mainly in North and South Africa – which willy-nilly pressed the Victorian states-men, those 'reluctant imperialists', against their best pragmatic instincts and treasury concerns for 'economy', to advance to tropical empire and a leading role in the African Partition.

How, then, does this view differ from that interpretation? The answer lies not in any great pedagogical disagreement, but rather in the analysis of the 'local crisis' in South Africa. Where Robinson and Gallagher were largely to trace that initial 'local crisis' to the dialectical relationship of instability between metropolitan authorities and the dissident Boers of the highveld, I have suggested a somewhat broader range of the forces of change pressing upon the Imperial Factor. Above all, this discussion gives a larger place to the interaction of white and black political communities in colonial South Africa. The local contest for African resources – in terms of land, labour and minerals – is here generally taken to be a fundamental determinant of the geo-political changes. The triangle of forces identified in Professor W. M. MacMillan's notable *Bantu, Boer and Briton* (first edition, 1929) would appear to come much closer to the realities of the local power situation with which I am concerned.

Yet even that designation does not perhaps take the analysis far enough. None of those three groups were at all monolithic. It is of the essence of the explanation offered below that the local 'politics of partition' gained much of its initial momentum and character from the fragmentary nature of the state-systems of frontier South Africa, coupled with the lack of over-lordship provided by the major Great Power concerned, Great Britain. Once it is perceived that a great deal of the dynamism for political change, and territorial conquest, derives from this colonial 'periphery' itself, it naturally follows that the behaviour of the major local frontier societies – be they Cape financial and commercial classes, Natal settlers, or trekking Boer pastoralists – in company with African political communities trying to protect land and independency in the face of a growing European invasion, becomes one of real significance in any overall explanation of the long-term origins and evolution of the Scramble in Southern Africa.

It also suggests the very considerable importance of the political behaviour of the local senior British imperial officials in the various regions of South Africa. The 'men-on-the-spot' have recently been elevated to an ever larger role in the politics of the empire; South Africa in the years of the Scramble offers powerful support for this view of the significance of the 'prancing proconsuls' in the inner dynamics of British imperialism and expansion. The role of the high commissioners – notably Frere and Robinson – was clearly crucial at certain periods in delineating, shaping, and even occasionally determining, the nature of British involvement in trans-frontier South Africa. They were also vital in influencing the techniques by which British rule and authority was to be maintained. And, below the level of these senior imperial proconsuls, there was an important colonial administrative corps in the service of the settler polities of the Cape and Natal, who also occupied significant roles in the coming and carrying through of Partition. Sir Theophilus Shepstone in South-east Africa was one such crucial 'local proconsul' whose ideas, actions and strategies, were to have results far beyond the administrative preserve he had created in the interior of Natal. All told, British proconsular officialdom was to be yet another variant on the theme of 'the frontier' as potent inspirer of much of the politics of Partition.[13]

To point to the significant role played by local factors and figures in this regional version of the general African Partition in the 1880s does not in any way, of course, lessen the need to take the New Imperialism seriously as a force for conquest, and as an animator of the process of white expansion already in motion in South Africa. 'Empire' in this environment was the ultimate expression of a highly complex meshing of metropolitan and local frontier-expansion. It is, in many ways, unwise to attempt a separation of these expansive forces of metropolis and periphery. The political and economic variables which came together, to develop the final Partition in South Africa, lived in close conjunction to each other.[14] We do not have to choose between a totally 'Eurocentric', or completely 'Afrocentric' explanation – such is an unreal choice, given the actual way in which the Scramble for South Africa developed out of a combination of long- and short-term factors embodying both sets of forces.[15]

This point of argument can be shown in specific and important ways in the South African context of the Partition. I have, firstly, absolutely accepted here – as Professor Stokes has well put it – that the role of the European Powers 'has to continue to be treated as an independent variable' in the study of the Partition, not least because of the 'essentially aggressive meaning' of Western imperialism in the African case.[16] The changing nature of capitalist societies, their economic needs and inter-state relationships, were all vital in the rise of the New Imperialism in international politics.

Yet that very European expansive force was also to grow out of the *existing* connections between the dynamics of the Western societies and the world of the colonial periphery, and became a development of it. Great Power rivalry, the changing balance of forces in Europe and the Middle East, the rise of imperialist enthusiasms in the societies of the metropolis – all the hallmarks of the New Imperialism[17] – were in fact non factors neatly and discretely isolated from the world beyond Europe. The Powers were drawn to participate in a Scramble for Africa, at least in part, because they were already increasingly involved in the undeveloped world. The map of Africa, even for Bismarck, did not really begin on the Rhine: it began, and was being redrawn, in Africa itself through agencies of the Great Powers, however 'informal' in character. As D. K. Fieldhouse has amply shown, it was because of lobbies of overseas traders, missionaries, emigration societies, land and shipping companies, geographical and medical researchers, that much of the public concern surrounding the colonial issue in domestic politics was initiated.[18]

In fine, it was because there had been an 'age of reconnaissance', followed by a progressive involvement of European agencies in the overseas world, that major events in international history could now find their source of animation around the great ocean rims of the globe.[19] The later nineteenth century was to see an intensification of this process, partly through the natural expansionist dynamic of European culture and capitalism, partly because after 1870 the continental balance of power was altering in radical and significant ways.[20] If imperialism was part of the age of nationalism, it was also an extension of the politics of the periphery. In the far flung localities of the globe, agencies of the West were increasingly in conflict with each other; increasingly active in reshaping the cultures of indigenous societies; and generally busy enmeshing their metropolitan states in the peripheries both by their lobbying at home, and through their expansive designs on the frontiers of conquest. The age of *weltpolitik* was thus also the age of frontier politics and expansion.

On the eve of the Scramble this is exactly what was happening in colonial South Africa. The area was already rife with European agencies of empire and expansion penetrating the remaining lands, markets, resources and authority of the African polities in the region. The aims of these groups could be couched in the terms of the strategic or economic expansion of the European states in the undeveloped world. More concretely, they can be traced directly to the quest to acquire more land and labour in the development of their own colonial polities of settlement and their private commercial houses. It was as a direct result of these *local* objectives that the frontier was so restive in the 1870s, as the settler states made their last great bid for resources. By the time the Germans appeared on the South-west African coast in 1884 – so potentially bringing Great Power rivalry to South Africa generally – the British had in fact already begun a series of important interventionist initiatives in the region. Frontier disturbance in South Africa, challenging British authority, had grown beyond tolerable limits. In Whitehall, and Cape Town, it was argued by Victorian officialdom that unless these military and expansive interventions were undertaken, the area would simply relapse into an almost endless series of border wars and internecine conflicts, stretching away into the future – a direct consequence of the activities of the local frontiersmen. Put very simply, before the New Imperialism the British had already responded to the phenomenon of 'local crisis'. This intervention was, in truth, the deepest origin of the Scramble to come.

It therefore seems to me that it is absolutely true, as the revisionist historians of free trade imperialism have argued, that the British played their central role in the Scramble for South Africa essentially because they were concerned to deal with a colonial region 'growing beyond their control'.[21] It is also vitally important to grasp, however, that the 'local crisis' to which the Imperial Factor was responding was not a static problem, nor one focused around any specific political challenge. Between 1877 and 1895 – the crucial high phase of the White Partition of South Africa – the 'local crisis' underwent a considerable metamorphosis. It began as a problem of frontier disorder and general instability; it changed into a series of militaristic challenges to imperial authority; it then, after 1884, escalated into an international problem of accommodating Great Powers in a single sensitive region of empire; and it finally reached its crescendo, in the later 1880s, as the massive highveld 'mineral revolution' began to have its manifold effects on both the domestic and international Scrambles already proceeding in South Africa.

The British policy-makers sometimes gave the impression that all their problems in South Africa found their origins in the independent behaviour of the frontiersmen, notably the Boers of the highveld. But the 'South African Question' was not centred on a simple breakdown of the relationships between the Imperial Factor and the recalcitrant Calvinists of the interior republics – in company with sympathetic and alienated Cape Dutch in the Western Province.[22] It was in truth an infinitely more confused affair. And indeed in terms of 'origins', the Partition can be seen to have ante-dated the revolt of the Afrikaners in 1880–81. The Boers were undoubtedly fundamental to the Scramble, but to their particular role must be added the problems of general frontier stability in the 1870s – notably in the borderlands of the Cape, centred on the Sotho and southern Nguni – and the effects of international rivalry and capital inflow after 1884–86.

In trying to make some sense of the 'tangle', it is accordingly perhaps useful to see the Scramble for South Africa in the light of a concatenation of long- and short-term factors, and of international and local forces. The 'local crisis' of 1877–84, which really formed the prelude to Partition, was in fact not an isolated eruption of disorder which called for imperial response and intervention. Rather, it represented the incendiary conclusion to a long expanding and changing British presence in the region; and to decades of 'sub-imperial' pressure on African lands by local settler agencies of empire.[23] This element was to run right through into the decade of Partition after 1884, and was to act as a basic theme over which could be played the increasingly complex variations of more immediate and short-term initiatives by the forces of the New Imperialism.[24]

It is for this reason that monocausal explanations just will not do.

The Scramble for South Africa was to be the expression of intense metropolitan, colonial and African politics intersecting within the decades of the 1870s and 1880s. It is in terms of context and sequence alone that we can discern motivation, pattern and meaning in the Southern African Partition.

Because the Scramble for South Africa evolved not only sequentially but cumulatively over the years 1877–95, and developed through what were relatively distinct 'phases' of Partition – each having its own particular characteristics and each shaping the nature of expansion to come – it has seemed sensible to arrange this analytic narrative around that natural historical structure. The aim has been to provide a simple lucid account of the Scramble while at the same time passing comment on the significance of events as they unfolded.

After this Introduction there is a section devoted to the first phase of Partition, covering the years 1877–84, the immediate prelude to the general Scramble for South Africa. It attempts a consideration of the political forces at work in 'frontier South Africa' at the end of the 1870s; and this is immediately followed by a linked chapter on the expansion of empire and local settlement, up to 1884.

The second section covers the relatively short but important phase of 1884–86. It is largely devoted to showing the consequences of Bismarck bringing the New Imperialism of international rivalry to South Africa; and, in particular, of the ways in which this expansion by metropolitan Germany quickened the already ongoing process of local Partition, as the New Imperialism intersected with Boer expansion towards the coastlines. British 'pre-emptive imperialism' symbolised the response of the Imperial Factor as overlord to these challenges to the *Pax Britannica* in South Africa of the mid 1880s.

The crucial years 1886–90 – the very heyday of the Scramble south of the Zambesi – are dealt with in the next section. This was a 'crisis period' for the British authorities. Not only did they now have to adjust to the presence of the Germans in South-west Africa, but they had to attempt to restructure their hegemony in the light of an economic revolution on the highveld which gave a dramatic new power to the republican Boer states of the interior. It is a period therefore delineated by the mineral discoveries in the Transvaal, the consequent frenetic local Scramble for resources, territory and supremacy, as peripheral and metropolitan factors came together with a vengeance working for a final White Partition of the region.

A concluding section considers the 'aftermath'. Interstate diplomacy and division now became conquest and exploitation 'on-the-ground', 1890–95. Where the politics of the New Imperialism had often meant the staking out of strategic claims, and the defence by the British of traditional interests, so now the older local imperialism of the frontier societies of South Africa advanced to incorporate, rule, settle and exploit these African lands and resources. The overthrow of the remaining independent and semi-independent African political communities of South Africa, in the mid 1890s, is considered in a chapter on the ultimate triumph of the settler and white entrepreneur – in Rhodesia, Swaziland, Zululand, Pondoland and Thongaland. The section is completed with a brief discussion of the closing of the last frontiers of expansion in 1895.

Connecting these several phases and surges of expansion in the Scramble for South Africa – and also connecting the sectional division of this study – was the very obvious role of the British Imperial Factor attempting to defend its authority and its interests as the great overlord power, in a vital region of empire; and also the less obvious but also fundamental force of local expansion by settler societies of frontier South Africa. In this way the real legacy of the Scramble is not to be expressed merely in terms of European or new colonies upon the map. What mattered most of all was that the *local* balance of power had tilted permanently against the authority of the African political communities in favour of the Europeans; that the peculiar modern political-economy of the region had been formed; and that the settlement patterns – particularly those of territorial segregration and the 'right to the land' – were ultimately decided.

The fact that South Africa entered the twentieth century not merely as a colonial territory but as a 'white man's country' was due in so many ways to the frontier legacy of the New Imperialism, and particularly the Scramble years 1877–95.

Prelude 1877–84:

frontier and expansion

'... at first the white man came and took part of this land [the Eastern Cape]; they then increased and drove them further back, and have repeatedly taken more land as well as cattle. They then built houses [i.e. missions] among them for the purpose of subduing them by witchcraft ... during his stay at Graham's Town the soldiers frequently asked what sort of country the Zoolus had ... that he had heard a far white people intended to come first and get a grant of land ... they would then build a fort, when men would come, and demand land, who would also build houses and subdue the Zoolus, and keep driving them back as they have driven back the frontier tribes.'

> Hlambamangi to Dingane, 1831 (reports by Nathaniel Isaacs)

'Though we abuse the Kafir, we want his service, and we want ... his land.'

> *Anthony Trollope, 'South Africa' (1878)*

'The great land question lies at the bottom of ... [frontier] policy.'

> Rev. J. S. Moffatt, 5 October 1882

'The chiefs well knew that ... once the die was cast [to rebel, in 1878–79] race hatred would blaze up, and that the blacks would strive to overwhelm the whites and drive them into the sea.'

> Resident magistrate, E. Pondoland 1881

'Government does not say to me like a man, I am going to take this and that privilege, but one by one my rights are stolen from me in the dark. Government is a wolf.'

> Chief Manthanzima of the Xhosa, 1884

I

'1877' – the annexers and the annexed

The Scramble for South Africa had its immediate origins in 1877. On 4 January Sir Theophilus Shepstone rode across the Transvaal border as special British envoy, accompanied by 25 Natal mounted police and leaving in reserve a corps of imperial troops, and a representative of the Standard Bank. Shepstone established himself in Pretoria, and made enquiry over the following months into the political, economic and administrative condition of the Boer republic. His activities in these crucial months have aptly been described as beginning with 'a sherry and champagne policy', to be followed – after altercation with the Boer authorities, Paul Kruger and the *Volksraad* – with relapse 'into a devastating silence'.[1] By 12 April Shepstone was ready to carry out the wishes of his imperial masters, which also happened to coincide with his own: annexation of the Transvaal to the British empire. The news of his action reached London on 6 May 1877.

This event did not of itself create the momentum for a Scramble in South Africa. Rather, the glaring fact of Transvaal annexation represented that demonstrable moment when the final Partition of South Africa first became manifest. The annexation drew its inspiration from the Imperial Factor's reading of the condition of frontier South Africa in the 1870s; and this bold, 'forward action', was intended to mark the formal beginning of a crucial new initiative by the British authorities – metropolitan and local – in reordering the political structure of the vast and unstable region. It was not to be an isolated forward action, of course; it was part of a larger strategy to solve local problems 'on a plan' – a plan of federation.[2] The plan ultimately failed, but the intervention soon led to extended involvement by the Imperial Factor in the politics of South Africa. Here was the very beginnings of Partition.

The Transvaal annexation is historically significant therefore not so much for the event in itself, but for what it revealed about South Africa in 1877: the problems of its inter-state frictions; its lack of any signs of sustained economic growth or 'development'; the disturbed state of its legendary frontier zones; and the methods and motives of the British as imperial overlords in dealing with these problems in the deeply complex, and often also deeply troublesome, portion of their overseas empire. A reappraisal of the Scramble for South Africa might well thus begin with this moment in 1877, and use it as a point of departure for exploring the meaning of South Africa to the British Imperial Factor, and the corresponding significance of the Imperial Factor in the politics of frontier South Africa.

Patterns of authority in frontier South Africa 1877

In 1877 not all of 'British South Africa' was British. Even more than in 'British India' – where some 38% of the sub-continent was ruled directly by traditional authorities – there were major areas and polities outside the control of the Imperial Factor; indeed some were apparently even beyond the legendary Victorian 'influence' in their obdurate anti-British postures. Undoubtedly, as in India, British metropolitan authorities saw themselves as possessors of the powers of 'over-rule' throughout Southern Africa; statesmen and bureaucrats alike spoke proprietorially of 'British South Africa'.[3] But the truth was that, on the eve of the Partition, large coastal areas lay open to foreign intervention; and, in the hinterland, the local agencies of colonial and Boer expansion harboured hopes of further frontier advances, which would allow them to extend their territorial settlements independent of the desires and interests of the British authorities.

This highly complex pattern of interposed British colonial, republican and African political communities, which was to turn the South African region into something of a nightmare for official policy-makers, owed its origins not least to the troubled frontier history of the area. The dominant *leitmotif* of the political history of nineteenth century South Africa had been the interaction between forces of the frontier and the Imperial Factor. The polyglot state-ststem, and settlement pattern, of 1877 gave concrete territorial expression to the difficulties experienced by the British in trying to devise viable techniques of empire for South Africa. No single or simple system of government had been found to be satisfactory in 'controlling' the area; and thus, short of ruling by the bayonet, the British had devised an infinitely complex structure of authority and influence – relying heavily on client groups, 'treaty associates' and collaborators – to secure their interests, both strategic and economic.

South Africa was surely part of the maps of Africa in the records of the colonial and foreign offices in London. Yet it actually required policy-treatment in a fashion closer to that of the most troublesome of the old colonisation settlements, British North America – with this exception, that South Africa offered all the cultural problems of Canada in conjunction with the race problems of New Zealand, the economic problems of Australia, and the politically explosive problems of administration in Ireland.

The British were, of course, not without experience in dealing with disaffected subjects, alienated settlers, defiant traditional rulers and voracious local economic pressure groups. But nowhere else in the empire of rule, or of influence, did they so completely face all these elements within a single geographical context, elements which lived in constant interaction with each other, and not merely discretely in relation to the Imperial Factor. Given this fact, it was pretty inevitable that, if this region became drawn into the more general machinations of the New Imperialism, it would provide quite the most complex case in the politics of partition and expansion faced by the British in Africa.

The difficulties and discomfort of the policy-makers animates the great body of official British records deposited by the late-Victorian governments and their bureaucratic agencies. From those records we can reconstruct their attempts to ride the tide of the New Imperialism, to balance an old imperial world in a period of quickening change – not merely in the balance of European power, but over the globe more generally as the age of *weltpolitik* burst upon the Victorian consciousness. Yet, the view from Whitehall is a limited one. The attitudes and behaviour of the British political and administrative elite may indeed provide the one guide-rope through the complexities of the expansion of the New Imperialism. But it is, in truth, only a point of reference in grasping the totality of the events of the African Partition. We need to know the local context to make sense of policy-decisions; we need to understand the pressures of the interest groups, whether economic or humanitarian, to grasp the forces working on British administrations; and we need, too, some understanding of those extra-European variables – such as the forces of the frontier itself – which also impinged on the development of events in a fashion 'contingent and unforseen'.

The central question at issue is clearly therefore: how did the British cope with *both* international and local factors in securing their interests in Southern Africa during the era of the Scramble for the last continent?

But before we offer some bold suggestions as to objectives, strategies and techniques of the imperialism in the region, it is just as well to get clear in mind the political situation in South Africa on the eve of the Scramble. What, then, were the constituent elements of the 'South African Question' as faced by the British authorities? The question can perhaps best be answered by a three-fold approach: a bare-bones statement of the political structure of the area in 1877; an analytic discussion of the agencies of empire and expansion – both 'metropolitan' and 'local' – operative in the struggle for mastery, land and resources in South Africa; and a brief comment of the ways in which the frontier itself, as a register of change, helped to impel the coming of a final Partition of South Africa, involving both regional forces from the settler societies and the Imperial Factor itself.

The most useful beginning in demarcating the political status quo of South Africa in 1877 is simply between 'British' and 'non-British' political units.

British South Africa   The formal contribution of South Africa to Victorian overseas empire was indeed a mixed bag in the year 1877. There were two settler colonies, at differing stages of constitutional development (the Cape had achieved 'responsible government' in 1872; Natal did not reach the same point until 1893), together with an ill-defined trusteeship responsibility – for Africans within the British colonies, as well as groups in the frontier borderlands of settlement, such as the Sotho of Basutoland and the southern Nguni of the Transkei Territories – in addition to even less well-defined claims to paramountcy over the northern Boer republicans in the interior Trekker states of the Orange Free State and the Transvaal. These various British responsibilities all found their focus in the office of the high Commissioner, Cape Town.

In practical administrative terms, the British authorities actually *ruled* very little of this polyglot set of political groups and states. The Cape colony was designated as a 'sub-imperial' agent of London in the African periphery, and ran its own local form of 'empire-state'. It was the Cape which increasingly administered the 'Ciskei' (largely the old imperial frontier province of 'British Kaffraria', of 1848–65, centred on King Williams Town); which ruled Basutoland (annexed by the British 1868, and passed to the colony 1872, though taken back by London in 1884) and which soon incorporated Griqualand West (originally annexed as a crown colony in 1871, after the discovery of diamonds at Kimberley) in 1880. The Cape did not as yet directly administer the Transkei Territories, but it did in fact operate a local 'covert', or 'informal empire', beyond the Kei River among the Xhosa; and it was very soon to convert that substantial interest and involvement into formal aquisitions under the 'Transkei Annexation Act' of 1877 – ending with the annexation of Thembuland and Pondoland in the 1890s. The Cape colony was also, in short order, to be urged by the Imperial Factor to take up its 'destiny' in Southern Bechuanaland, south of the Molopo River, when the British attempted to keep the Boers and the Germans out of the great 'Road to the North' in the mid 1880s.

Natal was not such a local 'empire-state' on the scale of the Cape colony; and the British were genuinely wary of its capacity to handle transfrontier 'native administration'. But this did not halt Natalians from having pretensions for the creation of a 'greater Natal': they had bid hard for Basutoland in 1868; they hungered for Pondoland; and they looked with more than keen interest on the best arable lands of the Zulu, the Swazi and the Thonga in South-east Africa.[4]

Non-British South Africa   Ranged alongside, and in many senses increasingly against British-administered South Africa, were two quite different groupings of political communities.

First in order of size and populations were the independent African polities. In 1877, we need to remember, not only were many minor chiefdoms still intact territorially, and independent in power, but so too were a majority of the greater African political communities of South Africa – the Zulu, Swazi, Mpondo and Thonga of South-east Africa; the Bapedi and the Bavenda of the Transvaal region; the Ngwato, Shona and Ndebele of the far interior. The next few years were, however, to be fatal to that set of political units and their independence. By 1884 only the Mpondo, the Swazi and hinterland societies could claim even a modicum of independence; and, in a number of cases – not least that of the Swazi and Mpondo – subversion of their authority, by local concessionaires, or frontier farmers, or diplomatic agents, had been set in vigorous motion. For the traditional African inhabitants of South Africa '1877' was in reality to be the last year of political freedom outside the rule of the white man.

These years 1877–84, the very prelude to the greater Scramble, were indeed the 'loaded pause' before the full impact of political subjection and administrative incorporation under colonial rule of various forms. The era of the Partition, after 1884 was, for the Africans of transfrontier South Africa, merely to be an intensification of the local Scrambles, conducted by the colonial and Boer agencies of white empire, with which they had been attempting to cope since the early nineteenth century, and which now suddenly surged forward immediately after 1877.[5]

The other important areas of 'non-British' South Africa were occupied by the Boer republican states. In 1877 they numbered two, both recognised in their status by the British, but with further unofficial mini-republics – spawned by the parent state – always a strong possibility. The Orange Free State had been acknowledged as an 'independent state' (*within* British Southern Africa!) as early as 1852; and the Transvaal had been accorded a similar status in 1854. But, of course, it was about to be stripped of that nominal independence (on 12 April) by an imperial forward action. The result was that, within a few years, it was soon struggling to return to its former status, through revolt against the British administration (December

1880 – March 1881) and treaty negotiation (the Pretoria Convention of 3 August 1881; and the London Convention of 27 February 1884). Further, the Transvaal was also shortly to express that revived sense of independence in the 1880s with amoeba-like expansion and segmentation, both on its western and eastern frontiers, when it allowed the creation of the freebooter republics of Stellaland (1882–85) and Goshen (1882–85) in Tswana lands, and the New Republic (1884–87) in the former Zulu state, by burghers from the 'Transvaal State'.[6] These petty political units were to appear only temporarily on the maps of the Partition; and most would disappear 1884–87 – partly by reincorporation into the parent Boer state, partly collapsed by British forces. Yet their very existence registered the long-term expansive dynamic of the Boer states of the interior, and the determination of the republics to play a major role in any final Scramble for interior South Africa. They also, in their pastoral, land and labour ambitions, pointed to the fact that the Partition south of Zambesia was marked out by an all too real struggle for African resources – both physical and human – and not merely a paper demarcation of European authority.[7]

An anatomy of the 'Old Imperialism'

Indeed, well before South Africa experienced the impact of the New Imperialism it had already been shaped, in its moving frontier and in its expanding regional economies, by the evolving power of what we might term an 'Old Imperialism' rooted in a tripartite set of forces: the impact of Victorian England – the 'Imperial Factor'; the sub-imperialist capacity and energy of the local British settler colonies – 'Cape Colonialism' and 'Natal Expansionism'; and the land pressures of the Boer states – 'Afrikaner republicanism'.[8]

These constituent factors of the Old Imperialism are worthy of some attention; in their capacity to create the local pre-conditions of a Scramble they were singularly important elements for generating the first phase of the Partition in South Africa 1877–84.

The 'Imperial Factor'   The overall intent of the British presence in Southern Africa, until 1886 at least, was abundantly clear and simple: the strategic protection of vital trading routes and interests in the Indian Ocean and Asian empire.[9]

On the eve of the Scramble for South Africa (1878) over £90 million worth of trade involved the Cape route (as compared to £65 million through Suez), and by that broad period (1880) Asia accounted for 23.4% of British exports (plus a further 5.9% to Africa itself) – and India alone had some

£270 million of British capital investment in the *Raj*. Little wonder that an empire authority such as Charles Dilke, could comment that, for *economic* reasons alone — quite apart from prestige and status as a great imperial power — loss of hegemony at the Cape 'would be almost fatal to our Indian empire and our China trade';[10] or, that a noted Royal Commission on Imperial Defence (September 1881) could state that 'this route must be maintained at all hazards and irrespective of cost'.[11]

This strategic-cum-economic commitment to the Cape route also implied commitment to the Cape itself and, in turn, to a degree of hegemony over the broader region of South Africa beyond. Two kinds of 'interests' were in fact involved *within* South Africa. There was the political commitment to defence and strategic factors, perhaps never better put than by the British colonial secretary in 1881 (Lord Kimberley) when he remarked that, 'It is a delusion to imagine that we could hold Cape Town, abandoning the rest. If we allow our supremacy in South Africa to be taken from us, we shall be ousted before long from that country altogether.'[12]

More difficult to categorise was a second set of 'interests' in South Africa — those associated with the settler societies and their economies, which also formed a British 'commitment'. It was not merely that the British had some £34 million invested in the region by the 1880s — mainly in the Cape, its diamond fields and public works — or that Victorian England did some £12 million trade per annum with South Africa as a whole, or even that they felt the area had turned the corner economically and commercially since the mineral discoveries of the late 1860s (with rumours of gold on the highveld). But rather that the Anglo-Saxon colonial societies of South Africa represented the technique by which the British imperial authorities were to sustain their dominance in the region. These settler communities also represented one of the colonised 'fragments' of the mother country — albeit less simply than, say, Australia, and more like Canada in its ethnic pluralism — and thereby created commitments of prestige and sentiment which also constituted an important aspect of British overseas interest. The Victorians were now a global people, and their external policies took the reality of colonial entities into account.

The overall result was that British involvement in South Africa was many-layered and deep; it began with the trade and naval interests of the Indian Ocean, and extended on through the dockyards and strategic harbours, into the settler societies about them, and then on into the hinterland of the region, as a dimension of an overall concern for an inviolate supremacy *around*, and *in*, Southern Africa.

Thus, despite being 'reluctant imperialists' in Africa and Asia — as the revisionist historians of free trade imperialism would have it — the British were locked into a situation in the South African context where the interests were so many, and so crucial, that they could not in fact hold back from 'forward actions' if either *external* foreign challenges interposed, or if *internal* threats to hegemony and stability arose. The British may indeed have wished to conduct their empire in this region by 'benign neglect'; but that was not to be allowed to them. A cruel path awaited the reticent imperialists. They proclaimed regret at each polity incorporated under British jurisdiction, and each acre annexed. Yet their advance was real and extensive.

The role of the British in the Partition years had, accordingly, been foreshadowed in the earlier history of their presence in South Africa since 1806 – they had, before 1877 and the Scramble, come to act out an almost 'traditional' role as defender of well-defined and oft-proclaimed interests. Indeed, put very simply: they did not have that luxury sometimes open to them in tropical Africa of pondering long whether an advance in juris-diction could be legitimised on economic or humanitarian grounds. In South Africa it was *ipso facto* accepted that certain coastal and hinterland areas were strategically or politically too 'sensitive' to fall into non-British hands; and also that the future development of 'South Africa' was heavily dependent on its peaceful evolution as a modern plural and capitalist society, in which the British role was clearly absolutely crucial. Challenge and response was a basic political law written into the imperial predicament in South Africa.

The preferred technique for accomplishing those ends, and defending that variety of British interests, was of course deeply complicated by the character of local politics and settlement. Essentially, however, as already indicated, it reduced itself as a problem in administrative politics, to con-ducting empire by settler clients and agents. The loyal white colonist was – in the acute phrase of Professor Robinson – 'the ideal prefabricated col-laborator'.[13] There were problems incipient in the fact that (a) the British colonies of South Africa contained a substantial proportion of Dutch settlers (in fact, a *majority* in the Cape); (b) that powerful transfrontier African political communities still existed, to influence and shape local politics; and (c) that the Boer states of the highveld created a potential for rivalry and disorder which mocked the hopes of British statesmen and governors alike.

But the British travelled in hope. The Cape Dutch appeared open to patronage and some forms of assimilation – quite as much as certain French Canadians, and more than the Irish – and through them connections were potentially open to their cousinship-community, the Boers. Further, if the white polities could be brought to see their common interests in a 'progressive' policy towards African societies, then the problems of frontier wars, labour supplies and land usage could be remedied in the interests of stability and development.

Such notions lay behind the progressive devolution of constitutional power to the Cape colony between 1853 and 1872; and they formed the stocks on which it was hoped, ultimately, to construct a South African state, within an empire context. If British North America could find its destiny in 'Canada', why not 'South Africa' from British and non-British Southern Africa?

The creation of a local empire of 'association' in South Africa, run by client assistants and collaborators, was not, it should be stressed, seen by the British as any negation of their interests, or their empire in this crucial portion of the globe. Quite the reverse. Far from these devolutionist thrusts indicating any desire to 'quit' the troublesome region, the Imperial Factor saw the emergence of a local associative empire as a subtle means of *strengthening* the British connection, and of safeguarding their multifarious interests in South Africa. In many ways, they looked at the situation as offering no other choice. It was not a case of direct empire or not; but rather one of associative empire or nothing. Both for treasury and for military reasons, British South Africa *had* to be ruled through the settler societies.

Making a virtue out of necessity, the British policy-makers soon pointed out that the larger the white client-group in South Africa, the more securely could the metropolitan government withdraw both its armed forces and veto powers concerning trusteeship over the African inhabitants, while yet feeling secure in their 'interests'. Broadening the base of British rule in South Africa ultimately involved not merely reliance on the Cape, but on winning republican Afrikanerdom as well to some kind of workable association; all the white settlers were to be called into participation in empire politics, and all were to be chosen over the course of time.

This was the broader context of the federalist policies and impulses which radiated out from the metropolitan factor in the three decades after 1870 – indeed, from Kimberley to Chamberlain as secretaries of state, and from Woodhouse to Milner as high commissioners. In his *Great Britain and South African Confederation*, Dr Goodfellow has suggested how individual Victorian statesmen and high officials could give policy a personal stamp of urgency and energy; and of how federation could lapse into inertia without these individual initiatives from, say, a Carnarvon or a Frere. Yet there was a remarkably steady commitment to this approach in the face of the problems of South Africa even by the more lethargic metropolitan or peripheral British authorities over the whole period 1870–1900. The alternatives to this approach were clearly very bleak indeed, while the advantages of some sort of federalised polity – acting to solve its problems within, but connected to the British empire – were vitally attractive.

The British often showed impatience with the 'unprogressive' character of the societies of South Africa; and they persistently determined to draw, or to press, the region along the paths of modernity, to a progressive and developing future. 'European immigration and capital flow slowly into countries under small and isolated Governments whose financial solvency is questionable, and where there is no adequate security for property and no confidence in present legislation', as one vigorous British secretary of state put it graphically for his cabinet colleagues in 1879, when advocating yet another attempt at federating South Africa under Cape leadership;

Federation would greatly improve and cheapen the administration of affairs in almost every branch [of government], and greatly lessen the probability of a demand for aid in the shape of Imperial money or troops. But the most immediately urgent reason for general union is the formidable character of the native question, and the importance of a uniform, wise and strong policy in dealing with it.[14]

The patchwork quality of the South African state-system was seen as the main enemy of both economic development and political devolution. Constructing a federalist state of association and collaboration had its considerable problems, of course: the white Cape politicians had to be brought to carry this imperial design, and the British metropolitan power might have to advance territorially before it could retire – by annexing non-British South African political units. The liberal ethic of empire disliked such a step. Yet it had to be faced. The local representatives of the metropolitan power – the 'men on-the-spot' – tended to accept this expansive necessity, in the cause of 'federation', more easily than did Whitehall. 'The British possessions in South Africa, as commanding the whole accessible seaboard', the Cape governor advised in 1868, 'must inevitably take part in, and control . . . the relations of the interior'.[15] The advice was taken at its most literal in the 1870s; and, in the hands of Carnarvon, Frere and Shepstone led to major British expansion, through belligerent onslaught on both independent Afrikaner and African power.

Federation failed to result. Afrikaners and Africans rebelled; the Anglo-Saxon settlers of the Cape did not warm to the burdens of being the only prosperous unit in an untidy collection of local states; and the Cape Afrikaners grew positively restive over the British initiatives. Federalism was put on the back-burner, for the time being: but the posture of creating a collaborative empire of loyal client associates continued, even if the structural character of the system was messier or less tidy than a federal form. The Gladstone–Kruger period of negotiation, 1881–84, was particularly important for it saw the Imperial Factor working the desperate politics of Afrikaner conciliation.[16] Not only did the metropolitan authorities dread a pan-Afrikaner reaction to the British connection but it was hoped that Hofmeyr's Cape *Bond* members could be brought into working alliance with the interests of *Pax Britannica* in Southern Africa. It was no chance that the newly designated British high commissioner – in succession to Sir Bartle Frere, with his Indian methods – was Sir Hercules Robinson, a less than 'prancing pro-consul', who had long experience of Anglo-colonial relations in prickly white settlements – notably New South Wales and New Zealand. He was also an outspoken advocate of the gospel of white colonial 'home rule', through empire devolution, to preserve the British connection in the face of potentially disruptive local colonial 'nationalism'.[17]

If British imperial policy in the Scramble era seemed confused in the South African context, it was because of these complex and apparently contradictory postures. The Imperial Factor was committed to the creation of an empire of collaborative association with the white-settler communities – notably the Cape – yet it was also compelled to advance whenever or wherever essential interests were threatened which could not be secured through its client agencies. The outward impression given was of a curious political dance, in which the metropolitan power would take one step forward in the hope of shortly taking two steps backward. The net result, however, was that the metropolitan imperialists became deeply enmeshed in the Southern African state system of inter-group relationships. In trying to draw the local societies in a net of British design – which would enable the Imperial Factor to 'reorder' the local situation along lines which suited the metropolitan power, preparatory to a controlled devolution of authority – the Victorians became caught up in the political forces of change which they had partly promoted. The Partition thus found them as cautious, yet principal agents of expanding empire in South Africa. They worked to defend British interests at the same time as they attempted to ease the administrative responsibilities involved onto loyal local colonial agencies of authority.

This apparently deferential posture in the face of the white societies of the periphery, by the metropolitan Great Power, had singularly important consequences for the character of the southern African Partition. The earnest desire to create a collaborative empire, gave the local white colonists of the Cape a pre-eminent role in influencing political developments in the periphery. London was inviting Cape Town to expand the powers of Responsible Government to the very fullest possible. Not only were the Anglo-Saxons to be courted by Whitehall, so too were the Cape Afrikaners of the *Bond*. The simple consequence was a strong encouragement to 'home rule' politics – especially trans-frontier – by the Cape authorities. In a short time, the growing dynamic of 'home rule' politics became an expansive force almost independent of metropolitan control – a 'sub-imperial' factor operating to extend its authority, administration and interests in areas as widespread as the Transkei and Bechuanaland. The Cape elite recognised the power in their hands, and called this force *colonialism*' as against 'imperialism' – for it denoted expansion based on Cape Town not London, albeit within a British framework.

It might also be remarked that, as the brunt of the Partition (in land and labour) was to be borne by African traditional societies, the rise of 'colonialism' – at the willing behest of the Imperial Factor – accelerated the shrinking authority of the chiefdoms. By working to strike a political alliance of collaborative association with the white colonists, the metropolitan power was negating its own powers of trusteeship. British ministers claimed that this was *not* so, and that the high commissioner still stood for African trusteeship rights. However, as the humanitarian critics of British policy quickly pointed out – notably John Mackenzie – the high commissioner was *also* the Cape governor. More, the particular officer in that appointment, Sir Hercules Robinson, strongly favoured the 'home rule' posture, to the extent of believing that colonists, rather than metropolitan officials, made the best agents of African administration. Whitehall could proclaim its humanitarian intent, by worrying over the excesses of Cape policy in the Transkei Territories – as the South African expert in the colonial office remarked, before the colony could incorporate African borderland territories, they had to satisfy London that there were 'reasonable safeguards against the prevalence in that district of deeds of revolting carnage and injustice'.[18] But once the Cape had 'matured', and once it had apparently learned its lessons in the 1877–81 disturbances, then Whitehall was surprisingly eager to believe that it possessed those 'reasonable safeguards' in sanctioning Cape expansion.

Yet perhaps not *so* surprising. British colonial policy surely drew from assumptions about 'race' and 'class' in the metropolitan society, and to presume that there would be more egality or 'justice' in such matters in a Victorian settlement 'fragment', than in the home community, is clearly a doubtful proposition.

After all, 'Liberty' and 'Progress' were presumed to spring from individual freedom in a competitive context, not from forms of legislated egality or social justice. 'All I want,' as even an arch humanitarian such as John Philip could remark early on in the century in this context, 'is that Hottentots be allowed to bring their labour to a fair market.'[19] The habits of social form, behaviour and rank were to evolve 'naturally'. Race and class were *not* to be criterions in law; but legislation might be passed – such as that for example which regulated employment practices, or the sale of drink – which clearly affected certain groups more than others. In the colonial context this was vividly illustrated in the Cape and Natal ordinances regulating master–servant relationships of contract – such as those of 1841 and 1850 respectively – and even in the property qualifications for the franchise. Race and ethnicity were naturally not mentioned; it was simply *presumed* that its group or 'class' implications would have the desired effects within the general social relationships of the colonial society.

Presumptions about race were indeed rarely set out in any systematised fashion in British imperial documents. But there are just occasionally glimpses of this great body of inchoate cultural values in the very techniques of empire adopted by the Imperial Factor in South Africa. It is abundantly clear, for example, that from the moment when an empire approach of devolved authority was advanced upon, there was scant chance that the imperial 'collaborators' and 'associates' in South Africa would be anything but European in origin – as 'nearly white' as possible. When the Cape was granted its form of self-rule in 1872, the permanent under-secretary at the colonial office remarked revealingly that it would be nothing short of 'culpable, to allow the establishment of Responsible Government without at the same time expressly disfranchising all persons not being three parts or at least one half, of white blood'.[20] Even outside specifically 'British South Africa', it is interesting to find that the Southern African expert in the colonial office could minute, in the midst of the crisis of 1884 in South-east Africa – when the New Republic of the Boers was being carved out of Zululand – that if the British did 'not stand too much' on their dignity, then the frontier Afrikaners would well 'serve as assistants in maintaining peace and order'; indeed rather than automatically oppose Boer expansion from the Transvaal, the Imperial Factor ought not to be swept away by humanitarian sentiment, and so 'turn would-be friends into dangerous enemies'.[21]

In short: the British entered the decade of the Partition unquestionably set to protect and defend their interests; to draw the polyglot political communities of the region into a working local relationship which would ensure laws, order and development; and yet also firmly committed to political compromise with the local white agencies of authority, on whom the ultimate responsibility for the administration of this empire-region was seen to rest. Thus while it is quite right to speak of the Victorian empire expanding in Southern Africa through the Partition, it did so in curious guise: the British continued to 'govern' but it was the local colonials who increasingly 'ruled'. The policy of devolution and association worked so well – too well for arch-imperialists – that it was the white 'collaborators' who came to dominate local Southern African politics in the 1880s. By 1889 Sir Hercules Robinson could remark, as high commissioner, that there was 'no permanent place in the future of South Africa for direct imperial rule on any large scale'. Indeed, all the Imperial Factor could now do was 'gradually prepare the way for handing native territories over to the Cape and Natal ... [with] advantage to all concerned'.

Cape 'Colonialism'   The Cape colony was *the* vital Afrocentric agency of white expansion during the South African Partition. Ultimately, by 1895, its administrative authority extended throughout the Transkei and Pondoland to the Natal borders, in one direction, and up into Bechuanaland below the Molopo River, in another. Further, it was Cape power and money which formed the basis of the great Rhodesian thrust into South-central Africa; and it was the hope of the British government that the 'protectorates', as much as 'Rhodesia', would finally be linked to a Cape-sponsored federated state. We should be careful, however, not to oversimplify the nature of Cape expansion by ignoring those elements in Cape politics indifferent to such an extension of formal authority, or the rather spasmodic character of Cape 'Colonialism'.

The emergence of the Cape as a 'sub-imperial' power of expansion and direct administration was relatively slow before the 1870s. The previous decade had found the colony indeed far from economically prosperous, and not a little politically stagnant. Events in Griqualand West, however, moved to change this situation pretty drastically. Diamonds were found in rich quantity in the late 1860s, and the British were moved to annex the area in 1871. Within the Cape's sluggish colonial economy, the Griqualand discoveries, and the rapid exploitation of the 'Diamond Fields', acted as a major stimulant to Cape growth. The 'Fields' – soon almost a state in themselves – were a wonder. Open farm country suddenly became a crowded urban and commercial area: in 1877 the Census gave the population of the Fields as over 17,000 of all races, earning wages in excess of £2 million annually; there were 160 miles of tramway; 350 steam engines; and the gross capital of the mines was set at £9,595,390.[22] An acre of ground in the 'Fields' cost £75,000. One nineteenth-century authority put a value of at least £35 million on the diamonds extracted between 1869 and 1885.[23] As the base of the British imperial presence in Southern Africa, the Cape not surprisingly began to pulsate with new economic well-being, climbing swiftly out of the relative doldrums of the 1860s. Public revenues rose from £711,360 in 1870, to £1,672,720 in 1875, passing the £3 million mark in 1881 – and based not least on the customs dues which the Cape could levy on the goods entering its ports for the interior.[24] A new sense of independence and authority came to Cape politics, hastened the grant of Responsible Government in 1872, and enlarged its potential as local British proxy agency of power.

Anthony Trollope, who made his extended tour of South Africa during 1877 — towards another of his famous travel books — is a valuable contemporary witness to these very themes. He commented on the Cape's new prosperity that it was 'due almost entirely to the diamonds, or rather to the commercial prosperity caused by the consumption in which diamond finders and their satellites have been able to indulge'.[25] Looked at in a long-term perspective which Trollope could not have enjoyed, diamonds may even be said to have begun the uneven 'modernisation' of Southern Africa, a process soon to be greatly accelerated by the gold discoveries on the Witwatersrand after 1886. What Trollope did catch, however, and singularly well at that, was not merely the drama of the great Kimberley hole from which the diamonds were extracted — 'it is as though you were looking into a vast bowl ... round the bottom ⌈ of which ⌉ are various incrustations among which ants are working with all the usual energy of the ant-tribe' — but the meaning of this capitalist enterprise for the Africans who came to labour as the 'ants' in the diggings:

Who can doubt that work is the great civilizer of the world ... If there be one who does, he should come here to see how those dusky troops of labourers, who ten years since were living in the wildest state of unalloyed savagery ... have already put themselves on the path towards civilization ... They come to work at six in the morning and go away at six in the evening ... They take their meals regularly and, what is best of all, they are learning to spend their money instead of carrying it back to their chiefs ... I have not myself seen the model Christian perfected; but when I have looked down into the Kimberley mine and seen three or four thousand of them at work ... I have felt that I was looking at three or four thousand growing Christians.

Because of this I regard Kimberley as one of the most interesting places on the earth.[26]

Trollope indeed hoped that colonial Africa generally would see other 'Kimberleys arise in various parts of the continent'.

We need not accept Trollope's Victorian faith in raw capitalism as agent of 'Improvement' in imperial Africa, to take the point that Kimberley stood for the new colonial situation being created in Southern Africa. The Diamond Fields, and all the secondary effects which they produced on the local economy — on everything from public works to railway and harbour developments, European immigration to black labour supplies — helped further to tip the balance of authority firmly towards the white political communities. They quickened and confirmed the trends of the later 1860s. In the furthest outlying districts of Cape administrative authority, for example, the magistrates happily reported on how the Diamond Fields had stimulated the 'forces of Progress', by increasing the range of Africans open to the influences of the work-ethic and the market-economy – the surest basis for breaking the thraldom of African cultural traditionalism, which the magistrates saw as the basic strength of African political resistance and disaffection. Indeed, the extension of the white political-economy appeared to hold out greater prospects of developing a 'new order' of society in British Southern Africa than the isolated actions of the missionary and the teacher. An examination of the regional origins of the African labourers employed at the Cape's Diamond Fields for example, certainly well reveals the power of the colony in the context of the whole region. Some 9,377 Africans laboured at the mines by the early 1880s, broken down as shown in Table 1, according to the Registrar at the Diamond Fields.

The statistical reports of the Cape Government in the early 1880s reflect even more broadly the same trends as the economic power of the colony expanded dramatically. In 1865 exports had totalled a mere £2,124,603 of which £1,680,824 was wool; by 1881, the real 'boom year' for the Cape, they reached £8,208,939 (over £4 million in diamonds and £2.2 million in wool) while a more average year, such as 1884, reflected exports of not less than £6,704,656 (£2.8 million in diamonds, £1.7 million in wool). Public expenditure, notably on railways, harbours and roads, as well as defence and interest on Government loans, also shot-up parallel to the new indices of economic activity and capital inflow. The *Controller and Auditor General's Report for 1885* showed that expenditure had grown, from the fiscal year 1876–77, to 1883–84, by nearly 250% over the decade: from £1,601,610 (in 1876–77) to £2,357,075 in 1879–80, to £3,375,682 in 1884–85. Indeed, he estimated that in the crucial political period 1 January 1870 to 31 June 1885 Cape public works had alone totalled £20,777,877; while the colony is shown to have raised loans largely on the overseas money markets to cover much of this physical expansion on which the interest paid (in the period 1876–85) was in the order of no less than £6,241,884.

It was certainly not a poor or undynamic colonial society which could, at the start of the 1880s, *annually* import over a million gallons of ale, 1.4 millions pounds of butter, 2.2 million pounds of candles, 1.2 million pounds of cheese, over 10 million pounds of coffee and chicory, some 950 million pounds of grains, 200,000 pounds of gunpowder, over 8,000 firearms, nearly 20 million pounds of rice, 7 million pounds of soap, 34 million pounds of sugar, a million pounds of tea and 2.4 million cubic feet of lumber. Nor was it a society which was only interested in buying essential

TABLE I '*Return of New and Old Hands Registered at Kimberley and Du Toits' Pan*'

Tribes	Kimberley	Du Toits' Pan
'Batlaros'	8	–
'British Basuto'	55	195
'Secocoenic Basutos'	309	1,177
'Bakwani'	57	79
'Batlapin'	8	18
'Bamangwato'	10	15
'Barolongs'	3	28
'British Zulus'	20	118
'Shangaans'	179	1,230
'Amaswazi'	1	12
'Transvaal Basutos'	14	–
'Lobenguelo'	–	–
'Matabella'	16	283
'British subjects of Cape Colony'	13	36
'Makalakas'	–	–
'Griqua'	1	–
'Koranna'	2	–
'Portuguese Zulus'	17	55
'Bakhatla'	13	193
Total new hands	726	3,439
Total old hands	3,528	1,684
Total	4,254	5,123

Source: Extracted from '*Report of W.J. Coleman, Registrar*', Returns of African Labour at the Diamond Fields for the year ending 31 December 1882, p. 20.

foodstuffs and basic supplies: 'haberdashery and millinery' is listed for the same year (1881) at £812,651; leather goods (including saddlery) at £624,320; woollen manufactures at £311,857; as well as 3,764,135 pounds of confectionery and 724,750 cigars.

Given the economic possibilities of growth open to the colonists and entrepreneurs in the 1870s, it is easy to see why the transfrontier African territories became such a focus of settler attention. Not only did they hold the potential labour force required for much of that development but, in their peaceful incorporation under Cape rule, there opened up great prospects in markets and general trade with the interior of Southern Africa. A growing Eastern Cape town, such as Port Elizabeth, manifested just such a deep concern with the evolving nature of frontier policy, and was constantly pushing both its own political leaders at Cape Town, as well as the British authorities in London, to expand the area of white rule in the cause of what they termed 'stability, progress and prosperity'. In 1876 the worthy fathers of the town indeed vigorously expressed their fears to Westminster that the transfrontier tribesmen were 'now far better armed, greater in number, and more confident than heretofore in their strength and skill, as well as in their ability, to take advantage of any opportunity to avenge wrongs, imaginary or real, and to inflict punishment' upon the white settlers of South Africa; and indeed, given the Afrikaner republican failures against the Bapedi there had been produced a 'pernicious influence on the other armed and warlike Kafirs and Zulus, who are massed on many parts of the borders, both of that country [the Transvaal] and your Majesty's South African territories, where they have waited to see whether any, and what, aid would be sent out to drive them back'. Accordingly, for economic as much as political reasons, they argued that African independency *had* to be ended:

The long unsettled condition and warlike desires of the natives have seriously retarded the advancement of public works, greatly increased the rise in wages, the cost of living, and the public expenditure for internal protection and frontier defence, and made it necessary for the government of the Cape to confer with Parliament now in Session how best to provide against a native uprising and against attempts at invasion.[27]

The British annexation of the Transvaal in 1877 was therefore greeted jubilantly by these settler-politicians: as far as they were concerned it represented a fundamental blow against African traditionalism and a major step towards the development of Southern Africa as a 'white man's land'. In their words, had it not been for the imperial advance in the interior,

The vast combination known to exist among all the tribes would have caused them to swoop down, first upon the white settlers in the Transvaal, and, extending their operations, mark their inroads by massacre, pillage and general destruction, and thus forcibly thrust back civilization in South Africa for many years, *to the great loss of the agriculturalist, the capitalist, the merchant and the distress of the colonists generally.*[28]

Eastern Cape settler opinion was accordingly deeply distressed when, in 1881, not only was the Transvaal annexation rescinded to a large degree (by the Pretoria Convention, with Kruger's republicans) but the Sotho Gun War disrupted trade with Basutoland, and the disturbed condition of

Southern Bechuanaland brought instability in commercial relationships with South-central Africa generally. Port Elizabeth public figures now strongly called for a policy of frontier control over all contiguous tribal groups – only then would 'the Colony be consolidated, the mercantile interests firmly established, and the repetition of rebellion be rendered impossible'.

The general advance in British territory in South Africa during the next decade of the Partition was therefore a man-made answer to somewhat desperate civic prayers. They delighted in the Cape's piecemeal expansion of rule into the Transkei Territories, the British advances in Zululand, Basutoland and the Tswana Territories, and they rejoiced in the founding of the BSA Company in Zambesia – together they secured 'very considerable advantages to the commerce of the Empire, and ... this Colony will also be largely benefited thereby'. Their interest in, indeed obsessive concern with, the railway strategies of the 1880s was thus bound not merely by the political challenge which the railroad expressed against the growing Kruger-axis in the interior, but also fundamentally focused upon the fact that it formed another dimension of the expansion transfrontier of general British interests which 'will have most beneficial results on the trade of the Colony'.[29]

This was, then, the general economic context of the political expansion soon to ensue. It was both a sign of the Cape's new sense of financial strength, and yet also of its nervous concern over the future progress of its commercial and mining development given the state of its frontiers, that this particular period – of the 1870s and early 1880s – was to be marked as the decade of major administrative extensions of authority over the African societies in the borderlands of the colony, beginning with the expansion into the Transkei. This process had begun earlier, with the incorporation of certain eastern frontier districts, such as British Kaffraria in 1864; but it now assumed very large proportions, and indeed between 1873 and 1879 the Cape expanded its administrative responsibilities, to include all of Basutoland (1873) and much of the Transkei Territories – Griqualand East (1875), Thembuland (1876), Bomvanaland and Emigrant Thembuland (1878), Fingoland and the Idutywa Reserve (1879). The new Chief Magistracy of the Transkei was also finally created (1879), and the Transkei Annexation Act (1877) was ready at hand to formalise by annexation these Cape 'spheres' of administrative authority operated by a small scattering of colonial magistrates. The proclaimed rationale for this new departure – and the constitutionally segregated 'administrative states', which the 'liberal Cape' cheerfully operated in these African territories – was law, order, authority and 'civilisation', in that order – although it is highly interesting that Cape land companies (quite apart from traders and labour agents) were already active in the Griqualand East area.[30]

The animating spirit of this *Pax Capensis* was provided by the redoubtable Charles Pacalt Brownlee (1827–90),[31] who held very distinct notions about the possibilities open to Cape administrative expansion. His private papers show that, despite a concern to practise 'cultural imperialism' very gradually, he looked upon African political communities in a far from neutral fashion.[32] He significantly opposed the 'Shepstone system' in Natal, as relying too heavily on African customs and authorities; and feared any return of the Imperial Factor to the administration of the African societies in 'British South Africa' – 'they may again build up chieftainship, by allowing the chiefs all the power which they formerly possessed; and which for the last 30 years we have been endeavouring to undermine'. Indeed, when it came to African political rebellions in the Transkei in the late 1870s, Brownlee was in no doubt that the 'forward policy' was the best policy to secure the colony:

We must either clear out of the country altogether, or make ourselves respected. And it does not matter where our frontier may be, for wherever we come into contact with barbarous tribes, the evil will be found. *Our only safe course is to bring the Natives under our control.* This is no doubt a difficult and expensive problem to work out, but it cannot be avoided. *We must govern the tribes to Natal, the Free State and Transvaal.* This is a difficulty we cannot avoid.[33]

Such views found official support in the colonial ministry which launched the disarmament policy against the Sotho, and which waged war against the southern Nguni, 1877–78. The Cape leader Sir Gordon Sprigg (premier 6 February 1878 – 8 May 1881) held highly belligerent 'civilising' views as the basis for his African administrative policies. 'The true philanthropist is the man who raises and civilizes the barbarian', he wrote in September 1879, on the eve of the Sotho 'Gun War',

And no race of barbarians was ever civilized by pandering to their weakness and passions, and by allowing them to do as they pleased under plea of liberty ... The expression of a barbarian is not civilization but barbarism. He does not require civilization – it must be imported to him, be expressed upon him, perhaps in spite of himself – for he likes nothing better than to be left alone.[34]

Sprigg's comments are particularly interesting for they probably represent not an exceptional set of ideas, but rather what was more likely the normative views of the settlers, and not necessarily those in the frontier areas of immediate contact and conflict alone. Indeed, it might be suggested that Sprigg's remarks are a valuable clue to the often unspoken 'cultural', or 'ideological' factors, which underlay Cape expansionism. It was, for example, widely accepted in settler society that the extension of white empire meant the extension of 'civilization' and the furthering of 'Progress'. As a petition from a leading town council in Sprigg's Eastern Cape region put it with stark simplicity in 1874, in advocating an imperial advance to Downing Street:

Experience has taught us that the prosperity of the native races are identical with the peace and happiness of the colonists. We, therefore, believe it would be wise of Her Majesty's Government to [take] ... over the tribes and their country lying between Natal and the [Cape] colony. Such protection would tend to their stability, progress and prosperity, and would meet with general satisfaction and approval.[35]

Social Darwinist idioms of race, culture and development also coloured the language of settler politics when it came to dealing with the 'Native Question' on the frontier. Sprigg himself happily referred to what he saw as a local law of progress: 'The European race marches forward; for good or evil, forward he goes, and when the white races come face to face with the black race, the controlling power of the white race asserts itself.' A more subtle exposition of these notions was also woven into the first authoritative account of Cape history, written by a contemporary of the events. The colonial historiographer, George McCall Theal (1837–1919),[36] has in fact left us with a sympathetic insider's account of this settler mentality. He too took Cape expansion to mean a grand amalgam of progress and development, not least expressed through 'civilization' and 'improvement' for the African societies so subjected to white authority. 'If by any chance they were left to themselves', he wrote of the Xhosa, 'they would not advance, but with civilization facing them and the leaven of a higher life working in the minds of some of themselves, they must conform to the law of progress'.[37]   The uneasy connection between 'might' and 'right' in Cape expansion also finds excellent exposition in Theal. African leaders who violently resisted the imposition of colonial authority, and were then subjected, brought this comment from the historian: 'Such is the inevitable fate of a barbarian ruler who endeavours to resist the progress of a civilized neighbour, *he must go under*.'[38]

Theal indeed saw Victorian culture and African traditionalism as natural enemies: the one exhalted individualism, self-help and progress; the other trapped societies in stagnant, pagan and communal values. He commented on one Herero group that, 'as they were extremely conservative in their ideas, a change to what the Europeans termed honest industry never once occurred to them. Naturally they and the Cape government were on terms of enmity.'[39] The word 'labour' crops up often as a synonym for progress in Theal's volumes, for it was by individual industry that many settlers believed the cake of custom could alone be broken among African societies. The expansion of such an enterprise as the Cape's railway network is thus described as not merely an advance for the colonial economy, but an improving agency for the Africans who labour in its making.

The rough labour in the construction of all these lines was performed by Bantu, who had now become quite expert in the use of the pick, shovel and wheelbarrow, though they could not perform as much work in a given time as European navvies. They were thus receiving an excellent education in the first principle of civilisation, the value of labour. They were also making use of the railways for travelling, and thus learning the value of time. A great change was taking place in the social life of these people in the colony, the men were becoming accustomed to work and to regular habits, and the women were relieved of much of the drudgery of earlier times.[40]

It was very much for these reasons that Theal – like a good majority of his Cape associates in the governing classes – brought down so hostile a verdict on Shepstone's supposed 'segregationist' approach to African administration in Natal.

This system did not tend to promote civilisation among the Bantu. In the locations they passed their lives in idleness, leaving the cultivation of the ground to the women just as in days of old, and only exerting themselves for a little when the time for paying the yearly tax came round. They were at liberty to indulge in all the vile habits of heathenism, without hindrance from the government.[41]

The Zulu war of 1879 was thus fought to achieve by the redcoat what should have been accomplished by the magistrate: 'The question was simply whether civilisation or barbarism was to prevail in the country.'[42] And 'civilisation' could not, ultimately, tolerate the adjacent 'barbarism' of African political communities.

There could be no security in the colony while tribes of barbarians were almost constantly at war with each other just beyond a fordable river border, and while many thousands of the same race were living in the colony itself . . . And so they were taken over, and the most strenuous efforts that were possible with so small a European element were put forth to lead them onward in civilisation and prosperity.[43]

In refusing to allow the independent African political communities to be 'left alone' – Sprigg's phrase – the Cape colony initially overreached itself. The retreat from Basutoland followed; and some colonial politicians had a fit of nervous hesitation over holding onto the Transkei. The mood passed. Basutoland offered least to the Cape, and was not 'reannexed'. Areas which promised richer possibilities in either settlement, or minerals, or labour, were held and expanded. Within three years of the Sotho fiasco, Cape authority extended deep into the Transkei; Griqualand West and Southern Bechuanaland.[44] Once the Transvaal challenge to local Cape hegemony began with the Witwatersrand gold discoveries, the mood of trepidation evaporated and the colonial leaders launched a series of expansive commercial, tariff, railway and territorial strategies designed to thwart the rise of Afrikaner republicanism focused on Paul Kruger. Henceforward there was no more talk of Cape 'isolationism' in Southern Africa. Rhodes and Hofmeyr were both, in their different ways, too committed to the larger political scene of inter-state relations to allow that. The Cape was, of course, to be encouraged in its extra-territorial activities by the metropolitan power. The ambitions of the colony meshed with the posture of the Imperial Factor in Southern Africa. If the Cape failed to play the leading role in local politics, the British would have to return to direct intervention, and abandon their hopes of a collaborative system of empire on the veld. The colonial collaborators forced their own price from the association in the end, however, and the British found themselves as partners in the great Northern Expansion into central Africa when they had only wished to secure their interests and hegemony south of the Limpopo River.

Cape Colonialism could thus be said to be the most potent of the local 'sub-imperial' forces of empire in Southern Africa during the Partition, and affected the course of events in at least three quite different dimensions. First, it was the leading 'British' economic force in the region, and through its labour demands, land needs and trading capacities, it was clearly a major factor in the evolving, if erratic development of the white colonial conquest of South Africa and its indigenous societies. Second, it was the major administrative power working for both British authority and white supremacy. The expansion of the frontiers of its government, market-economy, and Western values of civilisation – which had begun well before the Scramble years – continued after 1884, and formed the backbone of the British decisions to advance into the interior. Rhodes' penetration and settlement of Zambesia was essentially a product of Cape colonialism, rather than of metropolitan expansion. Third, it was a crucial political agency in the inter-state politics of South Africa. Through its local ambitions and its collaborative association with the Imperial Factor, the Cape acted as the central force of the British government and its local agencies. Taken together, they formed the operative factors of political transformation of the Cape borderlands – and further in the interior hinterland too – as their manipulations began to spring the forces of change at the centre of the initial phases of Partition leading into the Scramble after 1884.

Natal Expansionism   The settlers of Natal were also agents of British interests, and a force for change and Partition in colonial South Africa. But their capacity to impose their desires on a map broader than their own portion of South-east Africa was limited by the power which could be developed from their relatively small population and economy. Yet they did occupy a strategically important area of the coastline of British South Africa; they did nurture dreams of Natal as a co-equal rival in the future to the Cape; and their capacity to work mischief and disorder as they edged forward their frontiers of land settlement, and their set of labour demands, should not be under-estimated. And, in fact, in the coming general Scramble for South-east Africa, Natal was to play an unduly large role – partly through being the base of the strategies of Sir Theophilus Shepstone; partly through the opportunities opened up to the colony in Zululand in the aftermath of the British assault on the Zulu state; and partly through the arrival of foreign concessionaires on the coastline, which simply made Natal an important area in any proposed British Monroe doctrine applied to the coastlines.

In short, while not possessing the power of the Cape as a local sub-imperial agency of British empire, there existed in the attitudes of the Natal settlers towards African lands and labour resources, a potent factor for the impending Scrambles in and for South-east Africa after 1877. Particular aspects of the history of the colony in the nineteenth century were highly revealing of this potential role in any larger Scramble for South Africa.[45]

The settlers had come to Natal in a series of small waves. English-speaking traders had established the foothold in the 1820s. Dutch-speaking trekker pastoralists had arrived in 1837. Their Republic of Natalia had lasted for six years when the British government formally intervened in the region (1843), largely for strategic reasons, to assert British sovereignty against other Powers, and to cut off arms supplies to the Boer republicans – though the dignity of humanitarian motives was also cloaked around the action.[46]

The British occupation drove a majority of the Boers to *trek* again; they preferred their independence, and the hazards of existence on the highveld, to life under British administration. From the 1840s a trickle of British settlers came to replace the Boers in Natal, including the Rhodes brothers, Herbert and Cecil. By the decade of the African Scramble in the 1880s, Natal colony had less than 40,000 white settlers. They cultivated a mere 200,000 of its over 12 million acres, lived in isolated farm communities, very aware of their vulnerable status in the midst of a considerable population of Natal Nguni, who outnumbered them five to one, with the powerful Zulu state in the vastness beyond.

The white settlers of Natal entertained three obsessions, if their copious evidence before various government commissions in nineteenth century Natal is a reliable guide: fear over security, a constant land hunger, and a sense of continuous grievance over the shortage of black labour. Moreover, life in the plural society of Natal had not bred an overly tolerant attitude towards African peasants or traditional African culture[47] – as the series of colonial commissions on land, labour and the 'locations' were to show from mid-century onwards. Such attitudes are of historical importance as they were integral elements in the political and economic relationship of white Natal with African traditional societies.[48] The further development and modernisation of Natal could not go ahead if the labour and land shortages persisted. Yet Africans seemed quite content not to see the blessings of joining the white man in a cash-nexus relationship, much preferring to live within the self-sufficiency of traditional cultural communities and subsistence agriculture.[49] 'The natives are at present a farming population in themselves', as the Werner resident magistrate wrote succintly in 1882,

Each kraal cultivates land for its own use . . . It also owns and breeds stock of various descriptions . . . Thus the natives require a considerable extent of land for their own use, and are in a very different position from the labouring population of Europe.

So long as the natives are owners and breeders of stock, they will never, judging from an analogy with other races whose material wealth is stock, be a labouring population in the true sense of the word.

Indeed, only if the African traditionalists could be moved to 'depasture their stock' – by an alteration in land holding, or by labour taxes – would a 'great change in their mode of life and means of subsistence . . . take place'.[50]

The immediate focus of much of white colonial Natal's internal expansive dreams was therefore the traditional landed communities of the Nguni, in particular those Africans living in the six 'Locations' or 'Trust Reserves'. These were largely the creation in mid-century (1847–52) of Theophilus Shepstone's considerable administrative skills, and constituted the territorial basis of Natal's 'Native Policy'. By 1880 the locations constituted some 2,242,000 acres of land, closely settled by over 170,000 Natal Nguni. Shepstone's policies had established a paternal white overlordship of a unique personal kind – he was 'Somsteu' to his charges – in which he preserved African traditionalism through the inexpensive techniques of 'indirect rule' and 'segregation' from white colonial society. Later veneration of Shepstone by white Natalians – the man who 'understood the

Native' – should not blind us to the historical truth that for much of his tenure of office as Secretary for Native Affairs, 1847–76, he faced considerable criticism from the settlers as protecting Natal Africans against their vision of 'progress'. Put simply, many settlers felt the Reserves allowed Africans to enjoy far too much land, leisure and licentiousness.[51] Indeed the Reserves had hardly been established when a Natal commission commented in a most hostile fashion on their influence: 'The Kafirs are now much more insubordinate and impatient of control: they are rapidly becoming rich and independent, in a great degree owing to the polygamy and female slavery which prevails. They are better organised and consolidated, increasing in numbers by immigration, and more clearly aware of their real strength.'[52]

The 'opening up' of the Africans' Reserve lands and Locations thus became a popular political cry among settler Natalians, something Shepstone fought with great determination. In the eyes of the settler, however, the expansion of Natal to include occupation of these African lands, and ultimately of the 'unused' parts of Zululand itself, would 'solve' the chronic problems of labour and land shortages. Only in this way, equally, could Africans become progressive and civilised citizens in the colonial polity; for it was only by the spread of the work ethic and the gospel of individualism that Africans could be drawn from the thraldom of conservative and pagan traditionalism which locked them into old, unproductive and warlike patterns of life. 'The general lack of individuality prevents individual action', in the words of the resident magistrate at Umlazi (1882), 'and they still live on monotonously in a simple-minded acceptance of things as they are. Tradition, custom and the spell of habits, are still powerful forces.'[53]

Another important galvanising idea in white attitudes to the 'Native Questions' concerned the moral 'right to the land'. It was almost an axiom of faith among white settlers that the Natal Nguni were later 'immigrants' into the colony.[54] Yet as Dr Shula Marks has commented: 'That Natal was empty of Africans was always an illusion; though it was one that died hard.'[55] The earliest settlers had indeed entered South-east Africa to find Africans scattered and disordered due to the Mfecane. That situation, plus the fertility of the land and the ease of conquering the isolated Nguni communities, had joined to forge the idea of Natal as an open terrain for white settlement. In practical terms it meant, however, that the settler society was inclined to be unsympathetic towards African indigenous claims to Natal outside Zululand. It is a factor of no little import on the scale of the forces of political realignment in Natal in the 1880s.

Underlying this folk mystique of attitudes in the colonial society, were the fundamental facts about the land and labour situations. From the earliest days of colonisation, land had been alienated in a reckless manner – the Voortrekkers had established the concept of farms over 6,000 acres in size – while several speculative land companies had come to control vast areas of the colony. In the Scramble decade, one land company alone held nearly a million acres of good land, waiting for prices to rise as the demands of new immigrants, industries and railways, rose parallel to the expansion of the modernising agencies of imperialism. Further, a charmed circle of a few hundred Natal families owned a further six million acres. According to Professor de Kiewiet, by the mid 1870s over two thirds of Natal had been alienated. He adds shrewdly, 'European underpopulation and native over-population were phenomena with similar causes'.[56] Newer immigrants and small farmers found land very difficult to come by and expensive when available. Africans on the other hand were increasingly pressed outwards from their crowded locations and came to rent land from speculators – over five million acres by the 1880s – though there was a limit to that available. As Shepstone put it frankly in 1875, there 'is no land for them to go to in the Colony', and 'the locations are full'.[57]   His solutions, of course, lay in imperial expansion into 'open' areas of Pondoland and Zululand where 'his' Nguni could be resettled 'to provide for the wants of the natives in the Colony'.[58]

The 'labour question' was the other side of this somewhat desparate situation of settlement. White farmers demanded a large steady supply of cheap black labour and instead received an unsteady stream of workers, depending on the season. The cry for labour rose with the decades. The extreme expedient of importing Indian labourers had even been attempted, in the 1860s, with disappointing results. 'Labour is still scarce and high wages are demanded', as one magistrate wrote typically from a farm region in the early 1880s, 'the Natives retiring to their locations after a few months work, and the free Indians prefer the independence of [being] a farmer on one acre, to employment in European services. Indeed, the coolie has become the employer of labour, having Natives in his pay, instead of remaining the source whence labour should be obtained.'[59] Magistrate after magistrate echoed in their annual reports the comments of the Umvote official who wrote simply in 1882: 'The condition of the labour market has not improved; farmers find it more difficult every day to get the Natives to act up to the terms of their contract.'[60] A leading settler, John Robinson, writing in his *Notes on Natal: An Old Colonist's Book for New Settlers*, published in 1872, felt it necessary to warn of the scarcity of black labour and the 'natural idleness' of the Natal Nguni and Zulu.[61]

The degree to which there did indeed exist a crippling black labour short-age is, however, at least debatable. It seems significant that the lieutenant-governor of Natal could write in 1863 that, 'in fact, a very fair proportion of able-bodied male Natives of the Colony are engaged in the service of their white fellow subjects, although it is not very willingly admitted by the European population among whom it is the fashion to complain that the Kaffirs do not work'.[62] The contemporary reasons offered for the labour shortage thesis are therefore doubly interesting. Conditions of employ, a factual statistic of labourers needed, and raising low wage rates, are not touched upon. Rather, local officials and settlers were inclined to trace the roots of the 'shortage' to the continued existence of African traditional ways of life, both within the Locations and on rented farms. 'Native lessees naturally bring on their leases as many other Natives as they can get', the Newcastle magistrate argued. This was having dire results: 'it is in conflict with present notions respecting white and blacks – their political status and relative rights and duties – but also because it is considered that the system interferes with the supply and control of labour'.[63]

These 'squatter peasants' were however a minority part of the problem. At the core of the matter was thought to be the continued influence of traditionalism, under the sway of the chiefs. The latter were indeed characterised as the main bulwarks against 'progress', and the work ethic: 'The chiefs, as ever, are doing nothing towards improving their own condition or that of their people.'[64] In practical terms this meant, as another official commented, that 'not one [chief] can be pointed to as having endeavoured to elevate his position by improving his dwelling ... or inculcating by example or by precept, habits of industry.'[65] It might now be remarked that the reluctance of Africans to join the labour market *en masse* reflected on the resilience of traditionalism as it met African needs. Colonial opinion rejected such relativist notions. Answering the fundamental question of – why attack 'traditionalism' if it met the needs of Africans – one official gave this revealing nineteenth-century reply:

The Natives must at least see that a continuance of this easy, happy, idle sort of life, without those stimulating elements of labour and hardship and danger, which go to make a man a man, and a man a nation, must only end in degeneration and demoralization; and if the Native is to profit by the blessings which a civilised Government gives to him, he must learn to share its lot of labour.[66]

The continued power of the chiefdoms made such hopes of progress – both moral and economic – seem forlorn, while at the same time perpetuating the military insecurity of the sparsely settled white community.

The Zulu state played a symbolic role of singular importance in this white Natalian view of the situation. The independence of the Zulu was both a threat to the struggling colony and also an inspiration to the Natal Nguni under white rule. Shepstone put it best, in 1877, when he characterised Cetshwayo as 'the secret hope of every petty independent chief hundreds of miles away from him, who feels a desire that his colour should prevail' – adding that not until Zulu power was levelled would the Natal Nguni 'make up their minds to submit to the rule of civilisation'.

By the late 1870s, therefore, it could be argued that a good majority of settlers were convinced that certain developments in Zululand – notably Cetshwayo's struggles with his more militant younger army commanders, and the growing frontier conflict with the Afrikaners in the Utrecht area – betokened the coming of a final confrontation with the Zulu state. Many would also surely have accepted Shepstone's diagnosis (18 November 1878) that the 'Zulu Power is a perpetual menace to the peace of South Africa, and the influence which it ... is now exercising is hostile and aggressive'.[67]

Indeed, in the minds of a good number of Natal colonists, the late 1870s appeared to offer a pattern of growing, and co-ordinated reaction to colonial expansion and settlement, leading to a potential 'black front' of rebellion, from the Transkei Territories, Pondoland, and Basutoland, to Griqualand West, the Northern Transvaal and potentially to South-east Africa. In the rather alarmist, yet significant language of Shepstone, 'There are indications of the existence of a kind of common desire in the Native mind in South Africa to try and overcome the white intruders.'[68]

Firearms were an important factor in this situation. The white polities were 'gun societies':[69] firearms had been crucial in the establishment of settler hegemony. African leaders well took the point, and often eagerly attempted to acquire this destructive technology of the West. Certainly the ability of African political communities to resist white expansion in the nineteenth century was often to be intimately related to the possession of firearms – the case of the protracted resistance offered by the Xhosa groups of the Transkei,[70] and the resilience of the smaller Southern Sotho community of the interior,[71] being perhaps the most dramatic illustrations of this fact. The Zulu were suspected of harbouring a great cache of arms.

This is not to say that Natal Africans could by 1877 compete equally with the settler agencies of expansion: the British colonial administration restricted the sale of firearms to blacks; gunrunners tended to sell both out-of-date and expensive firearms; and the social conservatism of the traditional cultures prevented many African groups including the Zulu from maximising the effective use of such firearms as they did possess.[72] However, the fact that Natal Africans did acquire an increasing number of firearms – not least as a result of the cash-wages paid to them as labourers at the Kimberley Diamond Fields[73] – was to have major repercussions politically.

Firearms lifted black hopes of resistance and independency; they also made white colonial politicians increasingly nervous, yet authoritarian in their postures towards the chiefdoms. Indeed it was not long before Natal colonial leaders were agitating for a general 'disarmament' proclamation, or pressing for a rigorous programme of firearm 'registration', something actually accomplished in 1872. The fears and attitudes of the settlers were perhaps best, if crudely expressed, by the *Natal Mercury*: 'When the Kafirs get guns they fancy themselves the equals of their white rulers and neighbours, and they are prepared, as we have seen in the case of Langalibalele's people, to assume an attitude of contumacy and defiance which must end sooner or later in rebellion and bloodshed.'[74] Yet: who could doubt that among the major inducements to labour were the desires of Africans to obtain firearms; and who could equally doubt, as Sue Meiers has shown, that the gun trade was irresistibly attractive to certain colonial groups because of its high economic return, regardless of the political dangers?[75]

It was in this particular context that the 'Langalibalele affair' gained its considerable significance. Chief of the Natal segment of the Hlubi, Langalibalele had been settled on the slopes of the Drakensberg by the colonial authorities in the 1840s, and had thus enjoyed the independency of an African political community largely outside the daily influence and orbit of white magisterial interference. In 1872 Langalibalele expressed this sense of independence by ignoring the Natal promulgations to register firearms. The Natal authorities reacted fiercely, fearing any successful black challenge to their power. However, not only was Langalibalele militarily pursued across the entire Transkei, before being defeated and captured in Basutoland, but his chiefdomship was expunged, all stock seized, land confiscated, and his people dispersed among Natal farmers or labourers. As an incident it revealed the uglier side of nineteenth-century colonialism – including the distinctly questionable legal tribunal which passed sentence of banishment on the chief – and also the almost paranoid fears of the colonial society towards militant black reactions, together with the settler penchant for land and labour appropriation whenever and wherever possible.

In short, for both practical, and 'ideological reasons' – 'Natives like children, require leading', as one Natal official once wrote,[76] – settlers tended to view African societies, and their homelands in South-east Africa, from the perspective of an insecure, yet belligerent civilisation. From 1874 the colonists earnestly petitioned the metropolitan government for self-rule – in the form of Responsible Government – at first without success; Langalibalele and the Zulu imbroglio stressed the fragile situation of white Natal and its inability to conduct an African administration of respect.

In 1893, however, the colonists at last succeeded, and eliminated the 'Imperial Factor' in the local situation. 'To get control of the natives into the hands of the colonists', as one Natal politician remarked in 1891[77] had traditionally been a major goal since the Shepstone era. The Scramble years were to be the road to achieving that objective. The colonists were living up to the earlier dictum, of the senior imperial representative in Natal, who remarked pointedly in 1858 that 'it seems impossible for a body of white men to live in proximity to the coloured races, without adopting a conviction that as the dominant people, they have a right to command the services of the less civilised.'[78]

To bring about that situation, forms of political and social control of a major kind – including the reordering of the political geography of the region – were increasingly called for by the settler society as it attempted to develop. Before the metropolitan Scramble arrived in South-east Africa, the local forces of Partition were already assembled, their eyes focused on the 'unprogressive' societies and lands of the Natal Nguni and the Zulu. Prosperity, security and the frontier expansion of white settlement seemed inextricably intertwined with white dominance over black. Indeed, had not the leading Natal newspaper once commented that, 'We believe in the divinely purposed supremacy of the white over the black, and all history interprets and illustrates this belief'?[79] The patterns of political change in the nineteenth-century world of an expanding Europe appeared to make imperialism part of the 'natural laws' of Progress.

At the matrix of these contending political elements in the South-east Africa of the 1870s stood Sir Theophilus Shepstone (1817–93). He was highly sensitive to the play of forces, group against group. As 'Secretary for Native Affairs' Shepstone well felt the expansive pressures of Natal settler society, the Natalian desire for cheap black labour, together with white fears over Zulu militarism, and their concern to secure overlordship in all of South-east Africa. As 'Somsteu' to the Natal Nguni he was cognisant of the 'other side' of the settler frontier: the land shortage felt by the Africans, their fear of white expansion, and their problems in adjusting to the impact of modernisation. Lastly, as diplomatic intermediary with the Zulu state, and from 1872 counsel to Cetshwayo, he had a keen appreciation of the situation in Zululand.

This tripartite set of roles did not mean that Shepstone served all three groups equally. In truth, he served his own views first, and wished to manipulate the politics and settlement of the constituent groups in a fashion which would work towards his particular vision of the future. He fought against Natal settler expansion in the Reserves, yet was ready to channel

'Natal imperialism' towards the creation of an 'empire province' in which his views of group settlement, and intergroup race relations, would achieve fulfilment. He championed the cause of that Natal Nguni community against white incursions, yet ruled them as children whose political maturity was generations away.[80] He was deeply sympathetic to the traditional culture of the Zulu, yet was increasingly anxious to subvert the power of the House of Shaka – to produce a more malleable structure of Zulu political authority, one which could indeed be safely and securely integrated into the 'Shepstone view' of the ethnically plural but white dominated state of 'South Africa'.[81]

These apparently contradictory roles found their unity and rationale in Shepstone's political ideas, and in the development of his administrative politics. As an individual he was perplexing, complex, proud, secretive, austere, and authoritarian. An astute contemporary observer, Rider Haggard, could only describe him as a 'curious, silent man, who had acquired many of the characteristics of the natives amongst whom he lived'.[82] For the political historian concerned with analysing power and change, the 'mystery' of Shepstone would appear to be essentially with his personality, which was indeed opaque.[83] His public actions and administrative politics are well recorded, and here something more definite can surely be said.[84]

Shepstone was a paternalistic imperialist of the old utilitarian school.[85] He placed absolute faith in the direct government of 'good men', levying administrative justice, and offering leadership as magistrates, in close alliance with the traditional chiefs;[86] he had scant time for government by white farmers, or through modernised Africans.[87] He was also a Christian 'improver' and wished to lead Africans towards a progressive and civilised future over the bridge of gradualism, segregation and paternal guidance. He was ever eager to expand the orbit of *British* (not colonial) overlordship in South Africa, through the authority of the high commissioner, not the settler assemblies.[88] He claimed not to be aiming to create an 'apartheid society', and he pointed to his concerns for labour and education as preparations for African acculturation into Western life. But he fitted that within a perspective of social change among the Natal Nguni which was *very* gradualist:[89] in his extensive evidence before the noted Cape colonial 'Barry commission', on *Native Laws and Customs, 1883*, he remarked, 'I think it well to keep the object of improvement, and as far as may be, assimilation, in view as an ultimate goal: the danger lies in going too fast.'

It is important to stress Shepstonian ideas on African administration, for they formed the foundation on which he placed the superstructure of his wider British imperial vision in South Africa. Although it has yet to be fully explored by historians,[90] 'Shepstone the British imperialist' saw himself on a large scale, standing well above the various contending elements within the framework of local empire and the plural communities of Southern Africa. Sir Bartle Frere well caught this imperious dimension when he remarked that Shepstone was an 'Africander Tallyrand, shrewd, observant, silent, self-contained, immobile. Forty years ago he might have been great in continental diplomacy.' The fact is Shepstone clearly intended to carve greatness out of his actions on the African terrain in the service of empire, and to play a key role in determining the future of this vast portion of Africa: 'I have thought much of our position in South Africa as a Government.'[91] By the 1870s, a good many years before the Scramble, Shepstone had come to the opinion that major imperial actions were required in South Africa to ensure both the British presence and the steady, secure growth of the local plural society. These general notions had two fundamental thrusts.

He wished, firstly, to expand his system of African administration as broadly as possible – he simply desired to gain control of 'all Native matters in South Africa'.[92] Secondly, he yearned to extend British paramountcy to cover all of South-east Africa, and the hinterland of the highveld. His first purpose was to involve him in long-term strategies to reorder African settlement in South-east Africa generally and, in particular, to destroy Cetshwayo's authority, so that Zululand might also become a pliable element in his grand scheme, Shepstone's second concern led to his intimate involvement in the encouragement of British federation proposals in South Africa, which in turn involved ending the 'unreal independence' (his phrase) of the Boer states. In short, he wished to see nothing less than a step-by-step political revolution of the political scene in South Africa, along lines which he conceived as most likely to ensure the harmonious development of the area, within the fold of British influence and government.

The simple but dramatic result was that Shepstone's ambitions and strategies worked to loosen the existing framework of settlement and power, and to restructure local inter-group relationships. In so doing his machinations ultimately released latent forces in all the political communities involved, thus indirectly setting in motion an unparalleled process of political change, fragmentation and confrontation. This situation was ready-made for the expansive agencies of local colonialism to conduct a Partition, each settler group by the lights of its own specific desires and interests.

Many of Shepstone's attempts to restructure settlement and authority in South-east Africa before 1877 ended in failure. Yet they are signally revealing of the thrust of his political ideas. There is a pattern to his expansive political engineering. As early as the 1850s he was scheming to ease

African overcrowding in the Locations – 'a safety valve in the shape of adjoining territory has always been looked to as the only source of relief'[93] – by such proposals as an invasion of Faku's territory to the south, into which, like an old testament prophet, he should lead 'his' people. Governor Pine halted his ambitions in Adam Kok's eastern borderlands, in the 1860s, following on the 'Nomansland' annexation.[94] Further, Shepstone's hopes of establishing a 'greater Natal' by acquiring control over Basutoland in 1867[95] – a strategy actually agreed to by the British government – was only forestalled by the actions of the wily Sir Philip Wodehouse, Cape governor, who raced the Natal party for Moshweshwe's court, and won. Equally, Shepstone was frustrated in 1874–75 in his great scheme to establish a new Nguni 'homeland' on the disputed borderland territory between Zululand and the Transvaal Republic, plus 'a strip of Zulu country' about 20 miles wide, running from the sea along the northern border of Natal colony: 'this portion of Zululand is but sparsely inhabited by the Zulus', he told the anxious British authorities, 'and I have reason to believe that Cetshwayo's policy is to withdraw himself and his people more towards Delagoa Bay'.[96] That too failed to materialise as did his ambitions in Pondoland.

In view of these personal local initiatives, it is little wonder that a British high commissioner could later remark, that Shepstone 'shut himself up in an irresponsible isolation', and could be 'very dangerous in troublous times';[97] or that a British secretary of state for the colonies could draw back with some horror in 1874 at a particular Shepstone initiative – 'It must always be remembered that the very qualities and merits and past successes of Mr Shepstone in Native Affairs, tend to blind him to the danger of ... future complications, and make him set a horribly undue value on what he describes as British prestige.'[98]

That comment belonged to 1874. By 1877 with the British steeled to intervene vigorously in a forward fashion in South Africa, Shepstone became the very man of the hour. His larger view of inter-group and inter-state relations, his experience in African administration and his concern for British prestige were exactly what was wanted as the Imperial Factor moved on the Transvaal in its larger scheme to impose a pattern of peace and development on the potentially anarchic elements of plural South Africa, in alliance with its proxy agents, the Cape and Natal settler societies.

Afrikaner republicanism   Shepstone's concern to work for an overall re-structuring of the political order in colonial South Africa was certainly derivative of his desire to evolve a single 'native policy' – *his* policy – but it also developed out of his urgent desire to check and control the disturbing frontier activities of the Boer states of the interior, notably the Transvaal. Shepstone rightly saw the Boers of the highveld as naturally expansive forces of white settlement. They, too, must therefore be added to our local agencies of expansion, albeit of the most 'private' and unofficial variety.

A number of factors inherent to Boer society — political, economic and strategic — made the Afrikaners of the interior such a potent source of expanding frontier settlement. Indeed, the whole history of the Boer diaspora from the Cape after 1835, and the creation of the republican political communities of the interior plains, had at its core the restless outward expansion of zones of authority and settlement.

More Cape Afrikaners, of course, had *not* gone on the Great Trek than those who had actually joined the wagon parties of 'emigrant farmers' — as the politically and culturally disaffected Voortrekkers were soon termed.[99] Perhaps some 14,000 left British jurisdiction all told. By late 1877, and the eve of the Scramble in South Africa, the Shepstone administration of occupation in the Transvaal reckoned the northern Boer republicans at only about 32,000 souls — those in the Orange Free State as even fewer.[100] (The Cape then had some quarter of a million white settlers.)

Boer numbers however belied their power to engage in a local conquest of Africa. Technical factors assisted their survival and the subjection of opposing African forces: the mid-century conventions permitted the sale of firearms and gun-powder to the emigrant farmers, while denying them to traditionalist peasants. Sociological factors were equally if not more important. Afrikaners largely moved and settled on the highveld in groupings of extended family not unlike African clans. Strong patrilineal authority often gave charismatic leadership to these isolated groups bound together by kinship and the common enemy of African societies. Thus despite their small numbers, and the highly dispersed pattern of their farming settlements, the Boers were surprisingly well equipped to cope with the hazards of frontier existence. The commando system gave them military flexibility, and an ability to conduct the penetration of the interior, which their numbers and political divisions would not have indicated. They were *not* strong enough, of course, to subject the major African states: nor to impose a '*Pax-Afrikaner*' on the highveld. But they were able to carve out settlement patterns, and defend these in a state of armed co-existence with the African political communities of the area. They also, as 'Africans' (Afrikaners), played the politics of the interior as best they could by striking treaty alliances and inviting client relationships like any other political community on the highveld.

This still does not, of course, explain why the Boers were, decades before the Partition, attempting to create their own vast local 'empire' of settlement: it only indicates how they organised to survive. Here it is necessary to focus attention on the economics of the Boers. They were not cultivators but pastoralists; and pastoralists of a peculiar kind. Firstly, land and status were intimately linked. The Boer ideal was a farm for each son, often on adjacent land. Families thus had a way of expanding by generations, each generation leap-frogging over the former to set out new farms and homesteads on the *veld*. Secondly, the land required for these farms was extensive – some 5,000–6,000 acres was needed to sustain a Boer family. This was not because they developed a complex and cultured rural existence. Their homes were often no more than squared-off mud huts, their clothes were rustic, their food was simple to the point of monotony, and their social life beyond the farm almost non-existent. The size of the farms was determined largely by the relative inefficiency of their farming techniques. They were not peasant cultivators, and generally regarded manual labour in the fields as blackman's work. They largely subsisted therefore on cattle raising, though this hardly was of a scientific kind: over-stocking occurred (as it did amongst Africans) because the size of herds was intimately related to a man's theoretical wealth and status. They relied hardly at all on an export trade.

Further, they appear to have become landlords, on a fairly large-scale, to African peasant cultivators, taking back their rent in kind or in labour services.[101] As a system it came to be a notable feature of the Transvaal rural scene: as late as 1932 a Government Report (U.G. 22) could remark on the widespread nature of African labour-tenancy on Afrikaner highveld farms, defining it as the 'giving of services for a certain period in the year to the [white] farmer by the Native and/or his family in return for the right to reside on the farmer's land, to cultivate a portion of the land, and to graze his stock on the farm'.[102] Such a system required extensive land holdings, and implied the need for constant expansion to meet both population growth and economic demands.

So too, apparently, did their social structure. Although as a subject it remains ill-understood, and certainly requires demystification, some fascinating new research has now attempted to probe to the heart of the Boer state – the social and economic relationships of the emigrant groups gathered in their extended families – and has suggested that land was fundamental to status and patronage politics.[103] Far from the Boers occupying land in co-operative spirit, of communal settlement, the reverse was really true: land was very unevenly distributed among what were really greater and lesser families. In a kind of pastoral *ancien regime*, an inegalitarian landed social structure arose in which dependent relationships, marriage contracts, and general status, were all closely attached to the possession of land. Land usage was thus even worse than might have been supposed; and 'land-shortage' not nearly so strange a phenomenon as the low density of Boer pastoral population would at first indicate.

The internal history of the Transvaal, once written definitively, will provide a vital element to explain the dynamic of Boer expansion; until that time it might be ventured that it was this combination of agricultural inefficiency, labour tenancy, and the social importance of land as status, which did much to propel Afrikanerdom ever outward across the frontiers of original settlement into and onto adjacent African traditional homelands. It appears difficult to deny the conclusion of a modern twentieth century government survey which argued that there existed an expansionist dynamic inherent to Boer society on the highveld: 'To a people knowing only extensive methods in agriculture and pastoral pursuits, more land appears to be the natural and only cure for increasing economic pressure.'[104]

More certainly it can be said from the political history of the Boers, that the loose administrative authority in the Boer states meant borders to their political units which were somewhat elastic – determined more by the movement and settlement of the pastoral burghers than any constitutional convention. There was certainly no real central power to halt the landed expansion of the states' citizens – even if the nominal president's office had so wished. The Boers were also highly segmentary in their political behaviour, which is hardly surprising, given their groupings by family and personal leadership. The republics had been made by no less than seven quite separate Trekker columns of pioneers; while the Transvaal was, in fact, four small republics living in tense alliance until 1864, when they came together uneasily as one political unit. Much of their highveld expansion was often thus a function not of 'the state', but of one of its multitudinous kinship groupings.

Even with the creation of a 'national' presidency under M. W. Pretorius (president 1857–60, 1964–71) and Kruger (president 1883–99), the Transvaal failed to control its frontier-farmers. Pretorius indeed was eager to expand the state far westward into Tswana territory and northward into Ndebele lands (1868), while Kruger had ambitions in South-east Africa, notably in Swaziland, seeking both land and a strategic route to the sea. Joubert, Kruger's major rival to the presidency after 1881, was known to sponsor the Boer intrusions into Zululand, which led to the creation of the 'New Republic' in 1884. It was also axiomatic of Free State republican politics that the Boers should control the whole central plain, and war with the Sotho (and Griqua) for the best pastoral lands seemed endemic to the inter-group relationships. Only the intervention of the British in 1868, as trustees of Sotho rights, 'saved' Basutoland from subjection and 'partition'.

Although the major African chiefdoms of the Transvaal – notably the Venda and the Bapedi – were strong enough to hold off the Boers, the lesser groups were subject to the pressures of the burghers eager for their labour and land. The Transvaal's 'African policy' was essentially embodied in the person of P. J. Joubert. It was not without significance that he often concurrently held the posts of 'Superintendent of Natives' *and* 'Command-general'.[105] He became particularly adroit at African conquest and Transvaal expansion – exploiting political divisions among traditional groups, employing scorched-earth tactics, and deploying well-armed commandos where necessary – to produce a supply of indentured labourers and open lands.[106] This internal expansion of the Transvaal in fact represented its own domestic 'Scramble for Africa'. Its trans-frontier activities in the era of Partition were an addenda to this earlier belligerent activity on the highveld.

Until the 1870s the Boers failed to dominate and subject the whole of the interior only because of their own political weakness, in company with the opposition of the African chiefdoms. Beginning with the British annexation of the Transvaal (1877), the republicans ironically, however, began to strengthen their position. The British cracked down on their African rivals; the Boer revolt and victory at Majuba (1881) found common sympathy with the Cape Afrikaners; the British decision to withdraw from the Transvaal (1881–4) also involved abdication from control of the events of the interior; and the gold discoveries of 1886 gave the newly independent state a major economic base. Circumstances were thus propitious for Boer expansion, and the Partition decade found the republican burghers eager to extend their suasion over the interior, and over key areas of South-east Africa. The major African units had been largely subjected; the British were eager to conciliate Afrikanerdom, rather than face another pan-South African crisis, as in 1880–81; and, after 1884, Germany was present in the region, and not unready to play the 'Boer card' when it pleased against British foreign policy. To the traditional expansion of the Boers was added the political dynamic of 'Krugerism' – anti-British republicanism working for the domination of Pretoria, rather than Cape Town, in South Africa.

Not until 1899 did the Imperial Factor, as a result of Milner's machinations, frontally challenge republican Afrikanerdom. Through the Partition decade London attempted to strike bargains with Pretoria, to accommodate Transvaal territorial ambitions, and to undercut the growth of Afrikaner 'national' consciousness by acts of reasonableness and compromise. The results were crucial for the Partition. In the context of 'imperial Southern Africa', the British deliberately acquiesced in the expansion of Kruger's state, within certain defined areas. African societies in Swaziland, Zululand

and Bechuanaland, found themselves involved – more as bystanders than as participants – in an elaborate series of negotiations, between the Imperial Factor and the local white agencies of expansion, in which the lands of the indigenous societies were bargained away in return for grander political advantages. The British tended only to deny the republican Boers their territorial desires when Cape groups pressured London sufficiently vigorously, or where overwhelming imperial-strategic interests were put at risk.

The development of a 'greater Transvaal' in the Partition thus reflected on both traditional frontier expansion *and* on the British decision to kill the problem of the Afrikaner with kindness. If such a posture appeared to offer most to the imperialists and the frontiersmen, it offered least to African traditionalists.[107]

The rise of Afrikanerdom as a major force in the politics of South Africa owed not a little to this dialectical relationship with the British. It was the impact of British administrative practices and cultural elements which had first driven the Boers to become 'emigrants'; and it was the strategies of the Imperial Factor in the interior which had provoked into vigorous life the new sense of Afrikaner group-consciousness. In particular, the federalist policies of the 1870s, culminating in the Transvaal annexation and revolt, appear to have pressed Afrikanerdom into a new common bond against British overrule in South Africa – although oral tradition in the author's family has always spoken of the British annexation of Basutoland (1868) as the real beginnings of this Afrikaner identity against 'perfidious Albion'. Just when the Free Staters were about to expand their state in the much-coveted valleys of Lesotho, the British had stepped in and denied them their 'natural' local destiny. Republican policy in the Partition decade was best described by their political slogan, 'Africa for the Afrikaners'.

African political communities and the Partition

Reacting against this expansion of the white agencies – although just occasionally acting alongside the Partitioners – were the African political communities of South Africa.[108] Many of these major chiefdoms had already fallen to white authority by 1877; but there were others still sufficiently independent to possess the power which could alter or influence both the pattern and the pace of the Scramble for South Africa, as this narrative will reveal. Briefly, however, this can be introduced here in at least three distinct senses.

Firstly, it was the military strength of certain of the chiefdoms which shaped much of the initial *direction* and spread of white settlement in the interior. The Xhosa groups of the Transkei offered perhaps the most dramatic and long-term resistance of all African societies to the impact of the West in the whole history of the continent. It took over 100 years of frontier wars to 'break' traditionalism in the Transkei and this very fact was crucial in directing the flow of settler, *trekker* and Voortrekker. Further, it was the power of the Zulu in Natal, the Sotho in the central plains, the Bapedi in the Transvaal, and the Ndebele in Zambesia, which again influenced the patterns of white settlement. The strength of such African societies also posed a considerable threat in the minds of settlers and frontiersmen alike; the politics of the settlers often tended to find their focus in ambitions and strategies directed against the African political units. The development of Natal, for example, is unintelligible unless the Nguni are given an important role; or the founding of Rhodesia without close reference to Lobengula's Ndebele in 'Matabeleland'.[109]

Secondly, it was the *lack* of cohesion among the various major African political communities which largely assisted the white penetration and settlement of the interior. The sense of any common 'black front' – an identity of 'African' interests against the imperialists – was entirely absent. More: the settler intrusions of the 1840s found the interior of South Africa in a situation of some political and social disorder, resulting not from any European pressures but from the indigenous forces surrounding the *Mfecane*. We have only to read Professor Omer Cooper's noted study of the great event[110] to see the degree to which African political conditions affected the advance of the emigrant Boers. Had the major chiefdoms been enjoying peace, prosperity and the power which goes with such stability – let alone been in a position to unite against the white pioneers – it is hard to see how the Boer settlements could have got a secure foothold on the highveld. For several decades after the *Mfecane*, African states and statemaking itself, went through considerable phases of flux: leadership, power and territorial authority was violently contested, leading to political instability.

Settlers and frontiersmen were quick to take advantage of this fact. They feared, but never had to face, an African 'combination' against the colonial political units. They also found it possible to work the divisions – not only between, but *within* African societies – to the benefit of the forces of white settlement. In Theal's words, 'the dissensions among the clans presented a lever to work with'.[111] 'Client' and 'collaborative' arrangements cut into any potential African resistance to the European presence and also helped supply the white settlements and their economy with the vital flow of cheap black labour so necessary for the development of colonial South Africa.

The fact that several of the major African groups, such as the Nguni, were often segmentary in their own political development also, of course, favoured the intrusion of the white pastoralists. For the politics of resistance or collaboration merely quickened that fissiparous process at work, and further fragmented the African response. The white advances into the interior of Southern Africa thus moved forward in a highly complex manner: subjecting the weaker African groups, co-existing with the stronger chief-doms, or depending on the character of African politics to provide the suitable preconditions for frontier expansion through collaborative mechan-isms and divided counsels. Whether an African political community had the will or capacity to oppose the white groups was thus of real importance. The tactics adopted by an African leader could be fundamental in the sequence and development of the Partition. Within Southern Africa that response covered the whole range from armed resistance to 'concession politics', from scrambles for imperial protection to Boer-alliances. The highly complex and spasmodic character of the Partition's movement, and evolution in Southern Africa, thus involved the posture taken up by traditional African leaders as they faced the winds of change which sur-rounded the 'Scramble' for their lands and resources.

The Partition came to Africa too early to face any large-scale response of a literate African intelligentsia, which was only slowly coming to life and some small prominence in the later 1870s.[112] The major opposition to the European agencies of expansion therefore came from the chiefs. It is they who were forced to face the New Imperialism and the geo-political division of the tropical world. But it is still interesting to note that, even if the intelligentsia did not play a major role in the politics of partition, this was the period when a literate African response began to express itself, so projecting a new factor into the future public scene.[113] Mission-based vernacular journals already existed; mission-educated African teachers and priests had formed the 'Native Teachers Association' in 1875 and the 'Native Education Association' was to meet first in 1880; while the Ethiopian movement of African separatist churches soon connected with educated black opinion when Nehemiah Tile (a Wesleyan) seceded to create the 'Thembu National Church' in 1884.[114]

These were all symptoms of a growing African intelligentsia's response to the colonial society in which they found themselves. Only in 1884 how-ever did this small, largely Christian-educated elite, find a major spokesman, when John Tengo Jabavu (1859–1921) came to edit the Xhosa newspaper *Imvo Zabantsundu* ('African Opinion').[115] Jabavu was a moderate in Cape politics, really a 'Victorian liberal', and more a critical and questioning 'participator' than a radical 'nationalist'.[116] Professor Simons has remarked that there 'was a streak of Uncle Tom in Jabavu, but he was no white man's lackey'.[117] This is harsh, though containing an element of truth. Jabavu articulated African interests in a singularly hostile colonial environment; but he did so by the light of both his own missionary background and what he saw as pragmatically feasible for educated black opinion. He became the voice of the Westernised African,[118] and he spoke out strongly on the matter of the Partition, in which he fought for *imperial*, rather than *colonial* rule over the traditional African communities facing white conquest or incorporation into the settler states.

It might also be remarked that Jabavu's position on the presence and expansion of the West well reflected the general attitude of many of the educated Africans who had been acculturated. Certainly recent research into the activities of the African clergy in the public scene during the later nineteenth century,[119] fascinatingly suggests that the initial response of such Westernised individuals was to view the colonial society as one of beckoning opportunity, a widening of social, economic and intellectual horizons, rather than as a loss of identity and rights. There were not yet in evidence – not anyway in large degree before the formation of the separatist churches and the first 'nationalist' congress – signs that the African intelligentsia had perceived the limit of integration in fact acceptable to the white world of the Cape.

The Partition thus caught African society peculiarly divided: traditionalists were still, in many cases, at issue with each other over questions of land and authority as well as trying to close the frontier against Western influences; while the African intelligentsia was torn between some suspicion of what settler rule would mean for their native society (as the events of the Scramble soon harshly revealed), and considerable anticipation of the possibilities open to British subjects possessing an education, a skill, a trade, or, above all, a religious 'calling'.

The growing development and impact of the European Scramble certainly brought a new level of activity and consciousness to the emergent 'cells' of African political organisation representing black interests in an expanding white world of political authority and cultural values. But the manner in which these organisations responded to the sequence of frontier expansion, as symbolised by the Partition, interestingly reflects on the theme of divided loyalties mentioned above. *Imbumba Yama Afrika* (the 'South African Aborigines' Association') was founded in 1882, and the 'Native Electoral Association' two years later.[120] Both organisations took a deep interest in the character and expansion of white rule; yet their critical reaction was hardly one of outright opposition. Jabavu was instrumental in the creation of the latter association, and it is his ideas which dominate the main thrust of that literate response to the changing world of the 1880s:

fight against Cape colonial rule in the annexed transfrontier territories in favour of British guardianship; defend African rights and interests by agitation and pressure through participation in the colour-blind constitution of Cape politics; and work – partly through the local press as well as the missionary lobby at Exeter Hall – to remind the British government of their general trusteeship responsibilities in Southern Africa for the traditional societies.

The results were discouraging. While educated Africans did indeed come to play an ever larger role in the divisional politics of certain eastern Cape constituencies,[121] it still remains true that the impact of educated African opinion of the politics of the Partition was not great. Jabavu and his supporters rested their best hopes in the conscience of the Imperial Factor at a time when the British authorities were moving to create an empire of collaborative association with the settler governments of South Africa – administrations not dominated by the humanitarian sentiments of Jabavu's liberal allies, such as James Rose-Innes or Saul Soloman. The end result was that while educated African voices were now heard, reacting to the changing geo-political structure of Southern Africa in the Partition decade, such power as Africans possessed resided with their more traditional spokesmen. They alone could really influence the course of events, and although the Scramble would fatally undermine their independency this was still the era of the chiefs.

The frontier and the coming of the Scramble

It might have been presumed that the existence of such a plethora of agencies of European expansion, coupled with a lack of cohesion among the separate African political communities, would have produced a vigorously stable – even if highly exploitative – frontier world of white ascendancy and settlement. Exactly the opposite was true. The Natalian and Boer forces were not, until metropolitan intervention in the 1870s, able to establish an unquestioned hegemony; and indeed the Transvaal Afrikaners existed rather tenuously in the interior. Even the Cape was not in full command of its border zones in the 1870s, nor really capable of administering or controlling its transfrontier African responsibilities until well into the 1880s. Further, while the European agencies possessed the potential in the technology and fire-power to conquer all of South Africa, the very variety of the groups involved prevented the making of a unified white policy on the crucial issues of settlement, defence and African administration.

Thus it was that the mixture of official imperial power, plus highly unofficial private enterprise expansion from the colonies and republics, made for a frontier world of very considerable instability, unrest and disturbance. This volatile political situation on the frontier was to be a critical factor, for it was essentially in response to those local conditions that the Imperial Factor intervened in the 1870s; and it was that prevailing instability, rooted in the struggles for land and resources resulting in a 'creeping partition' of the region, which in fact escalated into a final Scramble for South Africa in the 1880s.

Why was the frontier constantly so disturbed? The British officials and statesmen favoured an answer which put the 'blame' squarely on the local frontiersmen and the African political communities, i.e. on the constituent elements of 'non-British South Africa'. And there was *some* truth in this thesis. The societies of the interior were prone to incendiary behaviour in their relationships, not least because as a leading South African historian his drily put it, settler and African claims to the land 'did not always coincide', and there were indeed 'many disputed frontier zones, where communities overlapped and rival governments competed for jurisdiction and allegiance'.[122]

Further, many non-British political groups had no 'core authority', and to suppose a political cohesiveness and a capacity to control all the sections or clans of a particular group – white or black – was often denied to its leadership. The grave of the early British 'treaty system' of the mid-century had lain in that illusion, as did its variant of the 'convention' approach, with the interior Boers. Even where a paramount chief existed, as amongst Moshweshwe's Sotho, sectionalism was part of political life; and in the case of the Tswana some nine distinct groupings were involved – some working alliances with the expanding white frontiersmen, others vigorously fighting that spread of settlement. Boer society was equally fractured in the character of its political authority: the two main republics had evolved from different columns and waves of migration out of the Cape, and thirty years after their foundation were still deeply segmented by region, family and personal leadership. The Transvaal was, for example really a cluster of smaller 'republics' bound uneasily together for survival. And it might be added, even 'British South Africa' was hardly a harmonious single political family: the Cape and Natal were rivals for paramount position; the Cape harboured a 'separatist' movement, based on the Albany district in the east; and the elements which should have drawn the colonial settlements together, could often divide them most – such as 'Native Policy' (involving as it did questions of labour and land acquisition).

In short: so long as the Imperial Factor declined to take up the burdens of direct administration, and regulate inter-group relationships in South Africa, the very contact, interaction and friction generated by the local

societies tended to keep up a chain sequence of political change and instability, resulting in a continuous process of frontier advance and partition.
That itself was one of the deepest sources of the piecemeal conquest and
subjection of the African societies of South Africa. The region was a classic
example of a frontier world creating its own political dynamic for unrest
and expansion.

The Victorian policy-makers groped towards this fact, but they were
somewhat baffled over the deeper sources of that frontier dynamic. They
perceived the actual context of the frontier only darkly. The century of
contact and conflict which had pre-dated the year of the Scramble had, in
fact, been absolutely crucial as a long-term factor in making a final Partition highly likely. Primarily, it created the curious leopard-spot pattern of
settlement in South Africa, in which white and black were not at all neatly
ranged on either side of a hard-and-fast 'frontier line', but were rather
juxtaposed in groups of unequal size and strength – so maximising the
potential instability and 'change'. The famed British 'frontier' of the Eastern
Cape, for example, operated not as an ethnic 'Berlin Wall' but as a long zone
of interaction – whites passing through as trek-Boers and missionaries;
blacks passing into the Cape as labourers, 'loyal' peasants and refugees
(often under humanitarian aegis); traders, smouse, prospectors, hunters,
and adventurers – not to mention cattle thieves – criss-crossing the zones of
demarcation and settlement.

The frontier was therefore a highly complex, evolving and dynamic context in colonial South Africa. It was porous, in allowing very considerable
traffic – commercial and human – and interaction. It was not so much an
area of sharp delineation between 'worlds' as a crucial zone of connection.
It was capable of movement – both as an expression of the 'advance' of British
authority, and as an expression of break-away settlements of whites in the
interior from the Great Trek onward. And it was a zone of change, settlement and barter which was an expression of all that was dynamic in the
colonial world to which it belonged: the work of Robertson, Neumark and
Legassick, for example, has in fact established that what happened on the
frontier was connected, in the most intense way, with the development of
the Cape colonial economy itself.[123]

It is also now becoming clear that the British cultural presence in South
Africa was of profound importance in creating tremors of unrest, change
and disturbance in the transfrontier world of the African societies of the
region. The other side of connecting the traditional African polities to the
new political economy of the Cape (and Natal) was the power to work change
and disturbance in the frontier zones and beyond. The Victorians were
often blind to this consequence of their presence – which they, not un-

naturally, saw as progressive and humanitarian in its thrust – and scholars since then have often been a trifle sanguine in analysing the consequence of the British influence on the frontier.[124] It would certainly be wrong to deny the very real humanitarian and liberal impulses which inspired, say, British trusteeship imperialism; but it would also be a very naive historical analysis which did not perceive that, to some degree, the Victorian political, economic and cultural impact in transfrontier South Africa could be profoundly unsettling. Because they were also improvers and empire builders they were also disrupters.[125]

This theme can be illustrated in a considerable variety of ways, and it does not require a radical or neo-marxist perspective on empire to accept the coming of the market economy, the creation of consumer demands, and the proselytising of ideas of individualism – whether in religious or land tenure terms – as corrosive of the stability of the cultures transfrontier. Nor to presuppose that the entry of well-intentioned agencies of British evangelical humanitarianism – mission Christianity, medical clinics, agricultural advisers and craft schools – was both to begin the development of 'traditional South Africa', and also collapse the working supports of the metaphysical world of the traditional cultures. In many ways, and despite their apparently oblique operation on the transfrontier societies, these active agents of evangelicalism and modernity did more to erode the political viability of the old African elites than the direct thrust of the Imperial Factor in any administrative or military guise – though that reserve of fire-power was always there if rampant traditionalism defied the administrator and settler over such fundamental issues as land, labour and 'law and order'. After the Blue-book and the Bible came the bayonet. As one young Victorian gentleman-traveller in South Africa put it with patent clarity in 1877, until there was 'better and more settled administration', together with the 'additional facility for locomotion', by way of roads and railways for commerce, there could be no rapid development. And, in practical terms for the frontier this meant cracking down hard on African politics and culture in colonial South Africa:

It is a fresh repetition of the old lesson taught us in India, in Central Asia, in New Zealand, wherever a civilised power comes into contact with an uncivilised, law and order must find themselves unavoidably neighbour to anarchy, civilisation cannot stand still, it must for its own preservation be aggressive, lest if law and order be not forcibly imposed anarchy may happily render both impossible.[126]

To point to this belligerent dimension of European imperialism or humanitarianism is not to suggest a blanket indictment of all British expansion and its methods; rather it is to recognise the complexity of the 'influence' of a great industrial power in an African context. 'The facts available show', as Professor Monica Wilson has sensitively put it – speaking from a South African 'liberal' and Christian perspective –

that when a once isolated people, with a limited technology and no writing, begins to interact with an economically more sophisticated people, with wide-scale relationships, a literature, some centralised form of government, and such military power as goes with economic development and centralised authority, then the culture of the once isolated people begins to change radically and some, at least, of their traditional institutions are likely to crumble.[127]

Such 'change', of course, could be induced by power, but also by the 'attraction of material wealth and social forms of the large-scale society'. The result, in functional terms, was that humanitarians as much as civil officers were often to become 'revolutionaries in traditional African societies'. Africans clearly often saw them as such; and they 'acknowledged it themselves. They sought to change society'.[128] This was certainly also how sympathetic contemporary Victorian observers frequently depicted their agents of empire in colonial South Africa: 'They . . . are bringing about a revolution among the natives', as one contemporary writer put it in 1877, 'of which it is impossible at present to estimate the good effects'.[129]

Those very presumptions, however, and the ways in which generally Europeans attempted to influence the evolution of South Africa, were linked with the very instability of the borderlands which they were attempting to control. 'Government', 'intervention' and 'influence' in South Africa could often have the reverse effect to that intended. Far from 'civilising' and 'controlling' the local indigenous societies, such influence often agitated the transfrontier communities, particularly as the British interventions tended to be spasmodic, shaped by surges of opinion, domestic politics and struggles with the treasury. The cumulative result was certainly one of measurable impact in the politics of South Africa. But it was an impact whose consequences could not be gauged or directed with any great certainty. Moreover, it was also probably true – to translate Dame Margery Perham's noted comment about the British in tropical Africa – that simply by being there imperialists changed things irrevocably. And 'change' was at the very root of the 'South African Question' as it confronted the Imperial Factor from 1877–84.

The Partition, developing progressively into a heated Scramble for the territory from the mid 1880s onwards, in so many ways represented the consequences and the extension of this earlier frontier involvement and expansion by the Europeans in South Africa. Contact and conflict on the dynamic, yet uncertain zones of authority – particularly in the late 1870s –

was about to let loose its own legacy on the political landscape. The greater Partition was undoubtedly to reflect a changing international balance of power. It was also to be the product of frontier empire, and of imperial agencies, older than the New Imperialism.

This can well be seen by examining the gathering dynamic of local frontier-expansion from 1877–84. For it was then that the 'South African Question' gradually turned into an international issue. Indeed, when 'expansion' became 'Scramble'.

2

The 'South African Question': frontier disturbance and imperial expansion 1877–84

The 'South African Question ... is a big one', a Victorian expert on the British overseas empire wrote in the spring of 1877 – in the very month of the Transvaal annexation – and indeed 'it is capable of working up into the worst cluster of native wars that we have yet had'. Would this be the 'starting point' of a great surge of reactive British imperialism, as Dr Marks once shrewdly suggested? The main purpose behind the several attempts at federating the South African political units in the 1870s had been to bring peaceful development to the troubled empire-region. The general thrust behind Carnarvon's determination to annex the Transvaal, through the agency of Shepstone, had been to attempt a bold stroke in that direction – by cutting the tangled skein of highveld politics, preparatory to making a more orderly political and economic arrangement out of frontier South Africa.

The British secretary of state attached 'the greatest importance' to this strategy: 'It solves a legion of difficult questions; it relieves us from many and real pressing dangers and it puts us, as regards African politics, in a more favourable position than any which we have as yet occupied.'[2] The federal architects' man-on-the-spot, Sir Bartle Frere, as high commissioner, very much concurred in that view and eagerly amplified the local significance of such formal expansion, which he saw essentially in terms of settler supremacy. He argued that only by firm imperial intervention in the local administrative patterns of authority could frontier South Africa turn the corner away from potential and endemic anarchy: 'Our great weakness has been the absence of vigour in organisation in many important branches of the Administration ... If the native population of these provinces is to be protected and advanced in civilization it is absolutely required that the European population should feel themselves secure'.[3] Shepstone, as administrator of the new British province of the Transvaal, also felt that overall British hegemony was the key to peace and development: 'Our relations with the native races is a question of serious importance, and one upon which the future prosperity, not only of the Transvaal, but of South Africa generally, very greatly depends.'[4]

Federation proposals, involving African subjection and Transvaal annexation, however, marked the beginnings not of peace and development, as was so earnestly hoped, but of disturbance, rebellion and war over a large part of the canvas of frontier South Africa. Not only were the Boers shortly to grow restive under British rule, breaking out in open revolt in December 1880 – when they symbolically refused to pay their taxes and then shot a British column to pieces for good measure – but in the tense years before that date, 1877–80, equally important rebellions developed in the trans-frontier African political communities of South Africa. This sporadic, but increasingly widespread pattern of disturbance and disorder, has been aptly described by an authority on one of those African rebellions – that of chief Moorosi of southern Basutoland – as the 'great armed outburst of African protest against the relentless pressure of white rule in South Africa in the late-1870s'.[5]

Again, 1877 was the decisive moment of divide, the point of departure for the dramatic political events which now occurred. By the end of that year the premonitions of Lord Blachford (formerly Sir Frederick Rogers) had come all too true: a great local African war was in progress. The sounds of frontier disturbance, and the acrid smell of burning villages and fields, scored the Cape borderlands from the Transkei Territories to the mountain slopes of Basutoland. And these initial disturbances of 1877–78 were to grow over the next few years from isolated pockets of unrest to large-scale armed African protests in areas as widespread as Griqualand East, Basutoland itself, Griqualand West, the northern Transvaal, and parts of South-east Africa involving Zululand. By 1881 the original disturbances in the southern Transkei appeared to have leapt, like a giant *veld*-fire, from one area of discontent to another. Colonists, imperial troopers and Afrikaner commandos launched a series of counter-offensives. Frontier campaigns of singular ferocity followed, in which the majority of rebellious African societies – all except the Bapedi and Basotho – were vigorously subjected, their lands often confiscated, and their peoples not infrequently dispersed to new areas of white supervised settlement. Not without justice did the colonial historian of South Africa, G. M. Theal, characterise these events as 'the most formidable attempt ever made by the natives of South Africa to throw off European supremacy'.

Although these 'rebellions' and wars have yet to find their definitive historian,[6] they clearly have considerable meaning in the political history of nineteenth-century Southern Africa. For the white settlers—whether Anglo-Saxon or Afrikaner – they were a frightening challenge to the fragile character of colonial authority over the great mass of African traditional groups, both within their administrative jurisdiction and in the border-lands surrounding the white settlements. For the African peoples they were, in all too many cases, a desperate and less than successful last-ditch attempt to resist the ever advancing tide of the white man's presence – whether through the farmer, magistrate, missionary or labour agent. Lastly, for the modern historian of the colonial empires – as the writings of Marks, Saunders and Benyon have compellingly argued, from different foci – these disorders explain much of the Partition to come in the next decade.

As a direct result of these intense years of disturbance and conflict, 1877–81, both the metropolitan and peripheral agencies of white empire were galvinised into expansive actions which involved further African subjection in the cause of white supremacy, frontier advances to extend administrative control, and a commitment by the Imperial Factor to involvement in the affairs of the interior as regulator of inter-group relationships. Even if the Germans had not appeared at Angra Pequena, as harbingers of the New Imperialism and created a Scramble involving Great Power rivalry, it would have been most surprising if the 1880s had not witnessed some attempt at a final Partition of Southern Africa by the forces of the 'Old Imperialism' situated in the British and Afrikaner white settlement groups. Colonial South Africa had reached a moment of great decision. White or black supremacy was being forced on the pre-existing patterns of political co-existence by the degree of contact, interaction and conflict which characterised colonial South Africa in the 1870s.

The Partition belonged in that sequence of events. Not only did it register the coming of international imperial rivalry to Southern Africa, it also stood for that decade of final African subjection in which an attempt was made to establish this colonial region as a 'white man's country', with its own peculiarly characteristic political economy.[7] The Scramble for South Africa, with all its international geo-political ramifications, was initially rooted in the attempts of an older imperial design to dominate and exploit African resources in the interests of both metropolitan and colonial society at the Cape.

The importance of that older imperialism in 'bringing on' the Partition and Scramble for South Africa before 1884 can best be understood by examin-ing the regional disturbances, and the response of the white agencies of empire, 1877–84. This disorder had its beginnings on the frontiers of the Cape Colony and within its ambit of 'influence' and 'informal empire'.

War, change and expansion soon characterised much of colonial South Africa.

'Government is a wolf': Pax Capensis, *African reaction and frontier advance, 1877–81*

The frontier disturbances which precipitated a major series of colonial advances had a great plurality of causes, some of them rooted in the internal structure of the African groups involved. Yet there is strong evidence to suggest that it was the steadily growing impact of the European presence, notably from the Cape, which actually played a crucial role in bringing on the unrest.

The piecemeal intrusion of colonial authority into African politics had brought instability to the frontier – the very reverse of what the colonial authorities had desired. Imperialism was producing conditions of disorder which would soon require even more determined advances of white authority. Local crisis on the frontier was creating the rationale for new empire; in their response to the settler and frontierman, the African tribesmen were to play a significant role in the surge of Partition politics in the late 1870s. Summarising the complex origins of these African risings is hazardous, but it certainly appears hard to deny the comment of Dr Benyon that 'this patterned sequence of African disturbances seems to have been caused more by the reinforced political thrust of whites in the late-seventies than by commonly experienced adverse economic conditions among the surviving tribal units, or by secret liaison for concerted action among blacks'; or the sharp complementary view of Dr Marks, who has depicted these events as 'the product of hopes raised amongst African by white gun-running and the despair engendered by their land grabbing'.[8]

Land, labour, authority and cultural values were the issues which most concerned the Cape as it viewed its transfrontier African neighbours; and these were also, naturally, the issues which were most deeply felt by tribal leaders as they faced the ever impinging world of the European. This latter view, from the 'other side of the frontier', was perhaps never better expressed than by the Mpondomise chief Mhlontlo, who commented in 1880 that he would 'rather die than endure what is coming'. His vision of colonial authority was indeed bleak:

The English Government has either entirely changed from what it was a few years ago, or it must be ignorant of what the [Cape] magistrates are doing. We are harshly treated ... Faith has been broken with us over and over again. We could, however, have put up with all this; but, it is what is coming that has led the black races to combine against the white man. Our cattle are to be branded; our arms are to be taken away; and after that our children are to be seized and carried across the sea [as labour apprentices].[9]

For other African leaders it was the administrative politics of the Cape magistrates which was indeed *the* objectionable factor – 'Government is a wolf', Chief Manthanzima protested at his progressive loss of authority[10] – something which even one of the magistrates indirectly supported in the aftermath of the revolts: 'In my opinion, there is a tendency to carry legislation for the natives too far', the Queenstown R.M. reported in 1880. 'They see this themselves and tell me, "the white man is oppressing us".'[11]

Others again felt threatened by the white man's interference with cultural traditions. 'Our people are hurt and shocked', the son of the great Sotho chief Moshweshwe protested for example when white priests appeared at a female initiation rite, 'just as Freemasons would be outraged if a woman went and saw their mysteries ... This is a matter touching our customs, like the greased cartridges in the days of the Mutiny in India, and I wish to bring it to the notice of Government.'[12] Certain Sotho leaders, faced with the Cape Ministry's ironically titled 'Peace Preservation Act', asked pointedly whether white farmers were also to be disarmed; and, if not, whether as loyal subjects of Her Majesty the Sotho were merely being singled out for the colour of their skin. 'I am only sorry that I am black today; I think that being black is a very great misfortune', one noted Sotho put it. 'The reason I say it is a very great misfortune is that although you may be following the Government ever so faithfully, it turns round upon you and says, "You do not belong to me", just because I have a black skin!'[13]

In essence, the disturbances and wars of 1877–81 focused attention on the clash of two political and cultural systems.[14] The unrest significantly began, in October 1877, with the attacks of the traditionalist Gcaleka-Xhosa upon the acculturated Mfengu of the Ciskei – the leading 'collaborative' group of Cape African peasantry.[15] The disturbance also subsumed internal violence between traditional cultivators and individual peasant farmers so beloved by the Cape administrative corps and missionaries: 'all the pent up feelings of animosity' with which the 'loyalist farmers' had 'been regarded by their countrymen broke forth with wanton acts of destruction', as the resident magistrate at Umtata graphically reported, 'their houses were demolished, trees which they reared under difficulties were destroyed, and any improvements they had tried to make on their farms were obliterated'.[16] Traditionalism had, of course, been placed under intense pressure by the steady advance of the Cape political frontier, and the piecemeal expansion of its white settlement and authority in the 1870s.

African territories were now over-populated, over-grazed and over-cultivated. The pressure on African men to undertake labour in the Cape proper was very great; and yet the inefficient system of white farming, and the low rate of wages, did little to benefit those who joined the market-economy. Many Africans thus came off the land, and merely moved from 'barbarism to pauperism', in Professor de Kiewiet's memorable phrase. The Cape policy of rewarding the acculturated African with land and peasant status, and of viewing the traditionalist villager with suspicion and distaste, only exacerbated the already divided political character of certain African societies within the orbit of colonial influence: Thembu and Mfengu forces joined the Cape war on the Gcaleka-Xhosa in 1877–81, and the wars which they prompted, thus obliquely reflected the reaction of a traditionalist world increasingly pressured and subverted by the agencies of white empire and 'Progress',[17] notably that of the *Pax Capensis*.

It is also quite possible that certain African political leaders were in fact moved to armed resistance by the well-publicised federation schemes of the British in the 1870s, which could indeed rightly be read as a potential coming-together of the white groups against the black societies in Southern Africa. Chief Sarili's comment on the situation perhaps best symbolised the needs of many traditional leaders: 'I am in a corner. The country is too small, and I may as well die as be pushed into a corner.'[18]

This unrest among the Gcaleka and Ngqika of the Transkei Xhosa was of course merely a beginning; much larger disturbances now followed. In February 1878, Griquas and Mpondos began their uprisings in Griqualand East, so sending tremors of unrest through most of the Transkei interior. Their actions were soon paralleled in time at Griqualand West, where more Griquas took up arms to recover their rights to the land – rights which had been cleverly removed from them by unscrupulous lawyers and land-agents. To the immediate north, African political communities followed their examples and soon Tswana of the Batlaping and Korana groups – joined by aggrieved Khoi-Khoi clans – were undertaking acts of violence in the Kuruman area.[19] Further afield, in the eastern Transvaal, the Bapedi led by Sekhukhune engaged in warfare with the Boer commandos of the Lydenburg District, in an intensified version of a conflict smouldering since 1876. In South-east Africa, the frontier friction between Zulu and Boer also began to reach new levels of intensity and which stirred African leaders to act; only Cetshwayo's determination to avoid a full-scale war against the newly-declared British state of the Transvaal halted a major conflagration.

The white colonial military responses to these challenges to colonial authority was, at first, fumbling.[20] In the Cape the small thousand-man body of volunteer Frontier Armed Mounted Police was inadequate to cope with the scale of the disturbances, being ill-trained and badly equipped. Their strategy was also less than successful. Falsely mistaking a Gcaleka tactical retreat for the end of hostilities, they began to disband only to have the traditional Xhosa warriors return in greater number. The 'Diamond Fields Horse' was rushed to the area, and the new imperial high commissioner took charge of the campaign, now conducted by regular troops as well. In the Transvaal Sekhukhune defied the commandos from his strongholds in the mountains, and it was not until after the Zulu war that the British regular troops finally broke the back of Bapedi's resistance. The Griqualand East disturbances were ended by Cape troops, but it took the Diamond Field's Horse, rushed back to Kuruman, to put out the flames of unrest. On the north-west frontiers the sporadic fighting continued, making some final conflict between black and white over Zululand even more likely. The methods of the colonial forces, and the *commandos*, in suppressing the rebellions were related to their fears of not merely loss of frontier territory, but the collapse of white authority itself in South Africa. The high commissioner, Sir Bartle Frere, was just as eager to bring law and order to the situation, but he was appalled at the boasts of the colonial troops that they took no prisoners, or the advice of the Cape attorney-general that rebels caught with arms could legally be executed 'without mercy or trial'.[21] Even the Cape colonial historian G. M. Theal found this a distasteful narrative to record: 'It is thus very likely that Kaffirs were shot who might have been made prisoners if sufficient trouble had been taken . . . And so hundreds were ferreted out and shot down as if they were noxious animals.'[22]

The 'peace-settlements' after these wars thus had a peculiarly local white-colonial stamp. Military surrender was not sufficient to ensure permanent African subjection. In the Transvaal the African rebel groups were broken up, their Reserves reordered in settlement patterns favourable to loyal clans, and the most obdurate of disaffected traditionalists scattered in small groups as 'apprentices' on Afrikaner farms.[23] For the Gcaleka and Ngqika the Cape Settlement was less shattering, but only marginally so. The Ngqika were removed from their Reserve, which was sold off as farms, having had their chief (Sandile) killed, despite his several requests for peace-terms; the Gcaleka suffered subjection, disarmament and the establishment of Cape magisterial control under newly designed administrative districts; and the 'loyal' Mfengu and Thembu rewarded with confiscated 'rebel' land, grain and cattle.

The significance of the war for the white settler society was rather different. The disturbances 'had cost the Colony the lives of sixty Europeans, £1,750,000 and a severe fright'.[24] The tenuous nature of white supremacy had, above all, been demonstrated; and the agitated warnings of the *Cape*

Defence Commission, which reported in February (1878) on the unprepared state of the Cape militia forces, now appeared to have been too near the truth for comfort – 'If . . . a combination of native tribes, so often predicted, should take place . . . the waves of barbarism would roll unchecked over the whole eastern districts . . . the Colony is living on a mine, that may at any time be sprung beneath its feet.' The Cape authorities accordingly determined never again to permit such a situation to arise.

The rationale for the severe peace settlement imposed on the 'rebels', and the very considerable expansive administrative advances soon made into the Transkei Territories, Basutoland, Griqualand West and Southern Bechuanaland, lay in their assessment of the events of 1877–78. The disturbances, in their widespread pattern and apparently sequential development, convinced a number of leading Cape administrative authorities of the ever present fear of a 'black conspiracy' against white authority, so long as independent chiefdoms existed. The magistrates' correspondence in the aftermath of the unrest is full of such foreboding and talk of 'plots'. 'This sectional rising is characteristic', the senior Ciskei official wrote from King William's Town to Cape Town,

The plan seems to have been to get one tribe, or portion of a tribe to rise, while others looking on were waiting the issue of the contest to shape their own course of action, and I believe that if the Gcalekas had succeeded in their attack upon the Fingoes at the first outbreak of hostilities in the Transkei, the Gaikas and all the other tribes would have joined to a man and combined to drive the white man into the sea.[25]

Another Ciskei magistrate who was convinced that the Transkei disturbances were due to a 'conspiracy of the chiefs', was quick to argue that 'so long as the system of chieftainship obtains the country can have no guarantee for a solid and permanent peace'.[26]

Events in Basutoland (and Zululand) 1879–81, were of course merely to add to these suspicions by nervous white politicians and officials. Against all good sense, and all the manifold advice they received to the contrary, the Cape ministry of Gordon Sprigg decided in 1879 to extend their Transkei disarmament policy to the territory of Basutoland, the object being – in Sprigg's own words – 'the establishment and maintenance of the supremacy of the European race in South Africa, which means the advance of civilisation, peace and security against barbarism, robbery and war'.[27] At an explosive final *pitso* with the Sotho, Sprigg did not hesitate to lecture the African leadership in offensive language. 'The Government feels that, like the rest of the natives in South Africa, you possess very much the character of children, and the Government knows that children cannot at all times trust themselves ...' Further, any attempt at resistance would simply be crushed. 'You know that the tribes which have gone to war with the Government in the Colony have been destroyed. The Gcalekas and Gaikas – where are they today? ... In every case where the black man has attacked the white man, he has ultimately ... gone before him'.[28] Thus when chief Moorosi defied Cape authority later that same year, Sprigg duly determined to show the mettle of his colonial ministry: he launched a military onslaught which only ended with the chief's death on 20 November, the subjection of his people, and plans to carve up the land into white farms. The Sotho watched all this with growing concern – a sense of anxiety and umbrage soon exacerbated by the announcement of increased hut taxes, and a general 'disarmament' in Basutoland.[29] By September 1880 over 20,000 Sotho had risen in armed revolt, using the very firearms the Cape forces had come to confiscate.[30] Months of indecisive warfare followed, and the official 'settlement' arbitrated by the high commissioner, registered a stalemate: Cape forces were withdrawn, but the Sotho were ordered to register their guns. In fact, the Sotho had triumphantly held off Cape belligerency and there was no immediate move made to enforce registration of firearms.

It was not the foolhardy and short-sighted character of this Basutoland policy which, however, produced the most significant contemporary comment in Cape official circles, but the place of the Sotho unrest in the apparent sequence of African rebellion. Reporting from the very district where Moorosi had begun his revolt, the resident magistrate put the rebellion down not to reckless Cape policy but African cupidity and conspiracy:

there was a deep laid plan entered into between all the principal chiefs within and beyond the [Cape] colonial border with few exceptions ... [and] there was to be a general rising against the white man, whose civilising influences and justness of his laws were estranging the loyalty of the people from their hereditary chiefs... The first outbreak of this combination was the 'Langalibalele' rebellion [of 1873 in Natal] ... The next sign of this combination was the Griqualand East revolt, Gcaleka War, and later on Gaika rebellion ... [Lastly, the Sotho] never intended when they asked for British protection ... that it should be permanent; it was simply a matter of expedience ... their allegiance was a necessity to be thrown off when the proper time came.[31]

Chieftainship was thus seen as the fundamental traditional institution at the base of the suspected anti-white 'combination'. 'It has once more been made apparent that if South Africa is to become a prosperous country, the tribal system must be destroyed', the Resident in Pondoland East commented. 'It is plain that the great object of the Chiefs has been to maintain the war spirit in the hearts of their people and to evoke it when it has suited their purpose. Until chieftainship is a thing of the past our native subjects can never become a peace-loving and industrious people'.[32] From the perspective of white colonial society it was indeed often easier to see the connections between disaffected traditional societies than their divisions by history and language. African political communities did indeed communicate with each other, but no 'plot' has ever been proved for the 1877–78 disturbances. The fact that the first sparks of the blaze were created by a purely internal clash, between Gcaleka and Mfengu following a wedding, further suggests that no well-planned combination existed. Yet even so senior and respected an official as J. Rose-Innes could write in 1878 that

The present outbreaks of Moorosi and Cetywayo are additional indications of this sectional rising, which we may be sure are being closely and anxiously watched by all other native chiefs and their followers, whose fidelity to us will depend upon the issue of these hostilities, and may be influenced by the success or otherwise which attends them.

From this point it is easy to understand how critical our relations with the natives must be and how readily they may at any time be seriously disturbed.[33]

The cumulative result of these disturbances for the various agencies of white empire – whether metropolitan or local colonial – was both coldly sobering and *also* a spur to attempt some final settlement of the 'Native Question'. 'The natives being now subdued and humbled under the effect of the late ruinous war', Charles Brownlee, the first Cape 'Secretary for Native Affairs' argued strongly in 1879, 'and ready to submit to the "word of Government", may now be acted upon more readily than at any other period of their history, and the present is a time most favourable for the introduction of changes so long urged upon Government, as necessary for the improvement of the Kafir races'.[34] Brownlee had always been an advocate of colonial security through the advance of the administration of 'civilisation', and he now best articulated the policy of Cape frontier expansion in the cause of law order and Progress: 'By taking over these tribes, they should be attached to us, the power of the chiefs would be broken up, and commerce and civilisation extended.'[35] Not all his fellow Cape settlers agreed; and once the fiasco of the Basutoland 'gun war' was over, the new colonial ministry of Thomas Scanlen was decidedly wary of undertaking the risks of extended African administration. Yet Brownlee's point, that the conquered Gcaleka and Ngqika territories should be annexed, could not be easily denied if further African unrest was to be avoided; nor could Sprigg's stress on establishing white authority in the disaffected borderlands be simply set aside. Cape administrative advances now began on the basis of the Transkei Annexation Act of 1877. A local Partition was in full and vigorous motion.

The imperialism of the proconsuls: Frere, Shepstone and the expansion of British authority, 1877–79

From the higher perspective of the high commissioner's office – the senior proconsul in South Africa – the disturbances and frontier wars also had serious consequences for the role of the British Imperial Factor in South Africa.

Sir Bartle Frere had hardly arrived at Government House, Cape Town, and was groping his way towards a viable administrative policy, when the disturbances began on the Eastern Frontier. His ultimate reading of the events was, not surprisingly, very similar to that of the permanent Cape imperial administrators and his senior advisers. He watched the growing, bloody frontier disturbances from close range, having quickly moved to the area of unrest, and characterised them as a 'general and simultaneous rising of Kaffirdom against white civilisation'.[36]

The frontier disturbances deeply offended his imperialism. Not only did he dislike these challenges to white authority, but the unrest summoned in him a fierce antipathy to frontier disorder developed over decades of service in the Indian *Raj*. These events also made mockery of his officially assigned mission of bringing the multi-state units of Southern Africa into a British-dominated federation. So long as white authority could be shaken, and so long as there were independent African societies strong enough to dislocate the settler states, there could be no progress towards a white federal dominion. From the outset of the Ngqika–Gcaleka war Frere was adamant that the Xhosa must be thoroughly subjected; and by the time that was accomplished he had already lifted his sights to envisage the subjection of the remaining symbols of African independency – Cetshwayo's Zululand, and the Sotho state. It was for this reason that he supported Sprigg's much criticised postures in Basutoland, 1880: 'This policy of general disarmament is, after all, only a branch ... of other greater and more complicated questions: Union or Confederation; self-defence against African enemies and good government, including settlement of the "Native Question".'[37] And it was for this reason that he was for action against any non-British political unit which failed to respond to his vision of a federalised Southern Africa under the Union Jack – whether African or Afrikaner. In 1877 he moved against the Transvaal; in 1879 against the Zulu.

These were not random urges. The problems of South Africa, Frere never tired of arguing, could only be dealt with 'on a system, and not by patching up'.[38] It thus seemed to him ludicrous that an African society, such as the Mpondo, should be left outside Cape authority once the Transkei annexations had begun in earnest in 1879; it was tantamount to the choices 'between a master who enforces order in his own school, and one who leaves the boys entirely to their own devices'.[39] From London the British secretary of state for colonies might try to hold back his local agents – the colonial secretary spoke in some horror of the 'enormous additions to the possessions of the Crown in South Africa during the last few years' and of the 'territories filled with masses of uncivilized natives'[40] – but the local momentum for white advance was no more easily stopped in short-order than some great Victorian steamship plowing along at full speed.

Further, the African disturbances 1877–81 had been no mirage. They were the strongest warning yet of the resilience and capacity of African traditionalism in the face of the imperialists. From a white perspective the logic of the situation demanded a strong common-front against the power of the chiefdoms and a policy of attempting to negate the ability of African political communities to challenge the development of 'British Southern Africa'. 'Unless and until this is done', the permanent under-secretary in the colonial office stated flatly in a cabinet memorandum in 1879, there 'is clearly no prospect of avoiding the periodical recurrence of wars carried on at great cost to this country and to the Colonies'.[41]

The same thought had already occurred to Theophilus Shepstone in the particular context of South-east Africa. 'Our relations with the native races is a question of serious importance,' he declared in 1877, 'and one upon which the future prosperity ... of South Africa generally, very greatly depends.'[42] His concerns had a very practical focus: the political situation in the Transvaal and Zululand.

He had long been unhappy with the condition of the highveld Boer republic, for reasons which related to both its internal structure, and its uncontrolled external frontier expansion onto African lands. On the first ground, he worried greatly over the consequence of a Transvaal collapse in the face of African disturbances, something he took to be increasingly likely after the victory of Sekhukhune's Bapedi over the personal Commando of President Burgers (1876), and in the prospect of major Swazi (and Zulu) onslaughts on the fragile Boer state. By early 1877 Shepstone was speaking of the 'fatal weakness' of the republic, and urgently warning that it would 'be destructive of the security of Her Majesty's possessions in South Africa to allow this seeming but unreal independence longer to tempt the ambition and cupidity of the native Chiefs and tribes within and without the boundaries of the Republic'. Indeed, by March of that year he was predicting that the Transvaal could be 'overrun and annihilated as a state' within six months unless some imperial action were not assured. Above all, he was at pains to stress that the Transvaal survived as a state because of the role of Natal's alliances and his own influence with African political communities, notably among the Zulu: 'If it had not been for the good offices of the Government of Natal ... [the Transvaal Republic] would have been overrun, and for these people [the burghers] to talk of their independence and freedom is simply to talk of enjoyments which they don't possess.'[43] After the Transvaal's annexation he remarked that 'the old nominally paramount Government, was but a shadow'.[44]

Shepstone was also very concerned with the external actions of the Transvaal state. In particular, he feared major unrest in race-relations arising out of the continual pressure of the Transvaal farmers outwards from the frontiers of their state, on to the lands of surrounding African political communities in South-east Africa. Between 1861 and 1876 some 18 requests came from the Zulu leadership to Shepstone petitioning mediation in that frontier struggle; in 1869 Mpande had even suggested the creation of a 'neutral' British buffer zone, in the disputed lands, to halt the Afrikaner encroachments; and in 1877, Cetshwayo, growing desperate in holding back his incensed warriors, begged Shepstone for a Natal agent to be placed in the midst of the frontier disorders so that it might be seen who are inclined to give more trouble – the Transvaal or the Zulu people.[45] The unsettled state of the borderlands finally indeed yielded not an agent but a Natal Boundary Commission of Inquiry (February–June 1878), which duly found in favour of the Zulu state. The Transvaal farmers, of course – notably those in the Utrecht region – simply refused to leave the disputed lands, and Zulu bitterness acquired a new militancy. For Shepstone the British annexation of the Transvaal (12 April 1877) was of fundamental importance not merely because it formed a stepping stone to a political confederation of the disparate states of South Africa, but because it brought under his control, as Administrator of the Transvaal, the most unruly state on the highveld. He could now begin to regulate both its internal inter-group race-relations – by the transplantation of his 'system' of segregated African 'reserves' and administrative justice – and also its external role, in inter-state relations.

Such an administrative and diplomatic vision had a powerfully pragmatic economic basis. Shepstone saw the annexation of the Transvaal as a means to encourage 'development' in the interior of South Africa – partly by stimulating more white immigration, trade and mining, even more by releasing a large body of much-needed black labour. This was the heart of his 'progressive native policy' for the Transvaal, and for any confederated colonial state of South Africa in the future. 'Measures are being taken', he wrote from Pretoria to the colonial secretary in London, after the annexation, with the ultimate object of bringing all the native tribes in the Transvaal under the control of intelligent Government officers . . . it will far more than repay any expenditure . . . not merely in the contributions by the natives to the revenue that will be regularly collected, but in the great impetus that will be given to the development of the immense resources of this country by the release of such a large body of labourers who are ready to work for wages the moment they are released from the thraldom that they are held in by the fear of inter-tribal wars . . . The agricultural and mineral riches of the country can best be made available by the free labour which these people are willing to give for moderate wages as soon as confidence in the stability and justice of the Government is established.[46]

In short: Transvaal annexation had deep significance for Shepstone within his larger vision of a reordered political geography in South-east and South central Africa, in which his concepts of government, development and empire could be implemented.

Shepstone's role in the coming of the Anglo-Zulu war of 1879 was also a further inter-locking piece of the same animating vision. His antipathy to Cetshwayo has already been noted; as has his desire to see some repartition of 'empty' Zulu lands for the resettlement of Natal Nguni. For Shepstone the natural condition of the people was a conglomeration of independent clans, who had been forced to live under the 'terrible incubus of the Zulu Royal family'.[47] The release of the Zulu from the 'pure military despotism' of Cetshwayo, by the suppression of the Shaka dynasty, he took to be a liberating and beneficient action. He viewed the independence of the Zulu state unhappily and had, by his own account, only reluctantly accepted the invitation to crown Cetshwayo as a means of influencing the conduct of the Royal Family: 'I felt bound, representing as I did the Government of a civilised race, to take advantage of the opportunity by endeavouring to ameliorate the condition of a people under one of the most oppressive despotisms in the world.'[48]

That was in 1875. By 1879 Shepstone was no longer even the unwilling ally of Cetshwayo. He was now an active opponent. As he remarked in 1877, he strongly favoured 'a more thorough control of the Zulu Country', whether this was 'gained by means of annexation or otherwise'.[49] He had, further, traditionally taken the authoritarian position that in dealing with barbarism might is right: 'it is in the power of the Government of Natal to annihilate the Zulu government by a simple order'.[50] Once established as grand-overlord of British authority on the highveld from Pretoria, Shepstone lost little time in joining the voices calling for an onslaught on the Zulu state. In a major despatch to the British authorities Shepstone argued vigorously that only 'when the Zulu Government is so changed as to be amenable to the demands of humanity . . . will the peace of South Africa rest on a surer basis than it does at present'.[51] It was a lesson he rarely tired of driving home:

'At this moment the Zulu Power is a perpetual menace to the peace of South Africa, and the influence which it has already exercised, and is now exercising, is hostile and aggressive . . . yet what other results can be looked for from a savage people, whose men are all trained from their youth to look upon working for wages and the ordinary labour necessary to advance the progress of a peaceful country, to be degrading; and to consider the taking of human life as the most fitting occupation of a man?[52]

Having come to this considered conclusion, Shepstone was adamant that the only real political solution necessitated 'the extinction of the Zulu power as it now is', for 'half measures will be useless'. Such a major and radical action he felt was utterly legitimate in the circumstances: Cetshwayo was a 'most cruel, bloodthirsty savage', completely unfit to be a major influence in South African affairs; his political demise was 'not only in the interests of the Zulus themselves, but in those which involve civilization and right, and the very existence of our position in South Africa'.[53]

The local ramifications of Shepstone's decision to throw himself into open opposition of the Zulu state were awesome. He helped to convince Sir Bartle Frere – the new high commissioner, and who needed scant urging to imperial gestures – that the Zulu state stood as the symbol of African independency and challenge;[54] and that until Cetshwayo's authority was broken, there could be no talk of safely confederating the various political communities of Southern Africa. Frere was already predisposed to major political actions on a large scale. He reported to London that he had found the local situation 'at the commencement of one of those eras of war and change'.[55]

Shepstone assisted in the focusing of the direction of 'war and change'. Not only did Frere quickly conclude that 'it will be found necessary, sooner or later, to extend the British Protectorate . . . over all the tribes',[56] but within that policy it was of primary importance 'to settle with the Zulus' once for all.[57] So well did he absorb Shepstone's lesson that he could in 1879 describe the Zulu state as 'a man-slaying human military machine',[58] and also deliberately delay the despatch of the report of the Natal boundary commission for over five months – so that he might have time to mount his case against the Zulu leadership, and Cetshwayo in particular.

On 11 January 1879 the British onslaught on the Zulu state began. The proconsuls – Frere and Shepstone – had together now secured metropolitan involvement in their local belligerent strategies.[59] The consequences of their 'success' were to be awesome for the African (and Afrikaner) groups against whom their strategies were directed. They were also to be deeply important for expanding the area of political 'change' and 'expansion' from the Cape borderlands to South-east Africa and, then, to the interior highveld of the Transvaal.

War and political change in South-east Africa: Zululand 1879–82

Events in South-east Africa, focused on Zululand at the turn of the 1880s, were to ensure that the local politics of Partition were not only sustained but given an explosive new ferocity. Zululand blew up like a powder keg, raining disorder, flux and disturbance over a wide environment. In the aftermath of these cataclysmic events, local colonial and Boer forces began a new series of scrambles for the land of the Zulu and Nguni.

Zululand was the cockpit of these happenings, for it was there that the strategies of the proconsuls had had maximum effect.[60] In particular, it was Shepstone's political actions which destroyed the very basis of Zulu external strategies – Cetshwayo's postures of co-existence, based on alliance with Natal, to ward off the Boers and the Swazi. The Zulu king was simply left dangling in a desperate situation. He felt deeply betrayed by his white allies – 'they have kept playing with me all the time, treating me like a child'[61] – and he now faced both external threats to his state from Afrikaners and colonists, together with internal challenges to his leadership, long simmering among the opponents to his posture of co-existence towards the whites. Most of all he felt betrayed by 'Somsteu'. Shepstone had been his nominal ally against the Afrikaner land pressures until annexation of the Transvaal, whereupon 'Somsteu' had entirely changed sides – the Afrikaners were now British subjects – and promoted the white claims to the Zulu borderlands as part of his grand imperial strategy.

Cetshwayo was driven back on a militaristic stance in which he had scant faith. He had thirty thousand warriors but not enough firearms, and no strategy to face the 'red-coats' except mass attacks.[62] So defensive was his counterpoise against Lord Chelmsford that the impis were given strict orders not to invade Natal colony. The king graphically described his predicament as comparable to 'a man warding off a falling tree'.[63] Professor Denoon has best caught the tragedy of the situation: 'Zululand was too strong to be ignored, but not strong enough to withstand a determined British invasion';[64] and there now duly followed what one indefatigable Victorian philanthropist in South Africa termed 'the ruin of Zululand', one of the most destructive yet graphically important events in the development of the Scramble in colonial South Africa.[65]

Zulu power went up in smoke with the attack on Cetshwayo's royal kraal of Ulundi on 4 July 1879. Shaka's bitter prophecy to his assassins that the 'swallows' (the Europeans with their mud homes) would inherit his authority, was about to come true at last.[66] The Zulu lost more than their political independence. The 'disputed lands' were given over to the Boers, whose local frontier-imperialism now increased, rather than diminished, with this British encouragement to expansion. The Zulu were also deprived of their 'national territorial unity'. The war being over the chief imperial officer administering the peace, Sir Garnet Wolseley, presented them with the 'poisoned chalice' of his own Settlement.[67] Wolseley claimed to have devised his Settlement in the spirit of simplicity and human justice: 'I have laboured with the great aim of establishing ... enduring foundations of peace, happiness and prosperity.'[68] In fact, it was to have results quite as disruptive and far-reaching as the war. In the apt words of Professor Thompson: 'No more astute device could have been found for setting Zulu against Zulu and thus consummating the military victory without further cost or responsibility.'[69]

Wolseley had been forbidden to annex Zululand outright as a British possession. He achieved his aim, of making a revival of the Zulu state impossible, by fragmenting power among thirteen 'kinglets', over each of which he set a new chief. Humanitarians could barely control their anger at the settlement. 'Having thus crushed the Zulu nation beneath his iron heel, Sir Garnet Wolseley passed on to find fresh fields ... for creating a striking effect', Colenso wrote with bitter irony, 'the usual subsequent collapse occurred, this time sooner than expected ... to reveal the black and dismal waste beneath'.[70] In the Settlement lay the seeds of the next phase of disturbance and the coming partition – the Zulu civil war and the Afrikaner invasion 1881–84.[71] The Usutho, direct followers of the royal house of Cetshwayo, watched with dismay as much of their status, land and cattle was stripped away, and then handed to their opponents. In particular, the Settlement rewarded collaborative African allies of Natal and the British – notably Uhamu, the 'traitorous' half brother of Cetshwayo, who was given authority over the Qulusi, noted supporters of the former king; Hlubi, who secured the lands of the Nqutu district, after supporting the colonial side in both the Langalibalele rebellion and the Zulu war (the fact of his being a Sotho chief added insult to injury); and the former white gunrunner and ally of Cetshwayo, the inimitable John Dunn, who had ambitions to nothing less than the Zulu throne itself, and who now gained a near 'kingdom' in southern Zululand.

Worst of all, there was the establishment of Cetshwayo's cousin, Zibhebhu, and his Mandhlakazi people in the very large Ndwandwe District north of the Black Umfolozi River. Zibhebhu had worked brilliantly for the Zulu state, until its collapse at Ulundi. Young and ambitious – he was born in 1841, and a man of considerable abilities – he now accordingly decided to take advantage of the aftermath of the war, and through his former association with John Dunn – who recommended him highly to the imperialists – Zibhebhu accepted office under British power. In return for his 'collaborative role' he was given extensive territory and authority. It even included general authority over much of the Usutho, as well as over Ndabuko and Ziwedu, plus Dinizulu – Cetshwayo's brothers and royal heir respectively[72] – who soon complained that Zibhebhu treated them like servants.[73]

The fundamental faults of the Settlement were obvious. It was artificial in ignoring the real patterns of Zulu settlement groups and power; it encouraged faction to fight faction for further partitions of land and cattle; and, in place of the centralising authority of Cetshwayo's office it offered a vacuum of power. 'The present state of affairs in Zululand satisfies neither the sagacity nor the pride of the people,' Shepstone protested to Frere, 'and every day's experience of it will add to their knowledge of the weakness of the rule that has been substituted for that of the king.'[74] Indeed, Shepstone was particularly bitter at the prospect of having waged the war for no purpose at all: the invasion had liberated the Zulu 'from the tyranny of Cetshwayo certainly, but we shall have handed them over bound hand and foot, to the tender mercies of a number of rapacious savages who have all along been . . . the instruments of the tyranny which we complained of in the king'.[75] White Natalians derisively referred to the 'kinglets' as the 'Kilkenny Cats'. Rider Haggard, an on-the-spot observer, thought the settlement an 'abomination and a disgrace to England'.[76]

From the Zulu perspective it was perhaps even worse. Inter-faction rivalry led to cattle-raiding and bloodshed, soon bordering on near anarchy and civil war. The Usuthu, humbled and bitter, watched their cattle 'eaten up' by their rivals. They decided to fight for the return of Cetshwayo – exiled to the Cape – and rallied round Mnyamana, Ziwedu and Ndabuko, forming the Zulu National Party in 1881 for that end.[77] Bishop Colenso's 'Bishopstowe group' aided their efforts.[78] The collaborative chiefs – especially Dunn, Uhamu and Zibhebhu – on the other hand watched these activities with some concern: the last thing they wished was the return of Cetshwayo and the old status quo. Dunn was said to have remarked in February 1882, 'As soon as I get sight of Cetshwayo I'll shoot him.'[79]

With imperceptible statesmanship being exhibited on the British imperial side, and with the warring Zulu factions struggling for power and cattle, Zululand was in a state of disorder not seen since *Mfecane*. 'I have been all through Zululand,' a reporter of the *Daily News* wrote in April 1882, 'and it makes me shudder to think of the misery now endured by these once happy people. They dare not complain or they would at once be "eaten up" by their kinglets or be killed.'[80] The British resident in Zululand, Melmoth Osborn also now openly admitted that he could not supervise a Settlement which had grown completely out of his control. In fact, he could not even *travel* in Zululand: 'The country from within a mile or two of this, right on, is in such a disturbed state, that even native messengers make a large circuit round to avoid contact with those in the pale of disturbance . . . I have no authority.'[81]

Some 'authority' clearly had to be applied or the area of violence would not merely consume more lives but must inevitably bring instability to ever wider areas of South-east Africa. Shepstone, the *éminence grise* of the situation, had logically been correct when he remarked that the post-war situation 'appears to be this':

the Zulu Government has suffered the total destruction of its Government; that Government was of an arbitrary and barbarous character; the natural and immediate reaction which follow [their] being freed from the restraint of such a Government, must be towards anarchy of a dangerous kind, and Natal as well as Zululand will be affected by it.

The destruction of this restraint has been the work of our hand, and we are bound, for the safety of the people whom we have conquered and for whose good we have professed to act, as well as for the safety of our own position, to replace the Government we have destroyed by one, less barbarous to be sure, but equally strong.[82]

This call was supported in a public campaign in England by Sir Bartle Frere, now forcibly retired from proconsular service by the Gladstone government. 'There is only one course which can secure peace in Zululand,' he wrote in the *Fortnightly Review*, 'and that is that the English Government should no longer strive to shut its eyes to the inevitable responsibilities of a great and powerful nation.'[83] Frere was joined by humanitarian cries for a British trusteeship annexation. 'For God's sake, my Lord,' Bishop Colenso thundered at the secretary of state, 'in common justice and mercy, take the whole land and *rule it*.'[84]

But the metropolitan authorities held back – despite the public excitement, despite the obvious failures of the 'Settlement' in Zululand, and despite the many entreaties for some kind of intervention by the Imperial Factor from various key figures in the public scene of South Africa. From Zululand itself came an almost constant stream of requests for abolition of the Settlement by the Usutho group – the Natal governor clearly had a painful time defending the status quo at a personal meeting in early

1881[85] – while from Cape Town came a steady call by Cetshwayo for restoration: 'I do not know what we have done, and I pray the Queen to let me go back . . . for though a man be allowed to breathe, he is not really alive if he is cut off from his wives and children.'[86]

The British metropolitan government stuck to 'benign neglect' as its policy for all seasons; and Cetshwayo was treated as an embarrassing liability from the past. Attending some 'highland games' at Rondebosch, Cetshwayo was nearly hit by a caber; the high commissioner commented, in an aside, 'Had it fallen on the king's head, a great problem would have been settled.'[87] Yet the alternative to restoring Cetshwayo was, in truth, establishing British authority. The imperial government tried to find a middle path – not least by deputing Sir Evelyn Wood to 'restructure' the Settlement in 1881 after his military services in the Transvaal,[88] with results which perhaps actually exacerbated the situation.

Wearily, but almost inevitably,[89] the imperial authorities thus turned to Cetshwayo, on whom fortunately the caber had not fallen, and who was now thought to be 'reformed' as a model political prisoner in exile. Lacking any viable alternate policy, the British looked to the broken Cetshwayo to remove their Zululand dilemma. 'All the Zulus wish him back', the somewhat desperate Osborn wrote in despatch in 1882.[90] The British knew this was not strictly true: the new Zulu authorities established under the Settlement had strong vested interests in opposing restoration. But the British authorities now schemed to reconcile the power elements of the Settlement – such as Zibhebhu's authority – with an Usuthu restoration. The colonial officials were encouraged in this policy by a declaration of the British premier, Gladstone, who now saw hope in Cetshwayo's possible return to South-east Africa: 'If it should appear that the mass of the people in Zululand are for Cetshwayo . . . so far from regarding him as the enemy of England . . . I should regard the proof of that fact with great pleasure . . . and that would be the sentiment of my colleagues.'[91]

In somewhat Machiavellian manner the deadly enemy of 1879 thus became the collaborative ally of 1882. Cetshwayo duly arrived in London in July, complete in morning suit, 'topper' and bare feet.[92] So desperate was he to return to Zululand that he disregarded his former treatment by the imperialists, and he now spoke of his role as a 'child' in the service of his 'mother' Queen Victoria. During the 'negotiations' at the colonial office for his restoration he made protest over a number of points – such as the size of a large 'Reserve' which the British intended to carve out of Zululand as a sanctuary for Zulu threatened by the Usuthu – but his resistence was token, and the discussion lapsed into rather one sided interviews in which the terms of his restoration were placed before him on a 'take-it, or leave-it' basis.[93] These terms forbade any reconstruction of the old Zulu military machine, or aspects of the old Zulu traditional order such as the 'washing of spears'.[94]

These conditions were, however, as nothing compared to the new settlement which the British colonial secretary had the Natal governor construct on the land. Wolseley's '13 kinglets' were gone. There were now Lord Kimberley's kinglets instead. Cetshwayo had agreed to restoration on the British terms without actually ever seeing a definitive political map of the new Zululand. Shock and dismay awaited him. The Reserve was indeed vast. Collaborative chiefs, like the 'traitor' John Dunn, still enjoyed their post-war status. New rival authorities to the power of the paramountcy were left intact: most important, Zibhebhu and the Mandhlakazi had acquired such power and authority in the post-war period that they could flaunt their status in Cetshwayo's face. In Rider Haggard's contemporary assessment, they 'alone of the kinglets now remained in an independent position'.[95] Equally distressing for Cetshwayo, and as an addendum to his problems with Zibhebhu, the local British governor Sir Henry Bulwer, was not an impartial observer of the restoration situation. As J. Y. Gibson, pioneer Zulu historian pointed out years ago, he was prejudiced against Cetshwayo's Usuthu, regarding them as the trouble-maker faction, and instead being sympathetic to Zibhebhu's Mandhlakazi whom he saw as England's best allies.[96] Cetshwayo, who could often characterise a situation better than any observer since, remarked sharply of his restoration: 'I did not land in a dry place. I landed in mud ... I came and found long-standing friends and bitterly opposed enemies. There are no new friends since I came.'[97]

The new era began on 10 January 1883, when Cetshwayo rode through the Indian Ocean breakers in a small boat from *H.M.S. Briton.*[98] Two months later he was in the midst of civil war.[99] Once again, as in 1879, a British initiative had merely exacerbated the situation. Cetshwayo found he was nobody's chief.[100] Old indunas, outlying chiefs, residents of the New Reserve, and above all, Zibhebhu, treated him as a British puppet, to be ignored, defied and challenged as the mood dictated.[101] The Usuthu precipitated the collapse of this 'Kimberley Settlement' when, smarting in their new and precarious status, they rose in defence of Cetshwayo's old authority and attacked the Mandhlakazi.[102] Zibhebhu showed his considerable military skills in counter-offensive: on 13 March 1883 over 4,000 Usuthu died in one battle.[103] Full-scale war with Cetshwayo was now likely. By July it was inevitable. On 21 July Zibhebhu scattered the last of the Usuthu forces, after considerable killing and plundering. Cetshwayo remarked simply that the bloodshed in his reign – for which he had been so criticised by the imperialists and colonists – was, compared to the period of the 'Settlement', 'as an ant in a pond of water'.[104]

Cetshwayo now fled for his life, into the Nkandla forests, where he was attacked and injured. He agreed to go 'into Mr Osborn's armpit', and accept British protection. Accordingly he was escorted to Eshowe in the British 'Reserve'.[105] He lived on, a curious 'exile' in his own land for a further eight months. When his death was finally reported on 9 February 1884 – officially of a heart attack[106] – it seemed unimportant. He had already passed into history. There was even laughter heard in the House of Commons when his death was announced.

The post-war condition – of flux, anarchy and the political vacuum in overall authority – had simply returned. The only independent power initiative in the situation was exercised by the British imperialists, and that was in an extremely limited and negative fashion. There was the metropolitan decision to defend the Zulu 'Reserve', where resided a British 'commissioner'. 'If we do not maintain the inviolability of the Reserve,' as one colonial office administrator remarked in extreme frankness, 'we had better clear out of Africa altogether, and never hear the word of South Africa mentioned again.'[107] The point was well made. British imperial initiatives in South-east Africa and the Transvaal had led directly to patent political failures: the much-vaunted confederation policy had now been responsible for the revival of Afrikaner national sentiment, and the destruction of African interests over large areas of the traditional chiefdoms. As a series of plural societies, Southern Africa was in an infinitely worse condition than before the grand vision of imperial federation had joined the local visions of Shepstone, and the sub-imperialism of the colonial communities, to reorder the basic framework of the region.

Zululand was again the cockpit of the situation. 'The maintenance of this Reserve . . . is the touchstone of our own position in South Africa', the same British official minuted in London, 'We shall never be trusted or believed again if we fail in this.'[108] The policy was soon to be severely tested and its limits exposed. When the Natal governor attempted to extend the area of the Reserve up to the Black Umfolozi,[109] to include Zibhebhu's territory in protective trusteeship against new Afrikaner incursions (May 1884),[110] the British drew back.[111] They would not accept 'a disguised protectorate', as they put it, preferring to allow all the latent and divisive forces in Zululand to have full play rather than be an external agency of order or responsibility.[112] Certain British officials pointed out that, having initiated the disorder, Great Britain had responsibilities of trusteeship. The cabinet would have none of it. Yet in private the British secretary of state admitted to the premier that the situation had him spinning in a gloomy spiral of indecision. 'What are we to do with that country?' he enquired:

Can we leave the whole matter alone? That is the simplest course: but it will lead to civil war and to a general disturbance among the natives ... I am afraid that we cannot wash our hands of the affair, much as I should wish it. Lastly, should we as a provisional expedient occupy the country temporarily up to Usibebu's boundary, to keep order till something permanent can be settled? You will not like this notion nor do I: but we cannot go on long as we are at present ... These seems no known means of getting the Zulus to say what they like best – they have not been used to being consulted. If you don't approve of my suggestion, can you offer one? I don't see my way.[113]

The Afrikaners, and then the Germans, were to help him make up his mind where Cetshwayo and the Zulus had failed to move the metropolitan government. Whether London wished it or not, general Partition was beginning to sweep over South-east Africa.

Boer rebellion on the highveld:
causes and consequences 1880–82

There was to be no peace for the Imperial Factor. At the moment when the British authorities were anxiously struggling to find settlement for affairs in Zululand, Basutoland and the Transkei Territories the Transvaal Boers rose in revolt on the highveld.[114] Yet another frontier war was about to be added to the disruptive disturbances which had already shaken South Africa since 1877, and which had made mockery of the British attempts to bring peace and development to this unstable empire-region.

The rebellion of the republican Boers was to be a crucial complication in the sequence of events in the early 1880s. Not only did they soon triumphantly flaunt British authority – by managing to capture and expel the imperial administration of the Transvaal province – but having done so, they added insult to British injury by celebrating their victories through expansion of their state into already troubled and explosive borderland territories. The cumulative consequences of their rising against the Imperial Factor were deadly: new waves of unrest flowed out from the Transvaal, which now became the epicentre for disturbance in South-east and South-central Africa.

The Boer rebellion certainly contained its own exclusive causes. These Trekkers of old had deeply, if rather silently resented the attempt of the British to draw them back into the imperial fold by annexing their republic in 1877 as part of Frere's 'systematic' moves towards federation. Their every instinct was anti-British: devoutly Calvinist, strongly anti-liberal, passionately individualist, against all bureaucratic systems and proudly republican. Out on their isolated farm districts, at their periodic gatherings for *nachtmaal* and market-fairs, they had grumbled against the return of the British overlords to their life. It had taken time for an anti-British leadership to emerge. But by 1879 Paul Kruger – and to a lesser degree Piet Joubert – offered an alternative national response to the more equivocal policy adopted by President Burgers two years earlier.

Kruger was the key to the internal Transvaal situation. He was easily misunderstood and under-estimated by British observers. The occupying administration tended to write him off as an oafish frontier Boer. 'Paul Kruger is an elderly man, decidedly ugly, with a countenance denoting extreme obstinacy, and also great cruelty', was the written portrait painted by the lawyer in Shepstone's regime;

His conduct at the public luncheon on Tuesday was ... 'gigantically horrible'. His dirty wooden pipe was visible, for it stuck out of his breast pocket; his scanty hair was in such a condition of greasiness that it lay in streaks across his head, the drops of rancid cocoanut oil gathering at the ends of each streak of hair, and thus rendering necessary the use of the pocket comb during lunch. The napkin was turned to strange uses during lunch.[115]

This was not how the Boers saw Kruger. Nor did it capture his power as a political figure. In 1877 Kruger was, in fact, in his prime. Only 52 years of age, he was a man of very considerable political skill and experience. Frere had caught something of this when he observed shrewdly, in the same year (1877), that Kruger was really 'a possible regenerator of the Transvaal'.[116] This is exactly what had happenend by 1880. Ambitious, fiercely anti-British – though controlled in his anger – populist and popular, a socially and theologically deeply conservative 'Dopper' Boer Calvinist, Kruger was peculiarly suited to lead the highveld Afrikaners in their hour of need. He had actually walked the Great Trek as a boy, and imbibed a powerful early passion against British rule and culture; he had political experience in the Transvaal 'civil wars' of the 1860s; he had military skills, developed in long Commando campaigns against African groups; he had unwillingly acquiesced in the British annexation of 1877, and he had led the protests against it in deputations to London and Cape Town; and his leadership of the Boers had the double strength of popularity, based on sentiment, and authority, resting on his frontier-war experiences.[117]

The Boer rebellion, and the brief counter-offensive campaign by the British in 1880–81, was also of course intimately connected to the other disturbances faced by the Imperial Factor in the South Africa of 1877–80. For a start, the much-maligned President Burgers had felt incapable of opposing the British annexation of the Transvaal when the Boer state was not only nearly bankrupt, but threatened with potential destruction by African forces – notably Bapedi and Zulu. The British annexation may have removed the 'sacred independence' of the Boers, but it had most certainly also removed the standing danger of African military threats through the imperial campaigns against the Zulu and Bapedi in 1879–80. Thus Kruger's rise to power, on the basis of an anti-British campaign, was staged against the backdrop of this new-felt security in the face of the Transvaal's traditional African enemies. The British had accomplished by column and howitzer what the Boers had failed to achieve by *commandos* and dynamite. The moment was accordingly propitious to 'thank' the imperialists by expelling them from the Transvaal and resurrecting the old Trekker republic.

The African disturbances to the south had also made this a superb moment to strike. The resolution of the Imperial Factor to intervene extensively and continuously in the inter-group politics of Southern Africa had been severely weakened by the degree of British involvement in the Cape's extra-territorial imbroglios and the Zulu fiasco. The unrest of 1877–79 cost the British Treasury over £500,000, with the prospect of further entanglements if the Cape regime failed in pacifying either Basutoland or the Transkei. Before the revolt of the Boers the British metropolitan government was already having second thoughts about the 'advances' inherent in the confederation policy; and from early 1880, with the accession to power of Gladstone's Liberal administration, the determination to impose an all-South African solution on the multiple problems of the area was further weakened. The earlier policy – of containing the Boers in the interior in 'splendid isolation', encircled by British possessions – had a revival of attraction. It was potentially a tenuous way to run an empire. But in the face of the ferocity of Boer 'nationalism', and the capacity of the highveld burghers to engage in land expansionism, it was thought to be the most pragmatic policy for giving the Imperial Factor a quiet life. The alternative was renewed conflict and war with the Boers of the interior, an unthinkable option at a time when the British government was facing major crises in Egypt and Afghanistan.

The apparent timidity of the Imperial Factor in treating the Boers with kid gloves, also owed some of its derivation to developments in Cape politics, where crucial British interests *were* involved. Not only was 'responsible government' tested to the full in these years at the turn of the 1880s –

when the high commissioner actually dismissed a colonial ministry over the right to conduct these disastrous frontier wars – but the Imperial Factor had to face an increasing politicisation amongst the Cape Dutch. The latter had evinced surprisingly strong sentiments of sympathy with the Transvaal Boers as a result of the annexation of 1877, and the consequent 'war of independence' on the highveld. Moreover, the Cape Dutch had also now begun to organise as a crucial sectional interest-group within the colony's political system. An Afrikaner 'home rule' movement soon emerged, parallel in time to the Parnell Irish challenge at Westminster, which was based on two quite distinct and important Cape Dutch organisations rooted in the rural districts of the colony.

It was Jan Hofmeyr who was instrumental in the creation of a farmers' protection association (*Boeren Beschermings Vereeniging*) to represent the rural Afrikaner interests in colonial politics, and the Rev. S. J. du Toit worked for the creation of a language league (*Die Genootskap van Regte Afrikaners*) to protect colonial Afrikanerdom from total anglicisation and acculturation.[118] The role of the imperialists in the frontier wars, and the federalist schemes, soon bore strong influence on the development of Afrikaner 'group consciousness'. The two Cape movements finally came together under Hofmeyr as the *Afrikaner Bond*, their aims being proselytised by two important local vernacular newspapers – *Die Afrikaanse Patriot* and the *Zuid Afrikaan*.

The *Bond* also began to spread on a pan-Southern African basis. Joubert and, to a lesser extent, Kruger welcomed the *Bond* into the Transvaal. By 10 May 1883 nearly a dozen branches existed on the highveld. The spirit of anti-British sentiment entered the *Bond* and was transmitted to the Cape. It did not make rebels of the Cape Afrikaners, but it did make them highly critical of the role of the Imperial Factor in South African politics. The *Bond* soon protested the British annexation of the Transvaal and defended the rights of Responsible Government in the Cape – perhaps best expressed in its determination to exclude any British interference in the transfrontier administration of the Transkei Territories. The imperialism of Carnarvon and Frere in the politics of the interior had, according to Hofmeyr, 'taught the [Afrikaner] people of South Africa that blood is thicker than water. It has filled the [Cape] Africanders, otherwise grovelling in the mud of materialism, with a national glow of sympathy for the brothers across the Vaal.'[119] When Kruger and a deputation of Transvaal Afrikaners called at the Cape, while *en route* to protest the Transvaal annexation in Whitehall, they were given a hero's welcome in meetings organized by the *Bond*.[120]

Protest failed, and the Boers launched a sudden and successful armed onslaught on the British authorities in the Transvaal. British hegemony was crumpled up in less than three months, ending with the fiasco of Majuba Hill (27 February 1881). Gladstone's cabinet pondered the merits of a major counter-offensive. Pride and prestige demanded subjection of the rebels: the *Liverpool Mercury*, for example, mordantly spoke of the 'Afrikaners' swords [sic] dripping with the blood of our best'.[121] The ministers of state, however, looked to the whole South African situation: they recalled the extensive and costly advances in the 1870s; they reflected on the rebellions and wars 1877–80; they considered the Basutoland situation where Cape administrative incapacity stared them in the face; they worried over the Transkei administration; they pondered gloomily at the lack of authority in Zululand; and they expressed considerable apprehension at the possibility of a pan-Afrikaner rising if the Transvaal were militarily subjected. Before Majuba their instincts had been to withdraw from direct administration of the Transvaal; they now moved to make this official policy by creating a Royal Commission to grant the Boers freedom within the locked doors of their state.

The retrocession was intended to allow the British to maximise their energies and expenditure on the other disturbed problems of Southern Africa. Yet the legacy of the Transvaal occupation, and the Boer rebellion, was to trouble them throughout the 1880s. Their federal initiatives had both broken the main opponents of Boer frontier expansion – the independent chieftainships – while at the same time encouraging the growth of a hitherto completely dormant sense of Afrikaner 'national consciousness'. By a curious tortuous and ironic series of developments the British attempts to regulate the inter-group relationships in plural South Africa – whose worst features had been exhibited in the series of wars 1877–81 – had made the local political environment even more unstable and intractable.

If the situation seemed highly unsatisfactory in 1881 for the metropolitan power, worse was yet to come. The Cape proved incapable of maintaining its trusteeship administration over the Sotho in Basutoland, and certain political groups in the colony now even agitated for withdrawal from the Transkei Territories – hoping to off-load both these considerable areas of African settlement onto the unwilling shoulders of the British imperial authorities.

Nor was that the end of it. The Transvalers, flushed with the pleasures of military and diplomatic success, happy to occupy the role of unchallenged authority on the highveld – the Zulu and Bapedi now humbled – celebrated the return of their old internal independence (at the Pretoria Convention, 3 August 1881) by reviving, on a new scale, their frontier expansions, both west and east of the state. The Tswana felt a revival of Boer and freebooter expansion, ending in the creation of the two petty republics in the lands of the Tshidi Rolong and Tlhaping in 1882. The invasion of Zululand by parties of Afrikaner farmers also began in earnest, resulting in yet another frontier republic in 1884.

As a culmination to these troubles for the British authorities rumours of a German interest in Southern Africa generally were given focus in 1884 after Bismarck's *Reich* appeared interested in South-west Africa. Afrikaner republicans were to be delighted, and welcomed the prospect of a non-British 'Great Power' in South Africa. Hopes were also expressed that a 'connection' might be made with the Germans, through either of these eastern or western expansive strategies of the Transvaal Boers.

Whether a 'German–Boer' connection would be made was a matter of conjecture in the early stages of Bismarck's annexations in South-west Africa. An undeniable fact was, however, the capacity of the Boer frontiersmen to continue and to expand their land scrambles. Frontier unrest and disturbance had created the most favourable of conditions in which a series of local Partitions could flourish. The dust of these disturbances had covered, to some degree, the fact that an ever-enlarging area of landscape was therefore being drawn into the realm of the settler and the frontiersman.

Boer westward expansion: Bechuanaland 1881–84

This covert development of private-enterprise expansion was superbly well exhibited in Bechuanaland, the next regional area to feel the impact of that ever-expanding local Scramble in South Africa.[122] Frontiersmen, tribesmen and humanitarians struggled to shape events in South-central Africa as the Imperial Factor kept a watching brief from the higher perspective of Whitehall. At the core of the matter, and this extension of the Scramble, was again the capacity of a local white agency (the highveld Boers) to conduct an almost continuous private Partition of Africa; and the degree to which this landed expansion drew in the colonial authorities and thus, ultimately, the British Imperial Factor as regulator of 'change' in Bechuanaland.

The Transvaal's 'informal empire' in the lands of the Tswana had certainly pre-dated the era of the Scramble proper; and Boer pressures had already become a fundamental feature of Bechuanaland's deadly politics of land and water resources. But these trends came to a new point of concatenation and crisis in the early 1880s, as the frontier burghers of the Transvaal began to test their degree of independence under British suzerainty through yet further lunges towards long-desired Tswana lands. It was, ironically, because the Transvalers no longer had to cope with internal problems of security – the British administration of 1877–81 having struck down the major independent chiefdoms – that the Boers could now harness their energies for an external Scramble for Africa in Bechuanaland and, shortly too, in Zululand.

The Transvalers had traditionally taken what can only be described as a happily expansive view of their frontiers of settlement. The Sand River Convention (1852) left the border vague; President Burgers had in 1868 accordingly claimed nothing less than the whole of the Road to the North, by drawing a Transvaal frontier which touched the Kalahari Desert; and the Keate Award (October 1871), which had attempted to demarcate zones of jurisdiction in the interior was, not surprisingly, rejected by the Transvaal as curtailing Boer interests in expansion. It was in the light of this history of Transvaal claims that the British laid considerable stress on the border when they came to negotiate the Pretoria Convention with Kruger's state at the conclusion of the Anglo-Transvaal war. That Convention – very largely the work of the British high commissioner at Cape Town – pushed the Afrikaner claims back across the Harts River, not so much to protect the Tswana as to keep open the great wagon-road to the interior for Cape trading interests. 'Bechuanaland is of no value to us', as the British colonial secretary put it;[123] but it *was* of growing value to the Cape. The interior African trade was worth some £250,000 to the less than prosperous colony and growing yearly. The Rev. John Mackenzie was later (1888) to speak of how the Cape interests were 'naturally much interested in the question of opening up the country to commerce'.[124] It also had crucial potential in labour supplies for the Cape's farms and diamond fields.

The Pretoria Convention was intended as a final settlement of the troublesome frontier; and also as a final statement of Great Britain's firmly limited responsibility to the Tswana. In fact, there was nothing final or firm about the frontier as decided. Local frontier forces in the years 1881–83, hungry for land, pasturage and water-holes, produced a situation of near anarchy and 'civil war'.[125] The white 'volunteer-freebooters' drawn largely from Boer frontier communities, lined up behind such chiefs as were eager for white allies in their local struggles for land and hegemony – notably Massauw (c.1810–85) of the Taaibosch Koranna at Marmusa,[126] and Moswete (1821–1904) of the BaRolong at Khurnwana[127] – and worked to create a world favourable to their own interests and against those of the chiefs supported by the humanitarians – in particular, Montshiwa (c.1814–96) of the Tsidi Rolong in the Mafeking District,[128] and Mankurwane (died 1892) of the Tlhaping.[129] It was not hard to guess the probable trend of events to come given the balance of firearms in the region, and the fact that the Imperial Factor declined to commit British power to the support of the humanitarians and their allies among the Tswana.

In 1881–82 the long-standing animosities between the various groupings in the area flared into open conflict. Some 600 Boer frontiersmen supported Massauw in the conflict and, in return for 6,000 acre farms, as well as a portion of the 'loot' of victory, defeated Mankurwane convincingly. The following year (January 1883) Massauw accepted the permanent place of the Boer volunteers in the region when the latter set up a mini-frontier republic at Vryberg – which was given the suitable Old Testament name of 'Stellaland' – under the leadership of G. J. van Niekerk (c. 1840–96), a Free State Boer who had drifted into the Transvaal and settled in the Christiana District before looking westward for new landed opportunities.

A parallel set of events had also overtaken Montshiwa in his struggles with pro-Transvaal chiefs and their white allies. His enemy Moswete, had acquired crucial Boer support, led by N. C. van Pittius, whose 'volunteers' in 1882 dealt a smashing blow to the Tsidi Rolong. Within the conquered area the Boer volunteers claimed their usual reward in land, and then established their own administrative jurisdiction in an area east of Mafeking and adjacent to the 1881 Transvaal border, in what was termed *Land Goosen* – the small republic of Goshen – around the farm *Rooi Grond* (red soil), with van Pittius president. Further Boer families soon poured in to settle the area, so extending Transvaal 'informal' involvement westwards and further undermining the fragile political status of Bechuanaland.

Throughout these events the Imperial Factor had maintained a posture of 'masterly inactivity'. The humanitarians had of course clamoured loud and hard on behalf of *their* African allies, the Tsidi Rolong and the Tlhaping, especially after the defeat of Montshiwa in October 1882. The Cape trading interests had also been vociferous in denouncing Transvaal border expansion, albeit for more secular reasons related to the trade, labour and the Road to the North. Yet throughout 1882–83 the British authorities managed to avoid acting in Bechuanaland, mainly by the simple expedient of letting the Boers have their way. The British inclination was not disposed to a Scramble against the Transvaal for South-central Africa, isolated as it was from vulnerable imperial interests on the coastlines.

However, it was that very successful local expansion which soon forced the metropolitan authorities to act, and to take some definite stand on the proceedings in Bechuanaland. The Transvaal leadership, chafing under even the loose restraints of the Pretoria Convention, sent a deputation to London in early 1884 with the express purpose of securing a new treaty-relationship with Great Britain; preferably a relationship of minimal obligations, and minimal British controls. A new and enlarged western border – to take into account all the informal expansion which had culminated in the 'republics' of Goshen and Stellaland – was a major practical expression of the general Boer demands for greater autonomy and for a 'greater Transvaal'.[130]

Much to the surprise of most contemporary observers, the revised Anglo-Boer agreement – the London Convention of February 1884 – made only minor concessions to the Transvalers in terms of that western frontier. Certainly the Kruger deputation secured substantial *internal* political concessions. But externally the Bechuana border line was fixed so as officially to exclude the Boers from the Road to the North, as well as the lands of the Tlhaping and Tshidi Rolong. According to Rhodes, who should have known, the origins of this firm decision lay with the Cape governor and high commissioner. Recalled to London to assist the British government, Sir Hercules Robinson had decisively stiffened the back of the anti-expansionist Liberal government. It was a rare achievement, Rhodes explained. The proconsul had

grasped the fact that, if Bechuanaland was lost to us, British development in Africa was at an end. He persuaded Lord Derby to deal with the Bechuanaland question, and induced Sir Thomas Scanlan [sic], the then Prime Minister of the Cape, to share in the obligations of the undertaking ... if the much despised Sir Thomas Scanlan [sic] had not taken this responsibility, Bechuanaland would have passed to the Transvaal, as Lord Derby was neutral on the question. Even though the Cape Colony [later] rejected this arrangement, it being made kept the matter open, and the interior was saved to us.[131]

The high commissioner, reflecting in 1895, confirmed the basis of this account.[132] British indebtedness to the Cape, coupled with a Cape offer of proxy aid, had tipped the balance.

The Scanlen–Cape offer was, however, carefully circumscribed. The colony only offered to assist in a *joint*-protectorate, conditional on Transvaal goodwill towards the idea.[133] But this offer was sufficient for the British authorities. They assumed that, in time, the protectorate would be handed over to the Cape. The German factor at Angra Pequena was *not* yet involved: Bismarck's proclamation of German South-west Africa was still several months off.[134] As Lord Knutsford later clearly explained: British Bechuanaland 'was only taken, in the first instance, on the understanding that the Cape would take it'.[135]

It also meant a tactical political advantage to the British government. John Mackenzie having waged an extended and effective public campaign on behalf of the loyalist Tswana in Great Britain,[136] it was to the advantage of the Liberal government to propose a policy of trusteeship. Dr Dachs has rightly stressed how John Mackenzie's public agitation had assisted Mankurwane and Montshiwa in gaining British support.[137] As a colonial office 'Confidential Memorandum' later stated, 'both were taken under protection in deference to an outburst of public opinion'.[138] The Cape colonial interests and their promise of assistance was, however, still crucial. 'In keeping back the Boers from the "Trade Route" and in protecting that route,' the same Confidential Memorandum stated unequivocally,

Her Majesty's Government had in view almost exclusively the interests of the Cape Colony, and the then Cape Premier (Sir T. Scanlen), who was in London during the negotiations with the Transvaal delegates, wrote ... giving more or less satisfactory assurances that the Cape Colony would in consideration of the Trade Route being kept free, bear its share of the expense of the Protectorate.[139]

On the basis of the Cape offer the British government now advanced the imperial flag to the Molopo River, declared a limited 'British Bechuanaland', despatched John Mackenzie himself to be the first 'deputy commissioner' in the protectorate, and waited on the Cape to implement the promise made by its premier. The colony however stood by embarrassed at the offer. Scanlen was soon repudiated by the Cape assembly. Responsibility for the situation in 'British Bechuanaland' accordingly thus fell hard on the reluctant Imperial Factor, and on John Mackenzie, its less than reluctant agent.

The Rev. John Mackenzie (1835–99) was a humanitarian imperialist *par excellence*. Deeply committed to African interests within the plural societies of Southern Africa, Mackenzie saw the Imperial Factor as the crucial regulating authority between the race groups.[140] With singular political realism he perceived that, in the face of settler colonialism, the best hope for African independency probably lay in British protection. He urged the extension of British rule over all the major African political communities with whom he was involved – whether Tswana, Sotho or Ndebele – as a humanitarian direction of the Partition. It was because of his faith in the benign imperialism of 'protectorate' administration, that he both strongly opposed Cape–Rhodesian colonialism in Bechuanaland and Mashonaland, and also argued for a separation of the offices of Cape governor and British high commissioner in South Africa. Ideally, Mackenzie wished to see African societies administered by imperial officials under the aegis of a high commissioner, totally divorced from settler interests in land, labour and resources. He especially feared Afrikaner oppression of African societies – simply 'because they were black'.[141]

Underlying Mackenzie's political views were equally strong cultural dimensions to his imperialism. He admired proseletysing Christianity in

Africa, and saw the 'civilising mission' subsumed within his gospel of empire. Mackenzie worked for an Age of Improvement in Africa, and his activities on behalf of the Tswana and Ndebele should be seen in this light. He opposed the traditional pagan cultures of the indigenous societies – 'a dead wall to the progress and civilisation' – placing his faith in acculturated Africans. In short: Mackenzie's vital role within the great Northern Expansion will only be fully understood if it is seen that he opposed not 'imperialism' but 'colonialism', to use the local political language of the 1880s. He thus vigorously pressed for the extension of the Imperial Factor in South Africa, seeing in this both political and cultural advantages for African societies. He fought against settler expansion – either Anglo-Saxon or Afrikaner – as being against African interests and not at all conducive to his ideas of Protestant progress against traditionalism. 'Not in Bechuanaland alone, but elsewhere in South Africa, our attitude ought to be to wean the people from their chiefs and induce them to put their trust in the Queen's Government.'[142] He was, of course, a man set against the tide of political events in South Africa during the Scramble years when the Imperial Factor was inclined to act strongly on the coastlines but allow the colonists to determine developments in the interior.

Mackenzie's chances of success were therefore not high. His enemies were many, both within the colonial office and the Cape colony. Above all, he stood for direct and expensive 'trusteeship' empire when the metropolitan imperialists favoured an 'indirect' collaborative empire of settler authority. His two volume work, *Austral Africa, losing it or ruling it* (1887) records his uphill struggle to work his ideas in Bechuanaland. Having campaigned for the introduction of British authority into the interior, Mackenzie eagerly accepted the offer of deputy-commissioner (February 1884) within 'British Bechuanaland', despite the range of enemies who opposed his ideas in Southern Africa. Dr Sillery has rightly remarked: 'He   undertook an impossible task and was given scanty means of attempting it.'[143] Plunged into the midst of the contending forces in southern Bechuanaland, Mackenzie's strong spirit and practical turn of mind allowed him only to make progress in regularising the land claims of some of the white volunteers in the freebooter republic of Stellaland and of establishing treaty relationships with the African chiefs.

It was an ill-omen for John Mackenzie's commissionership that the high commissioner – who had nominated him for the post – turned against his protégé. Sir Hercules Robinson had begun his conversion to Cape 'colonialism'. A colonial office minute noted sharply: 'Sir Hercules Robinson is smashing his idol and dancing on the pieces.'[144] John Mackenzie explained to his son how, from the moment of his arrival in March, the Rhodesian group in Cape politics – including the high commissioner – had worked to undermine his position: 'Fearing that my being a missionary will displease the Dutch-speaking colonists they have done their utmost . . . to get me superseded.'[145] He was later to characterize the Rhodes–Robinson association acutely as 'a sort of political and administrative firm',[146] working exclusively for Cape interests.

Sir Hercules Robinson was certainly in a unique position to prejudice the metropolitan authorities against John Mackenzie. The high commissioner's despatches depicted the missionary in the role of reckless imperialist, albeit for humanitarian reasons, bent on saving the Tswana from the Transvaal. This was despite the fact that the deputy-commissioner's 10 policemen hardly made him the most effective exponent of an expansionist policy. The Robinson–Rhodes pressures had the desired effect in London. The British officials came to suspect Mackenzie deeply of luring Great Britain to yet greater imperial responsibilities at the very time when the Cape was drawing back. The high commissioner's secretary at Cape Town remembered in later years how Mackenzie had come to be cast in this unfavourable light: 'Mr Mackenzie was a missionary and therefore distrusted. Moreover he was a political missionary of the extreme firebrand type, who had persistently agitated against the [Cape] Dutch and urged autocratic government and autocratic measures.'[147] This was unfair. But the point carried to London.[148] 'There can be little doubt that he [Mackenzie] must be got rid of', the colonial office now minuted. 'Mr Mackenzie acts like an honest schoolboy.' The kindest comment came from Sir Robert Herbert: 'Too old to be broken into harness.'

John Mackenzie resigned as deputy-commissioner on 19 August. 'My resignation has been accepted', he wrote to his friend Dr Dale, the famous Congregationalist pastor in Birmingham,[149] 'and I am now adrift. I do not know my future.' With Mackenzie out of the way, the Rhodesian element in Cape politics was eager to seize the opportunity for intervention, and to create a situation in Bechuanaland favourable to their interests. John Mackenzie was convinced that the Cape *Bond*, with its Boer sympathies, lay behind the colonial policy: 'It is said [that] everything is submitted to Hofmeyr in secret conclave, and ministers get what are practically orders.'[150]

Dramatic events now followed Mackenzie's resignation.[151] His replacement was none other than Cecil John Rhodes, who liked to tell the story of his appointment.

The Governor [Robinson] said: 'Oh, you can go up [to Bechuanaland] but I can give you no force to back you up. You must use your own judgement'. I replied, 'Will you allow me to do what I like?' 'Yes', said the Governor, 'but if you make a mess of it, I shan't back you.' I said, 'that is good enough for me'.

Rhodes departed to bé deputy-commissioner in a blaze of bravado. *He* understood the Boers; *he* knew the issues at stake; *he* could reconcile British, Boer and African interests. Humanitarians were appalled. London was cautious: 'He will do very well as a stop-gap, but, like Mr Mackenzie, he is inexperienced and untrained in administration work'.[152]

Rhodes had no intention of being a 'stop gap'. He soon entered the area of frontier contentions and conflicting groups, determined to work the situation to a solution which favoured the colonial point of view. Even this was mere window dressing. What mattered alone was the final clause of the Settlement: 'land titles to be recognised'.[153] This was Rhodes' answer for the problem of white frontiersmen in Bechuanaland. Buy them off with Tswana land, and turn them into Cape colonists as 'colonial associates'. Rhodes was well aware of what he had done, and of how he had exploited African interests for the advantage of the Cape, though he argued that contemporary circumstances had made this the only viable.policy. 'It is all very well for people now to criticise the agreement,' he wrote defensively to a Cape colleague early the following year,

but there was a period when matters were very different . . . and we had to work with the lights we then had. Apart from the whole of which, the occupation of Stellaland had gone too far to be disturbed, and if there was anyone to blame, we must lay that blame at the doors of the British government for their prolonged delay.[154]

But even this generous land policy failed to lure the republicans of Goshen into the Cape's orbit of influence. Rhodes was ejected from the most northern of these petty frontier states. In Goshen the 'Boers were rabid'.[155] Rhodes barely escaped with his life at the hands of the belligerent frontiersmen.

Transvaal informal expansion to the west of the parent state had succeeded remarkably well in the lands of the Tswana. They held the new frontier zones of conquest and settlement for the time being at least, until the New Imperialism and the Great Power Scramble swept over this earlier wave of white expansion in the later 1880s.

Boer expansion eastwards: establishing the 'New Republic' in Zululand 1884

But before that took place a very similar pattern of events was also to occur on the eastern borderlands of the Transvaal. With a pause in the successful Boer expansion into Bechuanaland, the energies and forces of the frontiersmen could now be directed at that other area of internal turmoil and opportunity for the land-hungry white man, Zululand – or the fragmented political region which had once been the Zulu state before its shattering fragmentation in an earlier European assault.

Yet again the crucial factor in the Scrambles and Partitions to come was a combination of expansive drives by Transvaal Boers coupled with the decision of the British authorities to 'accommodate' this local imperialism of the frontiersman – provided that Boer expansion kept clear of fundamentally sensitive areas of British or colonial interests. The local petty Partition on-the-ground accordingly moved forward with the British turning a blind eye to what was, in truth, yet another direct contravention of the very terms of the Anglo-Boer convention which had attempted to define Transvaal frontiers, and to isolate the Boer state in the interior of South Africa. But as even the practical architect of that convention, Sir Hercules Robinson himself remarked: 'Experience . . . has shown that mere treaty stipulations of this description are of little practical value. The attractiveness of Zululand and Swaziland for winter grazing is irresistible to the Transvaal farmers. Encroachments are now taking place which the Transvaal Government is either unable, or unwilling to present.'[156]

The frontier of the Transvaal state was indeed firmer on the map than on the ground. Steady agricultural encroachment on the disputed lands of northern Zululand had been paralleled by seasonal winter pastoral encroachment even more widely into the borderland areas of the Zulu and Swazi kingdoms.[157] These dual movements took on a new energy and permanency in 1882–83.[158] Moreover, apart from the forces in Transvaal – including the support of Kruger's rival, Joubert, for the frontier farmer's aspirations – the nature of Zulu politics at that time also aided the Boer incursion. In a desperate situation of conflict and struggles for supremacy, certain Zulu chiefs were eager to strike bargains with the Boer frontiersmen, inviting them to act as in Bechuanaland, as 'white mercenaries' in the cause of their particular faction or group. Both Uhamu and Zibhebhu made land deals on this basis,[159] although their engagements were of a limited kind.[160] Cetshwayo had also, as a last-ditch manoeuvre, held out the promise of 'grants of land on condition that they [the Boers] will assist him in the struggle of his party in the Zulu country'. With his death, the search of the Zulu factions for white 'advisers', and their modern firearms, achieved a new vigour. At the close of 1883 there were an estimated 45 Afrikaner families already farming in Zululand proper; three months later the number had doubled.[161]

Frontiersmen also began to pour in from colonial Natal and from the eastern plains of the Orange Free State.[162] The white intruders selected their 'employer' with a shrewd eye to the land they would acquire as a reward for their services.[163] The main group of Boers accordingly gathered around the Usuthu,[164] whose young leader, Dinizulu, was only too eager to sign agreements which might allow him to reinstate his people as premier Zulu group against Zibhebhu and Uhamu.[165] It was this desperate action by Dinizulu, involving essentially Coenraad Meyer's large party of Transvaal frontier farmers, which finally brought the Boers back into the centre of Zulu politics, and made them vital participants in the sporadic civil war then in progress, and in the new land partition already beginning.[166]

A critical moment had been reached. Only the external agency of British imperialism could have stopped this local Scramble for Zululand; and the British adopted a negative position aloof from events. 'I think we may wait', the British colonial secretary suggested in guidance to his lower officials. They took the lead. 'I should think it much safer not to recognise Dinizulu' as king of Zululand, the permanent under-secretary minuted rather cynically, 'It is impossible to say how much recognition of lawless acts by Boers and Zulus that would involve. The Boers may shoot him as soon as they have started their Zululand Republic.'[167]

A rather predictable sequence of events accordingly followed. The British high commissioner at the Cape, Sir Hercules Robinson, had indeed already (11 May 1884) written the scenario in a despatch of frank warning to the metropolitan government: 'the proceedings in Bechuanaland 1881–84 are about to be repeated in Zululand; both sides will probably enlist European volunteers who will be paid for their services in land, and a large part of the country north of the Reserve will eventually be parcelled out in European farms'.[168] He was to be correct in all details. First, Dinizulu became a captive of his own white allies. On 1 May the Natal governor was informed, by the Boer forces, that they had constituted themselves the 'Committee of Dinizulu's Volunteers' for the express purpose of 'protecting' the young king: 'Dinizulu . . . has in consequence of the continual shedding of blood within his territory, taken refuge with us, with the desire to see peace and quietness restored to his country. We have not come to wage war; our object is to restore and maintain peace in Zululand.'[169] On 23 May 1884 Dinizulu knelt in an open ox-wagon and was crowned King of Zululand through 'laying on the hands' by four of his white advisers.[170] Around them stood the leaders of all the major Boer families – Meyer, Uys, Spies, Laas, van Staden, Steenekamp, Fourie, de Jager, Jordaan, van Rooyen, Krogh and Esselen. The next day a formal treaty of alliance was signed with Dinizulu by those family heads as the '*Comite van Bestuur*'. The Boers were, indeed, as the Natal governor anxiously put it, 'in thorough earnest about the matter they have taken in hand'.[171]

That matter now involved immediate preparations for an assault on the forces of Zibhebhu and Uhamu.[172] The British poured 1,000 infantrymen, under general Smyth, into Zululand to defend the Reserve.[173] But they did no more than that.[174] The Usuthu and Mandhlakazi clashed on 5 June.[175] The combined Boer–Usuthu forces achieved a terrible victory over Zibhebhu. 'The defeat was in fact complete', the Natal governor wrote with obvious feeling. 'The cattle belonging to Usibibu's people, many thousands in number were looted, and the kraals burnt down. When Usibibu left, the work of destruction and plunder was still going on.'[176] Zibhebhu fled to the British Reserve and appealed to his allies, the imperialists, 'to give me armed assistance to enable me to return to re-establish myself in my territory'.[177] It was a hopeless strategy. 'It is good so far', the British colonial secretary remarked calmly of the situation, the Boers 'do not appear inclined to attack the Reserve'.[178] The Natal governor, Zibhebhu's strongest local white sponsor, was slapped down hard when he pressed for imperial intervention on behalf of the Mandhlakazi. Smugly an official in London minuted, 'Sir H. Bulwer appears to be slowly beginning to understand the situation . . . that the Boers are not going to invade the Reserve.'[179]

Outside the Reserve area, the Boers thus became the new determining power-force in Zululand. They behaved as victorious imperialists anywhere, and carved out a state which approximated to their cattle-culture interests and to their dreams of an independent outlet to the sea. On 16 August 1884 they had Dinizulu issue a Proclamation announcing to the world the creation of yet another Boer state in South Africa – the '*Nieuwe Republiek*' (New Republic). They were soon claiming over 3 million of the best acres in the former Zululand of Cetshwayo, stretching from the borders of the Transvaal to the Indian Ocean at St Lucia Bay.[180] A *Volksraad* was established to administer the new state; P. J. Joubert was invited to come down from the Transvaal and assume its presidency; 'locations' were established for Africans remaining within its boundaries; a tax of '5/-' per head was levied on adult male Africans; and white farms were both staked-out and 'registered' with the new Boer authorities.[181]

The reordering of settlement and inter-group relations, which had so fascinated Shepstone and the Natal colonists, had now largely come about. But this Boer Scramble for Zululand, in the wake of the British destruction of Cetshwayo, had meant a local partition *against* the loyal Anglo-Saxon Natalians and their old imperial ambitions beyond the colony. Not strong enough to block the Boer initiative, and certainly unable to intervene against the New Republic and its Usuthu allies, the Natalians could but look to Great Britain in the hope that the imperial government would impose a yet further 'Settlement' which might better serve the interests of the colony's white farmers, and check the ambitions of the Transvaal burghers. It was a slender hope, and the Natalians knew it. With not a little sense of pique, the *Natal Mercury* remarked of these events that the Boers 'at any rate, have shown that they can manage the Kafirs better than the British Government'.[182] More pragmatically, an imperial official admitted in a confidential minute that the Boers 'have done what we could not, or would not do'.[183]

It was now quite clear that unless the British imperialists did indeed stir themselves to intervene, this local Boer Scramble would stand as a major feature of the new repartitioning of the political geography of South-east Africa. The Boers were full of advice how this would suit imperial purposes and interests. 'The true policy,' their newspaper *De Volkstem* recommended, 'is to make friends with the Boers . . . by dealing fairly with them in respect of the farms they have under treaty with the King's party, acquired in Zulu-land . . . if that is done, peace is secured in Zululand for the next 20 years'.[184] This was largely the advice taken by the British. Despite claims to higher motives, the role of the Imperial Factor in this first phase of Partition in South-east Africa was confined to striking an agreement with the Boers, whom they had come to prefer as collaborators to the Zulu chiefs.

The British were not unaware, however, of the less than laudable side of their policy-decisions. There was a twinge of conscience over Zibhebhu – 'a faithful ally'[185] – and a degree of quiet embarrassment at the success of the Boer forces in the face of both Zulu and Natal interests made possible by Great Britain's crushing of Cetshwayo. Yet no positive response was to be offered. The senior Whitehall official had to admit, 'The proclamation of Dinizulu as King [by the Boers] is beyond doubt an insolent disregard of the position this country has hitherto claimed to hold in regard to Zululand; and as we have decided to acquiesce in it, it may be best to do so without words'.[186] Indeed, the British went to considerable lengths to avoid entanglement in Zulu politics, so facilitating the Boer expansion.[187] When the Natal governor pointed out that the Reserve area was so over-crowded that it had become less of a 'protected region' than a sprawling refugee camp, and that Zibhebhu's territory should also be declared to be under British trusteeship, he received a blistering rebuke, perhaps unequalled in imperial despatches.[188] Human-itarian opinion in England was most exercised over the course of 'Zulu policy', so much so that the parliamentary under-secretary, Evelyn Ashley, came to dread debating the official British attitude in the Commons – 'I know what a difficult task I shall have to defend the Government . . . in the House.'[189] There is even some evidence to suggest that the colonial office deliberately suppressed information which humanitarian pressure groups might have used as embarrassing ammunition. A critical sentence was, for example, struck out of the Natal governor's despatch of 16 December before it was sent to the printers and into parliamentary command papers.[190] Equally, the Cape high commissioner's modest suggestion, that a number of 'border agents and police on the eastern frontier [of the Transvaal], at the joint expense of the natives and of the Imperial and Transvaal Governments',[191] might stabilise the situation while some more permanent solution was found, drew no more enthusiasm than the cool comment, 'After a full consideration of recent reports and recommendations, Her Majesty's Government adhere to the decision not to extend sovereignty or protection over Zululand.'[192] They were 'prepared to defend the Zulu Native Reserve'. But they would 'not sanction any advance beyond it'.[193]

How should the British posture be interpreted? A treasury parsimony was certainly involved. So too was the uncertainty of the situation – which report was to be believed when all parties involved were pleading a case? For example, were there less than 100 Boers involved (as the *Times* of London correspondent claimed) or more than 800 (as the Natal governor asserted)?[194] An official minuted irritably in Whitehall: 'The number of Boers is somewhat variable, rather like Falstaff's men in buckram.'[195] Infinitely more important, in fact, was the overall imperial assessment of the meaning of the new order in Zululand for British interests generally. Neither humanitarian nor treasury questions here dominated. In the analytic language of the Liberal British prime minister, 'It is not for Empire, nor for humanity, that we have a concern in Zululand beyond the Reserve, but because it affords a solution for the native question in Natal.'[196] In other words, the British were essentially concerned with the nature of inter-group relations in South-east Africa as they affected imperial interests more generally. And once that *a priori* basis of policy was established, then there was scant hope of the British intervening – either against the Boers or for the Zulu.

It was not by absence of mind that the British practised neglect in Zululand outside the Reserve. They considered the pattern of partition taking place at the hands of the Boers, and they pragmatically decided to allow these local forces to have their way. In an ideal world, the British might have created a Zulu 'protectorate' – preferably one that could be handed to Natal as soon as possible. But this policy involved confrontation with the Boers, and it ran against the fact that Natal colony was barely strong enough to sustain its own development let alone take on a vast administrative trusteeship region. The territorial integrity of the Zulu kingdom had no special meaning in the imperial policy-makers' approach.

Accordingly, the British came to their decision: it offered most to the imperial vision of the situation, if least to the Zulu. Lord Kimberley wrote to his cabinet colleague Joseph Chamberlain on 25 September 1884: 'You will remember I supported Derby's proposal to annex Zululand as far as the

Black Umfolozi. The cabinet declined this, and it was evident, as Derby and I said at the time, that if we did not interfere the Boers would. We made our choice, and I would abide by the result, and leave Zululand beyond the reserve to its fate.'[197] With this action the first phase of Partition in Southeast Africa ended. The British machinations 1877–84 in Zululand and beyond had left as their most concrete legacy the destruction of Zulu political independence and the creation of the New Republic. 'Our policy,' as the British colonial secretary wrote privately to the Cape High commissioner, 'will be to hold on the reserve, so protecting Natal, and let the Zulus beyond it manage, or mismanage, their affairs as they please.'[198]

In concentrating on the harsh character of Anglo-Zulu and Cape–Sotho relations in these years, we should be careful not to miss the significance of the British posture towards the Boers of the New Republic. An extremely interesting and important aspect of nineteenth-century British imperialism is here exhibited. The imperial authorities were always aware of the possibilities provided by local collaborative agencies in conducting the politics of strategy, interests and colonial connections. The Zululand affair very well brings this out, in practical working-detail.

In the righteous days of 'Midlothian', 1878–79, Gladstone had campaigned on behalf of Cetshwayo's Zulu state by attacking Disraeli's imperial policy in South Africa. In particular, the Liberal leader had charged the Tory administration with pursuing a policy which, in the war of 1879, had involved the butchering of thousands of Zulu 'for no other offence than their attempts to defend against your artillery, with their naked bodies, their hearths and homes, their wives and families'.[199]

Now, in 1884, the Zulus needed protection against the imperial policy of the Liberal administration, in which the search for 'collaborative agencies' took precedence over humanitarianism. Despite the destruction of the Zulu as a political unit, the Liberal premier inclined to believe that there was now 'an opportunity for settling our Zululand difficulty by a friendly arrangement with the Dutch [Boer] element'.[200] Indeed, he went so far as to propose a 'general rule' for problems of British imperialism concerned with the government and future of African societies in South Africa:

Is it reasonable to think that as the Dutch [Boers] have Africa for their country, as they went out from the Cape greatly to our relief, as they have solved the Native question within their own borders, they are perhaps better qualified to solve the Zulu question outside the Reserve than we can in dealing with it from Downing Street.[201]

This was a view not confined to the British premier. An official Whitehall minute of the same period made plain the preference for white rather than African collaborators:

> if we do not stand too much on our dignity, [the Boers] may according to all appearances, serve as assistants, in maintaining peace and order in Zululand. There is no question now of driving the Boers out of Zululand and we ought not to turn would-be friends . . . into dangerous enemies, by refusing to recognise them as soon as they have established some form of settled Government.[202]

In the long-term, Victorian imperial officialdom indeed came to believe that such an approach was likely to be of use not merely in Natal and Zululand, but in relation to all the African societies of South Africa which adjoined the white state.[203] Never was this philosophy better expressed than in a note by the South African 'expert' in the British colonial office. Edward Fairfield wrote in mid-1885:

> The Native question cannot be solved except in friendly co-operation with the local [white] communities . . . All the mischief nearly that has ever been inflicted on the Natives in South Africa has been inflicted by Imperial officers . . . Once you get the Natives under the management of the much-abused . . . Colonists, and leave the . . . Colonists alone, everything goes right. They understand Native management much better than we do.[204]

Continued experience in handling the day-to-day conduct of Southern African material in the colonial office merely confirmed Fairfield in this view. Several years later he was to convey a similar opinion to a later colonial secretary, Lord Ripon, when the problem of British responsibility and the African societies of the veld was again being discussed.

> The fact is that the Boers have formed a way of settling with such tribes in other parts of their territory by the simple experiment of leaving them severely alone from year's end to year's end, and only interfering once in a way at very long intervals by punitive 'Commando' when the Natives are being recalcitrant.[205]

The frontier-Boers were increasingly endowed with new merits as the imperialists found new uses for them; and woe betide the person, or official, who argued against this approach. The Natal governor, and advocate of a larger Zulu Reserve, was derided in the colonial office as a bogus 'Cassandra'.[206] The British Resident in the Zulu Reserve was privately censured for identifying himself too closely with the Africans in his charge: 'He is too much of a white Kaffir'.[207] Likewise, attempts made by British pressure-groups to push the British government towards a policy of trusteeship for all of Zululand, met with a fierce resistance among policy-makers.[208] This, of course, merely harmonised with what one senior clerk noted on the Tswana question in Bechuanaland: 'We have more blacks in the Protectorate than we know what to do with.'[209]

Imperialism was very rarely the monolithic imposition of the metropolis on the periphery. The working connection in very many instances was filled by collaborative individuals or groups. Within the context of a plural society, such as 'colonial South Africa', the options open to imperialists on this basis were many and varied. With the parallel developments of resurgent African traditionalism, and the rise of nascent Afrikaner nationalism, the imperialists moved to make a fundamental decision for the future history of the peoples of South Africa.[210] They turned away from humanitarianism, to crack down hard on traditionalism and the independence of the chiefs.[211] At the same time, they began to set aside an earlier liberal distaste of colonists and Afrikaner frontiersmen, and to see in them the potential agents and associates of the British empire and a local whitemen's empire in South Africa.

Before the great Witwatersrand mineral revolution, which radically redirected the history of South Africa by attracting new settlers and capital, the imperialists had already begun to tip the balance of power locally in favour of the agencies of colonialism in the periphery, whether Anglo-Saxon or Boer. Not only had the metropolitan government's policies assisted the military power of the settler states 'by the large use of imperial troops armed with modern weapons, rather than by a great increase in the military effectiveness of local republican or colonial forces', as Shula Marks and Anthony Atmore have argued,[212] but by striking conciliatory alliances of convenience with the colonists and frontiersmen, they had also decisively helped to tip the scale of political authority in favour of the white colonial groups.

The return of the Imperial Factor to South African politics: the problems of Basutoland and the Transkei 1884

For how long though could the British authorities go on yielding to the desires of the local expansionists – especially the Boers of the highveld – before they lost any real control over the developing political scene in South Africa?

The British had accepted substantial Transvaal expansion in Zululand and Bechuanaland rather than thwart the Boer frontiersmen; and they had progressively moved to support Cape expansion, as a means of dealing with transfrontier African unrest and administration. In some senses, the British imperialists knew that feeding the crocodile was only defensible as a policy if they could satiate its hunger. '1884' was to deal harshly with this posture, revealing it to have been a policy based not on principled abnegation of power in South Africa but rather of penny-pinching weakness. The Imperial Factor was soon forced to adjust its approach to the political changes proceeding in South Africa – though it did not entirely abandon its conciliatory, 'crocodile' policy.

London was acutely aware, in fact, that by accepting Boer expansion in the interior it had gained Cape Dutch goodwill further south in the region which really mattered, so far as British interests were concerned. But the imperialists had also allowed the creation of serious problems of disorder as the frontiersmen carved new pastoral regimes out of African lands, and brought to a head the issue of trusteeship in the Imperial Factor's role in Southern Africa. Similarly, by moving with the spirit of Cape 'home rule' expressed concretely in the expansion of the colony into the Transkei Territories and Basutoland, they had also precipitated a crisis in certain key transfrontier African polities. At best, Cape rule had been vigorously autocratic; at worst, meddlingly incompetent. Occasionally, as in Basutoland, it had even become autocratically incompetent. As a direct result, the British were about to reap a bitter administrative harvest as a consequence of trusting the colonists to run a proxy-empire on their behalf.

The significance of this failure in policy-making was profound for the local continuing Scrambles in South Africa at the turn of the 1880s. It was also of vital importance for shaping the nature of Imperial Factor involvement in the politics of Partition in the whole region. Because of the British posture of abstention, and the unrest which stared at Whitehall and Government House, Cape Town, the British imperialists were now forced to move back into the mainstream of South African politics – partly to reassert control over incipient anarchy in the border zones, partly to protect their own interests now endangered by a combination of chaos and local expansionists.

The symbolic and practical key to these trends to come was Basutoland. There was not much the British could do about Boer expansion in Tswana and Zulu lands, beyond containing it within broad limits and thereby hoping to confine its power for disturbance of British South Africa. But they could not apply the same *cordon sanitaire* around Basutoland, the very regional centre of South Africa, touching on all sides areas of sensitivity for British relations with the broad area, and where Cape rule had completely broken down. As the British colonial secretary gloomily commented (1882), the colony could not be relied on 'to restore order . . . for a long time to come'; and therefore the Imperial Factor must do '*something*'. Events in Basutoland simply dictated that the British act as imperial overlords by intervention in South African administrative developments. The metropolis was accordingly now linked inextricably to the very patterns of local settler and Boer expansionism which it had hitherto found to be so distasteful.

It was the Cape colony's attempt to disarm the Sotho tribesmen, the Gun War which followed, and the political *modus vivendi* proposed at the end of those struggles – the Robinson Award – which had in fact so greatly exacerbated the political instability of Basutoland. Internal problems in Sotho politics also connected with the Cape policy to produce inflammable consequences. The 'paramount house', of the royal family, was dissatisfied with the rule of the Cape and stood out against registering its guns or allowing white settlers into Moorosi's old Quthing District.[213]

Moreover, the dissension and rivalry among Sotho factions on the death of the great old chief, Moshweshwe, reappeared after the 'Gun War' even more vigorously. A sporadic civil war thus flared up between those chiefs supported by the new Cape administration of J.M. Orpen (notably Letsie and Lerotholi) and those eager at building up their own power. Orpen himself was close to Moshweshwe's family and tried hard to reunite the Sotho around the old paramountcy, but he was not helped in this either by the contentious nature of Sotho politics; or the activities of his political masters in the Cape ministry who favoured exploiting Sotho divisions – in the words of one senior Cape member of the Scanlen ministry, 'We must therefore persevere . . . and endeavour to create a jealousy which will enable us to act on the old advice of "*divide et impera*". Orpen is not the man for this.'[214]

The lack of central authority in Basutoland, either created by Sotho leadership from within, or provided by strong Cape magisterial control from without, hastened the territory on to a new phase of instability and disorder. The Cape ministry's will to dominate Basutoland had dribbled away in the ignominious 'defeat' of the Gun War. In 1882 they simply admitted their incapacity: the Robinson Award was cancelled, and the infamous 'Peace Preservation Proclamation' finally withdrawn. The Sotho thus remained in possession of their guns and their country – white farmers were *not* to be allowed into Moorosi's old district. Rhodes now spoke of Scanlen's 'famous Basutoland retreat'.[215] Further *pitsos*, in March and April of the next year (1883) at which Cape authorities attempted to explore the problems of Basutoland with such Sotho leaders as would attend, failed to produce a solution except to garner the fact that the African leadership preferred British to Cape overrule. The Scanlen ministry was now 'all for scuttle'.[216] The Cape authorities had completely lost their nerve for Basutoland administration: Merriman, a leading 'scuttler', remarked that the colony should 'for a while postpone the luxury of empire', and even Rhodes favoured annexing 'land, not natives'.

The drifting character of Cape policy communicated itself all too quickly to the Sotho, and Basutoland exhibited all the signs of a state about to break into anarchy. Gladstone disliked the situation; but he disliked new empire even more, particularly in the aftermath of the recent African and Afrikaner troubles. Both the British high commissioner and the colonial secretary realised however that the collapse of Cape rule meant that the Imperial Factor had to act. So too did British humanitarian pressure-groups: led by the Rev. John Mackenzie they campaigned in London for direct trusteeship over the Sotho. Public opinion, warned the colonial secretary, 'will force some action on us, whether we will or no'.[217]

The British therefore moved, significantly, to devise a scheme which would meet the crisis of administration in Basutoland at the minimum cost. The Sotho would be taken back under the umbrella of the Imperial Factor, but administrative rule would be akin to that which operated in an Indian princely state. As the British secretary of state laid out their plan, in graphic simplicity – and with an interesting Irish metaphor thrown in for good imperial measure – the Sotho would be given '"Home Rule" but leaving them free in regard to internal affairs. This, I believe, is what they want.'[218]

It is certainly what the cabinet appeared to want. The high commissioner also supported it. Exeter Hall temporarily rejoiced. The Cape ministry was happy to part with its disaster in administration. Only the Sotho were left to be consulted. By the time they were addressed (at a *pitso* in late-1883) the policy had already been announced by the British colonial secretary (14 June); and the Imperial Factor had taken up its responsibility in the very heart of Southern Africa.

With the retreat from Basutoland there arose the question of whether the British should now add the Transkei Territories to their trusteeship responsibilities. Very revealingly neither the British nor certain influential Cape groups wished for that. Instead, there now took place an interesting 'bargain' in administrative burdens in colonial South Africa. The British would take up the thankless and economically profitless task of a Basutoland protectorate if the Cape accepted its responsibility to incorporate the Transkei region generally under colonial rule. Accordingly, in the very period when the colony was abandoning its role in Basutoland to the metropolitan government, it was in fact extending its role in the Transkei Territories. Local expansion was thus apparently masked by retreat, but it was very real expansion, and represented a determination to direct Cape administrative capacities and imperialism more closely, not to abandon them.

This important Cape expansion moved forward in two capacities, both revealing of the ways in which the local frontier crept forward in these years. First, it legitimised Cape informal expansion of the 1870s. Covert empire became overt administrative responsibility. In the cause of 'law and order', magisterial control was now expanded, to translate 'influence' and 'dependence' into formal responsibility, so that by 1886 only Pondoland stood outside Cape rule. Fingoland, the Idutywa Reserve, Gcalekaland, Thembuland, Bomvanaland, Griqualand East and·Xesibe land – all the main districts, in fact – now experienced the magisterial presence directly. This was done largely because there was no alternative to the dangers of a revived resistance by African traditional societies. Not even the anti-imperialism of the Scanlen administration, or the Basutoland fiasco, or the economic depression of 1883, or the warnings of the Barry Commission of the same year – against undue interference in tribal life – could halt this administrative advance into the Transkei Territories.

Cape expansion also, it should be noted, proceeded through the energy of a group of white settlers eager for land in the areas concerned. As part of the spoils of war, and as a security measure, white farmers were introduced into certain of the conquered territories. A Boundary Commission laid out farms in August 1882,[219] and also recommended that Thembu lands claimed by white squatters, from the Barkly East and Dordrecht Districts, be included in the Cape.[220] The white settler expansion into the Transkei was strongly supported by the *Afrikaner Bond*: Hofmeyr indeed favoured, as Professor Davenport has shown, the development of a 'broad belt of white settlement from Queenstown to Kokstad . . . as a means of bringing order to the tribal areas and extending the opportunities for the white farmer.'[221]

The fall of the Cape's Scanlen ministry, in May 1884, marked a change in the spirit of official Cape extra-colonial policy. More 'consolidationist' than really 'expansionist', the new Upington administration – strongly backed by the *Bond* – still determined to hold onto the Cape's African territories and to impose their authority. They were helped by the retreat from Basutoland; but they were men animated by a tougher vision of Cape development. They instinctively, as colonial 'home rulers', disliked the idea of giving up areas of authority to the Imperial Factor; they were more sympathetic to settler and commercial expansion into the Transkei Territories; and they were more empire-minded in seeing the future of the Cape in its transfrontier growth. Where the former Scanlen ministry had edged forward slowly in its Transkei administrative advances, the new Upington–*Bond* cabinet simply moved directly to convert its role of 'influence' in Thembuland, Gcalekaland and Xesibe country (July 1884–86) into full-scale annexation – a move from classic 'informal' to 'formal' empire. It also, somewhat protectively and jealously, watched the activities of German agents in South-west and South-east Africa. As early as July 1884 a metropolitan official could accordingly minute that the new Cape ministry was in an 'annexing mood'.[222]

Why did the British look so favourably on that expansion, given the all too recent lessons of a disastrous Cape administration of Basutoland? The reason is more subtle than mere expediency, though undoubtedly London preferred empire by settler than direct rule itself in Southern Africa.

The disturbances of 1877–79, combined with the recommendations of the Cape's vitally important *Commission on Native Laws and Customs* (1883), altered the thrust of administrative politics in the Transkei Territories, and so actually worked to speed up their incorporation into the colony. Prior to 1884 the Whitehall authorities had felt it vitally necessary to exercise a close supervision of Cape laws as they applied to African trusteeship administration. The civilising and expansive zeal of some of the colonial agencies was not above suspicion. The British indeed reserved the right to veto legislation affecting Africans even after the grant of responsible government to the Cape colony if it smacked of belligerent interference with African rights. The disturbances had, however, apparently taught the Cape several fundamental lessons in its transfrontier African administration. Not the least of these 'lessons' was a new-found preference for 'indirect rule', rather than direct intervention, to establish Cape authority. London approved. The post-1857 administrative manuals of India were to be adapted to the Cape's transfrontier rule. African traditional authorities were to be the 'clients', rather than the opponents, of Cape influence and authority.

The Barry Commission had simply brought 'theocratic Asia' – Professor Walkers' phrase – into the heart of Cape administrative policies. And in some ways the 1877–81 disturbances therefore compared interestingly with the impact of the Indian Mutiny on the administration of the *Raj*: in Dr Pandey's words, 'The British suppressed the mutiny and at the same time entered into an alliance with the forces that had caused it.'[223] The Cape certainly struck down the 'disloyal' traditionalists, but it did indeed now create an administrative system based on a close collaboration with the remaining traditional authorities. In so doing, it made the role of the Imperial Factor, as overseer of Cape administrative politics, that much easier. A recent study of the Cape colonial incorporation of the Transkei has shown how this assisted the British authorities in supporting the advance of Cape rule across the Kei – despite the disaster of Basutoland and despite the unrests of the colony's 'Ninth Kaffir War' 1877–78.[224] A leading critic of Victorian colonial societies in the tropics had once remarked (1877) on the dangerous potential of frontier colonists in creating wars in the periphery – 'being in contact with natives ... [they] manipulate the relations so as to compel the natives to compel the home authorities to fight'.[225] That fear was now to be set aside as a result of the Cape's experiences 1877–84, and the new administrative policies seen as a declaration of 'good intent' and safe procedures of rule.

Accordingly, and paradoxically, having taken Basutoland from the Cape, London could now sanction the development of a Cape colonial administrative empire not merely in the Transkei Territories but in Griqualand West and, soon, in southern Bechuanaland too. Lord Kimberley, as Gladstone's colonial secretary 1868–74, had once stated emphatically that if Great Britain gave the Cape responsible government and withdrew its imperial forces then, implicit in the situation, was the fact that 'the native tribes in that colony will be left to the control of the local authorities'.[226] This had taken place. The 'trusteeship element' in British imperialism in South Africa was by now, through the events of 1877–84, revealed in a starkly clear light. It was not 'all humbug', as its critics then or now would assert, but it was a humanitarianism much hedged about by restrictions. There were limits in financial commitment; it was shaped by Exeter Hall in the direction and focus of its attentions; and, above all, it was circumscribed by an underlying preference, in fulfilling any British trusteeship responsibility, for working empire through the proxy-agents of the Cape colonists. In cases where such an agency was not available, and where trusteeship involved extensive and expansive new empire – as in Zululand – the Imperial Factor was apparently even prepared to find merit in local administration by frontier Boers.

The peripheral parish-pump affairs of both Basutoland and the Transkei are thus of vital importance in discussing the coming of the Partition to South Africa. The role of the Cape, as administrative agent beyond its frontiers, had been central to the events 1877–84. In its reaction to the African traditionalist disturbances it had set in motion a local 'partition' of no mean order: it had ultimately established its authority in the Transkei Territories, by the subjection of the Ngqika, Gcaleka and Thembu, and the establishment of authority in alliance with 'loyal' traditionalists. The rationale for moving on Pondoland next was writ large.

Further, and even more important, by the success of the Sotho resistance in Basutoland, and the failure of Cape authority in that territory, the Imperial Factor had been forced back into the mainstream of local South African politics.

The legacy of the frontier disturbances and revolt:
triggering the Scramble 1884

In the coming politics of Partition, the year 1884 thus stood for more than the arrival of Bismarck's New Imperialism and the beginnings of international rivalries in South Africa. It was also the moment of the British return into Basutoland, the revival of Cape authority in the Transkei Territories, the establishment of Transvaal expansion beyond its borders – by frontier republic – and the major humanitarian agitation for imperial protectorates in South Africa. It was on the cards that some further British response to this evolving, and often disquieting, set of geo-political changes in South Africa would be required.

Pointing the way was, in truth, the advance into Basutoland. Henceforward it was to be almost impossible for the metropolitan authorities not to react vigorously when challenged either by disorder or rival authority. In the 'retreat' from the Transvaal they had set out the minimal holdings on which to base their South African supremacy. The British from now on could brook no erosion of this core of authority. South Africa was counted as 'the centre of the Empire' – according to the senior permanent official in the colonial office – and the measures to protect British economic and strategic interests in such an epicentre of power could, in truth, never be completely circumscribed.

The British, and their local collaborative agencies of empire – in the settlement colonies of the Cape and Natal – had of course been brought to this position in 1884 by the collapse of their imperial visions of federation at the hands of the local political actors who dominated regional politics. It was not Great Power rivalry which had set the stage for a final 'Partition' of Southern Africa but these inter-group squabbles and machinations in the state-system of the periphery. It was that set of relationships which had increasingly wrenched the initiative out of the hands of the Imperial Factor, and which had created a political situation intolerable to imperialists born to an empire of order, development and supreme Anglo-Saxon authority. It was the petty ambitions and strategies of the local groups who almost continually refused to let South Africa follow the 'natural' political and economic developments so readily perceived by metropolitan minds better acquainted with Utilitarianism, Progress, Improvement and the new Political Economy.

If the developments of 1884 seemed a long way from the disturbances of 1877, then there was still no gainsaying the fact that when the British did indeed move later that year to reassert their paramountcy in South Africa, by territorial advances and annexations – so becoming participants in the rise of the African Partition – they did so for reasons pre-dating Bismarck's challenge. The events of 1877–84 had possessed their own potency. The 'South African Question' had demanded not only vigorous attention, but its very composition had shaped the imperial responses, and had moved 'reluctant imperialists' to extended empire.

To lay stress on these local 'disturbances' 1877–84, in the making of Partition and Scramble in South Africa, is not to indulge in the mere novelty of sweeping revisionism. It is to revert, in fact, to an orthodoxy older than the recent contributions to the debate on free trade imperialism. Many years ago Professor E. A. Walker argued that the roots of the Scramble in South Africa lay with the 'breakdown of Cape native policy' – by which the Imperial Factor became 'entangled once more in Basutoland in the heart of the South African state system' – together with 'Transvaal restiveness and German intervention'.[227] That appears to be a fair summary of the origins of events post-1884. A most scholarly analysis of the role of the British high commission, in the colonial politics of South Africa, has also recently come to conclusions which appear to point in that same direction too.[228]

The Scramble for South Africa after 1884 was, in truth, a development from the politics of local contest and partition in the crucial years between the Transvaal annexation and reannexation of Basutoland. The struggle for South Africa had already well begun by 1884 when the broader international forces of the New Imperialism arrived to quicken that momentum of local Partition on the land.

The range of 'native wars', the rebellion of the Boers, and the frontier expansion of the local settlers, had indeed reaped a whirlwind. The 'frontier' had pulled in the Metropolis. The often-proclaimed reluctance of the Victorian authorities was soon to be set aside, so that the British could join the Scramble for South Africa as its masters and not its victims.

In 1877 the Imperial Factor had intended the various federalist strategies – including the subjection of Boer and African political units alike – to create the positive preconditions for a stable South African state, a polity from which the imperialists could begin a constitutional withdrawal by devolving power on a colonial leadership dominated by the loyal Cape. By 1884, however, the British stood poised to return to the somewhat desperate local politics of rivalry, pre-emptive annexations, and grand geo-political Partition. Given the character of the local frontier society of South Africa – with its propensity for inter-group and inter-state conflict – empire by proxy, 'imperialism on the cheap', had proved impossible, temporarily at least. 'I think it very likely that our resolute indisposition to annex up to 1877 was incapable of being maintained,' Lord Blachford had remarked at the opening of this period of local partition and empire-advance, 'and that we had run up a kind of *arrear of necessity* in that way.'[229]

It was across this highly volatile political context in colonial and frontier South Africa, that Bismarck's New Imperialism was accordingly to cast an ever-lengthening and worrying shadow in 1884. The British, as the overlord authority, initially claimed not to find this fundamentally disturbing. Gladstone was soon to welcome the Germans to the deserts of South-west Africa, just as Salisbury was later to wish the French well in the 'light soil' of the Sahara.

The character of local South African politics in 1884, brought to a new heat by the arrival of Germany in the region, soon however made British *sang froid* appear to be singularly ill-founded. More abrasive comments now followed. A first response was to blame it all on the expansive agencies of Boer frontiersmen whom – it was thought – were attempting to connect with the German presence. Even Gladstone gave voice to thoughts about the 'dirty Boers'; and the Conservative leader was later moved to denounce the Afrikaners as 'people whom we despise'.[230] They then turned to denouncing each other. The Liberal ministry which struggled with the beginnings of the Partition in 1884–85, was quite sure that Lord Carnarvon's grandiose federalist schemes had set the whole process of political reordering in action. 'Carnarvon has had a *cacoethes* of action, or stir in him, which has been at the root, I am sorry to say, of all these mischiefs in South Africa', Gladstone commented, 'I do not like to say this if I can help it, but it is my conviction.'[231] The Salisbury administration, of course, found its problems after 1885 directly attributable to the conciliatory postures of the Liberals in South Africa. 'There is no part of the world in which Mr Gladstone's policy has left more fruitful seeds of difficulty,' Salisbury stated unhappily, 'but for him, neither Portuguese, Germans nor Boers would be in a position to cause us any embarrassment.'[232]

Recrimination achieved little, and explained even less. Whether the British would have it or not, the local events of 1877–84 had drawn them into the swing doors of political change in South Africa. They were about to be spun out unsteadily towards a new and even more competitive age of power-politics in this colonial periphery of empire. It only needed Bismarck's introduction of a rival Great Power in Southern Africa to turn this quickening set of piecemeal Scrambles into a final and general Partition.

Beginnings 1884–86:
Britain, Bismarck and the Boers

'It is a dangerous complication of our position in South Africa that a foreign power should establish itself on this coast [of South-west Africa] . . .'

> Sir R. Herbert, permanent under-secretary
> at the colonial office, May 1884

'I want to secure South Africa *all round*, from the mouth of the Orange on the West, to the Portuguese on the East.'

> Lord Derby (colonial secretary) to Lord Granville
> (foreign secretary), 28 December 1884.

'Africa for the Afrikaners.'

> Transvaal political slogan, 1880s

'What we desire is [Cape] Colonial annexation, and not Imperial rule, in Bechuanaland.'

> Gladstone to Derby, 17 April 1885

3

The Scramble begins: the impact of
Bismarck and the 'New Imperialism' 1884

Bismarck brought the New Imperialism to South Africa.[1] His annexation of territory in South-west Africa, in April 1884, signalled the beginnings of a new phase in the local politics of Partition, and of the 'South African Question'.

The German presence at Angra Pequena, together with the possibility of its expansion eastward towards the Transvaal, and its appearance in the other 'open' areas of South Africa, lent a new and potent urgency to the Scrambles for land, resources and hegemony already developing, on some scale, in the region more generally. It was the creation of a German colony in South-west Africa which called into question the comfortable metropolitan policy-makers' vision of a 'British South Africa' stretching, in happy isolation from international politics, from the Cape to the Zambesi River, from the Indian to the Atlantic Oceans.

The arrival of the Germans in South-west Africa was thus a crucial factor in the development of the Scramble for South Africa after 1884. It began a new departure in the local Partition, by introducing an independent variable of great moment to the forces already engaged: the Imperial Factor took alarm for largely strategic reasons; the Cape colony feared loss of commercial interests in South-west Africa, and in the hinterland of South Africa itself; Natal was anxious for its own isolated place on the South-east African coastline, and its ambitions in Pondoland; and the Boers of the highveld took courage from the arrival of not merely non-British power, but a Great Power thought to be favourably disposed towards Afrikanerdom. The German occupation was ultimately to have an essentially symbolic importance in the overall Partition of South Africa. But its very presence, and the menace of its possible expansion – together with the activities of its eager local agents – was quite enough to give a heightened urgency to the Scramble.

The German impact in South Africa was felt most acutely in three distinct regions: South-west Africa, where an initial commercial enclave at Angra Pequena soon 'ballooned' into a huge semi-desert colony after April 1884; South-east Africa, in which, from later 1884, the 'German spectre' (Gladstone's unduly nervous description) came deeply to complicate the existent struggles for land between Victorian settler, Boer frontiersman and Nguni tribesman, and the British concerns for coastal hegemony, which duly led to pre-emptive imperialism of denial by Great Britain; and South-central Africa, focused on Bechuanaland, where the British were moved to serve Cape colonial interests against Bismarck and the Boers, in further expansionist actions, to secure 'British South Africa' as really British.

Each of these regional dimensions of the German presence in South Africa drew from the preceding one, acting in largely sequential phases. They were not to be discrete in their cumulative impact; but, given their evolutionary development and progressive significance in the 'South African Question', they can be discussed as such. This chapter examines the initial German occupation at Angra Pequena, and its immediate consequences – notably the local Scramble set under way, as the Cape colony actually attempted to rival Bismarckian Germany for the remainder of South-west Africa. A further two chapters in this part discuss the broader results of the German presence as it gradually impinged on the European Scrambles for South-east and South-central Africa in 1884–85.

Bismarck's imperialism and South-west Africa

German involvement in the Scramble for Africa was essentially Bismarck's decision.[2] The domestic origins of German imperialism have been the subject of much attention recently, notably in the valuable writings of Professor Hans-Ulrich Wehler and his critics.[3] These essentially metropolitan factors need not be rehearsed at length here. It is clear that at a certain moment in time Bismarck 'changed his mind' – to use Professor Turner's evocative phrase[4] – about the value of colonies in his working of German politics, and as a useful factor in his attempts to manipulate the forces of socio-economic change in the new state.

What has received less attention in a distinguished literature, has been the aspects in which Afrocentric issues intruded on the formulation and implementation of his emerging colonial policy. For, in fact, African factors entered from the earliest stages of the German expansion overseas. It was not least due to an existing interest in possible colonial possessions in Africa – among traders, missionaries, geographic and colonial societies – that the matter was initially pressed before a decidedly 'anti-imperial' Bismarck. Further, it was because of that evolving interest and involvement in certain regions of Africa, that the chancellor was directed to focus his embryonic colonial policy on specific points along the coasts of the continent when it finally came to take the step of annexation. Lastly, in the case of South-west

Africa, it was the clamour of local German traders for protection from local African groups and Cape syndicates, which squarely put the issue of the status and nature of the German presence in Africa before Bismarck in a manner which simply could not be ignored.

Indeed, since the 1870s, the chancellor had been well aware of the pressure and the desire of several German trading groups in the Angra Pequena area for official German state protection.[5] It had not initially suited his purposes to give such official assistance. Instead, he had merely offered a German consul to speak locally for their interests.[6] Beyond this he preferred not to go.[7] Later, when these German traders stepped up their demands for protection by the *Reich*, to secure their commercial outposts against African incursions, Bismarck turned the matter over to the *British* foreign office, on the grounds that the latter might add the German subjects to the British nationals who already enjoyed protection under the Cape colonial umbrella. Great Britain however declined to play local police-man for Bismarck. When the German request was repeated a few years later, it was merely set aside quietly by the British foreign office.

As a result of the activities of F.A.E. Lüderitz (1834–86),[8] a leading Bremen merchant interested in overseas trade, and increasingly involved in the coastline of South-west Africa, the issue however refused to be set aside. Through a number of local agents and German inhabitants in the Angra Pequena area, Lüderitz came to acquire commercial rights in the area from the Khoi-Khoi chief, Josef Frederik. Indeed, in return for a mere £100 in gold and some 60 rifles, Lüderitz came to 'possess' the whole harbour area (31 April 1883) through the energetic actions of the young German adventurer, H. C. F. Vogelsang (1862–1914).[9] The latter was not only filled with dreams of seeing the creation of German colonial possession in South-west Africa, but had gained the crucial support of J. T. Hahn (1842–1902),[10] the trader and linguist – son of a Rhenish missionary family long-established in the area, at the mission station of 'Bethanien' – and who provided the vital introduction to Chief Frederik, as well as detailed information on the resources of the region. The net result was that, in mid-1883, Lüderitz felt able to press the German chancellor for a monopoly of trade (*Alleinhandel*) between 20° and 25° south on the Angra Pequena coastline.

It was largely in response to this trading pressure-group – though partly also in umbrage at the casual and dilatory manner in which his earlier requests had been handled by the British authorities – that Bismarck now more strongly made representation to the Liberal government respecting the status of his traders in South-west Africa.[11] He received a relatively prompt, but decidedly unsatisfactory reply from London. He was informed that while Great Britain had no official rights to the region – and were thus not eager to undertake any security operations for traders – he was reminded that the region was 'reserved to the British'.[12] This despatch could not have been worse timed. As Professor Aydelotte has shown, in February 1883 Bismarck was still set against colonies in general, and against Angra Pequena in particular.[13] By the autumn he was beginning to shift his thought on the colonial issue. The presumptuous responses coming from London helped him on to make his colonial 'conversion'.[14]

Purely South African pressures also worked in the same direction. They moved Bismarck towards a more imperialistic posture, in a distinctly more hasty and forward manner than he had designed. The role of Cape commercial imperialists was crucial in this process. Although no better informed of the chancellor's ambitions at Angra Pequena, they suspected him more deeply.[15] In August 1883 the Cape sent its own gun-boat, *H.M.S. Starling*, to protect their interests on the coast, and to make enquiries about German trading activity. The gun-boat returned in a month with disturbing news. The local German merchants were defiant in their desire to secure annexation to the *Reich* if possible, 'protection' by the Reich at the least. The captain of the Cape gun-boat had left a caretaker on Penguin Island offshore, with instructions to raise the British ensign if the Germans indeed attempted an annexation.[16] The independent initiative of the Cape interests alarmed the British government and greatly irritated Bismarck. Sensing the dangers in the situation, the British colonial secretary despatched a royal navy gun-boat, *H.M.S. Boadicea*, to 'stop any possible friction' between the angry local German and Cape merchants.[17]

The actions of the Cape, which had precipitated this minor gun-boat crisis, were based on the simple claim that the area was under their 'control'.[18] They quickly produced a lengthy list of instances in which this colonial overlordship had been exercised, dating back to 1796 when a Captain Alexander in the sloop *Star* had taken the region on the Cape's behalf, including both Walfisch Bay and Angra Pequena.[19] Regular subsequent visits were also cited, notably from the 1860s, culminating in an official local annexation on behalf of Cape trading interests by another gun-boat, *H.M.S. Valorous*, in 1866.[20] This case had less substance, however, than the Cape interests were prepared to admit in public. None of these 'annexations' had ever been noted in London, nor had the Cape exercised its jurisdiction by administration on-the-spot.[21] Certainly the British high commissioner's brief for Southern Africa made no specific mention of South-west Africa.

The private correspondence and dealings of the Cape cabinet also betray the weakness of their position.[22] The Cape premier in the early 1880s, Thomas Scanlen (1834–1912), was for example most anxious over the area falling into German hands. 'Lord Derby thinks that the German Government has no intention of establishing a Colony', he wrote to a colleague from England in 1884, during his discussions with the colonial secretary at the London Convention negotiations,[23] 'and admitted that it would not be advisable for Great Britain to allow any European Power to get a footing there, or on the East Coast'. Other Cape politicians, such as John X. Merriman (1841–1926) had also for some years been trying to involve Great Britain in their South-west African ventures,[24] not least because, as he put it, the region had 'not hitherto [been] included in [the] jurisdiction of any civilized Government'.[25] The Cape case was also singularly self-centred. 'I do not want to touch any further annexations if it can possibly be avoided', Scanlen wrote to Merriman privately in November 1883.

> With our small population, [and] the impossibility to maintain forces necessary to ensure obedience and respect for our orders, a large expanse of territory is a source of weakness and humiliation. And just now our financial burdens and diminishing revenue forbid the incurring of grave risks. If the Imperial Government would aid, something might be done.[26]

Thus it was that when Great Britain finally gave the nod for the area to be annexed in late-1883 by the Cape colony, its leaders stood by embarrassed at the prospect of having to shoulder an administrative burden when they merely wished to exploit the trading potential of the area. 'They cried out like children for it,' the colonial office complained bitterly, 'and now that it is offered to them they hesitate to take it.'[27]

The German traders and the Cape

While the agencies of British expansion argued over the fate of South-west Africa, important local events had taken place, involving the German traders. From the Angra Pequena area there came rumours that certain African chiefs had signed concessions with the German trading syndicates, and the German flag had been raised, in return for 100 guns, powder and lead, and the equivalent of £200 sterling.[28] A despatch from the Cape's resident magistrate at Walfisch Bay, dated 26 July 1883, largely substantiated these rumours, and noted that the 'German Territory' now extended twelve miles inland. Further, Lüderitz's enterprise had been assured that it could 'count on the protection of the German government as long as its enterprises did not collide with the rights of foreigners'.[29]

The British were not inclined to be unduly worried. It was presumed in London that Bismarck was merely providing the kind of protection to the German traders which the Cape had declined to supply. The long-standing attitude of the British ambassador in Berlin still prevailed: 'The German

Government feels far more the want of soldiers than of colonies.'[30] This view was further buttressed by an important despatch from the British *chargé d'affaires*, dated 31 August, in which it was bluntly stated that

The amount of protection to be afforded is precisely what would be granted to any other subject of the [German] Empire who had settled abroad and acquired property. It would be a mistake to suppose that the Imperial Government have any present intention of establishing Grown Colonies ... I should mention that even in the press the Lüderitz enterprise is never alluded to otherwise than as a commercial colony – *Handelsniederlassung*.[31]

This was inaccurate. Bismarck was at this very time beginning to move towards a colonial posture. In retrospect the signs are there to be seen of this shift of policy. On 18 August Bismarck instructed the German consul in Cape Town to accord Lüderitz all 'assistance', and to extend his consular 'protection' to Angra Pequena. In September he had the German *chargé d'affaires* in London, Baron von Plessen, enquire of the British foreign office 'as to whether Her Majesty's Government claim suzerainty over the Bay of Angra Pequena'.[32] On 16 November the German ambassador in London, Count Münster, was instructed to press the British government for an unequivocal statement on the status of any British or Cape rights to Angra Pequena *and* its 'adjacent territory'.[33]

The British reply to these queries was surprisingly swift in arriving at Berlin, and distinctly offensive in Bismarck's eyes.

Although Her Majesty's Government have not proclaimed the Queen's sovereignty along the whole country, but only at certain points such as Walfisch Bay and the Angra Pequena Islands, [the chancellor was informed], they consider that any claim to sovereignty or jurisdiction by a Foreign Power, between the southern point of the Portuguese jurisdiction at latitude 18° and the frontier of the Cape Colony, would infringe their legitimate rights.[34]

The language appeared to be very sharp; but it was not so intended. The British still worked from the assumption that Bismarck's primary concern was not colonies, but protection for his traders. They therefore expressed the hope that 'it may be found practicable to make such arrangements as may enable the German traders to share in the occupation of the land at Angra Pequena'.[35] Such British concerns as existed pointed in other directions: they were anxious that the Cape merchants should not inflame the local situation now that the Cape had itself declined to annex; and they were eager to secure Bismarckian co-operation in respect of Egyptian affairs.[36] A German commercial enclave at Angra Pequena gave the British no qualms. 'I do not myself see why we should object to Germany ... occupying other parts of the coastline', as the British parliamentary undersecretary argued, 'It is a long way from everywhere.'[37]

Of course, it was not a long way from the Cape's trading areas. Their commercial interests were very eager to secure and develop the potential of the South-west African mainland, as well as the off shore islands near Angra Pequena. The Cape Town trading firm of 'De Pass, Spence and Co.' was highly active in this very area, developing a good traffic in guano from Ichaboe Island, fish from the surrounding coastal regions, as well as copper from the mainland. The head of this company, Daniel De Pass (1839–1921), was a leading figure in colonial society, having been active in Cape commerce since 1861, and a man not easily pushed aside by rival traders. He lobbied the Cape government vigorously, and fiercely fought any concessions to the Germans. Little wonder that a leading member of the colonial ministry could soon remark of Angra Pequena: 'As an inlet for trade, or on account of the hitherto underdeveloped mineral wealth, the possession of this coast might be of very considerable value.'[38]

The Cape premier heartily agreed, although he wished to exploit the region without actually paying for the costs in administration. His policy was simplicity itself: he wished the British authorities to acquire the area on behalf of the Cape, arguing that if it was in the Cape's commercial interest to control South-west Africa, then it was in the interest of British strategy and prestige to forestall Bismarck's Germany. 'I have been urging Sir R. Herbert, and public men with whom I came in contact, that England should at the very least go to the length of saying that between Cape Frio on the West and Delagoa Bay on the East, there should be a South African Monroe Doctrine', he wrote from London in late-1883 to a Cape colleague, 'and all European Powers should be given to understand that it must be "hands off"'.[39]

The crucial months: 3 February–29 May 1884

As much as the British were thus eager to close the question of Angra Pequena, so the Cape interests were determined to keep it alive. They put considerable pressure on Mr Mother-country, through their premier and their agent-general in London, to get the British government to take such action as to be 'considered paramount power on the coast ... even if such a definition only takes the form of an assertion of a right'.[40] The urgency of the Cape pressure increased with the month. 'I had hoped ... that intimation has been given at Berlin to the effect that we claimed the West Coast', Merriman now wrote to the Cape agent-general in England, 'Yet no intimation of this kind has been notified here, and meanwhile we are allowing these

[German] traders to acquire all sorts of rights which may be very inconvenient when the day of reckoning does come.'[41] His letter ended strongly: 'Get some Member of Parliament to put a question about [the] Angra Pequena question . . . We must have the Monroe Doctrine as far as England is concerned.'[42]

Pressures of a different kind emanated from Berlin. On 31 December Count Münster presented yet another 'Note' to the British foreign office, based on an extensive Memorandum sent to him by the chancellor four days previously. Given the Cape activity at Angra Pequena, and the obvious attempts of its commercial interests to control the area, Bismarck wished for a clear statement of the British home government's position before he himself asked to thwart the Cape at Angra Pequena. Indeed, he desired to know 'upon what title this claim to Angra Pequena is based, and what institutions England there possesses which would secure such legal protection for German subjects in their commercial enterprises and justly won acquisitions'.[43]

The British now made three fatal errors from which all else flowed. First, and most serious, they read the Münster 'Note' to mean nothing more than a yet more determined attempt by Bismarck to secure protection for his traders at Angra Pequena. Second, they attempted to make a final effort to press the Cape to accept administrative responsibility for both South-west Africa, and the German nationals therein, as a basis for a British annexation of the area. Last, they took nearly six months to answer the Bismarckian request, not least because it took them that amount of time to bring the Cape to accept the reality that Great Britain would not be involved in any 'Monroe Doctrine' for the coastline *unless* their local settler agency accepted the administrative costs of further empire.

The six months of British silence was crucial. While the British government struggled to secure an administrative commitment from the Cape imperialists, the chancellor grew ever more concerned that London was working to forestall him through its colonial agency. This gave a new urgency to Bismarck's colonial thinking, and forced him to bring forward his timetable of imperialism. Of course, the British *were* working for an annexation of Angra Pequena, via the Cape, but only because they believed this would appease both Bismarck and the agitated commercial groups in the Cape colony. The British were quite unaware at this stage that they were provoking a Scramble for colonial territory – or indeed were in the midst of any Scramble. Their position was plain. If the Cape imperialists failed to accept administrative responsibility in South-west, Great Britain would not act herself; Germany must rather be informed that the security of her nationals at Angra Pequena lay in her own hands. 'In such [a] case,' as the British colonial secretary himself intimated, 'it would appear difficult to resist the representation of the German Government that, failing other protection for German subjects at that place, they [the Germans] must assume jurisdiction over it.'[44]

The British therefore now made a concerted attempt to press the Cape interests to act. An official request was made to the colonial ministry on 3 February. The Cape declined to reply until 29 May. Why did the Cape imperialists allow such a time to elapse at so vital a stage of the matter? A number of purely local factors were involved. The first was the very strange story, never seriously contradicted, that when the Cape premier received the official telegram he read it, pocketed it, and forgot it. He later claimed he remembered 'receiving a telegram . . . while in Cradock, but he believed it related to Walfisch Bay alone, and not to the West Coast'.[45] Another complication lay in the nature of Anglo-Cape relations at this time. The British government was eager to involve the colonial agency in sharing an administrative responsibility in southern Bechuanaland as a part of the London Convention negotiations. The Cape was thus torn between a desire to protect its commercial interests, in South-west Africa and Bechuanaland, at the same time that it was withdrawing from Basutoland, having conducted an expensive and disastrous form of trusteeship administration, culminating in the infamous War of Disarmament which the Southern Sotho had certainly not lost.[46] Last, and most important, the Scanlen Cape ministry was breaking up. The premier had taken a harsh beating for his personal commitment to involve the colony in the administrative up-keep of Bechuanaland. On 12 May the Cape had a new premier, Thomas Upington (1884–98), an Irish immigrant and lawyer, known locally as the 'Afrikaner from Cork' because of his close ties with Hofmeyr's *Bond*.

The cumulative effect of these purely parish politics was important. South-west Africa, while strongly desired by certain Cape commercial imperialists, was set aside temporarily, and no decision was reached until August 1884. By that time the region had gone by default to Germany. The British high commissioner, who had enjoyed the unenviable task of trying to wring a decision from the chaotic arena of Cape political machinations in the first half of 1884, had read the signs correctly. 'I think that if the Cape does not care to have Angra Pequena,' he had written in the early phases of the affair, 'the Germans will be allowed to establish jurisdiction over it.'[47]

The 'Deutschfeindlichkeit' of the Liberal government?

Bismarck was not aware that he had indulged in a one-man Scramble for South-west Africa. He was cognisant of the British attempts to press the

Cape into South-west Africa and of the claims of the colonial imperialists. But he wrongly assumed that this all was an attempt on the part of perfidious Albion to keep him out of 'British South Africa'. The Liberal ministry was privately charged by the Bismarckian circle of handling their requests 'not only with indifference but with severity and deliberate injustice'.[48] By August 1884 Bismarck himself spoke of the '*Deutschfeindlichkeit*' of the British.[49] Indirectly, he became another victim of the tortuous activities of the Cape politicians; his sense of irritation and suspicion put him in just the right frame of mind to receive the schemes of the German traders. Lüderitz had recently returned from South-west Africa considerably agitated by a visit to Cape Town, where the governor's secretary had stressed the Cape involvement with Angra Pequena, adding that the local imperialists had at last found a document which proved their rights at the bay beyond reasonable doubt.[50]

Bismarck was not ready to be hustled by a small overseas trader. But with growing public interest in African colonies, and with the Reichstag elections of 1884 less than 6 months away, he was aware of the damage of his position if it was revealed that the German Empire had been thwarted at every step by a scheming petty group of Cape colonial entrepreneurs. The chancellor therefore moved to act in a fashion sufficient to forestall any British moves, yet without irrevocably committing him to a colonial empire. Germany declared 'an interest' in the West coasts of Africa;[51] Dr Gustav Nachtigal was appointed commissioner to the coasts, his duty being to secure treaties of friendship and concession from local African chiefs; and a firmer posture was adopted in the diplomacy of protecting overseas commercial interests.[52]

When Lüderitz next called on the chancellor, on 19 April, he detected a much warmer reception than ever before. Bismarck was said to have remarked, soon after, to a senior official: 'Now let us act.'[53] In fact he was prepared to take a first and most circumscribed step. He had always admired commercial empires of trade – such as the British had constructed by the John Company in pre-1857 India – and it was this kind of imperial expansion he desired. His inclinations were given practical basis in the South-west African case by two working documents. In a Memorandum dated 8 April 1884, Heinrich von Kusserow, a senior official interested in imperialism in the German foreign office, argued for expansion through that time-honoured British technique of the commercial company under charter.[54] This proposal, and its advocacy, clearly had its effect: 'Von Kusserow dragged me into the colonial whirl', Bismarck later remarked sourly. Some three weeks later, Lüderitz submitted his plans. He too eschewed the idea of a *Reichskolonie*, arguing instead for no more than a commercial possession under formal protection, *Reichsschutz*.[55] On this basis Bismarck launched Germany's first bid for colonies on Thursday, 24 April 1884.[56]

The unreality of British policy

The initial British reactions were decidedly confused. A minority element in the Liberal government shared the concern expressed by Herbert at the colonial office. 'It is a dangerous complication of our position in South Africa that a foreign power should establish itself on this coast, over which it has always been understood that this country holds undisputed authority, and we shall in future almost certainly have increased difficulty in dealing with both Boers and natives.'[57] It is interesting and significant that Herbert's fears related not to issues of prestige, diplomacy or the balance of sea-power, but to the *internal* Afrocentric consequences of the new official German presence on inter-group relations in Southern Africa. As he spelled it out, the 'German traders now at Angra Pequena, and others following them . . . will prevent us from controlling the supply of arms and ammunition to the Boers and natives, however urgent the necessity of doing so may become'.

A solid majority of the government, however, lined up behind the colonial secretary, who simply acquiesced in the situation – 'We have no choice. We cannot show any title'[58] – and took up the somewhat obtuse position that Bismarck's declaration signified nothing more than official protection for his traders. 'The Germans mean business', a junior minister warned.[59] But, the colonial secretary would have none of it. His first public statement on the question, in the House of Lords on 19 May, lifted unreality to the level of official policy. As far as he was concerned, South-west Africa was still a no-man's land, with a small German 'commercial enclave' at Angra Pequena. 'While we have not claimed the Bay', he stated categorically and misleadingly, 'we have claimed the right against Foreign Powers on the general ground of its nearness to our settlements, and the observance of any other claims.'[60]

British policy was now firmly rooted in nothing. By the logic of the senior ministers, there was no good reason why they should not still press the Cape to act on the coast, and so finally put the issue to rest. On 7 May another telegram of urgent advocacy was despatched to the Cape interests, reminding them of their failure to reply to the earlier request of 3 February. Dramatic results followed. The new Bond-dominated Upington ministry decided, in view of the growing German activity on the coast, that 'some such extension [of the Cape jurisdiction] seems to be unavoidable'.[61] They would accordingly extend Cape hegemony 'by means of commission similar to that under which Port St. Johns is now governed'. At last, the British had moved the

Cape to act. 'Yours 3rd February and 7th May', the high commissioner telegraphed on 29 May, 'Ministers have decided to recommend Parliament to undertake control and cost of coast line from Orange River to Walfisch Bay.'[62]

Nothing could be clearer: there was unbounded delight in London. The Liberal administration moved quickly to close the matter. On 2 June the foreign office was requested to arrange the despatch of a gun-boat 'without delay to Angra Pequena, in order that there may be no ground for alleging that the continued absence of British protection has rendered German intervention necessary'.[63] At the same time the British foreign secretary blithely informed the German chancellor that he was pleased to inform him that his request could now be met in full: the government 'have decided that arrangements shall be made for giving protection under the British flag to any persons, Germans as well as English, who may have duly acquired concessions or established [factories] on the coast'.[64]

The gap between British and German policy had become prodigious. Bismarck's far from clear diplomatic language allowed the British completely to misread his intentions. The less than rigorous analysis of the German 'Notes', by British officials in London and diplomats in Berlin, resulted in a policy of annexation through the Cape which increasingly angered Bismarck. By early June the British believed that they could congratulate themselves, and close the files. Great Britain was satisfied; the Cape was satisfied; presumably Bismarck was satisfied. Here was the rub. 'They first wanted to see if they could use it for themselves', he fumed on receiving a telegram from the Cape informing him of the intended colonial imperialism.[65]

The Scramble of illusions thus took on new proportions of misunderstanding. The British ambassador in Berlin implacably misinformed London of the situation in Germany. He acknowledged the rising interest in the *Reich* over the colonial question, but insisted that the chancellor had done nothing 'to satisfy their desires for colonies', beyond sending Dr Nachtigal on *S.S. Mieme* to 'report generally on the West Coast of Africa'.[66] Further, in respect of South-west Africa, the 'alleged assumption of sovereignty of that territory by the German Government is unfounded'.[67] In reality, as a direct result of the proposed imperialism by the Cape commercial interests under the British flag, Dr Nachtigal's sea voyage had taken on highly expansionist overtones. Bismarck had now instructed him to counteract any Cape imperialism in South-west Africa. He was to assume 'suzerainty' (*oberhoheit*) in the region, and seizure of possession (*Besitzergreifung*), as well as establishment of a formal state protectorate (*Protektorat* and *Schutzherrschaft*) over the new German colonial territory.[68]

A Cape bid for the coastline

The Cape interests finally revealed the true character and intent of Bismarckian policy to the British government.[69] The local imperialists moved quickly to attempt possession of 'British South-west Africa'.[70] The chancellor was therefore forced to request a British intervention against their own colonial agency of expansion. The foreign secretary explained to his bemused senior colleagues, after an urgent audience with the German ambassador on 7 June: 'Prince Bismarck wished him [Count Münster] to tell me confidentially that the German Government could not recognize such a mode of taking possession of these territories, and could not recognize the [Cape] right of doing so.'[71] The colonial secretary also grasped reality as a man emerging from a dream.

This seems to mean that the German government intends to lay claim to Angra Pequena as German territory. Of course they do not mean to include Walfisch Bay, which we have held since 1877 or '78 – they not objecting.

We must abstain from taking any action on the recommendation of the Cape Colony till the question of right is settled.[72]

Herbert Bismarck was despatched to London by his father for what became three noted conversations, with Lord Granville, 14, 17 and 22 June 1884. The British were forced to eat humble pie for their diplomatic blunders and their encouragement of the commercial interests at the Cape. 'It is very hard for me, as I have so much to do, that I cannot go into detail on these colonial questions', the foreign secretary admitted abjectly to Herbert Bismarck. 'Besides this, a part of the Parliamentary business falls on me as leader of the Upper House, in this difficult time. On top of this I have to conduct the awkward Egyptian negotiations.'[73] He further assured the German government that in the case of Angra Pequena he had throughout not intended to rival the Reich – 'on the contrary, he had acted in the belief derived from some of the questions which had been asked by the German Government, that it was their desire that the German settlers should receive British protection'.[74] Every effort would now be made to facilitate German colonial expansion.[75]

This personal assurance became official British policy with the meeting of the Liberal cabinet on Saturday, 21 June: 'it was decided,' Sir Charles Dilke noted in his diary, 'that Bismarck, who was greatly irritated with the Government, was to have all he wanted'.[76] At the same time the earlier policy of expansion via the Cape was put into reverse. 'Better not bring forward vote at present,' the surprised Cape governor was now informed,[77] 'in order to avoid any misunderstanding between Her Majesty's Government and German Ministry, with whom communications are proceeding.'

Bismarck viewed these developments with a happier demeanour.[78] The *Reichstag* was informed, at the end of June 1884, that German government 'had in view the idea of issuing . . . a letter of Protection, similar to the Royal Charter given by England to the East India Company, and lately to the North Borneo Company'.[79] His pleasure was to be short-lived. The Cape interests reacted violently. 'I cannot come to the conclusion that Her Majesty's Government has decided to hand that territory over, without paying the slightest attention to our wishes', the Cape colonial leader remarked bitterly on 2 July. 'If it is so, I can only say [that] I believe the almost unanimous feeling of this country would be that we have been treated with an amount of discourtesy we do not deserve.'[80] Their anger went beyond speeches. On Wednesday 9 July a strong deputation of Cape expansionists called on the governor. That evening he cabled to London reporting 'great uneasiness' in the Anglo-Dutch colony.[81] A week later the local ministry announced its annexation of all the territory *around* Angra Pequena before Bismarck had had an opportunity to delineate the frontiers of his 'commercial colony'.

Consternation followed in both London and Berlin. The British were emphatic in refusing to rival Bismarck for South-west Africa – '[we] are not in a position to oppose the intentions of the German Government . . . where no British sovereignty exists', the senior British official in the colonial office minuted[82] – and they prepared to 'fight' their own colony over the issue. Bismarck simply put on the uniform of imperialism and launched a hasty campaign of colonial annexations. On 7 August 1884 it was publicly announced that Germany had annexed Angra Pequena to the Reich as a sovereign territory: shortly after, when the scope of the Cape imperial design was learnt, the annexation was enlarged.[83] The German colony now included all the land from the Cape border to the frontier of Portuguese settlement in Angola.[84] By 26 August Bismarck had hastily acquired an enormous semi-desert colony, over 600 miles in length – partly to his own surprise, certainly to the anger of the Cape expansionists, and much to the bemusement of the British government, which was still trying to steady itself.

Anglo-German Agreement

This Scramble should have ended there. But complications soon abounded. The Cape imperialists declined to have their interests simply set aside. Herbert Bismarck complained to Lord Granville, on 20 August, of the Cape action as an 'unjustifiable and rash proceeding which has caused a great amount of ill-feeling in Germany'. Baron von Plessen was even blunter: he felt the Cape announcement was 'really calculated to injure the German undertaking'.[85] Germany was adamant that the British should do 'justice to the friendly sentiments of both Governments, by refusing their consent to the proposal of the Cape Colony'.

The British had hoped in July that they might set up an 'Anglo-German Commission to examine into, and decide all . . . claims on the spot'.[86] Events had now moved beyond this hope. The British colonial secretary found himself caught between two fires – both, in his words, 'equally unreasonable'.[87] Great Britain would have to choose between the declared and contending claims of Cape and German imperialists. The choice was obvious yet unenviable. 'Under all the circumstances it may be best to acquiesce in the German Protectorate over the whole of the coast from the Orange River to the Portuguese boundary', the senior British colonial official argued. 'It will be much better to have Germany satisfied than to have both Germany and the Cape dissatisfied.'[88] The cabinet agreed.[89] As one minister remarked:

I should meet Germany more than half way in the matter of the coast from the Orange River northwards – it is really of no value to us. Germany, if she really intends to colonize, will be as good a neighbour as anybody else – and the Cape, having delayed so long, can have no real ground for complaint if we give way to Germany there.[90]

The Cape expansionists felt they had every 'real ground for complaint' when the decision sweeping aside all their claims was conveyed to them on 22 September.[91] Nor were they the only critics of the policy of appeasing Germany. The Cape imperialists' cause was taken up in the British popular press. The *Pall Mall Gazette*, for example, asked 'Why did England give way about Angra Pequena?' and provided this answer: 'Because that was the price which Lord Granville had to pay for the consent of Germany to his abortive conference about Egypt.' By their logic it was a 'fatal policy, which [has] led us to sacrifice Egypt to the entente cordiale with France . . . [and] may yet cost us our South African Empire'.[92]

If there was this element of ransom in the decision, the British paid willingly, if with some indignation: 'when the Germans have chosen such territory as suits them, we have the audacity to take what they have left!', as the colonial secretary remarked. 'This is rather cool; even from Bismarck.'[93] All the substantive German claims were however fully met and recognised. The Cape commercial elite – led by the De Pass group – were left bearing a grudge; and the exclusive British right to manipulate the subordinate governments of colonial South Africa at will, was brought to an end.

Bismarck, as colonial victor, also had to pay a 'ransom'. He had acquired an empire, but it was not the empire he had first projected. As the senior British official in Berlin had once well expressed the chancellor's views on the agencies of imperial expansion: Bismarck was 'entirely opposed to the creation of colonies on what he considered a bad system, namely, to acquire a piece of ground, appoint officials and a garrison, and then seek to entice persons to come and live there'. Rather, he strongly preferred to 'leave the development of these colonies to the energy of the merchants'.[94] Local events had however hurried along his policies until he hardly controlled either the sequence of events or the character of the colonial expansions. His first, superior plan, of 'protectorates' (*Schutzgebeite*), worked by self-sustaining commercial enterprises, was soon lost. The actions of the settler imperialists from the Cape had artificially forced a Scramble on the chancellor, who had been driven to indulge in the hasty 'imperialism of denial'. As a result, the charter system was never instigated, while Lüderitz's enterprise soon collapsed in bankruptcy.[95] A new South-west company was formed, but it fought shy of accepting any administrative charter from the *Reich*, preferring trade to bureaucracy.[96]

Bismarck's imperialism on the cheap had failed. In less than five years he was almost totally disillusioned about the overseas venture. By 1889 he could declare: 'The Foreign Office either gets rid of colonial affairs or it gets rid of me.'[97] He fell that year. The colonial policy had been designed to secure his position in 1884. Instead, it helped to pull him down. The history of the colonial empire suggested he had paid a heavy price for very little. By 1914, the one million square miles of German colonial empire had less than 25,800 settlers, had yielded little in commercial worth, and sustained bloody African rebellions against German colonial rule.[98] As early as 1885 a leading British colonial official had minuted, not without a little relish, at the close of the British–Cape–German wrangles over South-west Africa, 'The German colonization scheme was a folly of [which] the Germans now appear to be tired, and it may be doubted if they will make any further effort to push their protectorate beyond the 200 mile limit proclaimed last year.'[99]

With the Cape removed from the issue, if not so silently nursing its grievances, an Anglo-German Commission drew up the final boundaries of 'South-west Africa' in July 1886. Germany secured all she desired; and the Cape was only partially compensated, with the award of the islands rich in bird guano off Angra Pequena itself. This was thought to be a safe decision. 'Whether the traders are German, or English,' an English minister commented in the mood of the unreality in which the Scramble had been conducted in South-west Africa, 'is a matter of perfect indifference to the birds.'[100]

The British government then took stock of the whole affair. It was felt they had muddled through to a reasonable, if not ideal, solution. 'Bismarck has not such a case against us as would appear about Angra Pequena', the foreign secretary concluded, in tracing the roots of the South-west African Scramble to the chancellor's diplomacy.

I think I was justified in acting as a medium of communication between him and the Colonial Office, instead of taking a more active part, as I should have done if I had known that the German Gov[ernment] t. attached importance to any question of German colonization, but I had constant assurances both from Münster and Ampthill that the reverse was the case ... But I hope this difficulty will be got over.[101]

Such a conclusion appears to have confused the progress of events with their real origins. Bismarck's diplomacy was far from clear. Yet, given the British attitude to South-west Africa, there would have been no Scramble had it not been for the intervention of the Cape imperialists. It was they who attempted to forestall Bismarck. It was they who pressed the British government to declare the coast a 'sphere of interest'. It was they who vacillated over accepting administrative responsibility for the area, and thus indirectly gave an aura of secrecy to British diplomacy in the months of silence which so worried the Bismarckian circle. As long as the Cape was bidding for the region the Scramble existed. Once the Cape was removed from negotiations the 'Scramble' immediately came to an end. The tail had wagged the dog. The character of the British liberal empire in Southern Africa – of imperial interests worked through loyal local agencies – made Great Britain vulnerable to such curious influence by her settler satellites.

A 'Mittelafrika' strategy?

The Angra Pequena question was not as easily 'got over' in South Africa, as the British foreign secretary had hoped.[102] The implications of Germany's new presence for the political communities of plural South Africa expanded rather than contracted. There was to be a growing anxiety – particularly in the years 1884–86 and 1894–97 – over further German territorial ambitions, something previously not given nearly enough attention by historians of imperialism. There was also to be a rising sense of troubled concern among British policy-makers at the influence which the Bismarckian presence appeared to be having on the republican Boers of the interior states of South Africa. In 1884 the 'Transvaal State' was busy negotiating its further independence from British authority, and was clearly eager to find diplomatic support from the German Empire. Further, from the western borders of the

Transvaal, *trek-Boers* were eagerly expanding on to Tswana lands, in the direction of the South-west African inland frontier.

The British premier fought to dampen fears over the Bismarckian presence: 'I want to give Bismarck every satisfaction about his Colonial matters, and I am ashamed at the panic about Germany in South Africa.'[103] Instinctively Gladstone dreaded being drawn into a Scramble for Southern Africa. He also placed the problems of South Africa below those of North Africa. 'No doubt we must be most cautious here as to Colonial alarmism,' he explained to his troubled colonial secretary in late-1884, 'but any language at Berlin appearing to convey sympathy with it at this moment does extraordinary mischief at one really vulnerable point, Egypt.'[104] If his government was searching for a definite policy for the future of 'British South Africa', Gladstone was happy to supply one: 'For my part I should be extremely glad to see the Germans become our neighbours in South Africa, or even the neighbour of the Transvaal. We have to remember Chatham's conquest of Canada . . . which killed dead as mutton our best security for keeping the British provinces.'[105]

The premier however found himself in a minority position in his own government. The manner of Bismarck's 'sensitive' annexation of Angra Pequena, the growth of his commercial enclave into a vast west-coast colony, and the rumours respecting his future ambitions, all kept alive a sense of insecurity in British official circles. Rather more typical of the majority view of the government was a comment from an administrator in the colonial office. 'It is rather too late to protest as regards the coastline, but no time should be lost in requesting the German Government . . . to declare *the limits inwards* of the territory under their protection.'[106] The secretary of state agreed: 'I think . . . Germany should draw a line to the eastward of their Angra Pequena territories, east of which they should not exert their influence, nor we to the west of it.'[107] Rumour abetted fears. According to a correspondent of *The Times*, Germany wished to 'push on into the Transvaal, Bechuana and Zulu countries . . .'[108] so making real the vague dreams of a *Mittelafrika* strategy.[109]

Searching for clarity and certainty in a confused local situation, the British asked assurances from Bismarck's Germany that they had no intention of leaning across the Kalahari to join hands with Kruger's republicans.[110] The chancellor declined to offer such comfort to the Liberal administration.[111] Indeed, Herbert Bismarck, speaking for his father, went so far as to inform Lord Granville that it was a 'question of mere curiosity . . . a matter that does not concern you'.[112] In a mood of some consternation,[113] the colonial secretary was soon speaking of the 'predatory proceedings' of Germany in Southern Africa.[114]

Germany and the republican Boers

Bismarck had no serious intention of becoming deeply involved in the political future of a disparate community of frontier farmers. The Victorians of 1884–85 could not be sure of this. Recent events had shown how difficult it was to assess German intentions. Further, local events, during the Scramble for South-west Africa, had drawn attention to the fact that the bonds linking Germans and Afrikaners had indeed been growing steadily with the years. That relationship, nebulous as it was, appeared to be pregnant with mischief.

As early as 1864 a Transvaal president had requested Prussian recognition of his 'South African Republic'. From 1871 German–Transvaal improved trading relations had been instituted. Attempts had also been made by President Burgers, Kruger's flamboyant predecessor, to find German assistance in building an independent rail outlet from the Transvaal to Delagoa Bay. It was clearly something of a one-sided friendship.[115] The Boers needed the Germans more than the latter needed the frontier republicans.[116] The earnest Transvaal attempts culturally to identify with the German societies of Central Europe – as a counterpoise to Anglo-Saxon influences – interested rather than convinced Bismarck. He declined to see the Afrikaners as a lost overseas branch of the German *Volk-stamm*.[117] In the later 1870s he was unmoved by the attempts of a German adventurer, Weber, to secure a German 'protectorate' for the Transvaal; or by the entreaties of the Afrikaner republicans to assist them in fighting the British annexation of the Transvaal in 1877.[118] His attitude began to change markedly in the 1880s. Bismarck was impressed with the Boer vigour in throwing off British rule in the 'First War of Independence', 1880–81, culminating in the Majuba victory.[119] Once his own colonial policy had begun to come to life in South-west Africa he was also not unaware of the diplomatic advantages of playing the Boer card in his diplomatic dealings with the British. A Bismarckian note of 1885 recorded: 'In view of the pro-German tendency of the Dutch farmers [of the Afrikaner Republics], England will not be pleased at the prospect of a German establishment four days away from Cape Town.'[120]

There was thus a degree of calculation in Bismarck's decision to invite Kruger to visit Berlin the same week that the colony of South-west Africa was announced.[121] Kruger was then in London leading the Afrikaner deputation which was negotiating the new Anglo-Boer convention of 1884. His departure from London for Berlin appeared to have symbolic importance.[122] The Afrikaner leader was given a warm welcome at Berlin's *Bahnhof*, and a state carriage took him everywhere. Bismarck honoured Kruger with a state banquet, and they were reportedly seen on several occasions having long discussions as they went for walks, their arms linked.[123] There was much discussion in the London *Times* over the significance of the visit.[124]

Kruger's Afrikaans biographer has described his return to Southern Africa, on 11 July 1884, after a '*triomf in Europa*'.[125] Allowing for hyperbole, there was at least some small significance in the commercial treaty signed by the two states,[126] and the sense of 'everlasting' friendship (Bismarck's phrase) which now existed between Germany and the Boers. British policy-makers certainly now worked from the premise that the republicans had found a patron in Bismarck.[127] Awkward questions arose. Was the Kalahari desert sufficiently big, and the coastal plains of northern Natal sufficiently wide, to keep the 'everlasting friends' apart? Would the new relationship encourage further German intrusions into South Africa, and further Boer attempts to reach out for the coastlines? A senior foreign office official indulged in the speculation of worst contingencies, and warned that if Germany took a foothold on the south-east African coast, 'she would at once be brought into the Transvaal and the headwaters of the Orange River, and so might stretch out a hand to the new settlement at Angra Pequena'.[128]

The consequences of the German annexation

Limited as were Bismarck's actual actions, they still had a far ranging impact in South Africa. In a moment new and disruptive elements had been introduced into the local politics of Partition.

First, and most obvious, major diplomatic issues were raised. Quite rightly 1884 has often been taken as marking a new phase in Europe's relations with Southern Africa. Bismarck's actions formed the first major intrusion by a Great Power in local political affairs since Great Britain had herself taken the Cape in 1806. By bringing South-west Africa into the German Empire, Bismarck had soon drawn all South Africa into the vagaries of international relations and politics. He had also partially challenged a fundamental presupposition concerning the isolation of the region as a British 'imperial preserve', so bringing to resurgent life the expansionist aspects of 'free trade imperialism', reacting in defence of threatened traditional interests.

The Bismarckian action also influenced Anglo-Afrikaner relations. The diaspora of the Boers in the Great Trek, and in subsequent family treks, had spelled political weakness and isolation for the republicans. The German presence, coming so closely after a reawakening of Afrikaner 'national consciousness' in the period 1868–81, culminating in the 1880–81 revolt against the British annexation of the Transvaal, helped along this new sense of cultural identity and unity; it encouraged potential independency outside

British influence; and it gave a further spur to that restless desire of the Afrikaner pastoralists to burst the boundaries of the old Trekker states, in search of fertile African lands on which to raise even further republics of God-fearing, negro-phobic, Calvinists. That very expansion also carried with it the latent dangers of promoting a German 'alliance' with those pro-German, and passionately anti-Anglo-Saxon inhabitants of the interior of South Africa.

Victorian officialdom was soon to be particularly concerned with the expansive drive of Trekker-groups towards Zululand and St Lucia Bay, where they would surely instigate further black–white frontier war, and where they might well invite further German attention on the east coast generally. 'Both Natal and the Cape Colony would be endangered', the colonial secretary stated flatly, 'if any foreign power chose to claim possession of the coast'.[129] Strategic supremacy in the interior was also thought to be involved. In the words of a British official at the colonial office:

That the Transvaal would be able to maintain itself as an independent state, I have never thought probable. That we should resume the Government of it is, I fear, a hope not likely to be realised. That Germany will take it under her protection, i.e. annex it, seems if we hold back, an almost certain contingency.[130]

The factual basis for such speculation was shaky. But there was no gain-saying the facts which stared at British officialdom from the changing political map of South Africa. Germany was at Angra Pequena, and spreading out to encompass a vast landscape in South-west Africa, which soon did not look nearly far enough away from the Afrikaner states of the highveld.[131] Also, by chance or deep design, the frontier-Boers were suddenly breaking into a renewed burst of enthusiastic local republican state-formation with expansion east and west from the interior republics. The political geography of South Africa was beginning to alter radically. In a single year a new political map had been written. Where at the beginning of 1884 Great Britain could call Africa south of the Limpopo her own, Germany was now present: and where there had been two isolated republican states of subsistence Boer frontier-farmers, there were now five republican polities, at least one of them eager to break the informal British cordon of isolation, and open windows to the world.[132]

Last, and most important of all, the German presence trenched on the dynamics of internal relations between the many cultural groups inhabiting South Africa, and their interaction with the imperial power. In the words of Sir Robert Herbert, the experienced permanent under-secretary at the colonial office, it was a matter of no little indifference to the British that 'a new Foreign Authority should be introduced and further complicate the already confused political questions with which we and the colonies have to deal'.[133]

Essentially, those 'political questions' concerned not merely white–white relations in Southern Africa (between Anglo-Saxon and republican Afrikaners) but also of course black–white relations, between settler and African polities. Any demographic movement by one group deeply affected those in the immediate neighbourhood, often sending tremors of unrest through the entire body-politic. Any major change in the overall power structure also of necessity set in motion a domino-like tumbling of the status quo, so inaugurating a situation of flux in which the more powerful, vigorous and expansive local political communities made new bids for land, resources and authority.

These several consequences of the German presence in South-west Africa were now to be vividly revealed in an ever-widening ambit. Just as the situation was in fact stabilising in South-west Africa – the British having met and 'contained' Bismarckian ambitions in South Africa, or so it was thought – so in truth a new regional 'front' of the Scramble was actually just opening up. It was now the already troubled context of Natal, Zululand and South-east Africa generally, which was to feel the impact of this new phase of the Scramble in South Africa. Indeed, the 'South African Question' simply declined to reach a point of rest in time, or remain isolated by region.

4

The 'German factor' in South-east Africa 1884–85

Germany did not repeat the annexations of South-west Africa on the parallel coastal region of Indian Ocean South Africa. But the British became deeply concerned, late in 1884, that Bismarck might do just that. Great Britain could look proprietorially on the entire South-east African coast – from the Cape to Natal, and from Zululand to Portuguese Mozambique – as under their imperial 'influence'. Yet it was an 'influence' not substantiated by territorial possession, even if the coastline was patrolled by the royal navy. Until that 'cordon of influence' was supported in a jurisdictional sense, it was simply open to alien intrusion by rival Powers; and by prefering this form of covert to overt empire in South-east Africa, the British made themselves vulnerable to challenge (by German and Boers) in a serious manner along the Indian Ocean rim of South Africa.

That 'challenge' duly took place. At St Lucia Bay, one of the hitherto annexed and neglected coastal inlets above northern Natal, the Old Imperialism of Boer frontier expansion threatened to make connection with the New Imperialism of Bismarck's Germany. To the south of Natal, private German concessionaires were soon at work trying to strike a treaty with the Mpondo, on which could be built a further German possession in South Africa, if Bismarck so desired.

It has traditionally been assumed that the British action in moving to claim the coastal belt parallel to Zululand was intended simply to deny the Afrikaners their dream of an independent 'window to the world'. This is true, but it is limited as a fully satisfactory explanation for that action. It is the thesis of this chapter that the ultimate rationale for the revival of the British 'stop–go' policy in south-east Africa, and its expression in direct imperial interventions through a series of coastal annexations in 1885, was intimately related to their reading of Bismarckian colonial intentions. The 'German factor' has been underrated in this phase of the Partition; yet, without its critical influence, it is hard to see why the British took such high alarm at the conduct of the sparsely populated New Republic at St

Lucia Bay; or indeed why, in short sequence, they began extending their coastal annexations southwards to Pondoland and the Transkei Territories.

Germans and Boers 1884

The frontier Boers took the first territorial actions and initiatives which rang alarums of danger in British metropolitan circles concerned with strategy and defence in South Africa.

'The plot thickens' the British colonial secretary minuted in the early stages of the Boer–Zulu entanglements.[1] In 1884 the expansive behaviour of the Boers now continued with a vengeance. The British themselves calculated that by February 1885 the Afrikaners controlled nearly 3 million of Zululand's 6 million acres.[2] Relatively early in the existence of the New Republic, the Afrikaners made it plain they had scant intention of invading the Zulu Reserve – which brought some relief to the British. But on 20 October 1884 they counter-balanced that policy with a major thrust towards the coast at St Lucia Bay, by claiming the remainder of Zululand outside the Reserve.[3] 'This is, I think, a desperate push to get hold of St Lucia Bay as a Dutch [Afrikaner] port', a high British permanent official commented.[4] The Natal governor agreed. 'The intention of the Boers is to take a strip of land about four farms deep, along the whole length of the Reserve Border, down to the sea', he warned in early 1884.[5] 'Their real object, no doubt, is to reach the sea, which has always been one of the cherished ideas of the Boers of the Transvaal.'

If this was true, what were its implications for British strategic interests in south-east Africa? Evaluations were begun. A good majority of senior Whitehall opinion expressed concern at this development in Afrikaner expansion, not least because British officialdom – both in London and Natal – saw dangerous implications of German involvement resulting. As one Minute expressed it: 'If we are to maintain our paramount power in South Africa it is very desirable that we should control this coast . . . Having taken the Zulu coast under German protection, Prince Bismarck may extend his aegis over the South African Republic.'[6] The British permanent under-secretary thought that alarmist; but he did think it 'extremely probable' that some German interest would be expressed in the coastline.[7] His ministerial chief, the colonial secretary, absolutely agreed. 'The feeling in favour of colonisation is just now exceedingly strong in Germany; and many people believe that Prince Bismarck is thinking more of humouring it, in view of the coming elections, than of real result', Lord Derby commented on 25 October 1884. He was cognisant of Bismarck's private anti-imperialism – 'It is well known that he is personally opposed to German colonies, thinking it reasonable that the strength of Germany lies in concentration, and that to scatter the forces of the Empire over the world is to weaken it'[8] – yet equally aware that German political considerations might lead the chancellor to further intervention in South Africa: 'The German Gov[ernmen]t. is making itself unpleasant to us in every part of the world: not merely showing great zeal in establishing settlements near to us, but rather ostentatiously affecting to disregard any prior claims of ours, except where actual possession has been taken.'[9]

The local African agents of the British imperial power not only substantiated these opinions, but added edge to the metropolitan sense of alarm by suggesting that Germany had ambitions beyond St Lucia Bay in Southeast Africa. The Natal governor, for example, was of the firm opinion that 'The Boers will, without fail, sooner or later, lay hands on St Lucia Bay – if indeed they are not anticipated by the German Government'.[10] More important, the much-respected British high commissioner for Southern Africa, Sir Hercules Robinson – not known as an alarmist, like Sir Henry Bulwer[11] – supplied this apparently balanced report from Cape Town:

For some time rumours have been circulating as to German designs on St Lucia Bay in Zululand. I need hardly say that a German port in that neighbourhood would be very inconvenient; apprehension is also felt about Pondoland. It would reassure people here if some authoritative statement could be made to the effect that the German scheme of annexation did not extend to the East Coast.[12]

As evidence of his concern, the high commissioner enclosed much local material in which the rumours were discussed, notably cuttings from the Afrikaner newspaper, *Die Volksblad*, which was full of 'information' on German actions and projections. Robinson also maintained a private correspondence with senior Whitehall officials, which further added fuel to British fears. As the colonial secretary was informed by his permanent deputy, 'Sir H. Robinson has, in a personal letter, recently expressed apprehension that the Germans may go to Pondoland as well as to the coast north of Natal. If they do, that will raise an irresistible storm here.'[13]

Standing up to Bismarck in Africa 1884–85

That feared political 'storm' derived largely from the earlier outcry at the 'secretive' manner in which Bismarck had annexed Angra Pequena, and now almost contemporaneously challenged British rights in New Guinea,[14] and stole-a-march on the British in annexing the Cameroons (September 1884).[15] This German overseas expansion, by sudden occupation, was singularly ill-received by the British. The secretary of state spoke angrily of the 'predatory proceedings of the Germans'.[16]

That anger was, it seems, fairly widespread in the Liberal government of the day.[17] 'Ch[amberlai]n and I are both very angry at the loss of the Cameroons', Dilke noted in his Diary, '... having thought we had annexed them – only to find that through F.O. and C.O. dawdling they have gone to Germany'.[18] Even the equable Lord Kimberley was roused to write to Chamberlain, 'I was as much surprised as you were at the German annexation of the Cameroons. After the decision of the [cabinet] Committee I thought the matter was settled ... I was quite ignorant of the reasons why our decision was not acted upon. "Too late", I fear.'[19]

To be 'too late' on the South-east African coast would, of course, be even more serious, as the senior permanent official now pointed out.[20] Thus when the Natal governor reported by telegraphic despatch that a German exploring party, led by a Dr Schiel, were openly marching through the St Lucia area – Schiel even dressed in a colourful Prussian military uniform[21] – the information was studied most closely. Schiel was apparently closely connected with the New Republicans, as well as having acquired a 60,000 acre concession from Dinizulu on the south-west corner of St Lucia Bay.[22] An associate of the Lüderitz enterprise, August Einwald, was also reported as active in the interests of the Germans, and making connection with the Boers. The links between the New Republic and the German empire appeared to be growing more tangible with each passing month.[23] The British permanent under-secretary was now of the opinion that the New Republic, being ramshackle, vulnerable and pro-German, would 'not improbably pass before long into the hands of Germany'.[24]

The records of the British colonial office for late 1884 also reveal that concern over the possible German presence extended beyond its potentially disruptive role on the Zululand coast. British metropolitan imperialists also worried how it would affect the politics of collaborative empire in Southern Africa based on the fulcrum of the Cape alliance. In October the cabinet was presented with a lengthy Memorandum on this theme,[25] by the permanent under-secretary, which argued forcibly that there existed at the Cape 'strong Colonial feeling that our interests abroad were being too readily surrendered to the Germans'. A private letter to the secretary of state amplified these issues.

When the Angra Pequena question is better understood, it will be patent that Germany has bounced and bullied us ... and I fear that if Germany is now allowed to interfere (at St Lucia Bay) when she has no locus standi at all, and we have to tell the Colonies that their wishes are set aside under German orders, there will be really serious Colonial disaffection.[26]

Sir Robert Herbert's views were surprisingly well received by an anti-expansionist cabinet. 'This is very important,' Lord Kimberley wrote to Joseph Chamberlain, 'especially considering the Dutch [Afrikaner] tendency of the present Cape government.'[27]

A strong 'lobby' in fact grew up in the cabinet for immediate strategic annexations. It would appear to have been led by the parliamentary under-secretary, Evelyn Ashley, who waged a private letter campaign of considerable vigour with his parliamentary chief, Lord Derby. Ashley's case was simple. He was ready to accept the Germans at Angra Pequena – 'as good a neighbour as anybody else'[28] – but only because it was an area isolated from British imperial interests. German intervention in South-east Africa raised far more consequential issues. He argued for annexation of 'a very short strip of coast taken from north of our Reserve territory, to a point just north of St Lucia Bay', which would 'save a good port, and reassure the Natal people, and British South Africans generally, who have got all their heads up just now – or rather down – at our supposed abandonment of that part of the world'.[29]

The British minister concerned, Lord Derby, was sympathetic to this view. He had, after all, remarked to the Cape premier over a year previously that 'it would not be advisable to allow any European Power to get a footing there (at Angra Pequena) or on the East Coast'.[30] But, of course, Angra Pequena *had* been taken by Bismarck in a 'surprise' action. The annexationist lobby feared that slow cabinet deliberations might see a repeat of that event. The senior ministers were in fact concerned over St Lucia Bay, but also at the 'danger of inconveniently irritating Germany if we were at this moment to take possession of any part of the coast between the Tugela [River] and Delagoa Bay which is not British'. For this reason, the annexationists stressed that they wished to move forward in a circumscribed way: 'it seems necessary to secure the British port of St Lucia Bay and the mouth of the Umfolosi from being annexed by Germany.'[31] The dangers of not acting were set out vigorously by the senior Whitehall colonial official: 'Parliament and public opinion would not overlook a second and much more serious surrender of British rights in South Africa. At Angra Pequena a foreign settlement is not directly and acutely dangerous: but Natal and the Reserve would be much weakened if foreigners had St Lucia Bay.'[32]

There also exists, in the private papers of the 15th Earl of Derby, that rare historical piece of evidence: a long, confidential letter from the senior civil servant to his parliamentary head, in which Sir Robert Herbert very frankly spoke his mind.[33] For him, St Lucia Bay was the 'nerve point' of the South African imperial position, *the* vulnerable area of British hegemony over the troubled plural societies of Africans and Afrikaners.

Our position in Zululand is at the present time, one of great weakness and danger, and if unfortunately the operations now being commenced [by General Warren in Bechuanaland] should lead to a serious break between this country and the Dutch [Afrikaners] of South Africa, our relinquishment of authority over Zululand might lead rapidly to grave results.

Herbert was particularly concerned at the prospect of any Afrikaner–German 'alliance': if Great Britain took up a strong position on any issue with the Transvaal Republic, it could well 'lead that State to appeal to Germany for protection'. He pressed home his case in a single and arresting concluding sentence: 'a hostile cordon drawn round the Cape from Angra Pequena to Zululand would effectually cripple us'.[34]

To some degree, these letters – both official and 'confidential' – were preaching to the converted. The colonial secretary accepted the main thrust of the argument, his only major reservation being the larger impact of such 'imperialism of denial' within British external policy: 'I don't think we can act without consulting F.O. as to the effect of such a proceeding on the Germans.'[35] That aside, he now tended to accept the logic of the expansionist group as expressed in the words of his deputy in the Commons, who argued that St Lucia Bay was 'so close to our borders ... (the Reserve is virtually British territory), that Germany cannot take offense, if we act'. Such a limited annexation would achieve the basic aims of the imperial power in South-east Africa: 'It would strengthen us in the Reserve, reassure the natives, satisfy the people of Natal and daunt the Boers.'[36]

Finance and empire

The power of the nebulous fear of sudden German forward actions in Southern Africa on the British official mind is also indirectly well shown in an interesting case-example concerning financial pressure groups and imperial policy in South-east Africa.[37]

In November 1884 certain business syndicates concerned with the African continent, and with overseas trade generally, held a well-publicised meeting at the Cannon Street Hotel, London. At this meeting resolutions were passed calling for a 'stronger' imperial policy in Southern Africa.[38] Sir Donald Currie, a well-known London financier, was selected to press the interests of the meeting on the Liberal government. Approaches were made to Downing Street, and Currie duly saw the British premier on Monday, 3 November. He informed Gladstone that, 'In 1882 the export and import trade to South Africa amounted to over 14 millions of pounds sterling. The exports reached were half this amount. But since the political unrest and uncertainty east and west of Transvaal, the trade of South

Africa has fallen off more than 15%, and is rapidly diminishing.'[39] Accordingly, Currie asked the premier for the 'adoption of a vigorous and settled policy', which would revive the trade figures, and dispel the uncertainties that lay over the political future of plural South Africa.

This was not an unreasonable request, from an important commercial pressure-group. But, of course, a 'vigorous policy' would have meant a large-scale imperial advance in South-east Africa generally. Here the British government pulled back, fearful of the responsibilities of African empire. Sir Donald Currie and the City group were duly informed that the imperial authorities had no immediate plans to annex further portions of Southern Africa simply in the cause of a 'vigorous policy'; but that, of course, the Liberal government would always keep its obligations to its own commercial interests well to the fore.[40]

Sir Donald Currie was not so easily fobbed off. On 21 November he dispatched to Downing Street a further long letter, laying out the importance of British trading interests in South Africa, and calling for all necessary imperial actions to support those interests.[41] Again his pressure was to no avail. The colonial secretary merely put aside his calls for direct imperial action, and a colonial office clerk filed his letter with a derisive minute about armchair politicians.[42] The rest of the government apparently felt much the same. When a third and last letter from Currie – all 19 pages – was circulated to ministers, it drew nothing but unfavourable comment. The premier's private secretary summarised that opinion: 'Gov[ernmen]t. do not share his apprehensions; and dissenting as they do from his principle, he will not be surprised if Cabinet form a conclusion different to his.'[43] The ministers indeed – on 22 November – moved to that decision. The imperial policy of the British state was not available as agent of City interest in defending, by formal empire postures, the 'informal empire' of laissez free trade.[44]

Two lessons stood out from this affair. Commercial pressures alone could not drive the British government to empire when it was not deemed absolutely necessary for the larger concerns of imperial interests. It also, in its negative fashion, revealed the degree to which the annexations which ultimately took place rested on other animating pressures – notably counterpoise against Bismarck's imperial ambitions.

Annexing St Lucia Bay, December 1884

Within a month of turning aside the City pressures, the British responded to the supposed German designs with annexation of St Lucia Bay and its surrounds.[45] A cabinet on 2 December discussed German ambitions at length;[46] and only two days later the colonial secretary circulated a note calling for opinion on the proposed imperialism in South-east Africa.[47] The document is revealing of official thinking on the mechanics of expansion.[48]

Northbrook If it is intended to maintain the right [to the St Lucia Bay area],[49] I think it would be better that the place should be occupied by some establishment on shore from Natal, and not only by the visit from a ship.

Kimberley: I would occupy it effectively.

Granville: I agree. The occupation should not depend upon the presence of a man of war.

Selborne: I agree; assuming that there is no reason to apprehend any serious international question or difficulties. It may, certainly, be a matter of great importance, that the seaboard of Zululand should not fall into hands which may be hostile to Great Britain.

Chamberlain: I agree with Lord G.

Harcourt: and I

Gladstone: I agree . . . in the view . . . and hope that the seaboard of Zululand will not be brought into the question unless it was included in Panda's grant.

Gladstone's reference to an earlier British treaty with Mpande in 1843, was to be important for the annexation to come.[50] The Zulu concession, which recognised British 'interests' on the Zulu coast, allowed the British to act in a fashion which claimed reassertion of rights, not a fresh annexation, and thus met any German objections ahead of time.[51] In a sentence out of the final despatch: 'The proceedings should obviously not be in the nature of an annexation, as that would imply a new acquisition . . . and merely the assertion of an old established right.'[52] It would be difficult indeed for the Germans, or the Boers, to protest an 'established right' – though the colonial office files show what the other powers could not know: the British had lost the Mpande Treaty,[53] and to their considerable embarrassment in Whitehall, had to confess this fact to the Natal governor. Very fortunately, Sir Henry Bulwer found a local copy in Natal, which did indeed support the metropolitan view that although Great Britain had not as 'yet made a claim on the strength of this concession' in over 40 years, nevertheless they had 'never, I believe, disclaimed or abandoned our rights'.[54]

Few legal or diplomatic niceties surrounded the actual British move on St Lucia Bay (18 December 1884).[55] The admiralty was instructed to hoist a flag, and to have it 'saluted at more than one place'. They were also to place British flags on numerous posts 'to be erected, painted red and blue, and supporting boards on which it should be stated that the flag was hoisted there by such and such a ship, and that the ground is British . . . the place should afterwards be visited at frequent intervals when opportunities occur'.[56] This was all accomplished by lieutenant-commander Moore, from *H.M.S. Goshawk*,[57] and the fact communicated to the Germans, the Afrikaners and the British colonists in South Africa. For an administration which was merely 'reasserting' an old right, it is hard to imagine how they could have been in even more thorough earnest over the St Lucia Bay area if they had been 'annexing' it in the face of a rival Great Power.

German concessionaires in Zululand

A theme which nagged at British policy-makers throughout this second phase of the South-east African Partition concerned the truth, or otherwise, of the contemporary evidence relating to German imperial ambitions.

Gladstone well personified this matter. He could talk critically of 'these rather undefined apprehensions' over German colonial policy; yet he could also, in time of stress, as the rumours of Bismarckian designs grew ever more frequent in late-1884, irritably write of a 'German spectre' which appeared to inhabit all the problems, and 'dark corners', of South African politics.[58] With hindsight, we know that British officialdom overdrew the dangers and likelihood of German involvement in the tangled skeins of Anglo-Afrikaner and Afrikaner–African relations. The British could not know this, and throughout the Partition on the South-east African coast a considerable debate continued: not so much over whether Bismarck had any intention of intervention – they did not doubt his image as portrayed in *Punch* as the 'hunter', colonial bag in hand – but what was sufficient, by way of annexation, to forestall his larger designs in South Africa.[59]

The issue was kept alive partly by the opaque quality of German diplomacy, which simply left the British guessing over Bismarck's plans, more specifically by the behaviour of the republican Boers in Zululand – who energetically appeared determined to forge links with the German *Reich*, or at least its local 'agents' – together with the mischievous role of those local German entrepreneurs, adventurers and explorers who were eager to draw Bismarck yet further into South Africa. On 5 December a deputation of Boers from the New Republic protested to the Natal governor at the British actions on the St Lucia Bay coast. Their leader, Lucas Meyer (1846–1902) was a fanatically anti-British Afrikaner, having fought the Transvaal annexation of 1877, distinguished himself in the Majuba campaign of 1880–81, and was now determined not to allow the imperialists to deny them the long-cherished independent outlet to the sea. He was supported in his actions by P. J. Joubert (1831–1900), then vice-president of the Transvaal, and leader of the frontier-expansionist group in the Boer state; his dread of a unified South Africa under the British flag drove them to work for 'Transvaal imperialism' in Zululand and Bechuanaland.[60] The New Republicans shortly elected him their president. As the Natal governor said, the links between the Afrikaner state in Zululand and that on the *high-veld* were indeed growing daily. Dealing with the New Republic meant, in fact, dealing with a colonising fragment of the larger republican Afrikaner state, with all the political complications that implied.[61]

The local German concession hunters were also singularly important for maintaining the unsettled state of local affairs. The Natal governor was particularly anxious over the conduct of two such individuals – Schiel and Einwald – with some reason. Adolf Friedrich Schiel (1858–1903) had come out to Natal in 1878 as a farmer, had married the daughter of a local German missionary, and then moved to the Transvaal. As he records in his autobiography, *23 Jahre Sturm und Sonnenschein in Sudafrika* (Leipzig, 1902) he returned to Natal in 1883, soon becoming 'secretary and political adviser' to Dinizulu in Zululand, and an associate of his fellow German countryman, August Einwald.[62] He duly secured a large land-grant from Dinizulu 'for services rendered', in the strategically key area around St Lucia Bay. Schiel was overseas attempting to secure official Bismarckian support for his enterprises when the British moved on St Lucia Bay, so undercutting his apparent ambitions to create a German empire in South-east Africa.[63] August Einwald (1850–1900) was an even more imperialistically minded local German concessionaire. A watchmaker from Heidelberg, he migrated to the Eastern Cape in 1880, and watched the German advances in South-west Africa with keen interest. He soon contacted Adolf Lüderitz, and began to work for a similar German concession in South-east Africa where he contacted Lucas Meyer and the Afrikaners of the New Republic. He pressed vigorously to forge Afrikaner–German links. Indeed, so aggressive was he in his enthusiasms that he appears to have alienated German officialdom in Berlin. The British action at St Lucia Bay also halted his plans in South-east Africa. But only temporarily: where Schiel gave up his designs, and returned to live in the Transvaal, Einwald merely changed his area of territorial hunting. He was next heard of trying to acquire the Pondoland coast for Germany.[64]

British metropolitan reactions to these far from satisfactory pieces of local news, was a curious mixture of relief and uncertainty. 'Our action with regard to St Lucia Bay has been taken just in time. Schiel is Secretary to the New Republic', one Whitehall official minuted.[65] Yet as the under-secretary of state pointed out, if it were true that Germany still had ambitions in South-east Africa, then 'we ought also to take the . . . coast between the

Umlatoosi [River, boundary of the Reserve] and St Lucia Bay. Otherwise we might find ourselves in the ridiculous position we are at Walfisch Bay – hung up *en l'air* – and looking foolish.'[66]

The politics of collaboration, as developed in the British acceptance of the Boers as useful 'associates' in Zululand, also now looked rather threadbare as a technique for assuring order and stability. The New Republicans, while certainly not attacking the Reserve, were at the root of the British problems, and had been allowed to strengthen their position by a calculated British decision. Rather forlornly, the senior British official in London had hoped that the Afrikaners might 'appoint a friendly president';[67] instead they had chosen P. J. Joubert. It had earlier been tacitly assumed that the British would officially 'recognise' the New Republic; now that policy was completely set aside. 'We had better maintain a masterly inactivity . . .'[68]

It was 'inactivity', however, which still worried the expansionist group in the British cabinet and colonial office. 'The fact is that, whether we like it or not, the annexation of Zululand is coming', Evelyn Ashley commented on the Natal despatches, 'to leave gaps in what we do take . . . such as . . . between Port Darnford and St Lucia . . . is I think unwise and unlikely to save trouble'.[69] Somewhat churlishly the secretary of state remarked to his deputy: 'I thought St Lucia Bay was the only harbour along that coast?'[70] An experienced clerk was sent to examine the charts most carefully. His report only lent support to the expansionist case: he found a most suitable harbour at the mouth of the Kosi river, 'which is outside the Portuguese limit of $26°\ 30'$ [south] and is therefore open to German occupation'.[71]

Would the Germans or Boers exploit such a gap? That was the moot question. Augustus Hemming, who had recently returned from attending the Berlin colonial conference for the British, had the final say:

From all I have heard in Berlin it seems to me clear that the Germans are almost certain to annex any place on these S. African coasts which we leave open for them. Our difficulties in S. Africa will be increased tenfold if we allow Germany to obtain a stand-point on account of which she may claim to exercise interference between us and the Boers.[72]

He also tended to kill any hopes which might have existed of undertaking a selective series of piecemeal annexations, rather than a blanket acquisition of the whole Natal–Zululand coast. 'There is no use in making two bites at the cherry . . . and having decided to annex St Lucia Bay we ought to complete the work by taking the whole coastline between the Reserve Territory and the Portuguese at Delagoa Bay. The cases of Angra Pequena and New Guinea should be sufficient warning against hesitation.'[73] 'I agree', was all the colonial secretary could add to these remarks, 'Propose this to the F.O., which I suppose is the first step.'[74]

In the midst of these critical departmental deliberations an extended 57-page despatch arrived from the Natal governor, each page saturated with local concerns over German ambitions in South-east Africa. There was detailed information on the explorer Einwald, and his escort of two German soldiers[75] – identified as from the General Staff at Baden, and the '76th Regiment' respectively[76] – together with his connections to Schiel and the Boers of the New Republic. They had apparently made extensive tours of Zululand, the New Republic and the coastlines, before sailing for Cape Town together, Schiel then returning to the New Republic while Einwald pressed on to Germany itself.[77] On top of this information, the Zulu Reserve Resident, Melmoth Osborn, reported that a 'trusty and reliable' German trader in his area, called Kraft, had 'received letters from Germany, from persons in authority there, requesting him to explore the coast of Zululand for minerals and to ascertain its general capabilities'.[78] He had declined. But Kraft had been approached yet again. To the Natal governor this merely gave further substantiation to the rumours he had heard respecting Einwald's activities and of the manner in which the Germans were going about preparatory to acquiring an interest in South-east Africa. 'Whilst Mr Einwald was in Natal he showed to a German settler here certain instructions which he said he had brought with him from Berlin, and which, among other things, gave him the authority of the German Government to treat for and acquire land anywhere in this part of South Africa.'[79] Indeed, one local source even said that Einwald had already acquired 'a cession on the Zulu coast in the same way as Herr Lüderitz obtained for himself a cession at Angra Pequena'.[80]

Rumour abetted rumour. Numerous such unsubstantiated, yet unsettling, reports came from Africa. Minerals, a strategic harbour, alliance with the Afrikaners – all were cited as the raison d'être of the 'informal' German interest. Even the local role of the Rhenish missions was soon dragged into the issue. According to the already agitated Natal governor,

The object of those interested in the introduction of the German Government into South Africa, has I understood, been to promote an appeal from the mission stations for protection by means of which their case may be taken up by the German Government in the same way as the case of the Rhine mission stations in Great Namaqualand was taken up.[81]

This suggestion could have been traced to the fertile imagination of the local rumour-mongers in Natal, but it was given some credence by the fact that at this very time there had been a series of savage attacks on mission stations by renegade Zulu.[82] Among those murdered was a noted German missionary, Dr Schröder. 'The most important part of this,' as the Senior British colonial office administrator minuted, 'is perhaps the grounds for German interference which are suggested – the murder of Schröder and the injury of the German missions.'[83]

There seemed, if all the rumours were taken into account, to be no limits to the political growth of the German possessions in Southern Africa. In mid-January, 1885, it was even strongly suggested that Germany had '*mittel-Afrika*' designs to include territory in Zambesia. 'If this is true,' the colonial office minuted in a mixture of incredulity and concern, 'it looks as if Germany really did intend to establish closer relations with the Transvaal.'[84] The South African expert in the British colonial office best caught the mood of the moment. 'According to the alarmists,' Edward Fairfield commented, 'a German can wedge himself in anywhere.'[85]

The Mpondo and the imperialists

The concerns of the 'alarmists' now extended outside Zululand. There was a constant, if nebulous worry, over Transvaal Boer strategies to secure a Bismarckian 'alliance'; there was also a distinctly more tangible series of events taking place south of Natal which suggested German interest in the coasts of Pondoland. Einwald, having failed in Zululand, was now active on yet another portion of South-east Africa.[86] He was soon joined by Emil Nagel, a former German military officer, who was attempting to play a similar role to the Mpondo Royal Family as that of Schiel to Dinizulu and the Usuthu.[87]

Mpondo politics assisted the intrusion of the New Imperialists. Segmentation was a noted feature of Nguni political society: by the death of the great paramount Mpondo chief, Faku (c. 1780–October 1867), the kingdom had split into two 'houses' – Mqikela (1831–87) headed the 'great house', and Ndamase, followed by his son Nqwiliso, became independent chiefs of the other political community. This division of authority also gave a greater sense of independence to the vassal groups subordinate to the Mpondo–the Mpondomise, the Xesibe and the Bhaca.[88] The situation was ready-made for white missionaries, adventurers and 'advisers' to work the expansion of Europe into Pondoland.

Earlier white involvement in Mpondo politics, by the Old Imperialism of Cape colonial authority, dating back to the 1840s, had also helped to loosen the cohesion of the Mpondo political unit, and so further assisted the extension of the New Imperialism south from Zululand. Through the critical decades of the 1830s and 1840s paramount chief Faku had, with considerable difficulty, skilfully maintained their independence in the face of the ravages of the *Mfecane*, and the threat of white expansion, notably Afrikaner *Voortrekker* state-making. His solution to the first problem was withdrawal south, and resettlement of his people over the Mtamvuma River, out of the range of Shaka's *impis*; to the second, after the Afrikaner attack on the Bhaca chief Neaphayi, in December 1840, reliance on his Wesleyan Missionary advisers, notably the Rev. T. Jenkins, to guide him to treaty-alliance with the agents of British empire in the Cape. On 7 October 1844 Faku signed an agreement with Great Britain. For the Mpondo it was thought to be a form of security; for the British it was merely a method of establishing order transfrontier through an inexpensive collaborative alliance – in return they recognised him as supreme authority over the large territory stretching along the whole coastal belt between mountains and ocean, from the Umtata to the Umzimkulu Rivers.

Faku's external policy of collaborate co-existence with the British at the Cape secured the immediate status quo, but ultimately led to a white subversion of Mpondo authority and encirclement of Faku's political community. Firstly, the 1844 collaborative treaty exacerbated internal Mpondo segmentation and inter-group conflict, by establishing Faku's authority over the Bhaca, Xesibe and Mpondomise lands, something which the latter had constantly rejected. Secondly, the treaty formed the basis for a slow but relentlessly steady process of drawing Pondoland in the British–Cape orbit of strategic and pacification policies. Step-by-step the world intruded on Pondoland: in 1861 Adam Kok's Griqua refugees were settled by the British in Nomansland, soon to be followed by white farmers, traders and more missionaries; from 1873 the Cape established magisterial authority in 'East Griqualand', which led to colonial annexation in 1879; from 1866 to 1878 numerous attempts were made to deprive the Mpondo of Port St John's; and throughout the 1870s, after Faku's death, the Cape pressured the Mpondo to sign a further treaty which would 'open up' Pondoland to 'commerce and civilization', and which would recognise the independence of the Bhaca and Xesibe, who had become allies of the local imperialists on their own behest. Lastly, the 1844 treaty created the initial lever by which the British came to manipulate Mpondo politics. By 1878 the collaborative alliance had grown to British 'overrule': Faku's weak son, Mqikela, was deposed as paramount chief by Sir Bartle Frere (5 July 1878) when the Mpondo refused to fall into line with imperial designs. Political fragmenta-tion now allowed the British to conduct their strategies without the inter-ference of the Royal House: Nqwiliso, son of Ndamase, gladly signed away the west bank of the Mzimvubu River at Port St John's in return for complete authority over 'western Pondoland'. Mqikela, as Dr Cragg has written, 'sullenly accepted a resident and nursed his grievances'.[89]

In the 1880s the politics of unhappy collaboration turned to the politics of defiance and confrontation, which were to have major consequences for the pattern of the Partition. The Mpondo had watched the Cape pacification of the Transkei 1878–81 uneasily: they resolved to resist ultimate subjection, and indeed to attempt to regain lost rights, notably their lands and authority vested by the Cape in the hands of the Xesibe and Bhaca.[90] Between 1881 and 1884 the Mpondo looked to all techniques short of war itself to thwart the pressures of the various agencies and thrusts of British imperialism: they rejected completely all offers of cash compensation for lands ceded out of their authority (December 1881); collected money to send two deputations to London protesting their position (1882, 1883); secured the Aborigines Protection Society assistance in agitating for their declining lands and rights (August 1883); placed a heavy duty on Cape merchandise entering Pondoland (August 1884); and unilaterally declared Port St John's a 'free port' (October 1884).[91] The British imperialists, both local and metropolitan, reacted most unfavourably for the Mpondo. The Cape threatened a war of pacification; the British in London declined to intervene as Mpondo trustees, and allowed the Cape to press its policies.[92] Backed into a corner, the Mpondo cast about in some desperation for allies. They found them in the German concessionaires.

This action was to be crucial for the introduction of the New Imperialism to Pondoland. It was a last-ditch counterpoise to the relentless advance of white authority from the Cape; and was largely the design of Mqikela's close adviser, Mhlangaso (c. 1845–1918). The latter was, according to the authority on Mpondo politics in the nineteenth century, 'virtual ruler of Pondoland' between 1878 and 1887, not least because of Mqikela's tragic addiction to white liquor.[93] Mhlangaso conducted treaty negotiations with Emil Nagel, and other German adventurers, in 1885, resulting in an extensive concession to a German company (June 1885). Nagel left immediately for Berlin, intending to use this document as a basis for requesting a German Protectorate. The concessionaires promised the Mpondo 'protection' against the expansion of the Cape; and Mhlangaso was offered a German education for his son Oscar, which he accepted.[94]

Events now quickly came to a head. The Upington ministry at the Cape protested vigorously over the Mpondo-German concession. Nagel arrived in Berlin, and began to agitate for a German Protectorate.[95] The Mpondo placed high hopes on the concession, and Mhlangaso took a defiantly independent line when he met the Cape authorities, during a Mpondo deputation to the colony, in October 1885.[96] The British resolved to act: they had no desire to annex the Mpondo, yet they now prepared to invoke the 'imperialism of denial'.[97] In the logic of one senior British minister of state, writing in an urgent private letter to the colonial secretary,

I would certainly, at once, proclaim British sovereignty over the coast between Natal and the Cape colony, i.e. the coast of Pondoland. We already possess the only port, the St John's River, and we have treaties with the Chiefs. We could not possibly allow any foreign power to interfere on that coast and it is better to put our exclusive rights beyond all doubt.[98]

Britain joins the 'Absurd Scramble'

'The recent German proceedings have created a good deal of temporary excitement in public opinion, or rather in public feeling,' the British secretary of state remarked of the political consequences of the local news from South-east Africa, 'and if Bismarck breaks out in a new place and annexes any more territory in the neighbourhood of our colonies, I think we shall have serious trouble.' He advised the foreign secretary:

Would it not be well for us at once to secure the coast of Zululand, and perhaps also that which lies on the south between the Cape Colony and Natal? There is no foreign claim possible in either of these localities. Yet the coast-line is not ours, and a German settlement anywhere upon it would be a nuisance if not a danger.[99]

He quickly received a most positive response; the Scramble gained pace.

My dear Derby,
    Your excellent Memo. and despatch have not mitigated the violence of the press, who think Bismarck must always be right and the British Gov[ernmen]t wrong.
    There is something a little ridiculous in the general scramble for colonies and I wish we could avoid taking a share in it . . . we are not jealous of Germany . . . I am ready to agree with anything you think necessary – But I have sent your note to the [Cabinet] Colonial Committee, as I am certain that Gladstone would require a Cabinet decision.

Yours G[ranville].[100]

The logic of the Partition in South Africa for the British 'official mind' was never better put than in the colonial secretary's reply to the above letter from Lord Granville:

I agree with you that there is something absurd in the Scramble for colonies, and I am as little disposed to join in as you can be: but there is a difference between wanting new acquisitions and keeping what we have; and both Natal and the Cape Colony would be endangered, as well as inconvenienced, if any foreign power chose to claim possession of the coast lying between the two, which is virtually ours, but not ours by any formal tie that other nations are bound to recognise.[101]

'Reluctance' did not mean inaction; scepticism of Bismarck's imperial design did not mean complete confidence in reading his intentions. 'I want to secure the South African coast *all round*,' he concluded, 'from the mouth of the Orange on the west, to the Portuguese on the east.'[102] Much as the colonial secretary did not wish to exacerbate Anglo-German relations, he did feel that Bismarck's imperial 'practice both in Africa and New Guinea has been very short'.[103] Certain coastal annexations were thus probably required as the only means to forestall German ambitions in strategically sensitive areas. Within a short time the British premier accordingly received a map from his secretary of state 'marking the parts of the coast which we ought to secure'.[104] This included 'the coast of the Cape Colony, which is ours already; that of semi-independent territory lying between the Cape and Natal (not as yet annexed or claimed by us); that of Natal, which we have, and that of Zululand'. In short, it amounted to nothing less than a blanket annexation of the whole sea rim of Southern Africa: if it were accomplished, Germany could not possibly create a colony on the seaboard for it would mean to the British, politically and strategically, 'our line of coast is complete'.

The 'German factor' is patent in all this; yet its ramifications were not simple. Indeed, there appear to be at least three distinct ways in which it drove on the British to annexation on the South Africa coastlines, 1884–85. The first concerned the pressures of public opinion, which from the German acquisition of Angra Pequena in April 1884 onwards had steadily mounted on a British Liberal government already deep in political troubles over Ireland, Egypt, India and Reform. This clearly impinged on the South-east African decisions, as this letter from the colonial secretary to the premier best suggests: 'I am afraid the colonial feeling of disappointment at the German annexation is running high. It does not seem to be reasonable but you will see by our newspapers that it meets with considerable sympathy here ... If the Germans seize either [coastline of Southern Africa] I would not answer for the consequences.'[105] Even Lord Granville, the foreign secretary, and a man not given to practising 'popular diplomacy', could feel the pressures of popular opinion. 'Our press has not been mollified by the *pièces justificatives* on Angra Pequena', he remarked unhappily to Gladstone at this time.[106]

The second indirect pressure operating in British official circles was the growing impatience with Bismarck and his overseas policy. Again, in the words of the British colonial secretary:

The more I reflect on what Bismarck has done, and his way of doing it, the more I am convinced that it is meant as a deliberate expression not perhaps of hostility, but of ill-will to England. The reason is less clear: possibly because we do not choose to take any step in regard to Africa that will embroil us with France – the result for which he has been working ever since 1877.[107]

Joseph Chamberlain was of like opinion. In what must have been among the seminal periods in the making of later 'Imperial Joe', he remarked:

Bismarck's action in New Guinea is, as I understand it, a piece of bad faith. It was agreed that we were to take the South Coast and discuss the position of the North (which we might have taken at any time) ... Instead of waiting the result of this discussion, and while in full possession of our intentions, Bismarck steps in and annexes. In these circumstances I do not think that we should allow him to forestall us again in South Africa.[108]

Lastly, the potential German advances into the complex web of metropolitan–peripheral relations in plural South Africa raised critical strategic questions for the British. Not surprisingly, the secretary of state for India was the most deeply concerned with the strategic importance of British hegemony in Southern Africa within the context of the great Asian ocean sea trading-lanes. He led that group of the Liberal cabinet who wished for a blanket coastal annexation, solely in the cause of British 'interests'. Not only did Lord Kimberley wish to annex the Mpondo and Zulu coasts, 'I would go further, and include the Amatongo coast up to the Portuguese border. Without this there would be still room for Bismarck to annex, and the presence of the Germans anywhere on that coast could hardly fail to bring serious trouble.'[109]

These several elements came together to press the British to advance their formal possessions in Southern Africa at the cabinet of 3 January 1885. A telegram was immediately despatched to the Cape high commissioner respecting the Mpondo area: 'Suggested that British Protectorate over all Pondoland should be renewed in explicit terms (see Frere's Proclamation, September 1878) to preclude foreign intervention. If your Ministers prepared undertaking control, H.M. Gov[ernmen]t. will probably consent.'[110] A decision was also taken to acquire any coastal lands lying *between* British territorial holdings: in no uncertain terms the British government wished to declare its control of the whole Southern African coast from the Orange River on the west to Cape Town, and then 'continuous on the east from Cape Town to the point at St Lucia Bay'.[111] The Queen was informed that it 'was decided to advise Your Majesty to annex to [the] Cape Colony the whole coast-line properly belonging to it.'[112]

Yet, what 'properly' did belong to British strategic interests? One anomaly stood out in these advances. The coast-line above St Lucia Bay was left open, leading to a yet further Scramble in the 1890s, when Thongaland became a focus of renewed Anglo-German confrontation in South-east Africa. The reasons for this all point to Gladstone. 'I think Derby is quite right in wishing to have a continuous line of coast in South Africa,' he stated definitively during the decision-making phase, 'but as to extending the terminus northwards, and (I presume) assuming the responsibility for Zululand outside the region which we have steadily disclaimed, I see great objection to it; and generally, considering what we have got, I am against entering into a Scramble for the remainder.'[113] Gladstone mounted a strong case in a cabinet which included noted anti-imperialists – such as Harcourt – arguing that a larger annexation on the Zulu coasts would tend 'powerfully to entail a responsibility for the country lying inland, which we think it impolitic to assume'. Further, if the British did 'go to Delagoa Bay, how can we be sure that the Germans will not negotiate the Portuguese out of that settlement, and be our neighbours whether we will or no?'

The expansionists had a modest revenge on the Gladstonians at the next cabinet. The colonial secretary raised again the matter of the Zulu coast along the Reserve, and carried the day. In Sir Charles Dilke's neat phrase: 'Mr Gladstone alone objecting to a protectorate, and being absent, it was decided to have one.'[114] This still did not, of course, include Thongaland. Dilke led the expansionists in sharp criticism of this 'half-way imperialism': 'I do not understand the reason for the delay in the matter, wh[ich]. will probably be serious to us.'[115] With studied patience he was informed by the secretary of state for colonies,

The reason is that the Cabinet, twice consulted, declined to give any opinion as to securing the rest of the coast up to the Portuguese frontier. And, in the face of the German protest against our claim to St Lucia Bay,[116] it seems hardly possible unless we wish to provoke a quarrel by making a fresh annexation in the same district.[117]

Dilke, and his associate, Chamberlain, were not easily put off. He now argued that, in acquiring the area up to St Lucia, Great Britain had implied an interest in Thongaland. 'I presume the Germans think that we have annexed the whole coast?'[118] The Gladstonians did not accept that argument. In annexing the coastlines of Southern Africa, from the German Southwest Africa to the new British possessions on the Mpondo and Zulu coasts, Great Britain had closed off one Scramble for Africa in the 1880s. By declining to annex Thongaland above St Lucia Bay, they had inadvertently created one of the major conditions for another Scramble in the 1890s.

The Anglo-German agreement on South-east Africa 1885

Britain's 'imperialism of denial' in South-east Africa had initially caused irritation in Berlin. Bismarck protested at the British 'reassertion of rights' at St Lucia Bay.[119] But his protests did not come from any deep sense of injury. German designs on South-east Africa were never substantive; essentially it was the local German concessionaires who in fact had attempted to draw the Reich into this additional region of South Africa. Bismarck merely disliked the British habit of 'locking up' areas for potential British annexations. Thus, over St Lucia Bay, Bismarck had felt no great umbrage in acceding to the British declaration of sovereignty. After all, he could hardly protest an annexation when he had made no official move. 'Even if the British title rested on no certain basis than the hoisting of the British flag on the 18th December last,' as the senior metropolitan official minuted in London, 'it would be valid against the objections of the German government, as that Government has not any . . . prior title to found itself upon.'[120] Such were the 'rules' of the Scramble. British officialdom was also not a little amused to discover that on new popular German maps of colonial Africa the St Lucia Bay area was 'marked as British'.[121]

Anglo-German rivalry in South-east Africa was among the leading topics during the informal discussions of March 1885 when Herbert Bismarck, the Chancellor's son, again came to London. He was suitably entertained and accommodated by the pro-German British Liberal Lord Rosebery (4–9 March),[122] during which time he also had extended discussions at the foreign office.[123] The British – notably the foreign and colonial secretaries – were pleased to settle the issue 'on the personal'.[124] Herbert Bismarck appeared eager to end Anglo-German friction in the colonial sphere, whether in Africa or the Pacific.[125] In the specific cases of the South-east African coastlines, this meant Germany simply admitted the inevitable. On 24 April Germany disclaimed any official connection with the German concessionaires, Einwald and Schiel; and on 7 May Bismarck gave a major undertaking which defined Anglo-German interests in Southern Africa generally. Germany agreed to 'withdraw her protest against the hoisting of the British flag at St Lucia Bay, and to refrain from making acquisition of territory or establishing protectorates on the coast between the Colony of Natal and Delagoa Bay'.[126]

This undertaking, of course, also settled the plans of Nagel for a German protectorate in Pondoland; when he appeared in Berlin in mid-1885, he was directed to approach the *British* authorities; in London he was turned back on to the Cape colonial government.[127] As his imperial designs were shattered, so too were Mpondo visions of independence from the Cape. Mhlangaso capitulated: on 9 December 1886 he negotiated a treaty with Sir Walter Stanford on behalf of Mqikela and the Mpondo, which pretty well gave the Cape what it wanted – short only of outright annexation.[128] The Mpondo lost the disputed lands of the Cape 'allies', the Xesibe; and the Cape secured the right to build vital roads into Pondoland, both for strategic and commercial uses. There were cash compensations for the Mpondo to cover the cession of the Rhode Valley (£600) and Port St Johns (£200).[129] Mhlangaso's attempts to develop Mpondo independency through the politics of defiance, and rival-alliance with the Germans, simply collapsed. His power slipped away rapidly after Mqikela's death (October 1887).[130] Mhlangaso might have achieved his aims if the imperialists had not come to an agreement among themselves.

Independent co-existence was largely only possible for nineteenth-century African societies in South Africa where the agents of white expansion remained divided. From the moment the Old Imperialism of Cape settler ambitions in Pondoland joined in compact with the New Imperialism of British strategic annexation policies, crisis struck Mhlangaso's posture. Worse still, once the German concessionaires were repudiated by their metropolitan government, his strategy turned from clever diplomacy into empty defiance.

By their entry into the politics of South-east Africa, the local German adventurers had undoubtedly played an important role in shaping the pattern of the Partition and its timing. Yet, for them, the results were singularly negative. Their role in the tangled 'Afrikaner – Zulu – British' triangle had resulted in pre-emptive imperial annexations of the whole Zululand coast, including St Lucia Bay. To the south, their involvement in Pondoland had merely hastened the demise of that independent African state. But in this curious fashion – through the impetus of the 'German factor' – the British imperial advance, the expansion of the Afrikaner New Republic, and the final political incorporation of the Zulu and Mpondo, all became part of the dynamics of the same system of political change in South-east Africa, involving 'Partition' and 'Scramble'.

5
Denying Bechuanaland to the Boers and the Germans 1884–86

The Scramble moved on to engulf Bechuanaland. There were factors similar to those involved in South-east Africa – notably the triangle of British defensive imperialism, Boer expansionism and German potential annexations. There were also elements that were peculiar to the region, the most important being the very considerable Cape colonial concern over the hinterland – what was termed the great missionary 'Road to the North', though it also carried more secular and economic elements of intercourse with the interior of Africa, in the form of traders moving northwards towards Zambesia, and black labourers moving southwards.

'Cape Colonialism' – the term used by politicians in the colony in the 1880s to denote the expansion of the Cape and its autonomous rule of transfrontier African territories – was to be a vital catalyst in moving the Imperial Factor to counter-poise imperialism against German and Boer ambitions in Bechuanaland, an area of great sensitivity in local inter-state rivalry. This force of Cape expansionism operated within the context of German and Boer ambitions in South Africa generally after 1884; it also found its motor engine through the dynamics of its own agricultural and commercial classes concerned for the overall development of the regional economy of South Africa.

Rhodes was the major spokesman for this local Cape Colonialism in the 1880s; but in fact, it had been a rising element in the politics of South Africa since the grant of 'responsible government' to the Cape in 1872. From Molteno to Sprigg, Scanlen to Upington, a sense of local Cape colonial 'independency' had been discernible; the Rhodes–Hofmeyr alliance of the 1880s was the culmination of this trend – they literally became a 'home rule' party within the larger context of the British connection for its rural interests; for the Rhodes group it provided a political base for settlement and commercial expansion; and they could jointly look to an increase in labour supplies in their extra-colonial activities, both for farmers and mine-owners. Rhodes expressed the nature of Cape Colonialism best, and revealed how it connected to the more general Scramble for South Africa. 'I am tired of this mapping out of Africa at Berlin, without occupation, without development, without any claim to the portion the various countries demand.' His answer for the interior of 'unclaimed' South Africa, was British expansion through the Cape: 'My belief is that the development of South Africa should fall to that country or countries which by their progress shall show that they are best entitled to it.'[1]

There was little doubt which polity Rhodes saw as the most likely to 'develop' the interior of South Africa; and the British metropolitan authorities were inclined to take a like view of the Cape in the hinterland Scramble. This did not mean that the Imperial Factor advanced to empire in Bechuanaland solely to please the exponents of Cape Colonialism; the British had their own strategic reasons for wishing to check any German–Transvaal alliances across the lands of the Tswana. But by appeasing 'Cape aggrandizement' – the hostile phrase of its main humanitarian opponent, Rev. John Mackenzie – the metropolitan authorities were hopeful of solving two problems with one tactic. They could secure British hegemony in the interior, as challenged essentially by the German presence in South-west Africa, through annexations which might then be devolved on to their proxy agents, the Cape colonists.

If this was a fundamental factor in the British advances in Bechuanaland after 1884, as they moved to fend off the dangers of German and Boer strategies in the interior, so it was also an important element in the coming Partition of the far interior, as the Cape expansionists began bidding for Zambesia. The imperialist postures and ambitions of certain Cape commercial and landed groups can thus be seen as a central theme, connecting the spasmodic advances of the British into South-central Africa, as the Partition in South Africa proper became the springboard for a Scramble in the hinterlands of tropical Africa beyond.

The advance of the British empire into Bechuanaland was, we might summarise, certainly in response to German and Boer expansionist threats; it was also a reaction to the closely related pressures of its local colonial allies, the 'loyal Cape', itself desperately concerned not to yield regional interests to agents of Germany or the Transvaal.[2]

Resisting Transvaal and German expansion 1884

It had been the humanitarians who had first campaigned to bring the British empire to Bechuanaland and the Tswana in the early 1880s. But they had struggled in vain, as much against the British treasury as the Liberal government of the time. In 1884, however, Bismarck and Kruger worked to advance the cause of Exeter Hall – an unusual but dramatically important turn of events.

The Germans quite suddenly extended their South-west Africa colony 20 miles inland, and declined to give assurances as to future interior intentions. Kruger, recently back from a successful visit to Berlin, mindful of Germany's entry into Southern Africa, and strongly pushed by his new and anti-British adviser, the Rev. S. J. du Toit (founder of the *Afrikaner Bond*, 1879) now moved on Bechuanaland.[3] The Transvaal issued a 'Provisional Proclamation' (16 September 1884) taking the petty frontier 'republic' of Goshen into the parent state, to protect its interests and to bring 'law and order' to the disputed area.[4]

This action merely formalised the informal Boer frontier imperialism in the lands of the Tshidi Rolong. But it stirred the Imperial Factor to angry reaction in a manner which had not happened in Zululand with the New Republic. The metropolitan authorities feared the potential of a Boer–German connection through Bechuanaland; the Cape commercial groups howled in protest; and the British also took umbrage at the obvious defiance of Imperial authority as established in Bechuanaland. 'It is of urgent importance,' the senior permanent official, Sir Robert Herbert, minuted in the colonial office, 'to make a distinct representation to Germany as to the British requirements in South Africa.'[5] From Cape Town the high commissioner deemed Kruger's action even more alarming: 'If in these circumstances British authority is not vindicated, we must clear out of the country [i.e. Bechuanaland]. I can see no middle course.'[6] Sir Hercules Robinson, indeed, went so far as to state that he did not think that 'a stronger case for forcible intervention could arise', the Transvaal leadership having given way to the 'extreme anti-English party whose object is land and loot'.

The British colonial secretary read the events in Bechuanaland and Zululand involving Afrikaner local imperialism as being directed towards one end: 'that the [London] Convention could be circumvented by the establishment, outside the [Transvaal] boundary, of small independent republics which, after a little time could be incorporated into the Transvaal'.[7] In other words, if Bismarck had provided an indirect threat to British interests in South Africa, Kruger had become a direct danger, by challenging the validity of British suzerainty, the core of the London Convention. As Sir Hercules Robinson warned, the British authorities had but two choices before them – 'the abandonment of the Protectorate and the Convention of London, or an announcement that existing engagements will be insisted on, if necessary by force' – which really meant no choice at all. Kruger could not be allowed his defiant annexation.[8] 'To eat humble pie once is one thing,' the British premier's secretary remarked, remembering Majuba,[9] 'to have a second helping of it is another.' The British high commissioner was aware that all Afrikanerdom was watching for the reaction of the imperial administration.[10]

Already weary of their Bechuanaland involvement, the metropolitan government thus found itself in a position where inaction would be folly, but where action would involve further African empire, *and* the dangers of worsening Anglo-Afrikaner relations. The advice from the high commissioner was, however, emphatic: 'All our troubles since Majuba have proceeded from the belief that [we] will not fight under any provocation. If the Home Government would only announce its determination to maintain the protectorate, if necessary by force of arms, I feel convinced our difficulties will vanish without having to move a soldier up country.'[11] Plain reasoning. Yet in London every reason was found for *not* acting. 'Sir Hercules is very angry with the South African Republic, naturally and deservedly,' Sir Robert Herbert minuted,[12] 'But would anything short of a strong army make the Boers see this?' Indeed, what most concerned the imperial administration was settling the Bechuana troubles in such a way that all the responsibilities devolved onto Great Britain, by alienating Cape Afrikaner opinion. 'Her Majesty's Government,' the permanent under-secretary made absolutely clear, 'in the case of Bechuanaland, as in Basutoland, has undertaken an experiment, the success and permanence of which will depend upon the sufficient co-operation of the [Cape] Colonial Government.'[13] In vain did the British now attempt to pressure the Cape into acting in Bechuanaland, in lieu of the imperial authorities: 'If the Cape Government and Parliament decline to carry out the policy pressed upon her Majesty's Government by the late Colonial [Scanlen] Administration, Her Majesty's Government will of course hold itself relieved from the obligations which it undertook in the interests of the Cape Colony.'[14] The Cape response, via the governor, was a telegram which placed the responsibility fully back on the imperial administration. 'Without presuming to dictate to Her Majesty's Government [the] line of policy to be followed, Ministers express opinion that in view of German annexation and other threatened encroachments calculated to cripple this Colony, decisive measures should be taken for maintenance of English authority in South Africa.'[15] In London, the British authorities shared the colony's fears without sharing the belief that a British interest alone was involved.[16] Surely it was in the Cape's interest to protect its own northern trade?

Just when it appeared that a stalemate had been reached, news came from Cape Town which suggested a way out for the Imperial Factor. The attitude of the Cape ministry softened. The high commissioner explained:

In long conversations which I have had with Mr Upington, the Cape Premier, . . . I gathered that in the present financial condition of the Colony, and looking to the State of the Eastern [Transkei] frontier, it would be out of the power of the ministers to help you in Bechuanaland with men or money – but they would give you all the assistance in their power, short of that, and as soon as British authority were established in the Protectorate, would relieve you of further responsibility of annexing the country.[17]

Here was a signal change in the Cape attitude. The colonial secretary noted on the despatch, 'This is more to the purpose.'[18]

More good news was shortly to follow. According to the high commissioner, Kruger's action had alienated Cape Afrikaner opinion,[19] which now supported a policy of 'standing up' to the republican Boers. 'I am glad to say that opinion is beginning to set strongly here against the Transvaal violation of the [London] Convention, and their allies, the Goshen freebooters. This feeling is shared, I am told, largely by the respectable Dutch of the Colony.'[20] Just how valid were the assessments of Sir Hercules Robinson was really a moot point. There is some evidence to suggest he deliberately misinformed the colonial secretary of the real Afrikaner feeling in the colony,[21] to the extent of having an English member of the Cape assembly[22] 'manufacture' colonial opinion, which the proconsul then reported to London as evidence of support for his own personal policy.[23] It was a highly dangerous 'game' to play. Yet the high commissioner was no ordinary British proconsul. His secretary has left us a portrait of an extremely capable, very determined, if not always scrupulous imperialist:

Sir Hercules had been so long a 'politician' that he had lost all sense of truth or loyalty. He looked at everything from the point of view of expediency . . . I consider Chamberlain a great actor but I always thought Sir Hercules better . . . Sir Hercules always remained behind the curtain, and sought to exercise power without being seen.[24]

Unaware of the high commissioner's tactic, the British still wished to avoid the responsibility for further empire west of the Transvaal, which the situation appeared to imply or demand. 'I distrust the natural inclination of all colonists for war', Joseph Chamberlain remarked on reading the high commissioner's despatches.[25] 'I fear we may be led into these heavy responsibilities which would be serious to any government, and fatal to a Liberal one.' Like all leading British ministers involved in the African Scramble, Chamberlain was pulled between his natural anti-expansionist attitudes in the tropics, and his reasoning of what had to be done to safeguard existing British interests. In conversation with Herbert Bismarck, on 24 September 1884, Chamberlain revealed the divergent pulls that made up imperial policy:

For us the whole of South Africa is simply a burden: if I had to deal with you, I should have said that we would have seen with pleasure Germany establishing herself in Africa. . . . I would tell that thorny Colony [the Cape] straight out, 'Take care of yourself and declare your independence if you want to'. All we want is Cape Town, and the Bay, for a coaling station.[26]

Yet in the very same week, Chamberlain pressed for a strong imperial advance in South Africa at the cabinet of 6 October:

It appears to me that whatever may be the excuses now made by the authorities of the South African Republic, there is really no doubt that they have connived at a flagrant and deliberate breach of the [London] Convention of 1884. It must be borne in mind that this breach follows on a similar disregard of the previous Convention in Pretoria; and I can conceive of no position more humiliating than that of the British Government continually making new treaties as, one after another, the old ones are violated by the contracting Party.[27]

Thus Chamberlain came, 'most reluctantly', to the conclusion that 'the limits of patience and forbearance have been reached' with the Boers, and that 'the time has come when more decisive steps must be taken'.[28]

The colonial secretary was inclined to agree with Chamberlain that a vital British interest *was* involved.[29] Yet this still did not make an expansionist policy any more palatable. 'The more I look at this Bechuana business the more unsatisfactory it appears', the colonial secretary wrote to the premier, 'it seems to leave no choice between accepting what is undoubtedly a humiliating defeat, or persisting in our refusal to recognise this new arrangement ... at the risk of the Boer War. And this when we have Egypt on our hands.'[30] The pessimism of the colonial secretary extended to the secretary of state for India. 'I wish I could resist the conclusion that we must interfere by force in Bechuanaland,' Lord Kimberley reflected,[31] 'but I see no other way out of that miserable business.' The British were being moved to empire against their best political instincts. The colonial secretary – a man who had 'no love for annexations' – well caught the mood of the moment in a letter to the premier: 'I am afraid we shall be forced to do something, though it is a most awkward and unpleasant business to meddle in. But *feeling at the Cape seems to be stirred up* – not that the colonists will help us – and the public here will sympathise.'[32]

If there was any doubt that an imperial gesture was inevitable, then pressure from the permanent colonial office, and war office officials, shattered that hope. From the latter came a long, extremely firmly argued 'War Office Confidential Memorandum', making plain the strategic British interests now placed at risk in South Africa by Boer and German action.[33] Working from a basis that 'the complete abandonment of the Cape Colonies to the Africanders [sic], or, as would probably result, to a German protectorate', was unacceptable to Great Britain, the war office argued that security for British interests meant securing more than the Cape itself:

It is impossible, for obvious political reasons, to create a Gibraltar out of the Cape Town peninsula, and that the permanent retention of this peninsula – essential to what the Royal Commission on Colonial Defence [1875–81] has pronounced to be the most important of the Imperial coaling stations – is dependent upon the maintenance of British ascendance in all South African Colonies.[34]

Rarely was there a better expression of the old-fashioned motives which pushed the Victorians to extending empire. Their inclinations ran one way; existing interests and necessity pushed the other way. They opted for security, the defence of interests, once there was no alternative policy. In so doing they responded not merely to their own assessment of the dangers to well-defined interests, but also to the pressures of that undefinable factor, public opinion. 'The British public just now is in a very aggressive and acquisitive mood,' the colonial secretary complained to the premier,[35] 'at least I find this the opinion of every person I talk to, and it is certainly that of every newspaper.'

Bismarck's actions had stirred a British public unhappy with British prestige since the failure at Majuba and the apparent challenge to Pax Britannica involved in the general Scramble for the tropical world now under way. Among the voices raised in protest against the 'reluctant imperialism' of the metropolitan Liberal government was that of the Rev. John Mackenzie. His second public campaign in Great Britain did not alone bring about an enthusiasm for British advances in South Africa. But he greatly helped to focus that sentiment on Bechuanaland and the expansive behaviour of Bismarck's Germans and Kruger's Boers. In this fashion, the rising floods of enthusiasm for the New Imperialism in South Africa contained within it not a few currents of humanitarian idealism.

Cape interests and northern expansion

'Public pressure' was also exerted on the metropolitan government by the forces of Cape colonialism.[36] It appeared that Cape colonial opinion was strongly in favour of an imperial gesture in the interior – against the Afrikaners if not for the Africans. The high commissioner reported: 'The public meetings which have been held throughout the country during the last week, and those still to be held, show that the English section of the community is thoroughly aroused as to the importance of maintaining the protectorate and enforcing the Convention.'[37] All that now held the British government back from taking what had gradually appeared to be the inevitable step of imperial advance in Bechuanaland, was a determination to carry the Cape colonial ministry with the policy. If there was going to be extended empire, then it must be empire acquired in the knowledge that it was destined to be 'off-loaded' onto the shoulders of the 'loyal' Cape colony. This meant acquiring Cape Afrikaner co-operation, not just local pro-English support. Thus, despite the Cape governor's reports that the Cape Afrikaners were loyal – 'During the last few days I have been trying to ascertain the Dutch feeling in this part of the Colony, and I am assured it strongly condemns the recent violation of the [London] Convention by the Transvaal. Even the *Zuid Afrikaan* admits the [Kruger] annexation Proclamation a mistake'[38] – in London there were still grave doubts. Whitehall had not forgotten how, after the promise given by Sir Thomas Scanlen, the Cape assembly had still refused to accept the Bechuanaland Protectorate as their 'inheritance', leaving Great Britain with an unwanted African trusteeship responsibility. Admittedly there *were* now imperial interests at stake. But the imperial administration still felt that the colonial ministry should bear its share for the local interests served by annexation. Sir Robert Herbert best expressed British reservations when he minuted: 'With the Dutch party now in power at the Cape the difficulty of operating effectively against the South African Republic would – unless the Colony pledges itself to co-operate thoroughly – probably be greater than at any previous time.'[39] What the colonial office wished was a firm declaration from the local Cape interests, and not merely assurances from the governor. 'I think,' the under-secretary advised his chief, 'that it is very questionable whether H.M. Government can rely upon anything short of a definite resolution of the Cape Parliament in favour of the immediate annexation of the whole of Bechuanaland'.[40]

In the end, they were forced to go forward with less of an assurance than they would have wished from the Cape assembly. Events in Africa would not wait upon the tortuous Anglo-Cape correspondence in progress, on the moot question of financial responsibility for new northern expansion. Nor apparently would the English public: 'English patience,' with Kruger and with Bismarck, 'is pretty nearly worn out', was the colonial secretary's reluctant assessment.[41] The premier was accordingly informed. 'I think opinion will force some action upon us, whether we will or no.'[42]

From the colonial office came a tentative northern expansionist policy, in which the British would make their actions 'dependent on that of the Cape Colony'. As a Confidential Cabinet Memorandum argued, 'We cannot hold a Bechuana Protectorate against the wish of the colonists, and even with their co-operation it would be difficult.'[43] A prime object of the Cape colonists was 'not to declare themselves, for if they see a chance of getting their object at our sole expense, they will certainly take it'.[44] But even this hope was to be dashed, or at least set aside.[45] Indeed, it was Chamberlain who pushed hardest of all for a policy of qualified advance, by circulating his minute on Bechuanaland cited above. The premier called a special cabinet for 6 October.[46] Chamberlain remembered in his 'Memoir':

In October [1884] the representations of the Government having proved insufficient to secure the withdrawal of the freebooters, and Lord Derby proposing to continue negotiations, I circulated the ... minute to the Cabinet. I was not present when it was discussed but Dilke informed me that although Harcourt strongly dissented from my views, the rest of the Cabinet came over to them, including Lord Derby and Mr Gladstone, and it was resolved to send an expedition.[47]

This well known account is slightly misleading, however, in failing to stress the fact that the policy agreed on laid very heavy emphasis on acquiring Cape colonial support for any expansionist policy. Chamberlain's own Minute concluded with the statement that, 'If the Cape Government should refuse to give any aid, of course the matter would be open to re-consideration.' The cabinet in fact decided, as the British premier's secretary recorded, 'To ask Sir H. Robinson, in concert with the Cape Govt. to call upon the Transvaal to disallow the incursion of the freebooters ... and to advise Home Govt. what steps should be taken.'[48] A telegram was despatched to Cape Town,[49] and a special portion was inserted into the Queen's Speech, of Thursday 23 October.[50] In all these statements justifying the coming imperial actions – including a debate in the Commons,[51] – the British were at pains to stress the Anglo-Cape aspect of the policy.[52] Derby indeed reminded the House that the 'Cape Government is at the present time a Dutch Government'; and that it represented the key to Partition in Southern Africa. Such was the power of Cape colonialism in the Scramble called the Northern Expansion.

The origins of the Warren expedition

The British prepared to advance to further responsibility in Bechuanaland. They did so in less than propitious circumstances:[53] they disliked the extension of African trusteeship; they worried over the Cape colonial vacillation in support; and they feared local confrontation with the Germans and with Afrikanerdom. A cabinet on 19 November fixed the financing on imperial expeditions in South *and* North Africa:[54] the Wolseley expedition to rescue 'Chinese' Gordon at Khartum; and the imperial force under general Warren,[55] to clean the white intruders out of Bechuanaland. 'An extra penny in the income tax is to be put on,' the premier's secretary wrote in his diary,[56] 'in order to meet the military charges of about £2½ millions for the Nile expedition and Bechuanaland.' This still did not make the imperial policy any more palatable to ministers.[57] Questioned on the reasons for the Warren expedition into Bechuanaland, the colonial secretary wrote cynically to the Queen's private secretary, in late November: You ask why?

(1) *The Opposition party*, in order to spend money and spoil our next budget.
(2) *The military party*, because to them the sending out of expeditions, anywhere and for any purpose, is the chief object of human existence. Besides, they have not forgiven Majuba Hill, and hope to pick a quarrel with the Transvalers.
(3) *The philanthropists*, headed by Forster, who want South Africa to remain a negro state, and see with extreme jealousy the inroads of white civilisation.
(4) *The Colonists*, to whom a war, or preparation for one, means fat contracts and double value for their produce.[58]

The colonial secretary's pessimism was to be given an added foundation when it was learnt that the British high commissioner had clearly misread Cape Afrikaner opinions. By 17 October it was clear that Sir Hercules Robinson had made an error of judgement, and was face-to-face with his colonial ministry. The Cape premier, a Hofmeyr–Bond protégé, declared that he had never agreed to support an imperial policy which was even indirectly anti-Transvaal. 'It is awkward that Sir H. Robinson urges a course which his ministers say will not be approved by the majority of the [Cape] colonists', Sir Robert Herbert complained.[59] From Cape Town came a curious letter of explanation.

You will probably have been puzzled at the change of front which has been executed by my ministers in the last few days. A fortnight ago they were all for the adoption by you of 'decisive measures for the maintenance of British authority in South Africa'. Now they are proposing to try what they can do in the way of negotiation, so as to 'avert bloodshed and race bitterness'. The explanation is, I fancy, that they have been called 'to heel' by their master – Mr Hofmeyr – who is alarmed by your determined attitude ... His sympathies are all anti-English.[60]

This was indeed news to the British authorities in London, who had come to see Hofmeyr as their link in collaboration with the Cape Afrikaners. The colonial secretary, then up at his country seat in Lancashire, Knowsley Hall, hurried back to London in alarm to handle the situation. A quick decision had to be taken. The colonial secretary did not hesitate. He could not offend the Cape Afrikaners. The high commissioner was to be informed, as the colonial secretary explained to the premier, that he was 'to allow the Cape Ministers to negotiate, but to make a show of military preparation in the event of this failure'.[61] The prime minister was quick to agree. The Cape Afrikaners must not be offended: 'There could be no more serious steps taken than to break our partnership with them.'[62] The British dreaded a 'nationalist' war against all Afrikanerdom. The Queen's secretary remembered a dinner conversation of that period: 'Chamberlain talked of war in Egypt as sad ... but a war in South Africa was a war against the people, and he did not see how we could come out well from that.'[63]

The Cape ministry was accordingly encouraged to send their own four-man mission to the troubled frontier area.[64] It included a noted *Bondsman*, and was headed by the pro-*Bond* Cape premier, Upington. It was *not* a marked success.[65] To no real surprise, the mission came out in favour of the white 'freebooters', and against the local African societies.[66] The colonial office neatly assessed the pro-Afrikaner findings as being derived from a fear of admitting humanitarian principles – 'lest their own natives should want the same treatment'.[67] Nothing had been settled, although the London *Times*,[68] and certain British ministers, thought imperial interests *had* been safeguarded.[69] Ultimately the cabinet decided they had not; and that, as an official put it, the whites had to be driven out of British Bechuanaland – 'They must go "bag and baggage".'[70]

The failure of the mission to settle the problem of internal paramountcy – the *Cape Argus* called the venture 'a hollow farce'[71] – had according to the high commissioner 'evoked an outburst of loyalty throughout the Colony which will greatly strengthen our hands in now going into Bechuanaland'.[72] Trusting that the high commissioner was correct *this* time, the British allowed the Warren imperial expedition to go forward.[73] The Queen was informed by the secretary of state for war:

It is proposed that Sir C. Warren should be authorised to raise 1,500 irregulars in the Cape Colony, a force of that description being considered most suitable for the task of expelling the settlers who have occupied positions of the territory recently declared to be under Your Majesty's Protection.[74]

It was with no small misgivings, however, that London prepared to despatch the imperial expedition. The colonial office's permanent under-secretary reported he had learnt that 'the anti-English party at Cape Town intend to get up riots among the very young Dutchmen in the Colony, in order to excite ill will against the [British] Volunteers'.[75] A colonial office minute went even further: 'It would not be surprising if all South Africa did rise against Sir C. Warren. They would undoubtedly have risen in 1881 had it not been for peace.'[76] In the anxiety of the moment, the British premier expressed himself 'as much afraid, at least, of Sir C. Warren as of the Germans'.[77]

A most interesting reflection on the new imperial policy came from the famed historian, Professor James Froude, who was then visiting South Africa and in correspondence with Joseph Chamberlain. He worried greatly over the British decision to advance into Bechuanaland.

As to what will happen, the impression is that the Dutch settlers in Bechuanaland will withdraw quietly over the frontier into the Transvaal, leaving the expeditionary force in possession. It can make nothing of the country or the native Chiefs. It will stop nothing, but create bad blood till we are tired of keeping it there.[78]

Faced with these bleak assessments, the Warren expedition advanced into Bechuanaland to contend with the local Partition on-the-ground.[79]

The Warren expedition and the British 'Protectorate'

The forces of Cape colonialism did not simply surrender to the situation. The Rhodesian group was emphatic in desiring colonial expansion over imperial advances. 'I solemnly warn this House that if it departs from the control of the interior,' Rhodes lectured his fellow MPs,[80] 'we shall fall from the position of the paramount state in South Africa, which is our right in every scheme of federal union in the future, to that of a minor state.' The Witwatersrand gold discoveries were still two years away, and Rhodes found support for his schemes less than complete. But he did gain a vital ally to the 'colonial position' in the high commissioner. It would appear that Sir Hercules Robinson had been shaken by the animosity shown among Cape Afrikaners to the Warren expedition; and he was also offended by Warren himself, who appeared to think he could act as independent agent outside the high commissioner's grand overlordship in Southern Africa.[81] Robinson's gradual conversion to 'colonialism' took another step. From the outset of the imperial expedition the high commissioner tried to bind Warren to operate from the basis of Rhodes' 'Stellaland Settlement'.[82] Initially Warren agreed – only to find on reaching Bechuanaland, that this would have been a negation of his own instructions, as Rhodes had simply secured most of the invading whites on the Tlhaping and Tshidi Rolong lands.

Warren's decision to reject that Settlement was crucial. It led almost immediately to the resignation of Rhodes as deputy commissioner; and it created an open breach with the forces of Cape colonialism, which now included the high commissioner. Warren turned for advice to John Mackenzie – who had returned to Bechuanaland, urgent to exploit the presence of an imperial expedition – and secured Mackenzie's enemies for his own. The 'political and administrative firm' of Rhodes–Robinson worked against Warren from Cape Town: Hofmeyr and the *Bond* called for his recall, on the grounds that his presence in Bechuanaland increased Anglo-Saxon–Afrikaner 'race' feeling; the Afrikaner frontiersmen were said to be stalking the expedition, ready to pick a fight in defence of their new farms;[83] while within the metropolitan government the old suspicions of enlarged African trusteeship responsibilities – *without* Cape colonial assistance – began to revive. 'I wish he may prove to be a Wolseley,' Gladstone remarked of Warren,[84] 'but he labours under Forster's high recommendation which usually smells of gun-powder.' He also cautioned the colonial secretary against imperial officials in Southern Africa – like Warren – who 'affect to make light of the Dutch element at the Cape'.[85] Only African chiefs and their subjects – such as Montshiwa and Mankurwane – whose lands had taken the brunt of the Afrikaner expansion, appeared to hail the Warren expedition as a welcome element in reversing the trend of informal white Partition in Bechuanaland.

As seen from London, the British were increasingly faced with making a choice between the policies of Cape colonialism or direct imperialism; or, put more crudely, between the Rhodes–Robinson 'firm' on one hand, and the Warren–Mackenzie 'team' on the other.[86]

An important meeting between Warren and Kruger – at '14 Streams' on the Transvaal frontier (24 January 1884) – failed to find a local concession with republican Afrikanerdom, and indeed made plain what had always been at the base of the situation: The British imperial authorities would have to choose between driving out the white intruders, or abandoning the territories of the Rolong and Tlhaping to the forces of local expansion. The conflicting nature of the policies emerging from Cape Town and the Warren expedition simply could not be ignored.[87] Warren claimed merely to be fulfilling his Instructions:[88] the vigorous establishment of imperial authority to challenge Afrikaner expansion and check German ambitions in the interior.[89] The high commissioner thought differently. Warren's actions, he argued, 'appear to me most injudicious and have been taken without consultation with me. His employment of Mackenzie in the face of the protest of [Cape] Ministers and of the Transvaal Government ... [and] his dismissal of Mr Rhodes, the only honest and wholly disinterested civilian he had about him, are all unwise acts.'[90] The high commissioner's opinion indeed confirmed the worst fears of the British government: 'The upshot of this line of action if persevered in, must, in my opinion, be to render necessary the retention of a considerable force in Bechuanaland for some time to come; and to leave Her Majesty's Gov[ernmen]t. with a troublesome and costly Crown Colony on their hands for an indefinite period.'[91] A special cabinet was held to consider the rival policies.[92] The colonial secretary expressed the opinion of the government when he wrote that, 'Both are able men, and both like their own way. Warrén had the public with him . . . But Robinson's is probably the more prudent policy.'[93] The premier agreed. 'Dilke was for giving Robinson unequivocal support and maintaining his authority and responsibility', the prime minister recorded after the special cabinet.[94] 'This is my own strong opinion.' His reasoning was plain if not humanitarian: '*What we desire is* [*Cape*] *Colonial annexation, and not Imperial rule, in Bechuanaland.*'[95]

In pursuing his own policy, General Warren now became the 'principal obstacle to [Cape] annexation', as the colonial office put it.[96] Accordingly the British decided to 'cut their losses', by recalling Warren once he had secured certain basic interests. On 27 January 1885, by an Order in Council, British jurisdiction was publicly announced to be operative under the Foreign Jurisdiction Act over the Bechuanaland territory 'east of the 20th meridian and south of the 22nd parallel'; and, on 23 March, Bechuanaland south of the Molopo River was declared a 'Protectorate.'[97] This staked the British claim to the region without committing the government to the modern connotations implied in the term – of direct administrative control. In case Germany should take umbrage at the action, the foreign office made it clear that Great Britain would 'not oppose the extension of German authority to the 20th [degree] longitude',[98] although in private the colonial office minuted that the Protectorate had been a directly anti-Bismarckian action – it 'was adopted mainly in view of the fear of the Germans'.[99]

The Warren expedition was deemed to have done its work. The free-booters had duly retired to the Transvaal, so keeping open the northern trade route, and a limited Protectorate had been marked-out, so securing British interests and paramountcy in the interior. Policy then radically swung round.[100] Every effort was now to be expended in trying to conciliate the unhappy Cape Afrikaners,[101] and in trying to lure the forces of colonialism to take up 'their inheritance in the interior' – Rhodes' phrase – so relieving the Imperial Factor of its unwanted newly born Protectorate. As the desire to impose British authority receded, Warren was left as an isolated and embarrassing reminder of an earlier policy.[102] At the British cabinet of 16 May 1885 it was decided to recall his imperial expedition immediately.[103]

Before this could be accomplished, however, local events further complicated the situation. The protection afforded the Tshidi Rolong and the Tlhaping by the Warren expedition led Kgama – in company with two other major chiefs – to 'Scramble' for imperial protection for his people as well. The British Protectorate was, in fact, announced from Kgama's capital at Shoshong; but of course it only included half his kingdom – that below latitude 22° south. John Mackenzie, his old friend and missionary adviser, encouraged him to call upon the Imperial Factor for protection over all his people and lands. Kgama needed little prompting – nor did Sechele of the Ba-Kwana or Gaseitsiwe of the Ba-Ngwaketse – for the energies of Boer frontier expansion began to impinge on northern Bechuanaland. Kgama well saw how events to the south could be repeated in his territory. He accordingly offered his state to the British empire – including lands for white (but not Afrikaner) settlement – in return for the sanctuary of imperial trusteeship, under British indirect rule.[104]

To General Warren the offer of Kgama, Gaseitsiwe and Sechele, was a 'magnificent opportunity'; to the British authorities in London it was only a political embarrassment. Undaunted, Warren submitted to London a detailed plan for developing a Crown Colony in Bechuanaland, with full civil service, and strong military force to ensure security against local white expansionists.[105] John Mackenzie's able hand had clearly touched the document. Despite its careful construction and humanitarian overtones, however, the plan was mercilessly torn apart: first by the British high commissioner[106] (assisted by Rhodes?), who suitably frightened Whitehall by estimating the cost of the Crown Colony to be at least £250,000 p.a., 'as well as risk of future wars in the interior';[107] then by the officials in the colonial office, who characterised the policy as aiming 'chiefly at insulting and alienating both parties at the Cape, and thus rendering the taking over of Bechuanaland by the Cape an impossibility';[108] and finally by the ministers of the crown – 'Her Majesty's Government have no intention of creating a Crown Colony in Bechuanaland', Warren was informed, and indeed British policy desired 'that the Cape Colony should ... assume management of the Protectorate without delay'.[109]

The British metropolitan authorities preferred Cape Colonialism to the New Imperialism. Thus it was that the high commissioner was fully supported in his relationship with Rhodes; and Rhodes in his alliance with Hofmeyr's *Bond*. The British colonial secretary indeed left no doubt how the high commissioner was to conduct future imperial policy in the interior: any separation in the 'administration of Cape and Bechuanaland [was] very undesirable', for it was vital 'to ensure the co-operation of the Cape Colony'.[110]

The problems of securing Cape collaboration

'Bechuanaland was saved by "Grand Mamma", I mean the Imperial Government,' Rhodes later remarked,[111] 'and the *Bond* today will own to its mistake.' Having watched the British secure the northern trade route for their colonial interests against nebulous German ambition and Transvaal expansion, the Cape politicians now decided to delay their acceptance of administrative responsibility for Bechuanaland. 'No prospect of [Cape] annexation this year', was the bleak news from the high commissioner.[112] Whitehall officialdom assessed the situation frankly, if crudely: 'what is to be done with this "precious possession" now that we have it, is a question which must stand over for the present'.[113] An official Memorandum summarised the limited choices for the new Conservative government, which had succeeded the Liberal administration in June 1885, as, '(1) Retire altogether; (2) . . . plant a European colony; (3) . . . maintain an indefinite protectorate . . . The first is admirable and cheap. The second is lunacy. The third must be understood by H.M.G. if adopted to include a grant of at least £120,000 a year for Bechuanaland.'[114] Salisbury, however, sought the same policy as pointed out by Gladstone: ease Bechuanaland onto Cape colonial responsibility. The new colonial secretary, Col. F. A. Stanley (by chance, brother of the outgoing secretary, Lord Derby), pressed hard to get the Cape to act.[115] Rhodes' work had clearly now had some effect. On 7 July the Cape indeed offered to accept Bechuanaland.[116] Delight in London was cut short on examining the Cape terms.[117] The colony was to control all future settlement and development in the Protectorate, yet the British government was to contribute at least £50,000 p.a. to defray administrative costs; and if the British declined to accept the Cape's terms, then the colonial ministry hinted broadly that it might 'give up' the Kalahari and Bechuanaland to Germany. Reaction in the British colonial office was unanimous and hostile: 'These proposals are wholly inadmissable, and are rightly described by Sir H. Robinson as impudent.'[118] As to the threat of 'calling in the Germans', the British were now less concerned: 'the Germans have found out that colonising swamps and deserts is a much more troublesome and less profitable thing than they supposed'.[119]

With Cape assistance temporarily ruled out, the reality of the British responsibility for the Protectorate had to be squarely faced. The colonial secretary again consulted the high commissioner. Sir Hercules Robinson advised that Great Britain secure their hold over the Protectorate (i.e. the area south of the Molopo River). As to the land above the Molopo,

it appears to me that we have no interest in it, except as a road to the interior. I would suggest, therefore, that we should confine ourselves to preventing that part of the Protectorate being occupied by either Filibusters or Foreign powers, doing, for the present, as little as possible in the way of administration or settlement.[120]

This advice was accepted.[121] Pending the halcyon day when the Cape would finally accept responsibility for Bechuanaland, in mid August 1885 the colonial secretary decided to turn the area south of the Molopo – the existing Protectorate – into the crown Colony of British Bechuanaland, while the lands north of the river, and up to 22°, were to be merely 'under Her Majesty's Protection'.[122]

This decision was conveyed to the high commissioner on 13 August, and announced publicly on 30 September.[123] A Land Commission was established, to enquire into the region's most pressing problem;[124] and an administration was tentatively constructed, under the new deputy-commissioner, Sidney Shippard. He was to be 'administrator' of British Bechuanaland, as well as 'deputy-commissioner' for the newly designated 'Protectorate'.[125] What was necessary had been done. The British were still in no doubt as to the policy which they ideally would like to have followed. They still spoke hopefully of 'the transfer of the new Colony to the old "faithful" Colony'.[126] Equally, the Cape colonial authorities were in no doubt over British policy. 'The Colonial Office has made up their mind to hold onto Bechuanaland for some time', the Cape agent-general in London explained from the blinkered perspective of the Cape view, to a colonial politician, 'that is after every attempt to shunt it onto the Colony failed'.[127]

Limiting imperial expansion in Bechuanaland 1884

The British metropolitan authorities had some reasonable grounds for feeling umbrage at the fickle or selfish conduct of the Cape politicians.[128] True the Imperial Factor had been driven to action in Bechuanaland by a concern for its *own* strategic interests in South Africa, against German and Boer postures; but it had also been encouraged and pressed to these forward advances by the vociferous calls of the Cape for action in South-central Africa. It was now the turn of the metropolitan authorities to decline to dance the tune of Cape Colonialism any further. Having secured what they deemed to be of absolute strategic need in the interior of South Africa, the British Imperial Factor determined to let the Cape fend for itself against German, Boer or even Portuguese ambitions, in Central Africa proper.

This view was shared by the British high commissioner at the Cape. He had been drawn to support Cape Colonialism in the Bechuanaland Question; and he had been burned, so to speak, in the process. He now accepted the British metropolitan argument that Zambesia was not crucial to the formal imperial presence in South Africa; nor did it substantively affect British hegemony.

If I remember correctly at one of the interviews with the [Transvaal] Delegates to the London Convention negotiations you gave them to understand that they would not be shut-in to the north. Lobingulo [*sic*] was considered strong enough to be able to take care of himself, especially as the lower part of his country bordering on the Transvaal is infested with tsetse fly. Besides, we had incurred no obligations whatever to the natives ... if we were free to shut in the Transvaal to the north I am not sure that it would be wise to do so, as it would close the only safety valve left to the restless spirits of that country.[129]

Hardly had the high commissioner penned this letter, however, when the colonial ministry suddenly took renewed interest in the northern expansion. It appeared that the Upington–*Bond* ministry had received alarming reports of renewed German activity in the interior, in particular above the northern 22° frontier of the Bechuanaland Protectorate. Rhodes was certainly very concerned too over German ambitions. The Cape premier now wrote a worried letter to the British permanent under-secretary for colonies, calling on the Salisbury government to check on the rumoured German advance.[130] A formal request followed to the high commissioner, pointing out that the Cape could not afford to be denied the interior.[131]

Despite the irony of the situation, both the British colonial office and the high commissioner gave the Cape communication serious attention. They still hoped to win Cape collaboration in Bechuanaland. Sir Robert Herbert carefully considered the Cape call to extend British influence north of the 22° frontier, arguing that it was 'very desirable to prevent the Germans from stretching such a "cordon" across Africa'.[132] And the high commissioner went to the trouble of writing an extensive Memorandum,[133] in which he now suggested closing the Transvaal Boers in to the north, and extending the British Bechuanaland Protectorate to the Zambesi. Such an extension would keep out the Transvaal, Germany and Portugal, and make economic sense of the existing Protectorate, which served as a trade route into Zambesia.

The suggestion was received remarkably favourably by metropolitan officialdom. The new colonial secretary in the short-lived third Gladstone government, Lord Granville, declared that he was 'quite converted to the proposal' – on the grounds that it was 'really not so much an annexation as a rectification of our frontier which is shown to be necessary'.[134] The permanent under-secretary agreed with Lord Granville's assessment that the extension would 'not practically add to our responsibilities'; he also agreed that a German entry into Zambesia would in fact be deeply embarrassing to the Imperial Factor – particularly in view of the efforts already expended in South Africa to safeguard British interests against Bismarck's colonial annexations. 'Unless the Foreign Office can soon obtain from the German Government a satisfactory assurance that they will not hem in the [Cape] Colony and its trade by advancing to the country directly north of it, it will be difficult to avoid protecting that country ourselves.' But before the colonial secretary's firm opinion could be acted upon, the third Gladstone government was sent from office on the Irish home rule issue, in August 1886. Salisbury was now premier for the second time, with Edward Stanhope as colonial secretary. The new government declined to see the logic of making this vast extension to the Bechuanaland Protectorate, particularly as in the passing of months since the original Cape alarmist letters there had been revealed no grand German design in Central Africa. The matter was accordingly simply shelved. Only the high commissioner continued to show any official interest in the idea, and he was strongly prompted by Rhodes.[135]

Unofficially, however, John Mackenzie was ever vigilant in the cause of the Tswana, and had again been active in trying to get the Imperial Factor to take up its trusteeship responsibilities in Bechuanaland more seriously. He met a blank refusal. 'Sir H. Holland has read your letter with attention and interest, but is not prepared to recommend the assumption by this country of the great amount of interference in, and direct responsibility for, the details of extra-Colonial affairs in South Africa which your letters appear to advocate.'[136] John Mackenzie did not easily give up. He stressed that he did 'not desire to impose on Her Majesty's Government further responsibilities, but ask you to face the discharge of those already incurred';[137] He clearly touched a sensitive point, for Mackenzie received an immediate and private letter from the colonial secretary.

There is unjustifiable 'interference' as well as a justifiable 'interference' – but the interference is not the less a fact. If we interfere at the request of Native Chiefs the the interference may be justifiable, and still more justifiable if the request of the Chiefs is supported by the request of intelligent Colonists. In each case H.M. Gov[ernmen]t. have to consider whether justifiable interference is desirable from the Imperial point of view.[138]

Mackenzie's old enemies in the colonial office also had their say. The South African expert, Edward Fairfield, still strongly preferred settler Cape Colonialism to direct British imperial expansion as the long-term answer for the administration of Bechuanaland. Pointing to the apparent tranquility of the Transkei Territories administered by the Cape, he suggested that this was 'a strong argument against "Mackenzieism" at the present time, contrasting as it does with the state of things in Zululand, where hostilities are in progress between the Natives and the Imperial Gov[ernmen]t., which took them under its authority to 'save' them from somebody else'.[139] In truth, Mackenzie's opponents had all too quickly forgotten the African rebellions against Cape rule 1878–81; and, as Joseph Chamberlain commented sympathetically to Mackenzie, the real parallel was not the imperial situation in Zululand, but the more recent disastrous 'Basuto experience' under the Cape settler policy and administration.[140]

So far as the British authorities were concerned, they had closed off the imperial advances in Bechuanaland and South-central Africa; they had also closed out the Boer and German ambitions in the region. The Partition in Bechuanaland was deemed to be at an end in 1885, by will of London.

London was to be defied. It was not at all the end; rather it was a beginning of immense chapter in empire advance. Instead of being a culmination of rival claims – British, Boer, German – the negative British expansion in Bechuanaland up to 1885 became a prelude to positive further Partition and an even greater Scramble for the interior of South Africa, by the local forces of expansion, in the years after 1888. A revival of Boer ambitions – based on the stupendous gold discoveries of the Witwatersrand – together with further speculations about the ultimate ambitions of the Germans in the interior, and renewed pressure from Cape commercial groups, worked to keep open and alive the whole question of further annexations by the British in South Africa's hinterland. The Imperial Factor looked to the short-term and met their own relatively specific strategic needs in Bechuanaland, by denying the region to Boer and German alike. In fact, they had taken the first steps in the direction of Central Africa. The Road to the North soon beckoned.

Heyday 1886–90:

Scramble for mastery and resources

'Until the neck of Kruger's [economic] policy is broken, all beautiful [tariff and railway] plans are so many soap bubbles ... the policy now followed among our people gives Kruger ... a dictatorship not only over the Transvaal, but over the whole of South Africa.'

Rev. S. J. du Toit to Jan Hofmeyr, 21 August 1888

'I am confident that a strongly constituted [chartered] company will give us the best chance of peaceably opening up and developing the resources of this country south of the Zambesi, and will be most beneficial to the native chiefs and the people.'

Lord Knutsford (colonial secretary) to Queen Victoria, 11 July 1889

'Rhodes is a great Jingo, but then he is a cheap jingo.'

Sir William Harcourt, October 1892

6

The highveld revolution: political and economic consequences of the Witwatersrand gold discoveries 1886–88

That which Milner termed the 'great game' of political supremacy in South Africa was about to enter upon an era of frenetic energy and crisis in the years after 1886. The gold discoveries of the Witwatersrand region of the Transvaal brought about both political and economic revolutions – 'revolutions' which gave new momentum, scale and direction, to the Scramble for South Africa.

Something like a quarter of all the world's known gold supplies were thought to lie under the veld and kopjes in the south of Kruger's republic. A dramatic new power was accordingly given to republican Afrikanerdom; the Cape colony experienced a corresponding loss of power vis-à-vis the interior states; the Germans were given an added incentive to make capital out of their association with the Boers; and the British were driven to re-consider the means of safe-guarding and furthering their interests in Africa south of the Zambesi River.

The combination of Witwatersrand and 'Krugerism' was in fact simply deadly in its potency to disturb the political and economic status quo in South Africa. In a myriad ways, it altered the whole future prospect of the region, and indeed became a great divide in the history of colonial South Africa. Above all, it had two primary effects within the politics of Partition.

First, it exacerbated and quickened the inter-state rivalry which had been at the core of the 'creeping partition' in frontier South Africa before 1886. But that already deadly-earnest interaction, of annexers and the annexed, now took on an even more ferocious intensity, contracting the expanding partition in time, and speeding up the whole process of conquest and incorporation, as the local white agencies of empire and expansion felt a great surge of new power.

Second, the highveld revolution completed what might be described as the 'internationalising' of the Scramble for South Africa. Bismarckian Germany's conquests in South-west Africa had both brought the spirit of the New Imperialism to the broader region of Southern Africa, and also created a situation of Great Power rivalry, soon to be one of Scramble. But that intrusion was on a modest scale at first, tending to be coastal in its preoccupations, and actually very limited in its ambitions in the hinterland. The rise of a great industrial mining industry on the 'Rand', and the emergence of a major financial centre in Johannesburg, now encouraged a new interest in the interior Boer state, and provided an impetus for developing a tangible German–Transvaal 'association'. Several European states were also now interested in the political and economic future of the Boers of South Africa; and the Boers were certainly interested in encouraging European involvement in South Africa.

Within a few hectic years of exploration, development and investment on the Rand 1886–88, the petty parish-pump politics of South Africa were transformed into the clash of great geo-political forces, as the region became yet another arena in the international spread of the New Imperialism. This did not mean that the old actors and the old interest groups – those identified with the pre-1886 Scramble for South Africa – just went away. Rather, it meant that their traditional, long-term struggles for local African resources were magnified, heightened in intensity, and given a further potency, as they intersected with the strategic and diplomatic interventions of the Great Powers involved. There was still continuity in Partition, through the ways in which the Scramble for South Africa, after the highveld revolution, merely extended those struggles for resources in the region. But it was now a Scramble derivative of greater reserves of power, with a corresponding increase in the passion for Partition.

The 'secondary effects' of economic change

It has been remarked, in a recent study of the economics of the nineteenth-century empires, that ultimately the Anglo-Boer War was an attempt to use political means to restore British political supremacy in an area where it was threatened by the secondary effects of economic change'.[1] The comment might well be taken back, and applied to the earlier British and Cape responses to the Witwatersrand economic revolution, 1886–95. By a series of railway and tariff strategies, the British imperialists – both metropolitan and local colonial – attempted to negate the possibility of the Transvaal republicans becoming both the economic and political arbiters of South Africa. Largely as a result of the successive failures of this strategy, the emphasis changed as the Rhodesian group at the Cape pressed for expansion up the great Bechuanaland Road to the North into Zambesia – again in the hope of counter-balancing the growing Afrikaner republican power among the various political communities of South Africa.

Subsumed within these themes of high territorial and tariff strategy were vital political and economic developments, rooted in the local situation, which again suggested how 'periphery' worked to shape the development of the New Imperialism and contributed to the Partition in South Africa. The conquest of the coastal belt, and its African societies, had revealed how the Scramble in South Africa was also a Scramble for its resources, by the agencies of settler expansion. The Scramble for the interior also contained this element.[2] Just as the gold discoveries were a power-house for republicanism, so the sheer demands of the new industry – partly in capital and emigrant skills, but more still in cheap black labour – gave a further dimension to the Partition as a crucial phase in the establishment of white supremacy. The Kimberley diamond discoveries had begun to tilt the scales of authority in favour of the white societies; the gold of the Witwatersrand confirmed that process in even larger degree. The manner of African political incorporation during the Partition was thus unique: first, the political independency of the chiefdoms was ended; then the forces of economic growth transformed the African 'reserve' areas into great pools of migrant labour. The external policy of the Kruger regime, within the inter-state relations of Southern Africa, thus assimilated to its interest in pastoral expansion a new energy for strategic railway outlets to the world, together with an added desire to acquire a supply of plentiful African labour. We should therefore remember that the Partition of the interior was, in its local dimension, more than the mere history of strategic encirclement of Krugerism by the Rhodesian agency of British imperialism.

Just how the republican Afrikaner began to capture the political initiative in Southern Africa can be best seen not by looking to a reading of the situation by the British 'official mind', but by examining the parochial struggles for economic supremacy and local human resources. The context of those struggles was the size and scale of the highveld mineral revolution.

The Witwatersrand

At 11 a.m., on 5 June 1885 – on a tennis court behind the Union Club in Pretoria – Harry Struben informed a gathering of the Kruger government, *Volksraad* and Transvaal business interests, of his favourable gold prospecting on the Witwatersrand in the previous two years.[3] His findings suggested gold reefs far richer than Carl Mauch's discoveries near the Olifants River in 1868, or Edward Button's finds at Marasbad in the Zoutpansberg (1873); and probably richer than the eastern Transvaal mines opened up between Pilgrims Rest (1872) and Barberton (1882).[4]

Just how rich the Witwatersrand resources were was only fully revealed two years later,[5] when the first stamp-mill commenced regular crushing of banket. By the end of the following year there were 688 such 'stamps' running, crushing 14,935 tons of rock monthly, with an annual yield of over two hundred thousand ounces of gold. Indeed, the first three years of mechanised development (1887–89) yielded no less than 642,803 ounces of gold. The scale of development was soon unprecedented in colonial Africa. The Witwatersrand had over 2,000 stamps in late-1894, crushing 2.75 million tons of banket and annually producing gold worth £7 million. The capitalised value of the mines was estimated (on 19 July 1895) to be £71 million, a figure which ran to £82.5 million by the end of the last boom month. According to one authority, '130 of the principal and working (including a few finance) companies, having an issued capital of about £25,000,000, represented ... a total value of nearly £103,000,000'.[6]

From being a struggling pastoral state, isolated in the interior of South Africa, Kruger's Transvaal thus found itself producing some 20% of all the world's gold supply. The rise in the value of the gold production – and the local status of the Afrikaner republic – had in short been nothing less than dramatic in the extreme.

TABLE 2   *Rise in gold production (value in £ sterling)*

1884	10,096	1891	2,924,305
1885	6,010	1892	4,541,071
1886	34,710	1893	5,480,498
1887	169,401	1894	7,667,152
1888	967,416	1895	8,569,555
1889	1,490,568	1896	8,603,821
1890	1,869,645		

Source: *Report of the State Mining Engineer for the Year 1896*, p. 5.

The world of international finance welcomed the gold discoveries, which helped to stabilise currency and ended the battle for a silver standard.[7] Investors in Europe and America took the opportunity to exploit what looked to be the most exciting speculation since South American railways. If Manchester was the 'shock city' of the European industrial revolution, as Professor Briggs has suggested,[8] then Johannesburg was the shock city of the 'New Imperialism'. Indeed, it soon became one of the great 'sights' of a century already conditioned to change and drama. 'As we drive across the tops of the hills, and gaze downwards, it seems impossible to believe it', as one Victorian visitor wrote in 1889,

Acre after acre, mile after mile, are covered with lordly buildings or the humble shanty . . . . Two hundred wagons a day come into the market place, each one carrying a precious freight of 7000 lbs. to 8000 lbs. and drawn by 20 patient oxen . . . There are some 700 members of the Stock Exchange, and all bargains are settled for the next day . . . At 10 am. all stocks on the lists are 'called', and the noise is deafening . . . Everyone anticipates a golden boom before the winter is over.[9]

The boom of 1889 duly came; then burst. Yet the progress of the mines continued in the 1890s, on an even larger scale. Deep level mining began in 1892, and the Main Reef was cut at 2,343 feet the next year, soon followed by the introduction of the new Macarthur—Forrest cyanide process for direct treatment of tailings, which much increased profits by raising the yield on low-grade ores. Further, between 1890—95 the rich coal deposits of the east Rand were developed, while the opening of major rail-outlets to the Cape (1892) and Delagoa Bay (1895) also helped lower overall production costs.[10] A great boom in gold shares — the second famous 'Kaffirs' speculation, of 1895 — soon followed on the London money market.[11]

The impact of the highveld revolution — as Dr Francis Wilson has shown in his essay on farming in South Africa,[12] and Leo Katzen has pointed out in his study of the role of gold in the modern South African economy[13] — was felt even more widely. The place of gold in the foreign trade of South Africa perhaps serves as the best simple index of that impact. The South African boom in railway-building 1880—1910 was also intimately connected with the mineral discoveries at Kimberley and on the Witwatersrand. Gold mining, in particular, led to a great surge in railway construction.

TABLE   3   *South   African   rail-lines   1880—1910* (*approx., in miles*)

1880	1,006	1895	3,200
1885	1,776	1900	4,000
1890	2,238	1910	7,000

An equally important human index of the economic power of the Afrikaner republic within its surrounding South African societies — though almost impossible to quantify accurately — lay in the question of labour. 'Johannesburg would not be Johannesburg were the nigger unknown', observed a British writer in 1889. 'He is the backbone of the country.'[14] African labour was a crucial element in the success of the industry almost from the beginning, and particularly after deep level mining began in 1892.

Not only did the mines require an ever larger number of African labourers – rising from 14,000 to 97,000 per annum between 1890 and 1899[15] – but the mine-owners wished to control and, if possible, lower African wages. In 1890 some 66 companies got together, and in three months managed to reduce African wages by nearly a third. This, however, affected the supply of labour, and it was soon clear that only some control over the flow of black labour, by determining the number of Africans coming forward, could alone assure the wages the Rand mine-owners desired to pay. The Chamber of Mines created a 'Native Labour Department' in 1893, not least to serve these purposes. Capitalists were hopeful. 'There is . . . the probability that wages paid to natives will eventually be reduced,' a guide to the mines in 1895 commented, 'through the unremitting efforts of the Chamber of Mines which, since its inception, has directed much energy to the question of the *reduction* of native wages and the *increase* of the supply of native labour.'[16]

The mines, however, found it difficult to co-operate on so crucial a matter as labour; they rivalled each other for black workers, with the result that wages were hard to control, and a steady supply of labour ever more difficult to devise. Increasingly, the Rand capitalists turned to the somewhat inefficient Boer administration to remedy their problems of labour supply – problems which their own inter-company rivalry could not sort out. The results, in the short term, were very mixed. By 1895 African labour costs were reputed to be 40% to 45% of production costs – though black wages were hardly over-generous[17] – and the Chamber of Mines grew urgent in its task. They pressed the Kruger government to increase the supply of labour from the Transvaal itself, where Africans were notably reticent in coming forward to join the wage-earning economy; and it called for more inter-state co-operation in the supply of labour. Its efforts had some small success: General Joubert worked to press more Africans from the Transvaal 'locations', while private Recruiting Agents directed an ever larger stream of labourers to the Witwatersrand from Swaziland, Zululand, Natal, the Transkei, Basutoland, Bechuanaland and the Portuguese colonies – often receiving as much as £4 per head as a fee.[18] Cape magisterial officials also co-operated in sending forward Africans for the mines. Further, as the Scramble expanded so too did the human resources of an African labour supply. The white colonial polities worked together closely in developing Southern Africa. Thus, for example, as early as 1891 the territory controlled by the BSA Company in Zambesia was supplying black labour to the Witwatersrand mines by the use of rather firm administrative techniques.[19] But when war broke out in 1899 the Rand capitalists were still grumbling over the labour question.

TABLE 4 *Foreign trade of South Africa – 1865–1900*

Annual average for period	Food and drink (£000)	Raw materials (£000)	Diamonds (£000)	Gold (£000)	Gold as % of total	Total	Average annual increase %	Total (£000)	Average annual increase %
						Exports of South African produce		Imports	
1865–70	112.7	2,251.8	35.7	–	–	2,520.6	3.5	2,334.8	4.4
1871–5	115.7	3,924.6	1,306.4	11.7		5,648.1	17.5	5,430.3	18.4
1876–80	92.0	3,740.9	2,268.7	30.4		6,613.9	3.2	7,808.2	7.5
1881–5	95.9	4,076.6	3,241.6	35.3		8,020.7	4.0	8,640.7	2.1
1886–90	87.6	3,924.9	4,091.3	890.1	9.2	9,855.6	4.2	9,215.9	1.3
1891–5	82.2	3,959.2	3,938.2	5,636.2	39.4	14,297.5	7.7	13,933.2	8.6
1896–1900	48.1	4,090.5	4,247.4	9,871.1	51.0	19,253.1	6.1	23,985.0	11.5

Source: adapted from Katzen, *Gold and the South African economy* (1964), p. 46; and C. G. W. Schumann, *Structural changes and business cycles in South Africa* (1938), p. 44.

The growing stream of mute unskilled African labour to the Witwatersrand was, however, perhaps the most dramatic register of the power of the Transvaal's new economy, and the impact of the local Scramble on the African societies of South Africa. Within the context of the periphery, Kruger's 'South African Republic' was becoming an empire-state in its own right.

Political dimensions of the Transvaal mineral revolution

'*Everybody* in South Africa speculates; the place is a living hell', remarked a Victorian traveller in 1889.[20] The sluggish economy, based largely on wool and wine, had since the Diamond Field discoveries begun to quicken its tempo; the Witwatersrand developments completed the transformation. Not surprisingly, such an economic revolution was matched by dramatic political consequences. This is best seen by looking to the changing status of the Cape in relation to the Transvaal.

The Cape colony had been the local 'parent society' of South Africa, and the base of the British presence; even the *Voortrekkers* were, in truth, a fragment of the Cape. As the most prosperous and civilised of the colonial polities which had developed in the nineteenth century, the Cape had since the 1840s enjoyed a position of comfortable condescension about the crude life of the Afrikaner republicans. In the later 1880s the Cape suddenly faced the prospect of becoming the poor relation, despite its British connections. This development had an air of irony surrounding it. Twice in the years immediately before the gold bonanza, the Transvaal burghers had approached the Cape, and appealed for the creation of a 'customs union'. Twice the Cape commercial interests had haughtily turned away from the republicans' gesture. The Transvalers were flatly told that the Cape colony had never, 'at any time, assented to the proposition that the inland states are entitled to a share of the Customs Duties collected at the Colonial Ports'.

Their logic was simple, if self-centred. The Cape enjoyed a stranglehold on most goods imported into the interior, while the Transvaal had economically nothing to offer such a 'union', and indeed was on its knees with its tiny budget hardly balanced.[21] With its diamond revenues, agricultural development and British investments in its public works – notably the vital harbours and railways of its economy – the Cape felt above the need to play a charitable role towards the Afrikaners of the north. The Transvaal frontier ambitions in Bechuanaland – across the Cape's trade route into the interior of Africa – also hardly endeared the Kruger state to the commercial interests of the senior colony. Three years of the Witwaters-rand, 1886–88, was enough completely to change this position.[22] The Transvaal was on a par with the Cape by 1887: by 1890 it had simply surged ahead.[23] The annual revenue of the Kruger state was over £4 million[24] – indeed it increased over 25 times between 1883 and 1895[25] – and its white population was (according to the Transvaal census of 1890) 119,128 – more than double that of ten years earlier. Of course, the Cape trade bene-fited from the demands of the new Transvaal economy, notably in customs revenues and foodstuffs, as the figures reveal.[26]

TABLE 5   *Cape trade statistics 1881–90 (in £ooos)*

	Imports	Exports		Imports	Exports
1881	9,227	8,396	1886	3,799	7,125
1882	9,372	8,506	1887	5,036	7,855
1883	6,470	7,151	1888	5,678	8,876
1884	5,249	6,945	1889	8,446	9,269
1885	4,772	5,811	1890	9,366	9,837

Yet these figures are innocent of certain vital economic and political dimen-sions of the Cape situation. They fail to show the fact the Cape was gaining only a fraction of the rich trade to be enjoyed with the Afrikaner state. They fail to indicate the steadily increasing public debt incurred by the Cape as it desperately tried to push its railways up to the north to cut into the heart of the Witwatersrand's commerce and 'carrying-trade'. They omit to show the failure of the Cape to draw the Transvaal into a customs union: Kruger's republic could now afford to play the part of the non-chalant, superior and independent family relation. Finally, these figures could not illustrate the specifically anti-Cape, and by implication therefore anti-British bias, which the Transvaal government pursued in trying for an outlet to the sea, via a rail-line to Delagoa Bay, which would be inde-pendent of the whole Cape customs and trading system.

To the Transvaal this latter policy was initially both economically sound, in avoiding Cape tariffs, and personally satisfying, in turning the screws on the Cape Afrikaners. From Cape Town – and to some degree from London – the republicans' policy was a nightmare come true. It appeared that the old 'Dopper' Boer was not merely becoming the arbiter of local affairs, but that Kruger was creating a specifically anti-British and republi-can axis in alliance with the Orange Free State Republic. He was fulfilling his determination to throw off the last restraining shackles of the London

Convention of 1884, and his desire finally to make the South African Republic the focal point for any unified state of 'South Africa' in the future. In fact, Kruger had stolen the imperialists' clothes. The hopes of many British secretaries of state for colonies might become a reality at last: a federated South Africa – as a self-sustaining 'union' – was not now an impossibility. But it would be a state based on sentiment, and power, united *against* Great Britain, and the empire; a state tied not to the imperial flag at Government House, Cape Town, but to Witwatersrand and the Boer *vierkleur*-flag which fluttered above Kruger's modest home in Kerkstraat, Pretoria.[27]

The Imperial Factor could also now reflect on the irony that some of the political problems posed by the Boers after 1886 might well have been avoided if the retrocession of the Transvaal 1881–84 had not taken place. In a perverse fashion, the 'Boer Question' reversed the otherwise universal consequences faced by the British in the expansion of the New Imperialism. It had been the problems of maintaining 'informal empire' in other parts of Africa and the Far East which had led to the formal expansion of the 1880s. In South Africa it had been the move from formal to informal empire on the highveld – overt to potentially covert imperialism – which was now at the root of the troubles faced by the British in dealing with the crisis of hegemony in the interior.

Challenging 'Krugerism': Rhodes in Cape politics

The power of the Boer state to become the pole-star in the constellation of local political communities initially alarmed the Cape leadership more than it did the 'Imperial Factor'. The British were generally inclined to place their faith in the flood of finance and *uitlander* migrants bringing about an internal 'annexation' of the Transvaal; the Cape political elite were less sanguine, for they felt the economic impact of the Witwatersrand most sharply on their commercial interests, and they also had some knowledge of the tenacity of 'Krugerism'.

It was the Cape elite, therefore, which was at the heart of the several railway, tariff and territorial strategies which were now deployed in the interior of Southern Africa, and into Zambesia, as a counterpoise against the power of Afrikaner republicanism. And it was the Imperial Factor – tied to the 'loyal Cape', as its leading agent in the development of an empire of association and collaboration in Southern Africa – which found itself being drawn into the politics of further Partition. Where the metropolitan imperialists were ready to rest content on the basis of their recent coastal advances, the local colonial imperialists of the Cape were urgent to meet and check the expansive economic power of the Afrikaner republic, even at the price of further Scrambles for African lands and resources. The first phase of this thrust into the interior was essentially concerned with tariffs and railway building; and found its focus in the Rhodesian group in Cape politics.

A young Cecil Rhodes (only 33 in 1886) was then becoming a leading figure in colonial affairs. He had come to the attention of the British authorities through his involvement in Cape frontier expansion, firstly in Basutoland, then in Bechuanaland 1883–84.[28] 'What information have we of Mr Rhodes?' the senior metropolitan colonial official enquired in mid-1884.[29] Back came the answer from the Southern African expert in the colonial office, containing the first picture the British government was to have of the imperialist. Rhodes was a young Kimberley mine owner and diamond speculator who 'has sat for Barkly in the Cape Parliament since 1882, and was Treasurer in Mr Scanlen's administration for a few weeks. He was President of the Griqualand West "Northern Boundary Commission" [of 1883] ... *a sensible man.*'[30]

It was Rhodes' involvement in the Bechuanaland affair which had crystallised his views on the Northern Expansion; it was through his role as diamond magnate, gold mining millionaire, and financier, that he came to lead the commercial interests in Cape politics. He did not alone design the colony's economic strategy; nor determine its implementation until he became Cape premier in 1890. But through him the Cape policy of challenging the republicans can perhaps best be followed. Rhodes himself was certainly not reticent in coming forward to provide leadership for the Cape commercial interests. More than any other Cape politician he spoke out on the gravity of the position in the face of the Transvaal economic power. 'We should be the dominant State in South Africa,' he flatly told his fellow colonial MPs in the Cape Assembly,[31] 'and should carry out the union of the South African States.'[32] That traditional Cape notion was however fast fading as Kruger's independent economic power allowed him independent trading outlets. As many Cape leaders saw it, and as Rhodes articulated it for this group,

if the Delagoa Bay Railway is carried out we shall not get a continuation of the line from Kimberley to Pretoria. Commercial people will be always inspiring or instilling into the rulers of the Transvaal hostile action against the Cape Colony. In other words, if the Delagoa railway is carried out the real union of South Africa will be indefinitely deferred.

Fundamental to the vital role which Rhodes played in the public life of Southern Africa was not so much his famed 'political vision' – much of it more rhetoric than anything else – but the alliance of Anglo-Saxon commercial interests and the Cape Afrikaner farming sector which he managed to stitch together in the late 1880s. Rhodes was only so powerful as this political alliance made him. This is not to belittle his political talents in creating the alliance. He faced the considerable problem of building a 'party-group' in a culturally divided white electorate – mainly Anglo-Saxon in the towns, commerce, administration and law; mainly Afrikaner in the rural areas and farming organisations. The latter were a majority in the white population, though seriously under-represented in the Anglo-Saxon dominated Cape Assembly. The rise of the *Afrikaner Bond* – not least in reaction against this last fact – merely sharpened the cultural and political divisions in the colony, for it was largely based on Afrikaner rural voters and spoke for the farmers' interests. Among the few personal reminiscences of Rhodes is a valuable account of his political strategy in forming the alliance with the Cape Afrikaners:

the 'English' party in the Cape Assembly was hopelessly divided and individually incapable. And it had nothing beyond that of serving office. On the other side was a compact body of nominees of what afterwards came to be called the Afrikaner Bond, who acted all together at the dictation of [Jan] Hofmeyr. Hofmeyr was, without doubt, the most capable politician in South Africa ... He was anxious to maintain the [British] connection, not out of any love for Great Britain, but because the independence of South Africa was at the mercy of whatever power had command of the sea. And ... his hatred of the Germans amounted to a passion ... Hofmeyr was chiefly interested in withstanding Free Trade and upholding Protection on behalf of the [Cape] Dutch, who were agriculturalists and vine growers. I had a policy of my own ... to keep open the road to the north, to secure British South Africa room for expansion.'[33]

In looking for his power base in colonial politics, Rhodes had no hesitation in choosing his 'side'. 'The Dutch are the coming race in South Africa,' he prophetically argued,[34] 'and they must share in running the country.' Hofmeyr may have been an unlikely ally in building a Cape expansionist 'alliance'; but, as Rhodes put it, 'I ... struck a bargain with him, by which I undertook to defend the protective system of [the] Cape Colony, and he pledged himself in the name of the *Bond* not to throw obstacles in the way of northern expansion.'[35] Indeed, Rhodes went out of his way to woo the Cape Afrikaner electorate into building a colonial 'front'. 'I like the [Cape] Dutch, I like their homely courtesy and their tenacity of purpose', he declared openly.[36] He lectured his fellow Anglo-Saxons on the necessity of white colonial unity: 'You cannot have real prosperity ... until you have first established complete confidence between the two races [English/Afrikaner].'[37]

Hofmeyr warmed to this unusual version of the 'beafsteak Englishman'. He remembered after the 1880—81 Anglo-Transvaal war,

I said to Mr Rhodes, 'It is an awful pity the war broke out'. I was surprised when Rhodes said, 'No, it is not ... It is a good thing. It has made Englishmen respect Dutchmen ...' Well, when an Englishman could speak like that to a Dutchman, they are not far from making common cause with one another.[38]

The failure of the Transvaal to accept the overtures of the Cape, extended through Hofmeyr, in the solution of common Southern African problems — notably in the matter of tariffs and the Swaziland question — disabused the *Bond* leader of his hopes for pan-Afrikaner unity. In the apt phrase of Professor Davenport, 'Rebuffed by the Transvaal, Hofmeyr walked into the arms of Rhodes just at the moment when the latter was most anxious to receive him.'[39]

Rhodes, of course, also took his steps towards the *Bond*. In a series of calculated speeches, in the rural areas of the Cape, he set out his vision of a 'British Southern Africa' which embraced the Afrikaner as equal partner in a white state. Appreciative Paarl Bondsmen, for example, heard him re-mark,

I was told this morning that the last time a banquet was given in this hall was on the occasion of the visit of the Transvaal Deputation [in 1880]. I believe there is a feeling of sentiment when I mention the name of the Transvaal. Where we have gone wrong in our actions ... is [in] our dealings with the Transvaal. We should be close with the neighbouring [Afrikaner] States.[40]

Such rhetoric was, in truth, unlikely to draw Kruger and his supporters closer to the local imperial vision of the Rhodesian group. But within the Cape itself, Rhodes' persistence in throwing overtures to the Afrikaners of the *Bond* finally brought about the creation of a colonial alliance ready to wage economic and strategic 'warfare' against the rising power of the Transvaal republicans.

Krugerism defiant: customs and railway rivalry

Achieving a Cape 'alliance' proved easier than challenging the rising status of the Transvaal republic in South Africa. For a start, the old Afrikaner president (Kruger was 71 in 1886) was not to be bought off with soft words from the Rhodesian group. He made it plain, for example, that his government would not hear of letting a Cape, or even Natal, rail-line into the Wit-watersrand, before they had completed their own independent line to Delagoa Bay. Kruger expressed his views in his usual dogmatic manner:

'Every railway that approaches me I look upon as an enemy, on whatever side it comes. I must have my Delagoa Bay line first, and then the other lines may come.'[41]

Added to that, the republican executive was firmly set against joining any Southern African customs union sponsored by the Rhodes–Hofmeyr alliance.[42] In the early months of 1887 the Cape despatched both telegrams, overtues and a personal deputation – led by Colonel Schermbrucker, as commissioner of crown lands and public works, and David de Waal, a *Bond* MP – to try and strike agreement on a customs union. All initiatives failed in Pretoria. Not surprisingly: Kruger infinitely preferred a *zollverein* of the republican Afrikaner states of the interior. A Transvaal deputation made a dramatic visit to Bloemfontein in October of that year, when Kruger spoke strongly of the need for 'closer union' between the Orange Free State and the South African Republic against 'British South Africa'.[43]

The Rhodesian alliance declined to let these obdurate postures of independence by the republicans hold them back from their economic counterpoise. Because of Hofmeyr's optimism in finding an eventual working compromise with Kruger, and even more because of Rhodes' dark warning against doing otherwise, the Cape colony began the great railway ventures into the interior in the years 1887–92. It was a desperate bid to secure a place in the economic and political sun of Southern Africa. It was also a less than successful bid. By 1891 the Cape had plunged itself into deep public debt to construct its vast northern railways onto the highveld.[44]

TABLE 6   *Cape railway investment 1886–94 (in £000s)*

	Investment	Railway revenue	Total Cape revenue
1886	14,130	1,048	3,039
1887	14,186	1,271	3,159
1888	12,214	1,451	3,426
1889	14,282	1,759	3,836
1890	14,665	1,896	4,430
1891	14,686	1,896	4,495
1892	18,557	2,248	4,971
1893	19,557	2,559	5,321
1894	20,092	2,713	5,390

Quite apart from Transvaal recalcitrance, numerous factors worked against the profitability of these schemes. The Cape colony had three rail systems, each feeling its way north from different regions and ports: Cape Town itself, Port Elizabeth and East London. The result was that, by 1894, the line from Cape Town carried less wares north than the other two lines combined.[45] Distances to the Transvaal were also vast.[46] As compared to the shorter distances covered by the Natal rail-line,[47] from Durban to the Witwatersrand, the Cape investment was a bad business risk. Return on capital was very disappointing.[48] It was clearly an economic venture with a basic political rationale.

The Cape line finally reached Johannesburg in September 1892.[49] Kruger had been forced to admit the railway to the Witwatersrand, partly due to pressure from the mining magnates, partly due to a loan from the Cape government accepted as a subsidy by his failing Netherlands Railway Company.[50] Even this, however, was a pyrrhic victory for the Cape alliance. By then they had failed to draw the Transvaal into a customs union. Attempts had been made in 1886, 1887 and again vigorously in 1888. Kruger listened to the Cape's case as put by Hofmeyr.[51] But behind Hofmeyr he saw Rhodes; and behind Rhodes he detected the British Imperial Factor. The Transvaal response was to draw closer to the Orange Free State. In October 1887 president Brand, of the Free State, had declined to commit himself formally to the cause of the Transvaal, 'the most unruly state in South Africa'.[52] Brand had however been recently succeeded as president by Francis Reitz. He was far more sympathetic to Kruger's concept of an Afrikaner republican alliance in the interior. The axis duly came into being in March 1889, when the South African Republic and the Orange Free State signed a defensive agreement: each Boer republic was now bound to defend its fellow in the case of foreign attack.

The only glimmer of hope for the Cape strategy came in 1889 when a customs agreement was signed with the poorer Afrikaner republic of the Orange Free State.[53] The Cape alliance hoped this might be a major step towards drawing the Transvalers into a similar economic union. They were to be disappointed. The republican defence-axis suggested the obdurance of the Kruger government; the Anglo-Saxon colony of Natal made it clear that it was moving closer to the Kruger state, and making its own tariff agreements;[54] and, most important, the Transvaal leadership declined to be lured into any Cape tariff sharing agreement when it still had a good chance of completing its independent rail outlet at Delagoa Bay.[55]

The Rhodesian group in Cape politics had always recognised this as a bleak possibility. Significantly, before the Cape railways reached the

Witwatersrand, they had already given attention to the possibility of securing a part, or complete controlling interest, in that vital Delagoa railway.

Cape finance and the Delagoa railway

The Cape began bidding for ownership of the line once it became clear that the Transvaal was in earnest in constructing the railway.[56] Kruger had in 1887 granted the concession for the Transvaal end of the line to a German company and for the Portuguese portion to an Anglo-American syndicate, headed by Edward McMurdo.[57] The Portuguese did not immediately reject the idea of the Cape buying a controlling share of the line. Rhodes and his circle grew hopeful that they might turn Kruger's dream of an independent outlet into a Cape-controlled 'tap'. Presumably they could then demand any commercial or political terms which they cared to name. In pursuing this scheme it was necessary of course to involve the British colonial office and, ultimately, the foreign office.

Here the Cape group came unstuck.[58] Money was no great problem. Rhodes was at this very time successfully amalgamating all the Kimberley diamond mines, into one Rhodes owned company.[59] But Lord Salisbury, as British prime minister, was less easy to win over.[60] Why? 'Lord Salisbury was old-fashioned enough to think it improper in principle to use British power for the buying and keeping of railways on foreign soil.'[61] Salisbury would not object to some private arrangement, by which Rhodes and the Cape group secured an interest in the rail-line. But he would not pressure the Portuguese to make an agreement, especially at a time when his primary diplomatic concern was the repairing of Anglo-German relations. Salisbury was also never entirely convinced of the Cape argument that the existence of the Delagoa line would automatically imply increased independence for the republican Afrikaners, or increased German influence at Pretoria.

Salisbury also took the long-term view. He argued that with the inflow of British capital and British enterprise into the South African Republic, Kruger's regime was doomed.[62] It was a view shared by the permanent under-secretary in the colonial office, who minuted on the Delagoa Bay correspondence in May 1889:

British capital and labour is at present prospering within the Transvaal, as much at least, as outside it; *and is gradually effecting a peaceful commercial annexation of the country*. The S.A. Republic would have its hands full with its eastern expansion and wretched sea port; and President Kruger's ambition to get down to the sea could be satisfied without any material injury, that I can see, to British interests.[63]

The South African expert in the 'office' indeed went so far as to find merit in having the South African Republic at the sea: 'Politically, it is always an advantage to England to have a Foreign State within range of its iron-clads.'[64]

Taken together, it was an attitude from which the British government refused to move – despite the entreaties of the Rhodes group, and despite the forebodings of Rand capitalists that the Delagoa Bay line would increase German influence at Pretoria.[65] To one persistent Witwatersrand mining advocate of British involvement, anxious to block Bismarckian overtures to the Afrikaners, Salisbury wrote in 1888:

I can quite believe in the probability of united efforts on the part of the Transvaal Republic and the Portuguese to diminish our influence in South Africa. Their power, however, to do so will not be very great. The more information reaches me, the more sceptical am I as to any real German action in the same direction.[66]

So that was that. The Cape could not move without British backing. Portugal would not take the overture of the Rhodes group seriously without that support. And Lord Salisbury would not be part of the scheme: 'On general principles H.M.G[overnment]. has always declined to place the power of the country at the disposal of individual investors.'[67]

Towards the North and the 'Balance of Africa'

Despite these enormous efforts and finances expended by the Cape leadership on the railway, tariff and Delagoa Bay strategies, they became increasingly side-issues in the hard facts of political Partition in the interior. As economic strategies they had bought the Cape time; but they were *not* a final solution to the deep question of authority, local paramountcy and future state-making in South Africa.[68] Rhodes was not alone in perceiving this, although he had warned of it earlier and longer than any other Cape politician. 'The mistake that has been made in the past is to think that a Union can be made in half an hour ... It took me twenty years to amalgamate the Diamond Mines.' In that long-term struggle to determine the political leadership and structure of South Africa, the Cape leadership of Rhodes increasingly pointed to the policy of territorial expansion northward, partly to outflank Afrikaner republicanism in its greater-state ambitions, even more to develop countervailing economic resources in the struggle for mastery in South Africa. Cape financial interests were desperately eager to expand their trade with the interior, to find rival resources of minerals, and to increase their supplies of labour for western Cape farms and the diamond fields. Again, these themes are all excellently exhibited by Rhodes himself – perhaps the 'representative politician' of the period in imperial South Africa.

The rhetoric of the Rhodesian expansion, a new and belligerent form of Cape Colonialism, was often florid – 'I knew that Africa was the last un-civilised portion of the world, and that it must be civilised' – yet the thinking behind the emotive language was decidedly hard-nosed. The Rhodesian group in the Cape well knew why they wished to 'undertake the civilisation of the black country'.[69] There was the nagging strategic issue of not allowing foreign intervention to strengthen the republicanism of the Boer state – without a northern expansion 'Germany would come across from her settle-ment at Angra Pequena to Delagoa Bay . . . [and her] ambitious objects . . . would be attained' – which, even if not proven, could not be set aside. More important, there was the defence of Cape trade up the Road to the North, which was intimately tied-in with the status and development of the colony within the South African inter-state system:

the Cape Colony should claim to hold the keys of the interior; as soon as possible we should take control of Bechuanaland; we should state by our own policy that we are prepared to take administration right through to the Zambesi; and that we should feel that [the] Cape Colony must be and shall be the dominant state in South Africa. If our possessions stretch from Cape Town to the Zambesi, no one can deny that assertion.[70]

More important again was the possibility of mineral resources in Central Africa being placed at the disposal of the Cape financial groups: 'I quite appreciate the enormous difficulties of opening up a new country but still, if Providence will furnish a few paying gold reefs, I think we shall be all right . . . as you know, gold hastens the development of a country more than anything . . . [and Mashonaland] is very healthy, full of gold and dominates the situation.'[71]

Lastly, the hinterland stood for Cape prosperity, in land *and* labour. The *Bond* supported the Rhodesians for these urgent local reasons, rather than for any larger sentimental commitment to the ideal of Anglo-Cape Dutch ties. It was this alliance of self-interest, in fact, which allowed Rhodes to remark in the same letter to W. T. Stead that he was 'working Northern Expansion with Cape sentiment'. The *Bond* and the Rhodesians might differ, in some degree, over the British connection; but over the rather more fundamental, immediate issues of economic development, they found close harmony. For example, both political groups primarily saw the expansion of *Pax Capensis* as the expansion of labour resources. The farm-ing interests of the western Cape never ceased complaining of the slow supply and the high cost of African labour, as the evidence to numerous colonial commissions on the matter reported; and as the financial interests of the Diamond Fields also decried, through their powerful representation in the Cape assembly. Never was this better vocalised that in Rhodes' highly revealing, if somewhat crude speech, on the Glen Grey Act of 1894 – a bill inspired by a Cape colonial commission of 1892, sponsored by the *Bond*, and pushed through the legislature by the Rhodes–Hofmeyr ministry.[72] Rhodes was at pains to spell out the value of a black citizenry to more nervous assemblymen:

the proposition he was putting to the House was that he did not feel that the effect of having one million of natives in that country was a reason for any serious anxiety. Properly directed, and properly looked after, he thought the natives would be a great source of assistance and wealth. At any rate, if the white population maintained its position as the supreme race, he thought the day would come when they would all be thankful that they had the natives – in their proper position . . . His idea was that the natives should be in native reserves and not mixed up with the whites. He claimed that in the interests of the whites . . . white people could not compete with black people in this country as regards labour. The black man was going to do the labour . . . The position therefore was that the lives of the majority of the natives must be like the lives of the majority of the old nations of the world – lives of labour (hear, hear).[73]

An imperial gloss of progress and improvement was given to this racial version of the new political economy – 'it was the duty of the Government to remove these poor children out of their state of sloth and laziness, and give them some gentle stimulants to go forth and find out something of the dignity of labour'[74] – but, at base, there was the frank admission that black labour was 'absolutely essential for the proper development of the country'.[75]

We do not therefore have to accept Rhodes' repetitious rhetoric – 'The North, the North . . . is my thought' – at face value, to accept the historical reality that 'the settlement of the South African Question'[76] after 1886 was intimately connected not merely with metropolitan strategies, but with the local imbroglios over labour, land and minerals in the inter-state struggle for mastery of South Africa. The local expansionists' fascination with maps which so amused Lord Salisbury – 'I think the constant study of maps is apt to disturb men's reasoning power'[77] – had a more serious and sinister reality, in fact; from the local perspective, the future *was* being shaped in the geo-political terms of a division of African resources. Each passing month reshaped the local balance of forces. Statesmen whose maps of Africa began on the Thames, so to speak, felt no special urgency to Scramble for an Africa they had not seen, and a continent whose resources were more legendary than proven. Within the inter-state rivalry of South Africa, however, a very real 'carve-up' of African resources was under way. The cold reality of possession or dispossession, of hegemony or of subservience, of economic development or of stagnation, stared at the local political elites. The very illogicality, exaggeration and emotion which characterised, say, the Rhodesian ambitions in South-central and Central Africa – and which offended the more refined sensibilities of Whitehall – were in fact a revealing manifestation of the urgent expansionist spirit which gripped the local white imperialists, for it was rooted in fundamental fears over the long-term economic and political future of South Africa.

The language of these annexers and expansionists also made the point that so long as there were 'unclaimed' African areas and resources open for seizure, there were likely to be local agencies of white expansion determined to move upon them. The power of these colonial and frontier agencies is accordingly not to be lightly set aside, especially in the Age of the New Imperialism. It may not have been true that 'If we get Mashonaland we shall get the balance of Africa'[78] – as Rhodes put it in a famed declaration – but this apparently 'absurd' bound into the interior, advocated by the Cape expansionists, seemed infinitely less odd when seen from within the inter-state conflicts of South Africa. It was still 'absurd' in its meaning for Great Britain and for Central Africa – as the modern history of Rhodesia has revealed – but there was no denying the fact that the Northern Expansion had its own logic within the context of the political and economic position of South Africa in the 1880s. And even for the Imperial Factor – which we are assured, by the historians of the empire was eager for a quiet life and not the drama of tropical advance – there were stark choices involved: if they wished to believe in such a concept as 'British South Africa', did they dare decline to support their local agents in the local Scrambles; and if they desired to safeguard British interests, both financial and strategic, was it not incumbent on them to intervene in the politics of the locality when the local situation appeared to be growing beyond the control of *both* their proxy agents, and their own influence?

Cast in this fashion, the great leap forward by the imperialists – both metropolitan and local – in the Northern Expansion appears rather more understandable, despite its undoubted complexity and apparent 'absurdity'. Internationalising the Scramble for South Africa had accordingly only accentuated the local themes of rivalry and expansion. The Cape feared an alien dominance of South Africa, first economically, then politically. Its involvement in the Road to the North, and the railway-tariff strategies, were all tied to the same rationale of who determined the local political economy. And just as land had once been the key feature of the earlier 'creeping partition' on-the-ground, so now labour joined it as the new *leitmotif* of expansion. The mining revolution had meant a staggering rise in labour demands. This ever-increasing employment of African workers on the mines soon exacerbated the labour shortages claimed by Natal and the Cape, where farmers and colonial politicians became yet more strident in their demands for labour, and still more vigorous in pressing for legislated social controls – such as direct taxation – to 'squeeze' a nascent proletariat from the reserve areas, out of the protectorates, and even off the legendary 'farm locations', all of which were suspected of harbouring an idle labour surplus.

The Imperial Factor became involved in this local version of the Scramble at three crucial levels. First, through its commitments to the colonists of the Cape (and somewhat less to those of Natal) as proxy-agents of British empire and interests in South Africa. Second, through the British concern to see that South Africa followed the paths of development, self-sufficiency and progress – rather than lapse backward into becoming a plural society forever at war within itself, and thereby inhibiting both capital investment and settler immigration. And lastly, because the Witwatersrand gold discoveries had, in fact, drawn a very considerable body of British capital to South Africa – Sir George Paish estimated it at about £350 million by the time of the Union (as compared to £375 million in Canada, £380 million in Australia, and £587 million in all of Latin America).[79]

None of these factors meant that the British *had* to annex anything; or that they suffered a sudden change in their intellectual metabolism, from cautious imperialists to rabid expansionists. But it did simply mean that they were not at all free agents to make free choices. These local factors pressed on them with varying degrees of intensity after 1886, pulled them ever more closely into the inter-state politics of South Africa, and pointed the way to some form of involvement in any Scramble for the resources of the region – whether those 'resources' were in the form of strategic harbours, settler farm lands, new mineral deposits, or supplies of black labour. As the agents of British interests – such as Rhodes and the high commissioner – never ceased to point out with pitiless remorslessness, if the British failed to support their economic and political allies in South Africa, then they would of necessity have to face up to the prospect of directly ruling the area themselves – or of abandoning it altogether.[80]

For reasons which therefore bore both on direct British interests, as well as on the very techniques of empire-administration in South Africa, the Imperial Factor came to play a central role in the transition from measured Partition to land-grabbing Scramble in the late 1880s. In the immediate aftermath of the gold discoveries of the 'Rand', the metropolitan authorities inclined to the view that the Transvaal could end up in an informal net of empire, through the operation of British capital, and skilled migrants. In Lord Salisbury's language, it would be the result of 'the action of internal forces'.[81]

That 'internal revolution' however failed to come about – and not even the fiasco of a Raid, of incitement by Rhodesian forces, could get it going. 'Capital' proved to be economically selfish and not at all patriotic; the Boer authorities indulged in fixing franchise qualifications, to assure their ascendancy in the economically booming republic; the mineral revolution generally skewed the whole regional economy of South Africa in a fashion which simply eroded the Cape–British position overall. The cumulative result was, accordingly, Cape economic and expansionist strategies of counter-poise which the British found absolutely necessary to support and facilitate. That was the real meaning of 'reluctant imperialism'. A Great Power was being progressively trapped and pressured by the narrowing options and circumstances of the local South African context.

7
The Road to the North 1886–88

In the aftermath of the highveld mineral revolution, the 'Road to the North' became *the* critical area of contention, expansion and incorporation in the developing Scramble for South Africa. 'Here are the politics of South Africa in a nutshell', Rhodes explained in 1888, having absorbed the lessons of that 'revolution' from the Cape and British perspective, 'Let us leave the Free State and the Transvaal to their destiny. We must adopt the whole responsibility for the interior . . . [and] we must always remember that the gist of the South African Question lies in the extension of the Cape colony to the Zambesi.'[1]

With some qualifications – the Rhodesians could *not* leave the Transvaal alone, especially after visions of gold in Central Africa evaporated in the early 1890s – this was a reasonable assessment of the main regional thrust now taken by the politics of the Scramble in South Africa after 1886. Bechuanaland, and its Zambesian borderlands, found itself the focus of the gathering forces of the Partition. This new dimension in the Scramble – and the fresh vigour given to the long-evolving Northern Expansion of the traders, humanitarians and frontier Boers – was derivative of the two sets of 'politics' operative in the South African Partition after the impact of the gold discoveries: the ever broadening sphere of international rivalry, and Great Power involvement, in Southern Africa generally; and the relentless advance of the local colonial societies towards acquiring African resources in their inter-state rivalry and development. The expansion of the Scramble, into the Road to the North, accordingly reflected the changing struggles for mastery now taking place in the changing political and economic balance of South Africa in the second half of the 1880s.

The Bechuanaland Protectorate as 'springboard'
to empire in Zambesia 1885–87

The prologue to the British advance into Zambesia, and the connecting element to the Scramble in South Africa before the highveld revolution, was to be the distinctly curious nature of the involvement of the Imperial Factor in Bechuanaland – curious because of its apparently strange combination of urgent imperatives to action, in the name of British interests generally, yet fumbling in the administrative techniques by which empire was to be carried forward.

At the root of the matter, yet again, lay the conduct and role of the Cape political and economic leadership. Cape trading and financial interests were adamant that the Road to the North should not fall into alien hands – whether Boer or German – to the extent that the Imperial Factor felt bound to support their expansionist postures in Bechuanaland. Yet the Cape declined to bear the administrative burdens of a portion of South Africa for which they had cried out so loud and so long. The colony preferred to allow that burden to fall on the Imperial Factor, while eagerly calculating the prospects in trade, labour supplies and mineral deposits, opened up by British control of Bechuanaland.

The Imperial Factor, of course, was not unaware of the self-centred tactics adopted by the Cape elite; and for this reason felt no desire to enlarge upon its already extensive administrative responsibility on the Road to the North. In the years 1885–86 the Partition of South-central Africa appeared, therefore, to have reached a moment of equipoise. The British would hold what they had already been driven to annex, in 1881–84, in the tortured politics of Anglo-Boer–Cape relations, but they would not advance another inch; the Cape wished to milk every advantage from that British initiative and the Protectorate which had been proclaimed, without itself sharing administrative costs; and the Transvaal burghers were so involved in the highveld revolution, and their push to create an independent rail outlet at the sea in South-east Africa, that they appeared to have given up serious involvement in the Road to the North and the struggles for Zambesia. In short, the Northern Expansion – so lively a feature of the Partition in 1884–85 – seemed to have ground to a premature halt.

In fact, it was not so much a 'halt', as merely a hiatus. The highveld mineral revolution changed the nature of local politics, and projected the Scramble towards the North, as the British agencies in South Africa attempted to counteract the power of the Transvaal state. Further, below the level of those high politics of supremacy, local forces of white expansion were still very active in agitating for concessions and expansion into Ndebele and Shona territory in Zambesia proper. As the forces of the New Imperialism prepared to involve Bechuanaland and Central Africa in their machinations, the activities of the older imperialism, of speculator and frontiersman, had already begun to create the conditions for a Scramble on the ground.

From Whitehall this was hard to see; but, from the vantage point of, say, King Lobengula's kraal at Bulawayo, it was all too clear.[2] By this very time Bulawayo was infested with concession hunters, not quite on the scale of Swaziland, but in a fashion sufficient to cause the Ndebele king some deep alarm. One such earnest concessionaire was, for example, Piet Grobler, a Transvaal burgher involved in the politics of frontier expansion, and who had duly obtained an important general concession from Lobengula (30 July 1887) which appeared to be the key to possible Boer intrusion into Zambesia. The following year Grobler died (July 1888) in a skirmish with Tswana forces from Kgama's territory. The Grobler treaty, and the contentions over his death – had his death been inspired by rivals from the Cape? – was an excellent symbol of the kind of local struggles already proceeding over potential expansion into Zambesia. It was also a warning to the neighbouring British administration in Bechuanaland of the complications which could arise if some sort of authority was not established in the hinterland. Indeed, the administrator of Bechuanaland, Sidney Shippard, took high alarm at this particular event in the general petty machinations of the concessionaires in Zambesia, for it potentially involved Transvaal interests. In Shippard's reaction to these growing contentions over the resources of hegemony of Zambesia there soon lay a powerful connecting force in the extension of British 'influence' – and accordingly the Scramble – into Central Africa.

Sidney Godolphin Alexander Shippard (1837–1901) was an Oxford trained lawyer, who had come to colonial South Africa in 1868. He had held a series of legal appointments under British authority in the Cape, and Griqualand West, before being appointed 'Administrator·of Bechuanaland' on 1 September 1885.[3] His colonial career had made him a convert to 'Cape Colonialism', and this was to be a crucial factor in his administrative politics. He was not at all an impartial representative of the Imperial Factor; even less a partisan friend of the Tswana, to whom he was 'Marana'maka' ('father of lies'). He was politically committed to Cape expansion into Bechuanaland, and personally committed to a close friendship with Rhodes, whom he had known since Oxford days. Shippard thus took an activist and expansionist approach to his role in the interior of Southern Africa. His alloted administrative duties concerned establishing law and order in Bechuanaland itself. In fact, Shippard spent much of his time outside the territory to the north. His presence at the court of Lobengula at Bulawayo – particularly in February 1888 – was to be absolutely crucial for the entry of Rhodesian interests into Central Africa. Shippard's assistant as deputy-commissioner, the Rev. John Smith Moffat (1835–1918) was also later to support Cape Colonialism, if it meant the opening up of Matabeleland to the influences of Christianity and 'civilisation'.[4] They both opposed the entry of the Boers into Central Africa, as the 'Grobler Treaty' apparently made likely.

Almost imperceptibly – and very 'privately' – British authority and responsibility was thus being drawn northwards daily by the small Shippard administration in Bechuanaland.[5] Operating for limited resources, Shippard tried to bring a degree of peace to an area still rife with concession hunters and land claimants. Order in 'British Bechuanaland', by Shippard's logic, involved some influence over events in the surrounding areas of contention, notably in Ndebele country. John Moffat was sent on a number of interior perambulations, partly to advise outlying chiefs and to regularise white claims, but also to strike good relations at Lobengula's court in order 'to promote at the same time the extensions of British influence and trade throughout Matabeleland and Mashonaland'.

If these 'Instructions' were not enough to produce a momentum towards further Partition in the interior, then the unofficial activities of Shippard were not unlikely to lead to such an expansion of the Scramble. Going beyond this official authority, he was soon urging on Moffat the need to check 'alien influences', such as the Grobler concession, by acquiring a monopoly treaty with Lobengula. As early as December 1887 the documents reveal him writing to Moffat:

You can point out to Lo Bengula [sic] the risk he runs of troublesome complications with Foreign States through the machinations of designing persons who will not scruple to make use of forged documents to obtain possession of his territory. You can also point out that Her Majesty's Government has no Sovereign rights and that if he desires to secure himself, against insidious attempts or open aggression without losing his independence, this result might be obtained if he could induce Her Majesty's Government to conclude with him a treaty similar to that recently entered into by Zambili [of the Thonga], a copy of which is enclosed.[6]

When Shippard was not worrying about Lobengula's security, and in case Moffat did not take his point, he was soon writing of the 'Treaty I should like to see concluded with Lobengula' – viz.: 'If we could once get as far as a Treaty *à la* Zambili we should be safe against all foreign interference in the country between the Zambesi and the Limpopo. It is this foreign interference that I so greatly dread.'[7] This was pure 'Rhodesian' thought; and it is no surprise to find that Shippard and Rhodes were in constant communication at this time. Rhodes waged a powerful propaganda campaign of personal letters on Shippard: 'I'm still working at my old idea and saw [the] Home Government about [the] Charter for Matabeleland [;] they appeared favourable', Rhodes wrote in a typical letter of mid-1888, 'but ... what I am afraid of is that Lo Bengula may give away his whole country to bogus Companies who will do nothing for Government [,] and what is left of that country will not be worth our De Beers Co[mpany]'s while to make an offer to pay [the] expenses of good government.'⁸ In the August, of 1888, Shippard received several such long letters from Rhodes, a man supposedly famed for his dislike of letter-writing. The most important of these letters was that of 14 August – which contained the famous 'Balance of Africa' phrase – and which also superbly well captured the nature of the Rhodes–Shippard relationship:

Rudd is going up to look at the country and see what he can do. He starts tomorrow and will see Newton at Vryburg. I am quite aware you cannot act freely with him but in [this] case he lays the ground work[;] the objects are the same, as[,] though he does not know [of] *our* big ideas, he will try and obtain what he desires for our companies, whose trust deeds I shall use for the objects I have in view.

You are perfectly right in your remark as to the point that in assisting me you are doing best for H.M. Government. . . . I sometimes think Kruger will fight for the interior but if he does we shall beat him[;] the great change is that the sentiment of the Dutch party in the Cape Colony is with us. They have been so badly treated by the Transvaal that we shall get their public support in any row that occurs over the Grobelaar [sic] matter and this is a total change as against the feeling during the Bechuanaland question.

My only fear is that I shall be too late with Lo Bengula as, of course, if his whole country is given away to adventurers, it is no use my stepping in for my Company to assist in the government of a shell. . .

If we get Matabelland we shall get the balance of Africa[.] I do not stop in my ideas at [the] Zambesi, and I am willing to work with you for it.⁹

Shippard was not, of course, the only recipient of these hastily written and ill-constructed Rhodes letters who was in the service of the British imperial administration. A similar 'campaign', of persuasion and flattery, was being waged on the British high commissioner in South Africa, and on members of his staff, notably F. J. Newton.¹⁰ But it was through Shippard, above all, that Rhodes and his financial syndicate could reach Moffat – being the 'man on the spot' the latter was the frontier agent most likely directly to influence the course of events, in the direction of further empire in the hinterland of South Africa.

The Moffat Treaty, 11 February 1888

The British foreign and colonial offices failed to see where this situation might lead. They described the crucial appointment of John Moffat, for example, with his ill-defined duties, as 'very innocuous'.¹¹ Gladstone might well have seen in it the almost certain egg of a Central African empire. For a start, John Moffat held strong views about the advance of European values in Africa; he also saw the Ndebele king as a militaristic tyrant. Schemes for the removal of Lobengula's influence were likely to win Moffat's approval; he saw Lobengula's fall as a means to advancing and civilising the mass of Ndebele people. Ultimately, he wondered aloud whether war alone would be able to bring this about[12] – 'it will be a blessing to the world when they are broken up'[13] – for although that might mean bloodshed, it would benefit 'tens of thousands of the subject races' of Lobengula.[14] He was later to find elements of the Providential Will in the arrival of the white Rhodesian pioneer column: 'I really begin to hope that it is God who is working out what has come about in a way that the will of no man could have accomplished.'[15] Despite the early history of the BSA Company in Rhodesia, Moffat continued to hold to that belief.[16]

Moffat wasted little time after he had been appointed to begin his work in the interior: he set out on a grand tour of his area of responsibility.[17] The journey, which was to last several months at the turn of 1887–88, culminated at Bulawayo.[18] On 11 February, the deputy commissioner and missionary not merely strengthened amicable ties between Great Britain and the great chief, but extracted from Lobengula the famed 'Moffat Treaty'. The chief promised to 'refrain from entering into any correspondence or treaty with any Foreign State or Power, to sell, alienate or cede ... any part of the territory under his chieftainship ... without the previous knowledge of the High Commissioner [at the Cape]'.[19] Rhodes was, naturally, delighted with Moffat's action. 'I am very glad you were so successful with Lo Bengula', he wrote conveying his congratulations through Shippard, 'at any rate now no one else can step in'.[20] The Treaty was to become the very stimulus for the further Rhodesian tactics in connection with the advance into Central Africa. For a start, it helped Rhodes towards acquiring the Trust Deeds which were to finance the enormous scheme. 'I [have] got my trust deed through', he wrote in April 1888, adding that he had met 'a little opposition at home', owing he suspected, 'to the wideness of the powers' which these Deeds granted him. But, if these powers went beyond the bounds of common sense, then the Moffat Treaty certainly went beyond Moffat's declared duties, in binding the British government to be responsible for all concessions in 'Zambesia'. One permanent official had partly foreseen the dangers of the tour: 'If we have a Commissioner perambulating the Protectorate in this way ... I doubt if we shall be long able to maintain an attitude of regarding the Protectorate as an external protectorate merely.'[21] The colonial secretary, Lord Knutsford,[22] had apparently no previous misgiving; but he now reacted sharply. He seriously doubted whether they should 'accept responsibility with regard to Lobengula and his country'. In fact, the more Lord Knutsford examined the Moffat Treaty the more he inclined to agree with his permanent officials, that the assistant-commissioner had shown an 'excess of zeal';[23] and he found it hard to fathom the 'reasons which have led Mr Moffat to conclude this agreement'.[24]

He was soon to be made aware of the 'reasons'. Not for the first or the last time, the redoubtable high commissioner, Sir Hercules Robinson, had been active on his own initiative. Interested, rather than devoted to the northern expansion,[25] he was convinced that it could never be carried out except by the Cape colony, or some local agency, bearing the financial and administrative costs. One significant conversation with Rhodes, in 1887, has been recorded. They were examining an African map together. Pointing to the 20° northern Protectorate frontier, Sir Hercules Robinson remarked: 'Well, I think that is enough ... And what a trouble it has been!' Rhodes disagreed. 'But where will you stop?', the high commissioner asked. Rhodes replied by pointing to the Tanganyika frontier. Robinson was apparently 'a little upset at this'. Rhodes talked on, and the high commissioner weakened; 'I think you should be satisfied with the Zambesi as a boundary.'[26] He was to be reminded of this and other statements in December 1887, when the Rhodes group became urgent for an extension of British authority to the Zambesi on hearing of the 'Grobler Treaty'.[27] In the company of his old friend Sidney Shippard, Rhodes rushed to see the high commissioner, then enjoying Christmas festivities at the old frontier-town Grahamstown, Eastern Cape.[28] Stressing the necessity for speed, and the irretrievable loss if Zambesia fell to the Afrikaners, Shippard and Rhodes finally won Robinson over[29] – but only on receiving certain financial promises from the Kimberley mining magnate. According to Rhodes:

His Excellency gave me a free hand, but he claimed from me a certain action when he considered that he had strained the responsibilities of Her Majesty's Government to the fullest extent. He claimed that I should take an obligation when we got to the 22nd degree of latitude, which was then the boundary of Khama's territory ... I found myself with the responsibility as far as the Zambesi – that is, so far as concerned the High Commissioner of the Colony, and far beyond, so far as the Foreign Office was concerned: I took upon myself these responsibilities because I thought it would come out all right.[30]

The details of this curious deal are largely borne out in Robinson's own published version of the story – in the *Times* of 7 November 1893. 'Up to 1888, Matabeleland was practically a sealed book', his inside 'history' of events recorded,

The country was unsafe for Europeans, and there were then resident in it only one missionary with his family and a few traders. A scramble for the interior of Africa had set in on all sides, and it was clear that the isolation of Matabeleland could not much longer be maintained. The Transvaal, as well as Portugal was casting longing eyes on the territory, and the former was striving to establish treaty relations with Lobengula. I accordingly early in that year, 1888, sent Mr Moffat up to Gubulawayo, with instructions to get Lobengula to sign a convention... To this Lobengula assented, and by the convention ... he undertook to refrain from entering into any correspondence or treaty with any foreign State or Power to sell, cede, or alienate any part of the countries under his chieftainship, or upon any other subject, without previous knowledge or sanction of the High Commission (in Cape Town).

Moffat was indeed so directed;[31] and the secretary to the high commissioner was to provide further documentation on this crucial initiative in his later 'Memoirs':

The territory then known as Matabeleland, ruled by Chief Lo Bengula, was known to contain gold, and both German and Boer concession seekers were fully aware of this fact.

Her Majesty's Government were not prepared to undertake the cost of the responsibility involved in the annexation of a territory far in the interior of South Africa. The Government of a barbarous people, given to raiding their neighbours, would have involved a constant military expenditure and the risk of a very heavy future expenditure in the case of rebellion.

As a result of interviews with Sir Sidney Shippard and others, Sir Hercules Robinson authorised Mr Moffatt [sic] to negotiate a Treaty with Lo Bengula which would bar the way to foreign concession seekers, and on the 11th February 1888 Lo Bengula signed a Treaty, binding himself on behalf of himself and people to refrain from entering into any correspondence or Treaty with any foreign state or Power, to sell, alienate, or cede, or permit, or countenance any sale, alienation, or cession, of the whole, or any part of the Amandebele country, or upon any other subject, without the previous knowledge and sanction of Her Majesty's High Commissioner for South Africa.

Such a Treaty effectually slammed the door in the face of Boer or Foreign ambitions.[32]

A startled British colonial secretary thus soon found himself reading an urgent despatch from the high commissioner which recommended strongly that the Moffat Treaty be supported – on the grounds that the treaty was essential if Zambesia was not to 'fall under influences adverse to British interests'.[33]

The expansion of the British 'sphere of influence'

After a week's consideration, the colonial secretary decided to uphold the high commissioner's action,[34] and to declare a British 'sphere of influence' in Zambesia, based on the Moffat Treaty.[35] Lord Salisbury stood by his colonial secretary,[36] once Lord Knutsford had made it clear to the foreign office that 'the present agreement with Lo Bengula is *not* in the nature of a Protectorate'.[37] John Mackenzie, who had been delighted at this apparent extension of direct trusteeship northwards, had his hopes quickly dashed. 'I think you are not quite correct in treating a declaration of "sphere of influence" as a declaration of "Protectorate"', the colonial secretary wrote on 9 December 1888. 'There is a wide difference between these terms.'[38]

What, then, did a 'sphere of influence' actually mean, and what did it cover? According to Knutsford, a British 'sphere of influence' was 'a notice to foreign nations that they must not interfere, but it falls short of a declared protectorate. It would, however, enable us to make such a declaration at any time, without giving just ground of complaint to foreign nations.'[39] An important colonial office Memorandum, on the 'Origins and Operations of the British South African Chartered Company',[40] explained the term as applying 'generally to such portions of Africa as Her Majesty's Government has considered that it might successfully claim as against other European Powers, to be reserved for acquisition under British administration'. It also stressed that it did 'not imply the existence of any British jurisdiction or Protectorate in such territory'.[41]

The actual area to be covered by this 'sphere of influence', was defined as 'the country north of the Protectorate and the Limpopo (or Crocodile) River, south of the Zambesi, east of longitude 20° E, and west of the Portuguese province of Sofala – that is to say, all the dominions of Khama and Lobengula'. The action was officially defended on the grounds that

the country became the theatre of a lively struggle between speculative groups almost too numerous to mention. . . In this state of things, Sir Hercules Robinson, who had been hitherto noted for his unswerving advocacy of a cautious policy in assuming responsibilities in the interior of South Africa, appears to have come to the conclusion that a step forward was the lesser of two evils, and that the Government should secure a controlling influence on the future of Mashonaland.[42]

John Moffat's actions, by this account, were merely 'confirming an old treaty of friendship entered into in 1836 between his father Mosilikatze [Umsiligaas] and the Governor of the Cape'.

Lord Salisbury finally concurred in this view. The declaration of the 'sphere of influence' was only intended to 'save (1) Matabeleland and Khama's country (2) the waterways of the Zambezi (3) the neutrality of Nyassa [from foreign interference]'.[43] It was, in short, a limited gesture towards a negative end. It kept Zambesia open, rather than placing it under any European administrative control. When the Portuguese objected to the sphere of influence, they were informed that the British Government 'do not recognize any claim of Portugal to Mashonaland, *which they hold to be under the rule and control of Lo Bengula*, and consequently under the influence of Great Britain'.[44] The sphere of influence, in its carefully limited terms, thus deliberately maintained the fiction that the political status quo had not altered in Zambesia. Lobengula was still ruler of Matabeleland. It also projected the even greater fiction that the action in no way committed Great Britain to further northern expansion into Matabele and Mashona lands.

In fact, as all too soon became clear, the declaration implied far more than it stated. One permanent colonial office clerk termed it rightly 'an entire novelty' in British policy;[45] and the high commissioner at the Cape claimed it was 'the most important point which has been gained by us for many a day [in Southern Africa]'.[46] Even the Confidential Memorandum cited above admitted that 'this treaty, from an international point of view, involved more than it expressed, being in fact enough to justify a claim to treat the country of Lo Bengula as reserved against other nations for Great Britain'.

This is certainly how the Cape,[47] and British financial interests viewed the declaration – quite apart from such non-British interest as Boer republicans, Germany and Portugal.[48] In declaring a 'sphere of influence', the British had in fact created an informal empire with all the potential for entanglements which such loose commitments invariably possessed in a period of rivalry and Partition.[49] Vivid illustration of this reality was soon provided by the two inter-related questions of the long-term administrative future of the British Bechuanaland Protectorate, and of the methods by which the 'sphere of influence' was to be secured against all alien groups.

Bechuanaland was hardly a self-sustaining colonial administration.[50] The British were in no doubt that they would ideally have liked to shunt responsibility for the territory onto the shoulders of the loyal Cape; but, the loyal Cape was, in 1887, busy fighting for its economic life against Kruger's republic. The Cape electorate was in no mood to carry imperial burdens into the interior of Africa at that time. All Cape politicians, whether of 'imperial' or '*Bond*' connections, were of like mind; and even Rhodes was heard to remark in the Cape Assembly that 'it is all bosh talking about interior extension; what we need is a railway to the goldfields'.[51]

Imperial attempts to lead the Cape towards Bechuanaland and Zambesia thus fell on their nose.[52] The railway and telegraph, which the Salisbury administration earnestly wished to see pushed up from the Cape colony, along the northern expansion, was duly begun – but it was directed towards the Rand. The vital artery that was to bring economic life, the pulse of blessed self-sufficient commerce and prosperity, to the moribund British possessions and options to the north of the Cape colony, was to be denied to British Bechuanaland. Sir Charles Mills, as Cape agent-general, voiced some of the increasing concern in London, in a private letter to John Merriman late in 1888:

Serious fears are entertained here that the Kimberley [railway] extension to the Vaal is hung up. Some three millions of money are ready for investment in railway enterprise towards the Zambesi, an enterprise which Her Majesty's Government have encouraged, and which has been patriotically supported in the City, to open up British trade through British territory to the British [Bechuanaland] Protectorate and its enormous mineral wealth.[53]

In the long-term, however, it appeared that if Zambesia were ever to be developed it would be through the heart of republican Afrikanerdom, now the centre of economic and railway activity in the interior of Southern Africa. From Cape Town the high commissioner prophesied a future of the darkest nature. Because the Cape colony had turned its back on railway extensions up the northern expansion, the value of Bechuanaland 'as a road to the interior will cease', and indeed the Colony will no longer even 'care to be bordered with that territory' – with the most dire results for the 'Imperial Factor', which will be faced with 'an expensive, valueless, inaccessible inland Crown Colony ... indefinitely on the hands of the Imperial Government'.[54] The only escape for the British government from this distinctly unwelcome situation was, according to Sir Hercules Robinson, to press Bechuanaland on the Cape administration at the earliest moment. That alone would pull the Cape politicians away from their obsessive concern with finding commercial agreement with the Transvaal. According to the proconsul, the British administration must abandon any talk of trusteeship in Bechuanaland, and ignore 'humanitarian' cries against the extension of Cape sub-imperialism:

[everyone] possessed of landed property in British Bechuanaland, black as well as white, would be better off, if it became part of the wealthy, self-governing Cape Colony, with a railway running through the territory, which would then have been the exclusive trade route to the north, than they would as the residents in an isolated impecunious Crown Colony, subsisting on Imperial grants in aid.[55]

But even this option went awry. Knutsford explained why in an anxious letter to Salisbury in October 1888: 'Sir Gordon Sprigg [premier of the Cape colony] said a few days ago that an offer from the Imperial Government to hand over Bechuanaland free of cost to the Cape was under consideration. This has excited writers in the press, and brought down strong attacks upon H.M. Gov[ernmen]t.'[56] This was putting it mildly. John Mackenzie and the influential humanitarian 'South African Committee'[57] had raised a howl at the prospect.[58] On balance, the colonial secretary came out against the idea, even though it had apparent advantages.

> In truth I am opposed to such annexation for the present.
> 1. Our possession, as a Crown Colony of Bechuanaland, strengthens our hold on the Protectorate beyond, and also on the vast territory which we have just declared to be 'within the sphere of British influence', and
> 2. I do not think the native Chiefs Montshiwa and Mankaroane would consent to the annexation; and we might have hereafter another Basutoland affair on our hands ... [where] the Cape Ministers mismanaged Basutoland – war ensued – and finally the Imperial Govt. had to resume the government of the territory.
> I do not doubt that it will some day or other be annexed to the Cape, but I would not in any way hasten such annexation.[59]

The gist of this argument was conveyed to the high commissioner,[60] who thought the British government had lost all sense of political reality; and he frankly told Lord Knutsford so.[61] The governor argued that the imperial government could not have its cake and eat it: it could not keep Bechuanaland, and still try and lure the Cape colony into being responsible for the future well-being of the northern expansion. Reviewing the correspondence and the general problem, Lord Salisbury came down on the side of his colonial secretary. 'I was very glad to receive your letter about Bechuanaland,' he informed Lord Knutsford;[62] 'I was getting quite frightened at the positive assurances in the newspapers.'

But if the colonial secretary was prepared to stand firm on Bechuanaland, he was determined to conciliate the Cape leaders in every other way. Some British ministers in the imperial cabinet committee furiously opposed the idea that the British government should sanction a Cape entry into a local customs union,[63] on the grounds that this would merely draw the colony within the engulfing maw of republican Afrikanerdom. Lord Knutsford declined to accept such a view,[64] though he did wonder why the Cape could not 'consider other modes of offering equivalent [commercial assistance] to Orange Free State for construction of railways'.[65] Knutsford soon knew why. The Cape ministry threatened extreme actions if the metropolitan imperialists did not accept the colony's railway and customs policy. The Cape premier telegraphed the colonial secretary in emphatic terms, on 9 February:

> The position is critical. The issues embraced are wide ... upon the Customs Union also depends Railway Construction and the existence of our trade. If it be not

assented ... I shall then resign. The result will be that the Imperial Government must then give way, or will have to face the question of the severance of the Colony [from the Empire].[66]

HM Government were in no position to argue with that sort of language. Knutsford, anyway, had never intended to oppose the Cape. The risks were too great. Salisbury was thus informed that 'to refuse, perhaps even to delay sanction of the engagement given, would tend to throw the Orange Free State into the hands of the Transvaal Republic and greatly strengthen the Afrikander party. It would be a serious thing to break up the proposed Customs Union between Cape and Orange Free State'.[67]

The Customs Conference, of course, fell through. Kruger preferred to place his faith in an independent outlet to Delagoa Bay.[68] Yet because of this failure, and because of Cape umbrage at Kruger's attitude, the high commissioner had been able to get the Sprigg ministry to think seriously of a colonial rail extension towards Bechuanaland.[69] A bill was in fact narrowly passed in the Cape assembly – the 'Bechuanaland Extension Bill' of late 1888 – only to be dashed to earth by the imperial government's attitude over the administration and settlement of Bechuanaland. The British government was back at square one.

The imperial predicament in the interior, however, only began there. Not only had the British failed to involve the Cape colony in the maintenance of the Protectorate and the defence of the 'sphere of influence'; they now also faced the diplomatic difficulty of preserving British rights and interests in Zambesia against several local challenges.[70] Something of the nature of the imperial predicament was reflected in the private reports submitted to Lord Salisbury by an eminent Victorian, J.E.C. Bodley,[71] who had recently toured Southern Africa. According to the premier, Bodley had assessed the situation as:

1. No hostile German influence.
2. Pondoland should be annexed.
3. Joubert is anti-German.
4. Delagoa Bay splendid harbour[;] opening it up would *ruin* Natal ...
5. Portuguese map includes Matabeleland.[72]

This analysis, and in particular point 5, was strongly supported by the high commissioner.[73] Robinson had, in May 1888, sent the colonial office a Portuguese map, showing Zambesia as under the sovereignty of the House of Braganza.[74] This provided the background to the official Portuguese rejection of the Moffat Treaty,[75] and of the British 'sphere of influence' itself.[76] Originally, neither the British government – which doubted the vigour of Portuguese imperialism – nor the Cape colony's leaders – who described the Portuguese Royal House as a 'monarchical myth'[77] – took seriously Lisbon's claim to Central Africa. A sudden renaissance of Portuguese imperial energy, backed by English capital, and German and French diplomatic support, changed that impression.[78]

Salisbury approached the problem in his usual pragmatic way; and the fact that he basically believed the Portuguese to be a 'very unreasonable people'[79] did not allow him to abandon his sensible posture in conducting foreign policy during the 'New Imperialism'.[80] Working from the basis that what the British government were exclusively concerned with was the area of the 'sphere of influence' (i.e. that land *south* of the Zambesi), together with protection for the extensive Scottish missionary endeavour in Livingstone's province of 'Nyassa', Salisbury proposed that Great Britain and Portugal should divide their central African empire along the line of the Zambesi.[81] The colonial secretary agreed,[82] and the matter was proposed to the Portuguese authorities,[83] with only two added provisos on this bald scheme: first, that the Zambesi must be open to free navigation;[84] and, second, that the colonial governments of the Cape and Natal should agree to give up any ambitions in the region north of the Zambesi.[85]

Portugal rejected these proposals[86] – living up to Salisbury's 'unreasonable people' tag – hoping to get all of central Africa through the action of their own local proconsuls and adventurers.[87] Abandoning hope of any easy amicable settlement – 'they [the Portuguese] have no policy except one of purposeless delay', Salisbury later remarked[88] – he embarked on a more forceful policy, symbolised by the appointment of Sir Harry Johnston as an 'emissary extraordinary' to Lisbon. As Salisbury told it, Johnston's task was to press the existing policy strongly in person: all Great Britain asked for was a recognition of the 'sphere of interest', and the neutrality of the mission provinces around Lake Nyassa, in return for acknowledgement that 'the territory north of Zambesia . . . [fell] exclusively within the Portuguese sphere of influence'.[89] But, as Johnston told it,[90] Lord Salisbury had given him instructions to keep Portugal entirely out of Central Africa. The instructions had been given personally by the Premier:

I entered Lord Salisbury's room. 'Since we last met', he said, 'there has been a change in the affairs of Nyasaland . . . The Portuguese seem now determined to push the matter forward to a settlement north of the Zambesi, either by taking as much as they can, or coming to terms with us over Nyasaland. D'Antes, the Portuguese minister, was here yesterday . . . [and] I suggested to him I might send you over to Lisbon to . . . see whether it is possible to come to an understanding about parties which would keep the Portuguese out of the Shire Highlands [Nyasaland] and central Zambesia . . . it would be a capital thing'.[91]

The Johnston–Portuguese informal agreement, however, did not even follow this account of Salisbury's instructions.[92] Johnston preferred to give up the legacy of Livingstone's missionary field in the Shire highlands for the area of northern Zambesia, on the grounds that this settlement would allow the grand vision of the Cape-to-Cairo link to be carried out, whereas securing Nyasa and losing the area immediately south of Tanganyika would close it for all time.[93] Johnston always claimed to have been the original architect of the Cape-to-Cairo scheme,[94] and it was not without significance that before he left for Lisbon he spent a whole night – from dinner party to breakfast – talking euphorically with a new acquaintance, Cecil Rhodes, then in London.[95]

Salisbury was not swept away by the Cape-to-Cairo vision; nor was he in the slightest degree enthusiastic about Johnston's negotiations.[96] As he told his colonial secretary,

As far as the North of Zambesi is concerned, it seems to me we gain absolutely nothing by Johnston's arrangement. The North West of Nyassa is not what we want – and if we did, we could always take it whenever we could get at it.

In order to gain this very shadowy present, we renounce all rights ever to claim the lower part of the Nyassa shore, on the banks of the Shire, or the banks of the Zambesi ... I do not see why we should execute this gratuitous renunciation and get nothing in return: especially as it is on the lower Nyassa and the Shire that are the settlements of the Missionaries and the Lakes Com[pany] – who will holloa [sic] out frightfully if they are handed over to Portugal.[97]

Knutsford, for once, disagreed with his premier. Closer to the Cape high commissioner, and therefore closer to colonial opinion, he saw merit in the Johnston arrangement denied to Salisbury.[98] In particular, Knutsford was aware of the strong Cape commercial interest that still existed in the area to the north of the Zambesi; and, therefore, for purely political reasons at the Cape, he argued that 'the advantages which we should gain north of the Zambesi are considerable'.[99]

Rhodes was then in London to gain public support for retaining an option on northern Zambesia, and to talk privately of financial support of the administration if the British authorities kept all of Central Africa, including the Shire highlands, out of Portuguese control.[100] Rhodes' gesture could not have been better timed. The British were faced with the difficulty of meeting the Portuguese claims,[101] yet balancing them against Cape sensitivity over their region.[102] They also had, more seriously, to contend with the vigorous challenge from Kruger's state. The republican Afrikaners had already refused to accept the 'sphere of influence',[103] and had indeed rejected outright the Moffat Treaty on which it was based.[104] Transvaal objections, which were largely based on the Grobler Treaty,[105] were given added importance when Grobler was murdered in the most mysterious of circumstances.[106] It was alleged, quite without foundation, that Rhodes and the Cape interests had connived at the murder to deny the Afrikaners' right to Zambesia.[107] Invalid though these Transvaal–Grobler claims were,[108] the high commissioner still took the matter of the Afrikaner concession most seriously, mainly on the grounds that in the London Convention the British government had failed to bind the Transvalers from expanding north-wards.[109] Highly alarmed, Lord Knutsford stated firmly in reply that the Convention *had* contained the Transvaal:

it was a principal aspect of H M Government in concluding that Convention to secure that the trade routes to the northward . . . should not lie within the Republic. In fact, the northern limit of the Republic was in that Convention definitely fixed, with its other boundaries . . . In the same Convention (Article V), in consequence of the troubles which had occurred with the tribes to the eastward and westwards of the Republic, it was expressly stipulated that the South African Republic should make no treaties with those tribes except with the previous approval of Her Majesty's Government.[110]

In lecturing Sir Hercules Robinson – a leading architect of that Convention – Lord Knutsford was in so many senses whistling to keep up his courage. To Lord Salisbury he admitted that the existence of the London Conven-tion was not enough to ensure that the Afrikaners would not expand into Zambesia, as they had into Bechuanaland, Zululand and Swaziland:

This is an important question, and must now be dealt with. It was touched upon at the last Cabinet and Sir M. Hicks Beach was in favour of letting the Boers extend to the North . . . His view is not consistent with the strict terms of the Convention of London, though I am not sure that any objection was felt at that time to the Boers extending to the North of the fixed boundaries of the Republic. But, whatever may have been then thought upon this point, the position of affairs is now different; and I apprehend that we intend to prevent the *annexation* of Matabeleland by Boers or any Foreign Power, although we are quite willing that all should trade freely there and get mining and other concessions.[111]

Yet how was the British government to halt an Afrikaner policy of encroachment, if the Transvaal contested the interpretation of the London Convention through frontier-expansion? By another Warren-style imperial expedition, which would rouse Afrikanerdom and make the politics of collaboration at the Cape yet more difficult? Hardly. The colonial secretary knew this. His response was an intriguing insight into the position which the British imperial authorities felt themselves to occupy in dealing with Afrikanerdom within Southern African politics.

We should be much abused in this country if we let the Boers annex Matabeleland and Mashonaland, as they are rich territories, and concessions by Lo Bengula are held by some influential people; but we shall have to face considerable danger of conflict with the Boers, if we bar them from extension to the North. I should be inclined to compromise with them, by letting it be known that if they come to terms with Umbandine [of Swaziland] we shall not prevent them from protecting or annexing that country.[112]

It was a poor foreign policy which found it necessary to resort to the principles of a 'territorial bribe', to secure an interest based on a recognised international claim in the 'sphere of influence'. But Southern Africa was hard on both imperial proconsuls – it was known as the 'graveyard of reputations' – and on imperial policies.

At almost exactly this time, just when the British were casting about in a state of policy-making disarray, searching for that elusive approach which would secure their interests in the interior, check the Transvaal Afrikaners, yet also find support from the *Bond* alliance at the Cape, the Rhodes group put forward a local initiative which gave new direction to events, and which also pointed the way out of the impasses faced by the Imperial Factor, by raising the possibility of empire by chartered company.[113]

The Rudd Concession, 30 October 1888

The British authorities had seen the 'sphere of influence' and the Moffat Treaty in essentially negative terms; a way of holding the position in the interior against rival forces. The local expansionists, in contrast, perceived these actions as but the prelude to formal empire in Zambesia. They determined to convert the option obtained by the Moffat Treaty into a positive act of possession and conquest before rival concessionaires determined the fate of Zambesia by actual piecemeal occupation and concession.

Why did the Rhodes group succeed then where so many other contenders had failed? There was in fact little that was particularly heroic about their success, and a number of more mundane administrative and political factors must be brought into play in analysing the actual development of the Scramble. Three elements in particular deserve comment: the role of the local British administrative corps in South Africa; the external policy of the Ndebele state; and the place of the missionaries in the development of Lobengula's diplomacy.

The close connection of the Rhodes syndicate to the British representatives-in-the-field was crucial. Soon after the Moffat Treaty was recommended to Whitehall by the high commissioner, a Rhodes team of Charles

Rudd, Rochfort Maguire and 'Matabele' Thompson left almost immediately to race for the court of Lobengula, where Shippard and Moffat waited. 'They are of course going up to see the King and hope to be able to obtain something from him on behalf of Mr Rhodes (really De Beers Company) which would make it worth his while to invest a large amount of capital in that country', a member of the high commissioner's staff wrote privately to Moffat, so exposing the whole Rhodesian tactic.[114]

> You know yourself what an enthusiast Rhodes is in the matter of the extension of British influence northwards; in this case he is doubly enthusiastic, viz. politically and financially. I had a good deal of talk with him both in Kimberley and Capetown and he is I am sure prepared to do everything that Lo Bengula and those around him may wish; if the King will trust him and make an extensive concession.

This letter, from Newton, also revealed the fact that the high commissioner's office was utterly behind the private Rhodesian syndicate, to the cost of all other rival enterprises. Most improperly, Newton continued:

> Without the slightest wish to hamper you or make any recommendation, I can only say that Mr Rhodes' enterprise is genuine, and that, if the King sees what is inevitable, viz. that capital is necessary to develop his country, no better man could be found to supply him with it.
>
> Of course I write this purely in a private capacity and rather as a friend of Mr Rhodes, who however has not suggested that I should do so, either directly or indirectly, and I trust you will forgive me if you think I have paid too much. I confess I should like to see a thorough Imperialist and good man of business at the same time, as he undoubtedly is, get a good footing in that country. Much more can be done by private enterprise than by lukewarm advances of the Colonial Office at home.[115]

To the speed and vigour of his actions, Rhodes thus added the secret support of Government House, Cape Town. It would have been unusual if he had now failed in his immediate task – replacing the Moffat Treaty with a comprehensive concession. Shippard 'happened' to appear at Bulawayo – from 16 to 22 October – during the crucial negotiations with Lobengula. He claimed impartiality in his role, but it was clear that when the Rudd Concession was signed later that month (30 October 1888)[116] his position had not been one of detachment. 'Shippard and Moffat did all they could for us', a member of the Rhodes team wrote happily to F. J. Newton at the close of the negotiations with Lobengula.[117] Shippard was certainly to be delighted when Rhodes received a charter the next year; and Shippard later joined the Board of Directors of the BSA Company after his official retirement.

Further, the high commissioner himself placed his influence and stature behind the Rudd concession. 'When this concession was submitted to me in Cape Town,' Robinson reminisced very frankly soon after in his retirement,

it appeared to me, although a monopoly of the kind was not free from objections, it was, on the whole, in the interests of the Matabele that they should have to deal with one set of *substantial* concessionaires instead of, as in Swaziland, with a number of adventurers of different nationalities, who would have quarrelled amongst themselves and with the natives, and who would have been amenable to no practical control.[118]

In such a situation, and bearing in mind Robinson's political closeness to Rhodes, he immediately supported the Cape syndicate: 'I . . . recommended that the Rudd Concession should be recognized by Her Majesty's Government, and directed Mr Moffat to take up his residence at Bulawayo and assist Lobengula with his advice, and to keep the High Commissioner informed of the progress of events.'[119]

If the influence of the local imperial authorities had tended to favour, rather than hinder the Rhodes group, this still does not explain why the Ndebele agreed to the Rudd document.[120] After all, Lobengula had successfully kept at Bay a myriad of concession hunters over the course of some years.[121] Why did he now make the tragic error of signing away his country through treaty and concession such as those possessed by the Rhodesian expansionists?

The answer is relatively clear: Lobengula did not think he was 'signing away' his country. Lobengula was not 'Scrambling for protection', in the fashion of Kgama or Moshweshwe; but he *was* trying to regulate the character of his external relations, through treaty-agreement with the leading concessionaire groups, or their parent states. In this sense, he followed the policies of his father: Mzilikazi had told a missionary in 1862, in answer to a question on the number of Afrikaners active in Matabeleland, 'Oh, they come to trade and hunt and then they go about their business. It is to people settling in the country that the Matabele object.'[122] Missions were also tolerated within the state, under strict terms; they were useful as a source of advice on the outside world, and Ndebele traditionalism was so strong they made almost no converts. This apparently fragile policy, of holding the whites at bay by select treaties, and of holding back the *amatjha* (unmarried soldiers) eager to wash their spears, worked remarkably well until the 1880s. But, in the shrewd assessment of one historian, the Ndebele 'then entered the dangerous world of the Scramble against a history which in a sense was too successful'.[123]

Independent co-existence had come to mean isolation: rivalry with

Tswana chiefs meant no likely African allies: deep suspicion of the Afrikaners' ambitions in Central Africa had made a Transvaal alliance unthinkable. Lobengula was not in fact well placed to handle any surge of the European stream into his country: he had sufficient power, based on his past successes, to continue his select concessions, but not enough to conciliate the increasing white pressures without falling victim to an internal coup from his watchful *indunas* and army.[124]

After 1888 the Scramble in South Africa proper began to impinge on Zambesia, as an ever greater number of adventurers and filibusters looked eagerly on the lands of the Ndebele and Shona. Lobengula's problems now became acute, and the hidden fragility of his earlier policies was starkly revealed. Short of either resisting – as his conservatives wished – or attempting to secure British protection, there was no middle way once the forces of the white frontier pressed north. Yet it was that 'middle-way' which Lobengula still attempted. Moffat quite correctly surmised that, at base, Lobengula wanted 'to be left alone', and deeply suspected signing extensive concessions 'from a fear of being entrapped into something more than he really agrees to'.

Yet he could not simply ignore the whites, especially the Afrikaners. In February 1888 Lobengula signed the Moffat Treaty: he did so with distinct reluctance, after careful scrutiny of its limited terms, and on the strong advice of a trusted missionary – John Moffat.[125] It appears that Lobengula saw it as a treaty of friendship with the British, and a useful counterpoise to Afrikaner power. He did *not* see it as a request for British overlordship or intervention; nor of course did the metropolitan British authorities, who still saw Lobengula as ruler of Matabeleland. It was only the local forces of colonialism and frontier expansion who saw this document as the thin edge of the wedge into Lobengula's territory.

It was the almost overwhelming flood of concession-seekers which after 1888 then brought great crisis to the Ndebele state. Moffat reported that Lobengula was considerably afraid of the developing situation: his reaction was 'to aim at a Chinese isolation from the rest of the world', and to 'concede less and less to [the] Europeans' who pestered him from concessions.[126] He was not to be allowed his isolation. Rumours of Transvaal ambitions in Zambesia abounded in 1888, and the concession-seekers camped on the edge of Bulawayo in a relentless vulture fashion. Moffat now played a critical role by advising Lobengula that 'it would be an advantage for him to act in concert with one powerful company who would simplify matters for him'.[127]

The Rudd group, apparently strongly backed by the local British authorities, was offering just such a deal. A single, 'super-concession', would rid Lobengula of all the petty concessionaires *without* losing his political sovereignty: the British syndicate would merely exploit the minerals, and only bring in such whites as were needed for the technical operations. This was probably the only kind of concession Lobengula would sign, or his people would allow him to sign. In return for allowing the British agency to 'dig a hole' – as Ndebele oral tradition has it[128] – Lobengula believed he had solved the problem of the concessionaires *and* the Afrikaner political threat. His tragic mistake was not in signing the Rudd Concession – which indeed made no mention of a white settlement colony – but in believing the intentions of the Rhodesian group as they explained them in the verbal assurances spoken over the Concession document.[129] This strategy is pretty well the advice Rhodes had given Rudd in getting Lobengula to sign the document. He told Rudd to stick to the '*"Home Rule" trick*' – 'Go on the lines of becoming his Gold Commissioner and working for him' for 'he will not understand Companies [and] you can apportion it afterwards'. Above all, 'Stick to Home Rule, and Matabeleland for the Matabele [;] I am sure it is the ticket.'[130]

It was indeed. The Rudd Concession eventually formed the very basis of the White Partition of Central Africa and the subjection of the Ndebele. Rumours of how the Rhodesians intended to use the Rudd Concession – particularly the loose phrase 'full power to do all things necessary to win and procure' minerals – as a basis to 'open up' Zambesia for colonisation, soon reached Lobengula and the Ndebele *indunas*. The concessionaires were bitterly denounced; the Concession itself was suspended; and finally, on 18 January 1889, repudiated by the Ndebele leadership. Lobengula also despatched two leading *indunas* – in the company of one of Rhodes' opponents, E. A. Maund, of the Bechuanaland Exploring Company – to protest the Ndebele case to the Queen's government in London. Desperately Lobengula tried to remove the noose which he felt settling around his society. His best hope now lay in securing a British promise not to sanction any white advance into the 'sphere of influence'; and that, as we shall see, was not a realistic hope. From the moment the imperial government decided to deploy Cape colonialism as part of its larger South African imperial strategies – through the technique of a charter for Rhodes – rather than exclude it from Central Africa, the Ndebele were left to face the European incursions in isolation. Lobengula had lost the struggle for 'a Chinese isolation'.

In the evolution of that situation, the 'missionary factor' was also of importance, though it was not simply one of helping the concessionaires to trick Lobengula into making unfavourable agreements for the Ndebele, or using their quasi-official roles as British agents to steer the chief towards concessions for the Rhodesian syndicate, as is sometimes alleged.

The Protestant ideology of the missionaries, their proselytising zeal and humanitarian instincts, all pressed them towards support for the 'opening up' of Zambesia to Western cultural influence, and to 'cracking open' the pagan societies of the interior to Christian values. Yet many missionaries also feared the chartering of a private white agency of expansion as a means of bringing 'civilisation' to colonial Africa. 'I am conscious . . . that there is a good reason for saying that the missionary interest has been on the side of the Chartered Company', as the Rev. R. W. Thompson of the London Missionary Society commented in 1893; 'The fact is, some of us who have been pretty closely connected with work in Matabeleland for many years past, have been sorely troubled as to the attitude we ought to take.'[131]

Some humanitarians, like John Moffat, accepted the chartered company as the best agency of civilisation – though *not* the ideal agency – and placed their faith in a carefully circumscribed charter to protect human rights. They were pushed to set aside their misgivings over the Rhodesian group by their antipathy to the Ndebele state – 'a miserable people . . . [who] have made myriads of other people miserable too' (Moffat)[132] – and the resilience of such African cultures to the improving influences of individual missionaries or traders. 'It is where the political organisation is most perfect, and the social system still in its aboriginal vigour,' as John Moffat once well expressed it, 'that the missionary has the least success in making an impression.'[133] Only the conquest, and subjection of such societies, could indeed open them up to the Protestant gospel. Again, John Moffat's thoughts are highly pertinent: 'I fear there will be no change for the better until there has been a breaking-up of the Matabele power and a change in the whole regime.'[134] The temptation to see in the charter policy the best hope for creating a new social order in Matabeleland thus made many missionaries the unlikely yet undoubted allies, of Rhodes' Cape colonialism. 'We, on the spot,' one missionary wrote from Zambesia, 'hail the Charter with joy, as a God-sent deliverer.'[135]

Not all missionaries, of course, came to the same conclusion; not all joined with John Moffat in August 1889 in urging the swift grant of the charter, so that the imperial company might 'the sooner get to work in the field'.[136] John Mackenzie, for example, despite equally passionate feelings about Ndebele pagan cultural forms, still refused to believe that the agency of a company so intimately connected with Cape colonialism was adequate, or proper, as the means to civilising and converting the Ndebele to a Protestant way of life. His experience in local South African politics had convinced him of the necessity to keep African societies out of the control of settler assemblies. Mackenzie was adamant that the BSA Company meant domination from Cape Town, not London. As in Bechuanaland he favoured direct British imperialism, and absolutely opposed local 'colonialism'.[137]

This division among the humanitarians was also important as an element in the coming of the Scramble to Zambesia. It meant that the humanitarian lobby in British politics was divided, and in its division there lay opportunity for the expansionist syndicates. Further, by finding some support among the missionaries, the aspirants for a royal charter could claim humanitarianism as one of their avowed 'civilising' objectives in Zambesia. 'The merits of the case are shortly these', Rhodes flatly explained in 1889, the Rudd 'concession has led to the Charter, which will result in the civilizing of the interior'.[138] It also allowed the British authorities to recommend BSA Company to Lobengula as agents of responsible imperialism – 'The Queen repeats that the Chartered Company are the friends of Lo Bengula, and she gave them the Charter because they would keep peace between Matabele and the white men'[139] – and for George Cawston to claim on behalf of the company that one of its primary objectives was serving the interests of the Africans. The London *Times* happily celebrated the founding of the BSA Company as a supreme example of the progressive combination of 'British capitalists and philanthropists'; while the *Pall Mall Gazette* spoke grandly of 'Civilization by Company'.[140] Rhodes gleefully, and more pragmatically, spoke of 'philanthropy plus 5%'.

The missionaries were thus deeply important in the chartering of the imperial company. The founders of that company welcomed missionary support – Rhodes was pleased to tell a missionary with the Ndebele, 'if there is anything needed for your mission, be sure to let me know'[141] – especially when it could be secured from well-known members of the humanitarian community, such as John Moffat. Indeed, Moffat's ultimate support was doubly important: it assisted the BSA Company founders in pressing their otherwise questionable 'civilising' claims so strongly, while out in Africa itself, as the Scramble gathered momentum in the Road to the North, it was Moffat's role as imperial emissary from British Bechuanaland which had been of such value in securing the crucial concession on which this further dimension of the Partition in South Africa could soon roll forward.

A trigger had been pulled; local and expansive forces had been encouraged and released; some sort of British imperial province in the heart of the hinterland of South Africa was now a very strong likelihood in the politics of Partition. Although they possessed similar facts, the metropolitan authorities preferred not to see the local events in the Road to the North as leading to that conclusion. But the makers of that series of local thrusts in the Northern Expansion knew exactly what they were about, and indeed harboured dreams of economic exploitation and development, by settler colonialism from the Cape, on a scale which would have left even the most ardent of metropolitan imperial enthusiasts aghast.

Certainly the Imperial Factor felt no great enthusiasm for Zambesia in the light of the Rudd Concession; at that very moment, however, the local expansionists were ecstatic. 'Our concession,' as Rhodes excitedly wrote, 'is so gigantic it is like giving a man the whole of Australia.'[142]

8
Empire by chartered company 1888–89

The British expansion into Zambesia formed one of the great events in the general Partition of Africa and of the Scramble by the New Imperialism for the tropical world beyond Europe. Yet it had about it – in its origins, technique and consequences – peculiar and individual qualities which equally well tied it to a narrower regional context of events, and to a closer localised South African political context.

The advance of the British empire into Zambesia was to be expansion rooted in the existent Partition of the Road to the North and the 'sphere of influence' declared from the Bechuanaland protectorate. It was to be undertaken not by metropolitan officials but by the agency of a chartered company having strong South African support. It was intended as a means of solving problems of hegemony south of the Zambesi quite as much as meeting the demands of the rivalry implicit in the New Imperialism's impact in Central Africa. It was to be expansion expressed not merely by foreign office representation, but by the arrival of a column of settlers, para-military police, and mineral speculators in the 1890s – all largely drawn from the colonial societies of South Africa. And it was to be a uniquely personalised empire: the very fact that the new territory was, in an unprecedented action, to be given the name of a living Cape politician and capitalist had its own revealing significance.

Empire by chartered company in Zambesia was thus an important development in the Scramble for Africa; it was also a large post-script to the final Partition of South Africa which had been moving forward, with gathering momentum, since the 1870s. It certainly had about it all the hallmarks of the process of local conquest and rivalry: the role of private enterprise forces active in African lands, seeking concessions and 'alliances'; the vigorous activism of Cape economic interests; the somewhat desperate attempts by African leaders to find security, or buy protection, against subjection; the pressure of Boers and frontiersmen to expand their state, and the Cape colonial counterpoise to that informal expansion; and the determination by the Imperial Factor to solve its problems of international strategic needs and prestige, while at the same time working to secure the Cape Colony as its major proxy-agent in the politics of South Africa.

To say that is clearly to give Rhodes and his supporters – both financial and political – a very important role in the extension of the Scramble to Zambesia.[1] He was by the later 1880s certainly 'a phenomenon' – James Innes' memorable phrase[2] – in the politics of South Africa: he stood at the head of the Cape economic interests concerned with the evolving regional patterns of development, and he was the crucial link-figure in the metropolitan–colonial axis of local empire politics. Yet his role too needs careful definition and refinement.[3] The motivation for his imperialism was, beyond certain important ideological and cultural inclinations about British dominance or influence, at least partly financial and personal. The development of his emphasis on the need for expansion under metropolitan aegis into Zambesia was part and parcel of his activities as a South African mining capitalist: the uncertain fortunes of his Witwatersrand investments inclined Rhodes to an intense interest in the possibility of a 'second Rand' in Zambesia, and the failure to find such a mineral resource in the early 1890s simply returned the focus to the Transvaal.[4]

Rhodes' power was, however, not exclusively financial and his motives more complex than personal gain or private 'ego-satisfaction'. He was fundamentally a Cape expansionist, his power residing in a less tangible form than his capital: namely, the power generated by Cape Colonialism in South African politics. The charter was ultimately granted to representatives of that 'British' expansionist force, and not merely to the best capitalised of the syndicates eager to conquer and exploit Central Africa. Rhodes' connection to Hofmeyr's *Bond*, and the Cape Dutch interests generally, was crucial – as also was the support given the Rhodesians by the British high commissioner at the Cape.

To arch imperialists it was a sorry way to conduct an empire when a Great Power became so indebted to local agencies to maintain its interests and further its mission. According to Milner, after the mid 1880s the British resolution to deal with South Africa began to 'wobble', and the Imperial Factor 'allowed the Cape Government, bowing to the influence of the Dutch party, to take the starch out of our resolution'.[5] Yet, to the British metropolitan and local authorities in the era of the Scramble, it was the only workable political strategy, other than direct imperial rule with all its fiscal burdens. Accordingly, from at least 1886 onward, the British administration accepted the necessity of giving primacy 'to the views of the colonial governments of the Cape and Natal in respect of the external affairs affecting the Colony'.[6] In so many ways, the choice for the Imperial Factor, in the case of the expansion into Zambesia, was therefore not really between chartered empire and trusteeship protectorates, but rather empire by company, or not at all.

Further, the new political slogan of the highveld – 'Africa for the Afrikaners',[7] south of the Zambesi – also sounded infinitely less menacing when blunted by an alliance between the Imperial Factor and Cape Dutch, worked through the political association of Rhodes and Hofmeyr. The charter for Zambesia was developed in that overall context of South African collaborative empire politics in the later 1880s.

The British were indeed to be very watchful that any new departures in frontier expansion should not be in the form of trusteeship protectorates if this could be avoided at all; their ideal of 'expansion' in Southern Africa was through local agents, preferably Cape Colonialism. They desired no more Basutolands and Bechuanalands. It was in this area of administration, the very technique of empire, that the aims of the British policy-makers meshed with the ambitions of the local settler expansionists.[8]

These several themes were all to be exhibited in the chartering of a company to conduct empire in Zambesia – in the name of British interests in South Africa generally. This chapter follows the tangled course of the evolution and making of the charter policy 1888–89, not by treating it as a separate case-study in the Partition of Africa, but rather within the broad context of the evolving Scramble for South Africa in the later 1880s. Empire by chartered company, in the far hinterland of the region, was simply the latest manifestation of the local Partition of the interior which had developed since the 'highveld revolution', Boer expansion and the German annexations, had focused attention on the 'Road to the North' and South-central Africa.

The beginnings of imperialism by financial syndicate 1888

'You will see', the British colonial secretary wrote to his premier (1 May 1889) in some awe at the capitalised power and projected ambitions of the Rhodes group for conquering and administering Zambesia, 'that he proposes to help you'.[9]

Lord Salisbury was not, of course, automatically won over. He was suspicious of colonial politicians who came bearing gifts – especially when the 'assistance' was related so closely to their own financial and expansionist ambitions in Africa. But the idea of empire by charter, imperialism by controlled and self-sufficient British agency, danced before the eyes of penny-pinching Whitehall in a fashion both tempting and dazzling. As a policy or technique for empire it had its great hazards:

the memories of the consequences of other charter policies – not least in the India of 1857 – were still sharp; and the humanitarian lobby in British politics, firmly rooted in the legendary 'non-conformist conscience', was not lightly to be shrugged aside in an age of party flux. Yet for all that, empire by chartered company was distinctly attractive as a notion, particularly if the suitable syndicate could be found: 'suitable' so far as its financing, leadership, humanitarian respectability and political credentials in colonial South Africa was involved.[10] Clearly the personnel of any proposed chartered company would be a matter quite as important as the actual concessions possessed in the lands of the Shona and Ndebele. What was above all crucial was the need to combine respectability and responsibility with free enterprise and economic exploitation.

Given these prerequisites, there were in the end only two major contenders for a charter. One was the Rhodesian group, which possessed excellent concessions, the involvement of certain finance capital interests in the Kimberley and Johannesburg mineral 'houses', and the likely political support of Cape expansionism and the British imperial high officialdom in South Africa. The rival group, led by Lord Gifford and George Cawston, had small Cape or local imperial support and weaker concessions; but they did have better personal credentials than the Rhodesians with respect to both London money and general public acceptability in British political circles – they were supported by noted English and continental financial houses, together with a certain influential section of the humanitarian lobby, including members of the 'South African Committee'.

Rhodes was indeed to get his charter in late-1889, but only after he had convinced Salisbury of his political and economic credibility within Cape 'colonialism'; only after he had faced a concerted agitation by John Mackenzie's humanitarian group; and only after he had used his talents, as the 'great amalgamator', to the full, in making alliance with the rival 'Exploring Company' syndicate. These difficulties faced by the Rhodesians were larger and deeper than most of Rhodes' biographers have indicated; yet they are an integral part of the politics of Charter imperialism in Zambesia.

The Gifford–Cawston syndicate had evolved from a concession granted by Kgama, in 1887, to the 'Northern Gold Field's Exploration Syndicate of Cape Town' of Frank Johnson and Maurice Heaney. They were bought out, in April 1888, by the Bechuanaland Exploration Company – with Paris and London money – which worked to exploit the Protectorate and to develop a rail communication with Cape Town. It was this Bechuanaland company which spawned the 'Exploring Company' later in 1888, with the express purpose of joining the Scramble for concessions in Lobengula's territory.[11] Their agent in Bulawayo, the ubiquitous Edward Arthur Maund (1851–

1932), initially failed to acquire a concession equal to that of the Rudd document. But Maund was hopeful of working the anti-Rhodesian feeling, which had soon grown up in Bulawayo, to some advantage.

That advantage came surprisingly soon. Within two months of the Rudd Concession being granted, Lobengula was deeply suspicious of the Rhodesians, and Maund was present and ready to assist him in that thinking. Maund's real opportunity thus came in November (1888) when Lobengula asked him to take two of his trusted *indunas* to London to protest the Portuguese encroachments on his country, and to ask advice on the general white encroachments. Maund had high hopes that this mission could be used to discredit the Rudd Concession, and eventually lead to the grant of a new 'super concession' to the 'Exploring Company'. At the very least he hoped to acquire a large concession in the Mazoe Valley region.[12] Maund took considerable comfort from the fact that Lobengula personally assured him (24 November) that there would be no further concessions signed until the London deputation returned to Bulawayo, and that anyway the Rudd agreement was most circumscribed in what it granted.[13] Maund had good reason to feel confident as he hurried off to London, accompanied by the two *indunas*: he carried with him a written despatch from Lobengula protesting the Portuguese imperialism – which happened to include the Mazoe Valley – and a secret oral message from Lobengula concerning the white concessionaires, which clearly could be given an emphasis which discredited the Rhodes–Rudd strategy.[14]

Awaiting Maund in London, the directors of the Exploring Company had also gained advantages for their enterprise in 1888 as well. The Gifford–Cawston syndicate had impressed the metropolitan authorities with their financial and personal credentials, while their enthusiasm to build a rail-line into the interior to develop the Bechuanaland Protectorate had a special appeal at the colonial office.[15] Outside official circles, the syndicate was also gaining considerable support from noted humanitarians. So strong did the Gifford–Cawston group feel that they now laboured over the drafting of a charter for an enterprise to be called 'The British Imperial Central Africa Company'. A copy of this intriguing document resides in the Maund Papers, and is dated 6 September 1888. Maund has added this explanatory marginalia:

This draft of a Charter . . . was drawn up by Lord Gifford and Messrs. Cawston and Maund in September 1888, and finally in March 1889, before Mr Rhodes came from S. Africa, and so before any amalgamation of the Rudd–Rhodes interest with Lord Gifford's 'The Exploring Co. Ltd.', which proved that the Chartered Co., 'British South Africa Company', was not Mr Rhodes' scheme but was formed under the auspices of the Exploring Co. C. J. Rhodes and Alfred Beit joined the Board of the

Exploring Co. and the charter was carried through, the name being modified, 'Imperial' and 'Central' being left out, B.S.A. remaining.

[Initialled] E.A.M.[16]

Gifford and Cawston also, naturally, took extreme pleasure in Maund's work at Bulawayo, and awaited his impending arrival in London, with the *indunas*, in a state of some delight. It seemed that they were on the way to success where so many others had failed in their plans to exploit and develop Zambesia. Maund received the most warm of letters from Gifford in respect of his work in Africa for the syndicate.[17] At the very least, the London syndicate was now, as an authority on Rhodes has recently suggested,[18] in a position to frustrate the Rhodesian designs – an opinion supported by Rhodes himself: 'Everything was going well . . . when Mr Maund turned up.'[19]

The high commissioner and Cape 'Colonialism'

Gifford and Cawston might well have secured a charter for Central Africa had they faced only Rhodes. But the British high commissioner in Southern Africa, Robinson, was in fact the crucial advocate of the Rhodesian group at the Cape, and the policy of expanding local colonialism within official circles. It was he who constantly stressed the need for an agency of empire in the 'sphere of empire', and the necessity of seeing that such an agency was based on the Cape, with local political support from the Rhodes–Hofmeyr alliance. His role in the granting of the charter to the Rhodesian group was simply crucial, and has hitherto not received the attention it deserves, although both the humanitarian lobby led by John Mackenzie, and the Gifford–Cawston syndicate, strongly suspected his critical influence in favour of the Rhodesians.

Robinson had early in his tenure as high commissioner evinced sympathy for expanding the powers of local responsible settler government to its fullest 'home rule' potential; and also revealed considerable sensitivity towards the political sensibilities of Afrikanerdom. Since Majuba and the Pretoria Convention in 1881 he had favoured winning non-republican Afrikaners to the British connection by a policy of conciliation and association; since the troubles over the Warren expedition in Bechuanaland in the mid 1880s he had strongly advocated colonial as against imperial expansion in the Scramble for the interior of South Africa; and since the emergence of the *Bond*–Rhodes alliance, together with his own personal commitment to Rhodes, he became the leading advocate of 'colonialism' with the metropolis. By 1889 he had moved close to converting the high commissionership into an agency of the Cape interests, and made private, unofficial 'alliance' with

Rhodes. The result was, as he declared in his retirement speech in 1889 to a euphoric Cape audience, a highly devolutionist view of empire south of the Zambesi.

The true British policy for South Africa seems to me to be what may be termed *Colonialism, through Imperialism*: in other words, colonial expansion through imperial aid, the Home Government doing what the Colonies cannot do for themselves, having constitutionally no authority beyond their borders. There are three competing influences at work in South Africa. They are Colonialism, Republicanism, and Imperialism. As to the last, it is a diminishing quantity, there being now no permanent place in the future of South Africa for direct Imperial rule on any large scale . . . All the Imperial Government can now do in South Africa is, by means of spheres of influence, protectorates and Crown colonies, to gradually prepare the way for handing native territories over to the Cape and Natal . . . [with] advantage to all concerned.[20]

Just how Robinson first came to develop the charter idea 'as a dimension of his thesis of imperialism through local agencies is not absolutely clear, though we can say some pretty definite things about when he moved to this policy. Rhodes may have initially put the idea, of empire by chartered company, before Robinson; or, it is even quite possible that Robinson had the notion proposed to him by Rhodes' great rival – Maund's discussions with the high commissioner could well have included reference to the proposed 'Imperial Central African Company', for the Exploring Company syndicate clearly needed Robinson's support to succeed in London, and Maund was anyway hardly the best man to trust with such a large 'secret'. By July 1888, however, Robinson was firm in favouring expansion by commercial agency. He pressed his views on the metropolitan administration with force and close argument in a series of despatches. His basic argument was easily grasped: he wished to defend the 'sphere of influence' against other influences, and he saw little hope of achieving this by recommending a further 'protectorate administration'.

The alternative before us as regards Matabeleland is to recognise a monopoly [concession], which may possibly develop into a Royal Charter, or to follow the Swaziland course, of allowing a number of competing concession seekers of different nationalities to establish themselves in the country. Lo Bengula would be unable to govern or control such incomers except by massacre. They would be unable to govern themselves; a British Protectorate would be inefficient, or we should have no jurisdiction except by annexation; and Her Majesty's Government, as in Swaziland, would have before them the choice of letting the country fall into the hands of the South African Republic or of annexing it to the Empire.[21]

Such a choice, Robinson reasoned, was no choice at all. The 'protectorate system' was, to him, a less than viable option for policy:

hitherto annexations and Protectorates seem to have been decided on only to be followed later on by a perpetual wrangle with the Treasury for the means of maintaining a decent administration.

I think the position of British Bechuanaland at this moment, after nearly four years of Imperial rule . . . is a forcible illustration of the effect of attempting to administer a Crown Colony – if I may be permitted to use the expression – 'on the cheap'.[22]

The high commissioner's enthusiasm for such a 'charter policy' was not, of course, from mid-1888 dissociated from Rhodes' efforts towards the same end, although Robinson once claimed in retrospect, 'Rhodes did tell me some story once about taking me up an exceeding high mountain and showing me all the wonders of the Northern Expansion: but the truth is, I saw the Northern Expansion before ever I saw Mr Rhodes.'[23] It is however possible to determine when the high commissioner first joined Rhodes in formally pressing the scheme.

The local imperialist and the British proconsul had a long private discussion, in Cape Town, in July 1888. Robinson had no hesitation in sending the secretary of state a confidential account of their discussions.[24] It seemed that Rhodes had already formulated his scheme to use the recently amalgamated De Beers Consolidated Company as a means of opening up the interior. An exclusive concession was to be obtained from Lobengula, to exploit those regions of Zambesia which were not 'in the occupation or use of the Natives'; and a commercial enterprise was to be formed, 'for the development and government of the unoccupied territories surrendered to the company by a Royal Charter somewhat similar to that granted some years ago to the Borneo Company'.[25]

The high commissioner immediately supported the idea. He did so for the now traditional reasons that it would operate in favour of British influence at the Cape, and general British interests in Southern Africa: 'the extension of British interests in the interior of South Africa *by a chartered company with Cape associations* would be more in unison with the Africander sentiment than if the same result were attempted by the establishment of another inland Crown Colony.'[26] It was, as he described it, a policy for all seasons. It would involve the Cape colonists in the interior, by creating 'a very general feeling here amongst Dutch as well as English Colonists, that instead of being dependent on the caprice of the Republic, the true policy to pursue would be the *gradual expansion of the Cape Colony to the Zambesi*';[27] and it would be a policy of wise devolution in strengthening the base of prosperity in that interior region of South Africa.[28]

It was largely for these reasons, and because of Robinson's influence in London, that the initial attempts by the Gifford–Cawston syndicate to explore the possibility of finding official support, for a mission to Lobengula, were directed by the colonial office to Cape Town –

it is the province of the High Commissioner to decide what advice he should give to a native chief entitled to his advice... [and] that Her Majesty's Government would give no countenance to any concession or agreement unless it were concluded with the knowledge of an approval by the High Commissioner ... if you, and those associated with you, decide to proceed with the undertaking which you contemplate you will do well to be prepared to satisfy Sir H. Robinson of your strong financial position.[29]

– and also why later attempts to secure British governmental interest in a charter for the London syndicate were declined by Knutsford. In a helpful, but negative letter,[30] the colonial secretary explained that a charter could not be contemplated for an enterprise which lacked Cape colonial support – Hofmeyr's *Bond* was set against its Imperial overtones in Bechuanaland[31] – and whose concessions did not, after all, include an agreement from Lobengula. By inference, a syndicate with all these attributes might indeed secure official blessing in advancing into Zambesia.

Well aware of these manoeuvres by Rhodes' rivals, Robinson had no hesitation in playing a distinctly partisan role in supporting the Cape syndicate, at almost any price. This is best seen in relation to the Rudd Concession, which promised fire-arms to Lobengula as an inducement to signing the document.[32] Such a promise was most improper, and a flagrant breach of British policy, which aimed at containing the number of firearms held by African societies. Robinson, however, explained away the offer most ingeniously,[33] on the basis that if Lobengula's Ndebele were not supplied with British arms they would soon find 'friends' in rival governments (he could only have meant the Afrikaner states) all too eager to oblige, in return for concession favours.[34] Rudd wrote with some relief that, 'The Governor was very pleased to hear the result of our mission, and raised no difficulty as to the guns.'[35] This was very fortunate for Rhodes, who had worried over the matter, and who had yet also come to the opinion that the guns were *the* key to any bargain with Lobengula. 'I shall not approach Lo Bengula without the guns,' he wrote to Rudd at the time, 'and they will have to be filtered through the Cape Colony, through Bechuanaland, through Khama[;] they are the essence of [the] question.'[36] The imperial secretary in Cape Town has also in fact left us an interesting 'inside' account of the tactics followed in Government House over the firearms. Sir Graham Bower records in his unpublished 'Memoirs':

It was clearly illegal to deliver Martini-Henry rifles to a native chief. On the other hand unless the rifles were delivered the contract was not complete and the concession was invalid.

Sir Sidney Shippard solved the problem by issuing a permit on his own authority and informing the High Commissioner, Sir Hercules Robinson, in a private letter that he had done so. Sir Hercules showed me the letter and said, 'We will take time to answer that'.

I do not of course defend such a shirking of responsibility, but a hunted man with all his senses in full cry for official life may be pardoned some of his weakness.

But the fact that the law had been broken came to the knowledge of the Cape Parliament and the opposition attacked the Government.

Sir Gordon Sprigg, the Premier, asked for the facts and the papers, which I refused to give. I knew Parliament had only a few days to live and if I could gain time I would be able to shield Sir Hercules from the charge of guilty knowledge.[37]

It is a good example of how the work of the Rhodes group and the high commissioner's office complemented each other. One controlled the financial and local political aspects of the charter policy in Africa, the other provided the crucial channel to influence official opinion in the metropolis. 'I shall bring what you much need in a great undertaking, the "sinews of war", both in my private fortune and my Trust Deed, with twenty millions behind it', Rhodes once remarked to Shippard.[38] Robinson however could deliver something equally as impressive – nothing less than the possible political support of Her Majesty's Government.

The high commissioner's vital role was made simpler when Rhodes and the London syndicate suddenly came to an agreement. It has usually been assumed that Rhodes financially 'squared' his rivals; and then absorbed the Exploring Company into his syndicate. But Professor Galbraith has most convincingly constructed a new explanation. It was the colonial office which urged the rivals to merge, and it was to this overture that Rhodes responded when he met Maund in Cape Town and began the formal association of the two syndicates – later known as the Central Search Association Ltd.[39] 'You will have learnt from our telegram of the action which we have carefully followed,' Gifford wrote to Maund on 24 May, '[and] as we have joined R[hodes] we must all therefore pull loyally together.'[40]

This agreement meant that Robinson could now remove his hitherto implacable opposition to the Ndebele deputation to London, and indeed even suggest that, with careful control, it might be of use to the policymakers.[41] He could, further, of course, all the more strongly advocate the new combined syndicate, with its Rhodesian leadership, as representing London interests yet *also* having a secure Cape political basis. The power of the high commissioner was felt most dramatically by the Gifford–Cawston group: in January 1889 they made no headway in London, and had their approaches directed to Cape Town; by March they found themselves poised to succeed in both London and Cape Town. Securing association with Rhodes clearly meant finding the support of the influential high commissioner as well.

Humanitarians against the charter

Success appeared to stare at the amalgamated syndicate in early 1889: Gifford exuberantly wrote to Cawston, 'I am convinced we are going to win, it is a grand game.'[42] In fact, a tantalising spring and summer awaited the entrepreneurs, in which one complication after another delayed the issue of the charter. Rhodes, for one, was reduced to the depths of despair at times.[43]

These obstacles first found their focus in the initiatives of Lobengula, and his humanitarian friends in London, to counteract the impending Scramble in his country.

The Ndebele deputation which Lobengula had despatched, in Maund's company, arrived in London on 27 February 1889.[44] It could not have come at a more propitious moment to complicate the negotiations. The colonial secretary was thrown into a whirl by the whole matter. Initially he had deplored the deputation:

Mr Maund, who chaperons them, is a man of no position, but a clever man . . . He has doubtless represented himself to Lo Bengula as a person of influence, and induced him to send over these headmen . . . We can, I think, in no way recognize them . . . I propose that . . . they should have an interview with me, and that they should be allowed to see the Queen as she drives out. She can hardly be asked to grant them an interview. All the rest of the entertaining (Tussauds; the Tunnel, etc.) I think we must leave to Mr Maund.[45]

The impending amalgamation of the syndicates, however, gave Maund and the *indunas* a new stature. Suddenly they had to be accorded a magnanimous welcome. Not only were the *indunas* warmly greeted at the colonial office, but the secretary of state was forced to miss a cabinet to be at court when they were presented to Queen Victoria, at a formal lunch – the gold plate was used, according to Maund – and also cornered into sending a singularly damaging letter, in the name of the Queen, to Lobengula, in response to the 'oral message' concerning white concessionaires. It placed all previous concessions – including of course the vital Rudd document – in a very curious light. It could be read, by opponents of the Rhodesians, as a basis for rejecting the charter policy:

In the first place, the Queen wishes Lo Bengula to understand distinctly that Englishmen who have gone out to Matabeleland to ask lease to dig for stones, have not gone out with the Queen's authority, and that he should not believe any statement by them or any of them to that effect.

The Queen advises Lo Bengula not to grant hastily concessions of land, or leave to dig, but to consider all applications carefully.

It is not wise to put too much power into the hands of the man who came first, and to exclude other deserving men . . . A King gives a stranger an ox, not his whole herd of cattle, otherwise what would other strangers arriving late have to eat.[46]

The amalgamation of the syndicates was now complete, and so too was their dismay at this turn of events. The Imperial Factor appeared to be joining the humanitarians in encouraging Lobengula to oppose the policy of sub-imperialism by financial agency. In the letters of Rhodes at this time it appears that Maund was thought to be the main malignant influence between the Ndebele, the metropolitan authorities and the new syndicate. 'It rests with you to help and get the concession through with ⌈the⌉ King,' Rhodes lectured Maund,

and not to attempt any sub-signatures with him. We have the whole ⌈area which⌉ they recognised by the Queen, and if eventually we have any difficulty with ⌈the⌉ King the home people would now always recognise us in the possession of the minerals⌈;⌉ thus quite understand that savage potentates frequently repudiate ⌈concessions⌉. I hope I shall hear of your success.[47]

The Rhodesian group did their very best to make sure that Maund worked to strengthen the Rudd Concession, and to support the interests of the newly amalgamated syndicate.[48] As late as September, when the charter was already drafted, Rhodes was still suspicious of Maund and feared he could yet trip up the whole great scheme by playing on Lobengula's fears of the interpretation being placed on the Rudd document.

My dear Maund,
. . . Of course I know you have to hold apparently to an independent position but you must help us as much as you can. Jameson will show you the Charter⌈;⌉ it fully recognises our concession and whatever Lo Bengula does will not affect the fact that when there is white occupation of the country our concession will come into force provided the English and not Boers get the country. You must do your best to get the concession through.

Yrs,

C. J. Rhodes.[49]

Maund gave verbal assurances, before he left for Bulawayo, of his good intent; and he even delayed that return journey (he did not reach the Ndebele capital until August) to facilitate the advance of the charter policy. By June of the next year he had done very well for the syndicate at Bulawayo.[50] However, the fact that he felt bound to deliver the 'ox herd' letter from the Queen, rankled and worried the concessionaires. At his worst moments of anguish, Rhodes gave way to despair over the results of the Ndebele deputation, feeling that the whole charter scheme was lost. He told Cawston, in a very unguarded letter,

If it was not so serious it would really be laughable to think that our own servant should be devoting his brains at our expense to destroy all our plans. You remember how much he hid in that room of mine and said there was no such [damaging] message in the Queen's letter. If he had told the truth we could have remedied the evil, but he deliberately denied there being any such expression. I saw a letter of Moffat's saying the mischief to us done by the Queen's letter and that from the Aborigines' [Protection] Society was almost irreparable. How the Government could have sent such a message at the very time they were thinking of giving us their support I cannot understand . . . I must own that one's liberal views received a nasty jar on finding out that whilst trying to do everything for them they had quietly done their best to give me a quietus with Lo Bengula [–] the object of it I fail to see if they are really desirous that we should develop the interior.[51]

Lobengula's initiative in sending the *indunas* had undoubtedly produced major effects. The worries of the amalgamated syndicate were to be continually fed throughout the summer of 1889, as the British humanitarian lobby, led by the South African Committee, supported by the Aborigines' Protection Society, (APS), and having as its spokesman the redoubtable John Mackenzie, took the occasion of the *indunas*' visit to launch a major public agitation against the charter policy. The campaign took its lead from Mackenzie – 'The country up to the Zambesi is now in our hands to make or mar'[52] – and it is he who best expressed the humanitarian issues involved. With incisive analysis he argued that the Imperial Factor was at the parting of the ways in South Africa: they had to choose between 'colonialism' and 'imperialism'.

The first policy . . . is connected with the name of . . . Sir Hercules Robinson, and involves the speedy elimination of the imperial Government from all trans-Colonial territories. We are told that Swaziland might be handed to the Transvaal, South Bechuanaland to the Cape Colony, and North Bechuanaland to the administration of a trading company; and the Imperial Government retire from South Africa.[53]

The alternative policy, of direct empire – 'imperialism' – involved the British government in recognising its obligations of trusteeship to African societies:

it is the duty of the Imperial Government . . . to consider thoughtfully the disposition of native territories under imperial protection, so that a federation of European Governments in South Africa under Great Britain may become practicable in the future; and therefore South Bechuanaland and Zambesi[a] should be administered as separate colonies of territories until such time as he wishes of their respective inhabitants ... [are] made plain.[54]

Where the Imperial Factor had been working steadily to involve the Cape colony in the interior, John Mackenzie of course wished to exclude the white Cape colonial influence altogether:

They would 'hammer' the natives, and rob them of their land, and never recognise their right to own land, or to possess any civil right except to pay a hut-tax. They would 'level-down' the Cape Colony constitution to the condition of those republics where a man, no matter how good he is, or how much he knows, or how much he has, in character, knowledge, or property, can have no citizen-rights, because he is a native African in his own country of Africa.[55]

Mackenzie's sensible and compassionate arguments also had an almost prophetic aspect. From the very beginning of the charter scheme, he warned the British authorities that 'it cannot be too distinctly remembered that, while the British South Africa Company is British, it is not the British Government';[56] and he foresaw the inevitable BSA Company–Ndebele clash of arms: 'The British Government and the British public can afford to exercise patience with native prejudices; a commercial company is not likely to be so inclined to want patience in view of the treasures of Mashonaland.'[57]

The humanitarian campaign embarrassed and irritated metropolitan imperial officialdom – the colonial secretary privately described the opposition to the charter policy as 'generally the negrophils'[58], although their public response to the petitions and deputations, which Mackenzie's group directed at Whitehall, kept fixedly to questions of finance: 'Her Majesty's Government do not feel that they would be justified in inviting Parliament to provide the very large sums which would be required' for direct administrative responsibility.[59] Thus, as Mackenzie was ominously informed by the senior colonial office administrator in August, they were 'considering what may be the best mode of advancing the British interests under Imperial control in the territories of British Bechuanaland and of the Transvaal'.[60] Quite rightly Mackenzie took these guarded phrases to mean a growing commitment to Robinson's policies of 'colonialism' and the Rhodesian charter.

Not that the humanitarians easily took 'no' for an answer. Mackenzie, for example, kept up a vigilant criticism of the British charter policy throughout 1889 – and even after the BSA Company was sanctioned. Further, Lobengula continued to play an independent role of intervention, and launched another initiative against the Rudd Concession, this time in even more specific and damning language. His letter provided superb support to the humanitarian campaign. 'Some time ago a party of men came into my country the principal one appearing to be a man called Rudd', Lobengula wrote to Queen Victoria on 23 April,

They asked me for a place to dig, and said they would give me certain things for the right to do so ... About three months afterwards I heard from other sources that I had given by that document the right to all the minerals in my country ... I will not recognise the paper as it contains neither my words, nor the words of those who got it.[61]

A moment of some crisis arrived with the delivery of the letter in London on 18 June. Lobengula, and his humanitarian allies, were forcing the Imperial Factor to declare its support for the charter policy and Cape Colonialism, or repudiate the amalgamated syndicate in favour of the imperialism of direct trusteeship.

Rhodes in British politics 1889

The crisis for the syndicate deepened before it departed. In being pressed to make a firm decision on future policy for the interior, the British metropolitan authorities were moved to examine the supplicants for the charter closely. It was then that serious misgivings were expressed in official circles over the proposed agency of sub-imperialism. In particular, it became clear that in the granting of the charter a major obstacle surrounded the political and financial activities of no less than Rhodes himself. It was true that the great amalgamator did indeed have singular advantages in the eyes of the British government: his wealth, his standing with the Cape Afrikaners, and his easy relationship with the British high commissioner. But he had his disadvantages. It was not simply on the grounds made out against the Cape imperialist by Lord Harcourt – 'Mr Rhodes is a very reasonable man. He only wants two things. Give him Protection and give him Slavery and he will be perfectly satisfied.'[62] Rather, it was much closer to Chamberlain's contemporary assessment – 'I know only three things about Rhodes, and they all put me against him: (i) he has made an enormous fortune very rapidly (ii) he is an Africander ... (iii) he gave £10,000 to Parnell.'[63]

Leaving aside the matter of Rhodes' financial methods for the moment, it is now clear that Rhodes' political sympathies were sometimes seen to be as much a hindrance as a help. It well demonstrated the ambivalence in imperial attitudes: the British authorities wanted loyal colonial collaborators at the Cape, yet baulked at the fact that Rhodes did indeed have strong Afrikaner *Bond* support. Salisbury initially described Rhodes as 'rather a pro-Boer M.P. I fancy';[64] and Lord Knutsford suddenly had qualms that

'Mr Rhodes is not liked by the [English] Cape Ministers',[65] presumably because of his Hofmeyr alliance. Similarly, the British government while apparently pleased with a policy of 'colonialism' and political 'home rule' at the Cape, backed away from a man who could give £10,000 to the Irish 'Home Rule' Party. In fact, the money was given to Parnell by Rhodes in the hope that he could bring Gladstone to *retain* the Irish M.P.s at Westminster in any future Home Rule Bill.[66] The Unionist government failed to take this point. Even the colonial secretary suddenly began to look at Rhodes with very critical eyes. 'Any suggestion from Mr Rhodes (who I may advise in passing is the gentleman who presented Mr Parnell with £10,000 when he was in this country),' Lord Knutsford had written to the premier in January 1889,[67] 'must be treated with some suspicion.'

In the coming months this initial suspicion deepened, for a second political reason, when it was suggested that Rhodes might have been subverting the independence of the British high commissioner, by the use of his well-known cheque-book and 'despatch-box' of shares. Clearly Sir Hercules Robinson and Cecil Rhodes had long espoused much the same general policy as concerned Zambesia and the northern expansion. But what particularly worried the senior members of the British government was the manner in which the high commissioner had come to use his office to champion the personal cause of Rhodes' financial syndicate against all others. The matter had been brought to a head by the fact that Sir Hercules Robinson was due to retire that very year, 1889.[68] Rhodes had been appalled at the suggestion, and campaigned for Robinson's term of office to be extended. The imperial government felt their suspicions were being confirmed. Hitherto, remarks concerning Robinson had been highly complimentary – 'his services are admitted to have been more conspicuous than any governor of late years'[69] – but now Salisbury was to comment that he was perhaps *too* close to colonial opinion,[70] and to hope that a baronetcy might see him safely into retirement.[71] The colonial secretary, whose policies had been virtual carbon-copies of those evolved in Robinson's despatches,[72] surprisingly tended to agree with the premier:

Dear Lord Salisbury,
I do not think it would be at all desirable to extend Sir H. Robinson's term of office, which has in fact already been prolonged for 2 years ...

It is supposed and with good ground, that Mr Rhodes is working with Mr Rudd as to getting large mining concessions from Lo Bengula, and that Sir H. Robinson favours Mr Rudd as against others who are trying to get concessions in Matabeleland. Only this morning I received a protest against the conduct of Sir H. Robinson from one of these gentlemen ...

Both Smith and Goschen are inclined to suspect Sir H. Robinson of being influenced too much by Rhodes and Rudd, and I am disposed to agree with them.[73]

Before the Charter was drawn up, the cabinet had already selected Lord Loch as Sir Hercules Robinson's successor.[74]

In all the proceedings, the permanent colonial office staff, who had also come to rely heavily on the persuasive advice of the high commissioner since the war of 1880–81, followed the example of the colonial secretary. They deserted Sir Hercules Robinson with some speed. As early as 8 January 1889 one leading clerk could speak emphatically of Rhodes and Robinson being 'in league' at the Cape,[75] and could also suggest that Rhodes had infiltrated the British administration of Bechuanaland, by using Robinson to bias the actions of the senior civil servant, Sidney Shippard.[76] Commenting on a Robinson despatch, analysing rival concession hunting groups in Matabeleland, the colonial office minuted sarcastically, that all 'combinations are unscrupulous, and the Rhodes' combination strictly scrupulous – that is about the sum of Sir H. Robinson's philosophy on this question'.[77] It was no great surprise to these officials, therefore, that three years later the *Daily Chronicle* published a sensational article,[78] in which it claimed to prove that the financial connection between Rhodes and Robinson was finally laid bare. By checking the share register of the Central Search Company (dated 4 October 1889), it was found that Sir Hercules Robinson had 250 shares to his name. These shares had apparently been acquired in May of that year, while Sir Hercules was *still* high commissioner, and adviser to HM Government. Further, in the year immediately after Sir Hercules Robinson's retirement, 1889–90, he was found (on 21 November 1890) to possess 2,500 shares in the new Rhodes Company of United Concessions, a shareholding that increased to 6,250 by the following January, 1892. The colonial office was in little doubt as to the financial origins of these shares: they were a delayed Rhodesian payment 'for his past advocacy of the Rudd claims'.[79] This was never proved. More likely is the probability that Robinson subscribed some £250 to the Central Search Association, on the advice of Rhodes, when the proconsul was told that he was to be replaced as high commissioner in the course of 1889. He then found, to his delight, that the Search Association had been acquired by United Concessions, paying 10 to 1. Robinson thus now had 2,500 shares in the new company without having speculated a penny further. Buying and selling modestly in retirement – he was appointed a Director of the BSA Company, the Westminster and Standard Banks – he built the shares up to 6,235 in number, before selling them in January 1893 at a considerable profit. The suggestion that he had been 'bought' by Rhodes was unfair; but, their relationship was, all the same, as one permanent official expressed it, 'fishy'.[80]

This explanation of Robinson's financial dealings with Rhodes is further borne out by the fact that Rhodes behaved in much the same way towards fellow Cape MPs when canvassing colonial support for the Northern Expansion. What he offered was not illegal; what they accepted from him was not unconstitutional. But it remained questionable.[81] Men of principle, like Sir Graham Bower, who were approached by Rhodes, declined his overtures. Another, who also said 'No', was Sir James Rose-Innes. He left a graphic picture of Rhodes at work:

> When Rhodes became Premier, he was a phenomenon, a man of great wealth, prepared to expand it in furtherance of a political ideal . . . He had come to regard money as the great source of power; it had stood him in good stead in the past; rival concessionaires had been bought out, and competing interests amalgamated . . .
> He [now] offered members of parliament, and other prominent persons, the opportunity of subscribing at par for parcels of chartered shares then standing at a considerable premium. It was delicately put; the idea was to interest the selected recipients in northern development. Of course the recipient paid for his shares, but equally of course they were worth far more than he paid. In effect it was a valuable gift, which could not, one would think, be accepted without impairment of independence. Yet there were acceptances in surprising quarters.[82]

Rhodes, of course, saw nothing wrong in this: men could always say no. Yet it remained a less than admirable reflection on his politics. His fortunes gave him 'entire freedom in regard to details and method', as Rose-Innes well put it, 'Those were matters for his conscience, which was not a non-conformist conscience.'[83] Whether such an individual, at the head of a major British imperial enterprise, should be given a royal charter, was thus a very real question for the British authorities as they contemplated the future of the Southern African hinterland in mid-1889.

Why the charter was granted

Given these various factors working against both the charter policy generally and against Rhodes individually, why was so all-embracing a charter awarded to the BSA Company from an obviously suspicious imperial government? A Confidential Memorandum of 1893 – which set out the questionable financial techniques which underlay the BSA Company's foundation – also tried to face this question squarely. The official Memorandum ultimately concluded that four factors had outweighed all others. The Rhodesian syndicate was thought to be the only agency which could be expected to (1) greatly strengthen the British political position in Southern Africa, and make connection with collaborative Cape Afrikanerdom through support of 'colonialism'; (2) save the British taxpayer a very considerable amount of money in the administration of central Africa; (3) put an end to the growing rivalry among the swarm of concessionaires at the Ndebele court, itself a source of instability in the 'sphere of influence'; (4) render some form of immediate and practical law and order to this disturbed region of the interior where African, Afrikaner and concessionaire Scramble continually for rights and authority and resources.

To this set of reasons several other historical factors can now be added. The humanitarian campaign failed partly because the British 'official mind' was closed to advocacy of expensive trusteeship in the interior; but also because of the division among humanitarians. John Mackenzie fought the Chartered Company, but John Moffat had of course finally thrown his support to the Rhodesians. 'Some such Company as that to which Mr Mackenzie refers, and to which he so much objects, might be the best solution to the problem. It would have no territorial or judicial rights, and could be left to make its own terms with the Chief, always recognising him as the Chief of the country.'[84] So too had some members of the APS as a result of the determined effort of the BSA Company founders to attract a highly responsible looking board of directors – including no less a sympathizer of humanitarian causes than Earl Grey. He told a deeply disappointed Mackenzie, in July 1889, that he had accepted the appointment 'after considerable hesitation', as a policy of direct imperialism was very

evidently beyond the thoughts and intentions of the present Gov[ernmen]t. and as they have made up their minds to grant Rhodes a charter, it is I think desirable that one like myself, who is in close sympathy with you and the S[outh]. African Committee should be on the board. I am very hopeful that the action of this company may prove instrumental in developing and stimulating on a very great degree Imperial interests in South Africa.[85]

Obviously in a position of some strength as a result of humanitarian divisions, and the 'capture' of Grey, the BSA Company authorities had no hesitation in declaring, to the surprise of many in Exeter Hall, that the syndicate 'had been formed mainly in the interests of the natives and of[the] missionaries, to prevent unprincipled white men going in and ruining everyone'.[86] The fact that such statements could now be made in some confidence itself reflected on the division in the humanitarian response to the charter, and on the isolated position in which Lobengula and the Ndebele found themselves to be.

It is also important to note not merely negative but also positive factors in the ultimate failure of the opposition to the charter application. Above all, it should be stressed that while Lord Salisbury never did warm to Rhodes personally, he did finally set aside a number of his graver suspicions about the Cape expansionist and financier; while Lord Knutsford and some of his permanent officials would appear to have been won over to Rhodes as a suitable imperial agent. This transformation in Rhodes' position is not easy to set out, but the official documentation suggests how progressively the amalgamator managed to calm the worst fears about his shortcomings, and even work up some very positive personal support.[87] Rhodes was relatively unknown when he was first mentioned in connection with a charter, and when the opposition was begun by Lobengula and the humanitarians. Lord Knutsford at first indeed even thought he was 'Secretary to the High Commissioner',[88] then admitted confusing him with a 'Mr [Graham] Bower'[89] – the true secretary to Robinson. In March 1889 Rhodes came to London and began to change that impression by establishing some personal credibility. He even captured a few old enemies. 'I believe,' a watchful Knutsford duly informed Salisbury,[90] 'he has managed to win over Mr Chamberlain and Mr Labouchere.' Rhodes explained away his embarrassing alliances at the Cape and in Ireland, and propelled himself into a firm alliance with Imperial interests. Labouchere, who had once called Rhodes, 'an Empire jerry builder . . . a mere vulgar promoter masquerading as a patriot . . . the figurehead of a gang of astute Hebrew financiers with whom he divided the profits',[91] was later to change his verdict to 'an entirely honest, heavy person'.[92] Rhodes undeniably had that curious charisma. He also, more important, gave the impression, with Lords Salisbury and Knutsford, that he could be controlled. It was a fatal misjudgement, from which all else now flowed.[93]

Chartering the Rhodesian syndicate

The final cabinet decision to grant a charter (10 July 1889) was based on all these elements; yet the rationale leading to that action is perhaps best captured by examining the working documentation by which the policy was implemented. What is supremely evident in that narrative is the simple fact that, well aware of the limits of both charter enterprises as such, and of Rhodes as its possible head, the British authorities saw it as the best option open to them in the administration of the interior. Milner perhaps put it better than anyone else when he wrote in a kindly, yet firm way, to John Mackenzie (20 June 1889): 'I don't say it is an ideal solution, but it is better than letting the whole thing out of our fingers.'[94] Thus it is clear, for example, that as early as February 1889, the colonial secretary and his senior staff had accepted the advice of the high commissioner; given the circumstances in the interior of Southern Africa, together with the charter syndicates in formation, 'it may become possible and desirable to entertain the idea of a strong Chartered Company for Matabeleland and Mashonaland'. Indeed, as Knutsford plainly minuted at that time, 'A strong company with a Royal Charter, under the concession fair and reasonable in terms although wide in extent, would have an advantage to Lo Bengula and his people.'[95] Such a company might also, as Robinson quickly pointed out, undertake the development of the long-delayed rail communication to the isolated Bechuanaland Protectorate[96] – a suggestion which greatly appealed to the colonial office which had utterly failed to secure Treasury support for such a railway or even a modest telegraph line.[97] Beyond all these factors, the local British administration in Bechuanaland pointed a grim picture of growing lawless chaos in Zambesia. 'Matabeleland seems in a seething state', as one London official minuted on the African despatches.[98] All these reasons seemed to point towards the advantage of a responsible chartered imperial agency in the interior.

The financial syndicate, of course, was not unaware of the advantages which it offered to the British government in return for the royal charter. Using Lord Gifford as the public head of the new enterprise, the Rhodesians applied for a charter in return for: (1) extending the railway and telegraph north to the Zambesi; (2) encouraging English immigration and colonisation in Africa; (3) developing the mineral resources of Mashonaland; and (4) establishing British trade and commerce in the hinterland.[99] As the newly amalgamated enterprise of London and the Cape interests, their application carried considerable financial and political weight. The momentous document read simply:

> The Gold Fields of South Africa, Limited,
> 2 Gresham Buildings, Babinghall Street,
> London, E.C., April 30, 1889.

My Lord,

Having perused the letter of this date addressed to your Lordship by the Chairman of the Exploring Company, Limited, with regard to the development of the territories to the north of the Cape Colony, we beg to state that we are prepared, as representing the Matabeleland Concession, and having a very important stake in South Africa, to cooperate cordially with the approval of Her Majesty's Government, in carrying out the scheme proposed. Arrangements have been made to that effect between the Exploring Company and ourselves.

We have, etc.,

> C. J. Rhodes
> A. Beit
> Thomas Rudd
> Chairman of the Gold Fields of
> South Africa Ltd.[100]

This vital correspondence was sent on to the British premier the next day. Clearly Knutsford's doubts about Rhodes had by this date been removed, and he was now ready to support the Cape imperialists:

You may like to see the enclosed from Mr Rhodes, who with Mr Rudd got the large concession from Lo Bengula, and has now disarmed opposition to that concession by giving his opponents a share in it . . .

His plan is now to form a large Company with a Charter, if possible like the Niger Company, and thus to work the concession south of the Zambesi . . . you will see he [also] proposes to help you North of the Zambesi.

He and his colleagues are well backed up in the City, and he himself is the richest man by far in S[outh] Africa: this Company will construct the railway through B[ritish] Bechuanaland, and hint, if they get a Charter, of extending it to Shoshong.[101]

The official reply to the Rhodes—Gifford consortium was suitably restrained. Lord Knutsford declined to say 'yes' to such a proposal until he had further details — 'much would depend on the *personnel* of the directorate, and on the provisions made for securing the right and interests of the Europeans and Natives'. But, in private, Knutsford and his officials were as enthusiastic about the scheme as the high commissioner. The Rhodesians were going to remove all their financial struggles with the Treasury. The permanent under-secretary began to talk grandly of a British administration in Zambesia, 'the funds for which could be provided with the assistance of a Chartered Company';[102] and the colonial secretary waxed enthusiastic over the fact that, in his eyes, the proposed BSA Company would merely be a financially self-sufficient arm of imperial policy, controlled from Whitehall:

if such is incorporated by Royal Charter, its contributions, objects, and operations will become more directly subject to control by Her Majesty's Government than if it were left to these gentlemen to incorporate themselves under the joint Stock Companies Acts, which they are entitled to do. In the latter case, Her Majesty's Government would not be able effectually to prevent the company from taking its own line of policy.[103]

Rhodes however was ready to be bound by the strictures of a royal charter. Knutsford's enthusiasm for the scheme soon knew few limits. The charter supplicants were proposing and making effective the apparently impossible — secure administrative empire in tropical Africa on the cheap: 'The example of the Imperial East African Company shows that such a body may to some considerable extent relieve Her Majesty's Government from diplomatic difficulties and heavy expenditure.'[104]

That happy prospect was clouded by the arrival of Lobengula's second letter of protest to the Queen on 18 June — the day before Gifford proposed to forward a draft charter as proposed by the BSA Company,[105] some 21 days after Knutsford had informed his premier that he was strongly committed to the charter policy, and some 14 days after the foreign office had agreed to give the draft charter attentive examination.[106] In obvious embarrassment, and some consternation, the colonial office forwarded Lobengula's letter not just to the Queen, but to Rhodes as well.[107] He replied by urgent return post.[108] He said that he had with him Rochfort Maguire, who had recently arrived from Bulawayo; and Maguire was pleased to assure the secretary of state that the letter was probably not genuine, and could well have been written by an 'organised opposition [in] a certain section of the white inhabitants of Matabeleland'.[109] The British authorities were apparently so relieved that they made no further enquiry to verify Maguire's opinion; perhaps the fact that, like Lord Salisbury, Maguire was a Fellow of All Souls, simply established his credibility. Work on the charter thus proceeded, despite the fact that Lobengula had now repudiated the concession on which it was to be based.[110] The Queen was informed by Knutsford,

I am confident that a strongly constituted Company will give us the best chance of peaceably opening up and developing the resources of this country south of the Zambesi, and will be most beneficial to the native Chiefs and people. Such a company has been formed, and all the capital subscribed without going to the public.[111]

The British premier's response was rather more restrained – 'Lord Salisbury agrees with Lord Knutsford in thinking that Lord Gifford's proposition deserves attentive consideration'[112] – but he too was gradually won over. On 1 June the Rhodesian syndicate began to show their financial strength: they dazzled penny-pinching Victorian officialdom with an offer of an immediate £30,000, to start work on the telegraph line to the north, and a further £4,000 towards the appointment of a British resident at Lobengula's court.[113] The colonial office was suitably impressed: they saw the proposal 'as affording a safe and efficient means of providing for the more pressing requirements of the case, pending the consideration of the application for a charter'.[114] Rhodes was so informed – though his cheque was not accepted until the charter had been granted.[115]

A draft of that charter was now submitted for approval by the Rhodes syndicate.[116] The imperial administration began to look on the proposed BSA Company as even more of a solution to their problems than at first envisaged.[117] As the colonial office enthused, when forwarding the draft charter, to the foreign office:

Lord Salisbury will observe that the Charter as drafted will incorporate the company for the purpose . . . of trading, and working the various concessions . . . and will empower the Company, if and when it acquires from the Native Chiefs grants of territory or parts of government, to assume such functions of Government as Her Majesty may think desirable to undertake.[118]

The thought of converting the commercial BSA Company into a form of 'chartered administration', in areas of British Central African responsibilities, firmly took hold in the mind of officialdom. 'Mr Rhodes called here on Saturday', Sir Robert Herbert informed Lord Knutsford from the colonial office,[119] and 'confirmed Mr Fairfield's understanding that the Company does not propose to go to work actively at present in Bechuanaland . . . otherwise they would be strongly opposed by the Rev. John Mackenzie and his followers'. The permanent under-secretary saw the sense in this – 'I think the Company are right not to court that opposition' – but Sir Robert Herbert still hoped that, 'in settling the Charter we should see that it contains power to HM Government to place under the Company any native territories over which it may be thought expedient that the Co[mpany] should have control'.[120] Far from trying to find means to curb, control and restrict the activities of the Rhodesian syndicate, the British authorities thus now appeared in fact to be looking in the opposite direction: how to build in as many administrative responsibilities as possible into the royal charter – even if, for the moment, that charter were to operate only south of the Zambesi.[121] Salisbury was emphatic in keeping Rhodes out of the Nyasa mission-field[122] and northern Zambesi[123]. He reasoned that there were quite sufficient for the Rhodesian syndicate to undertake as already outlined.

A royal charter was issued on this basis. It was signed by Queen Victoria on 29 October; Rhodes however had been given the news as early as 10 July, in a brief letter from Sir Robert Herbert,[124] based on the cabinet decision of the previous day.[125] Rhodes secretly visited the foreign office on 11 July, and had the exact terms of reference in the proposed charter carefully explained to him.[126] He agreed, for the moment, to limit these activities south of the Zambesi, and to work in the Shire Highlands through John Moirs' African Lakes Company.[127] The final wording of the charter was agreed on, in a lengthy correspondence between Rhodes and Sir Robert Herbert.[128] It then went to the law officers,[129] who returned the charter to the foreign office in mid-August. By 29 August it was ready for the printers.[130] A map, showing the area of operation, was agreed between the colonial office and the foreign office,[131] and consideration was now given to communicating the charter to interested countries – an unfavourable reaction, for example, was anticipated from Germany.[132] It was only left to the colonial secretary to obtain the Queen's signature (29 October), [133] and to explain the nature of the charter to the new British high commissioner at the Cape, Lord Loch (14 November).[134] The BSA Company Charter was, according to Lord Knutsford, based on 'precedents, so far as they were applicable, of the North

Borneo Company's, the Royal Niger Company's, and the British Imperial East African Company's Charter'. The new Company was not to operate in British Bechuanaland, but was rather confined to Zambesia, the area of the sphere of influence, where it was to 'enact ordinances, and to maintain a police force', to allow the peaceable mining of minerals. The Company administration was to respect local African religions, 'except so far as may be necessary in the interests of humanity', and in its day-to-day 'administration of justice, to have regard to Native customs and laws'. But, above all, the high commissioner was to ensure that the Cape colonial ministry worked with the BSA Company, for in the charter-policy lay 'perhaps the best prospect of developing the interior of South Africa in a manner advantageous to all interests'.[135]

The Ndebele were now informed of their fate. At last, on 15 November, a response was despatched to Lobengula's suspect letter of 23 April; and the BSA Company was recommended to the Ndebele as a responsible agency of progress and development 'The Queen has caused inquiry to be made respecting these persons, and is satisfied that they are men who will fulfill their undertakings, and who may be trusted to carry out the working for gold in the Chief's country without molesting his people or in any way interfering with the kraals, growers or cattle.'[136] Ironic words with the bloody Ndebele war of conquest less than three years away. Yet not *so* surprising: the letter bore the influence of the BSA Company. A draft of the communication had been suggested by the syndicate,[137] and was drawn on by the colonial officials in writing the despatch.[138] The new British high commissioner, Lord Loch – who was not uncritical of the chartered company – found himself in the unenviable position of defending the Rhodesian policy to the disgruntled Lobengula.

My friend,

... You are mistaken in supposing that your country is being cut up and given out. ... I add for your own good this advice which has already been given to you in the words of the Great Queen, the Chartered Company are your friends and the Queen gave them the Charter because they would keep peace between the Matabele and the white men. Those who tell you otherwise are not to be trusted.

I am, your friend,
Henry B. Loch[139]

The chartered scheme was thus duly launched. Despite the assurances of the British metropolitan authorities and the high commission, the charter as published revealed that awesome power had been placed in the hands of the BSA Company's local agents. The BSA Company syndicate were empowered to negotiate treaties, to promulgate laws, and to preserve the peace by maintaining a company police force. They could also acquire new concessions; and, where necessary, could construct roads, or railways, and undertake other public works. Finally, of course, they could engage in mining (or any other industry), establish banks, make independent land grants, and in fact carry on any lawful commerce, trade, pursuit or business not illegal under the terms of the Charter. Men like John Mackenzie were appalled. It confirmed his worst fears: 'I am persuaded that without direct and wisely exercised diplomatic arrangements with the Chief Lo Bengula, the history of a chartered company will prove a stormy and disastrous one.'[140] Even Lord Knutsford had his qualms. 'I hope Mr Rhodes will better himself,' he minuted, 'and win over Lo Bengula.'[141]

It was a vain hope. A great commercial and financial syndicate was about to be given almost free rein in Central Africa, with powers not far short of those of an occupying force. When the question of an official insignia for the new BSA Company was mooted, one permanent official minuted in London – only half in jest – that the motif be 'one of their picturesque policemen, with the skeleton of a rival concessionaire in the foreground'.[142]

John Mackenzie was also to be vindicated, to the extent that the early history of the occupation of Zambesia revealed that while metropolitan authorities claimed the BSA Company to be the Imperial Factor in action, it soon became patently clear that it was not. By the end of the decade even so confirmed an imperialist as Milner could thus be moved to bring down a hostile verdict on the Rhodesian administration in Zambesia: 'the blacks have been scandalously used'.[143]

The fact that the Partition in Zambesia was, in truth, really the triumph of the *local* expansionists – rather than that of the metropolitan government's New Imperialism – suggested that the Scramble here had evinced a very specific meaning. First, far from being a major success in British imperial policy – as the early histories of Rhodesia were inclined to indicate – these events could be seen as suggesting just the opposite. They registered a metropolitan failure to resist the 'sub-imperialism' of Cape Colonialism, and admitted the need to conciliate the Cape leaders in the larger politics of supremacy in plural Southern Africa – at the price of further frontier expansion by the local colonial society. It was also a sign that the Imperial Factor had simply failed to find other and more responsible means of conducting a viable policy in Bechuanaland and the Zambesian 'sphere of influence', short of trusteeship empire. The Salisbury government looked to the suspect administrative techniques of empire by charter rather than meet their obligations by direct authority and formal empire. But, then, perhaps 'empire by charter' was the ultimate administrative and economic development of the Victorian imperial ideal of 'informal empire'.

Aftermath and legacy 1890–94: conquest and closure

'The object of my political ambition . . . is the expansion of the Cape Colony to the Zambesi.'

C. J. Rhodes, 28 September 1888

'If you aggrandise the Cape Colony . . . you sacrifice with your eyes open the interests of the Natives and you place the whole country [of the interior] in the hands, and at the disposal of, men utterly opposed to ourselves as to justice and fair dealing between man and man.'

Rev. John Mackenzie to Colonial Office, October 1892

'I have white men all round me. By force they have taken the countries of all my neighbours. If I do not give them rights here, they will take them. Therefore I give them when they pay. Why should we not eat before we die?'

King Mbandzeni of the Swazi

9
The triumph of settler expansion 1890–94

'Partition' now became occupation. The Scramble for the interior of South Africa underwent a broad change of character as it entered the 1890s. Where it had often formerly – especially since the impact of the German presence and the 'highveld revolution' – been focused around questions of strategy, political hegemony and 'paper Partition', so it was in the future to be represented increasingly by an expansion of local settlement groups and economic agencies, all conducting their own grab for African resources. Where the New Imperialism had finally decided questions of jurisdiction, so these sub-imperial forces of the periphery could now follow through with on-the-ground expansion.

The success of the white settler and the Afrikaner frontiersman in conquering and acquiring lands long desired in Swaziland, Pondoland, Zululand and Zambesia in the early 1890s was thus a far from happenchance event in the overall impact of the Scramble. The incorporation of these African territories into the white colonial and Boer polities formed the logical conclusion locally to the international diplomatic struggles over South Africa in the 1880s. The consequences of the greater Partition after 1877 was this lesser but very real Scramble *within* the periphery itself. And the natural development of the British desire to maintain an empire-hegemony in South Africa through sub-imperial proxy agents was in fact the expansion of those very agencies – partly to fulfil their particular economic aspirations, partly to develop and 'control' the lands which the Imperial Factor had annexed but which Whitehall had no wish to administer directly.

This chapter explores the ways in which the essentially negative Partition by the Imperial Factor – the 'imperialism of denial', in the name of British hegemony and interests after 1886 – was converted, by the colonial and republican states of South Africa, into a genuine 'Scramble' for Africa itself. These years were to evince the highly complex conclusion to the Partition in Southern Africa. But they were also to well demonstrate the simple truth that at the core of much of the political changes which had marked the Scramble in South Africa there was a readily identifiable source – the relentless energy of the white frontier communities attempting to create a colonial world in Africa favourable to their own interests and future. This energy and determination in fact sustained and perpetuated the Partition on-the-ground when the metropolitan imperialists were ready to call a halt to the Scramble, and were eager to strike mutually acceptable agreements – respecting their various zones of possession and interest – thus facilitating both an end to African frictions in international politics, and a return to European preoccupations in their diplomacy.

The 'abdication of the governors'

The fact that the policies of the local and metropolitan imperialists now ran in different directions was to be of enormous importance for this final phase of the Scramble in South Africa. The very determination of the British, above all, to stage a calculated retreat – having attempted a series of federal postures, and also having directly intervened by expansive annexations in the 1880s to secure basic interests – meant that the forces of local expansion were given maximum opportunity, free of metropolitan trusteeship restraints, to act out their desires and ambitions. Indeed, in the case of the local British settlement colonies – not just the Cape but 'maturing' Natal – there was to be positive encouragement to take up transfrontier territory annexed by the Imperial Factor on behalf of Whitehall. 'In the self-governing colonies', as Lord Ripon superbly well expressed the principle behind the policy of trusteeship devolution in the 1890s, 'the more fully we can accept their self-government in the fullest sense, and leave them to deal with the natives in their own way, on their own responsibility, the better for our relations with them and for the maintenance of their loyalty'.[1]

This 'abdication of the governors' (to adapt Carlyle's famous phrase) created the conditions in which Partition could be readily and rapidly converted into settler occupation. The classic example of this trend of events was the departure of the pioneer column of settlers for Rhodesia and the occupation of Mashonaland in 1890–93. But that was merely a simple and direct expression of what was taking place less tidily over a wide range of the frontiers of South Africa. The Cape colony had, for example, since 1886 been encouraged by the Imperial Factor to enlarge its role as proxy-agent of empire by taking up Walfisch Bay on the west coast, and by converting an informal imperialism and 'over-rule' in Gcalekaland and Thembuland into formal administrative responsibilities through acts of annexation on the east coast borderlands. By 1890, from that advanced vantage-point in the Transkei, the Cape administrative corps was restive to extend its responsibilities to include Pondoland – which they did in 1894, at the point of a gun, behind which stood the Rhodes ministry.[2]

The Afrikaners of the highveld were also active in conducting their own local expansionist drives as part of the territorial adjustments at the core of the Partition in South Africa. They consolidated their holdings in Zululand, and by the late-1880s had joined the 'New Republic' to its parent state – as the district of Vryheid – so really creating a 'greater Transvaal' state. Having achieved that local Scramble for African territory, the Boer energies increased in Swaziland: by 1890 that African kingdom was well on the way to being drawn into the net of Transvaal authority.

Lastly, in colonial Natal, the long-term ambition of the white settlers to control the Nguni was also achieved. Responsible government was granted in 1893; four years later the remainder of Zululand came under colonial authority. They had acquired all they had wished in Zululand or Basutoland or Pondoland. White Natalians had at last gained, in land and labour, much they had yearned for since the 'era of Shepstone'.

The mechanics by which this local expansion of settler and Boer was achieved is worth discussing. It is revealing of the manner in which Partition soon shaded over into a local Scramble for occupation of the annexed lands in the 1890s; and it is indicative of the way in which the forces of the New Imperialism acted in a manner complementary to the local expansive ágencies, to produce a situation of increasing African incorporation within the polities and economies of colonial South Africa.

The occupation of 'Rhodesia' 1890–94: the BSA Company as imperial agent in Zambesia

The early history of the BSA in founding 'Rhodesia' – as Zambesia was styled after 1891 – was not the marked success of empire by proxy-agent desired by the British metropolitan government.[3] Indeed, the very opposite. The BSA Company did not prove itself to be the responsible agency of administration which had been somewhat naively anticipated; and violent disturbance was always possible from the moment that the pioneer column of some 200 founding settlers and police snaked its way up through Bechuanaland from the Cape in July 1890, skirted Matabeleland, and came to rest in Mashonaland in September. The motives of the settlers were a mixture of adventure and expectation, 'but the ruling passion was gold'.[4]

Lobengula's court and his warrior advisers could now well assess the direct consequences of the chief's attempts to buy isolation by a single super concession to Her Majesty's appointed agents. The Ndeble leadership grew restive as they watched the proceedings of the BSA company settlers and officials. Lobengula was driven to put the most optimistic interpretation on the Rudd document and the manner of the occupation in Mashonaland: 'I am going to give the white men a hole to dig', he was said to have told his unhappy *indunas*, 'you told me you were afraid of guns against you – the white men will bring guns and horses. If you go against me I will have to call the white men to help me.'[5] Lobengula desperately hoped that by steering the white pioneers away from Matabeleland to Mashonaland he could both secure his own state and also win time in his continuing struggle to contend with the white people who pressed on his society and land. This strategy could work only so long as he could restrain his army; and, equally important, only so long as the local white agency of empire did not move against Matabeleland.

Here Lobengula's policy came unstuck, with awesome results for the Ndebele. Not only did many of the whites have ambitions over mineral resources in Matabeleland, but many of the company's officials argued from the beginning that 'Rhodesia' could only be developed securely once the 'threat' of Ndebele power – 'the Matabele Question' to the whites – was removed. The BSA Company officials had not come to dig a hole but to make a colonial state. This fact simply ruined Lobengula's authority. 'If he attacks us, he is doomed,' as one company official wrote as early as January 1890, 'if he does not, his fangs will be drawn, the pressure of civilization on all his borders will press more and more heavily upon him and the desired result, the disappearance for ever of the Matabele as a power, if delayed is yet the more certain.'[6]

By 1893 some of Rhodes' close associates were actually looking to a conflict. 'We have the excuse for a row over murdered women and children now,' Jameson reported from Mashonaland, 'and getting Matabeleland open would give us a tremendous lift in shares, and everything else'.[7] To his brother, Sam, Jameson was even less guarded in wishing for an open conflict with the Ndebele, for 'though expensive and troublesome in the meantime, it will be a quicker way of making the country go ahead, than by peaceful policy of gradual absorption of the Matabele amongst our black labourers'.[8] Jameson got his war that same year. Even Lord Grey could now write of how well the BSA Company forces were 'crumpling up' the Ndebele – a necessary, if ugly thing, 'for once the black cloud at Bulawayo is cleared away the development of Mashonaland will proceed space'.[9]

For our purposes of political analysis what was to be striking, in this none too creditable process of Scrambling for Zambesia on-the-ground, was the reaction of the Imperial Factor to the role of the BSA Company in Central Africa 1890–95. The colonial office had moved to the charter policy well aware of its limitations. 'The existing system of chartering,' one clerk minuted in early 1889, 'has not been such a success as to make it augur well for its extension to a poor inland country, the seat of political troubles.'[10] These reservations were not removed by the early history of the BSA Company – indeed the reverse had taken place. 'I regard the system of administration by Chartered Companies as essentially bad', Knutsford's successor, Lord Ripon, commented in November 1893 to Gladstone,

These companies are really speculative, got up mainly for stock exchange purposes, and a good deal blown up in that aspect of their existence. The British South Africa Company has been very near bankruptcy, from which probably their success in [the] Matabeleland [War] will save them for a time. But anyhow they are not pleasant instruments of administration.[11]

The uneven quality of that early administrative practice was well summed up by Milner writing in 1897:

I am dead against any attempt to rip up the past, but, between ourselves, it is a bad story. On the one hand, land was alienated in the most reckless manner to Companies and individuals, on the other hand, a lot of unfit people were allowed to exercise power ... with regard to the natives, in a manner which cannot be defended.[12]

Between 1891 and 1893 the British metropolitan authorities were also disabused of their faith in the financial structuring of the BSA Company by its founder. The colonial office soon complained bitterly that whereas in the case of the 'Royal Niger', 'East Africa' and 'North Borneo' Companies, they had been dealing with men 'of the statesmen and philanthropic class ... actuated by no baser motive than a vague hope of something like a star or handle to their names', in the case of the Rhodesian venture it was all rather different: 'when we deal with the British South Africa, we are dealing with men who represent the latest development of the Limited Liability Acts working in a sphere which is the paradise of the monopolising financiers'.[13] The directors of the BSA Company had indeed taken every opportunity to enrich themselves, not least by the manipulation of shares in which one company was capitalised upon another, so creating an even larger pile of 'paper capital'.[14] It was not exactly 'proper' financial behaviour, and it certainly placed an unreal value on the shares issued for public investment, but it was legal.

Far more questionable yet was the use to which the founders of the imperial company had put the Rudd Concession in floating the chartered enterprise. What the amalgamated syndicate had done, in the simplest terms, was form a company on the basis of the Rudd–Lobengula agreement – the 'Central Search Association', later the 'United Concessions

Company' – which had then granted a *lease* on the concession to the proposed BSA charter company. This had obvious advantages in safeguarding the concession if the chartered enterprise failed. The 'catch' in this perfectly legitimate arrangement was that the founder of the chartered company allowed the Imperial Factor, and the Chartered shareholders, to presume ownership of the concessions by the new imperial company. In fact, the BSA Company had to pay a charge of 50% of its profits, to 'United Concessions', in return for use of the concession. These facts surfaced in 1891, and were given wide circulation in a sensational article in Labouchere's journal, *Truth*, on 23 April of that year: 'All these transactions are very much on a par with those that characterised the South Sea Bubble.'[15]

It took some two years however before the British authorities had fully documented the matter. A Confidential Memorandum was drawn up on the origins of the BSA Company, and submitted to the British cabinet.[16] The memorandum had no hesitation in stating that,

Her Majesty's Government were misled as to the real position which the Chartered Company, on its formation, was to occupy, and the nature of its interest in the concession or concessions which it was believed would constitute its assets, the actual arrangement being of a nature contrary to what was understood, and apparently incongruous with the particulars of the position recited in the preamble of the Charter.[17]

Most of all, the imperial officials were naturally concerned over the ownership of the Rudd Concession.

It is understood that the concession from Lo Bengula never actually passed, in full proprietory right, to the Chartered Company, but is leased by the 'United Concessions Company' to the Chartered Company, for a payment of one half of the net profit of all their present and prospective undertakings, which, however, have to be conducted entirely by and at the expense of the Chartered Company.[18]

According to the senior official in the colonial office, if this fact had been discovered in 1889 'The Charter would certainly have been refused'; and he wondered 'whether the announcement of it now [in September 1892] does not render it necessary to consider whether the charter should be revoked'.[19]

In short: by the end of 1893 the British authorities were faced with a chequered history of administrative and financial practice, and the question had indeed to be faced whether the BSA Company should not be stripped of its imperial support and its charter. Very significantly, the British government decided against this course. 'Although I think we have been misled by the British South Africa Company's founders,' the colonial secretary wrote wearily, 'I am not prepared to take any steps towards putting an end to the Charter.'[20] Why? One strong reason was financial. Harcourt spoke of Rhodes as 'a great jingo' but 'a cheap jingo'; while from within the colonial office came an explanation of how Rhodes' wealth would release officialdom from the close supervision of the Treasury, which only worked to 'thwart and delay, and an Audit Office to worry . . . with queries about the microscopical irregularities of the local accounting officers, which you are expected to explain satisfactorily on pain of being had up and badgered before the Public Accounts Committee'. Further, cancelling the Charter 'would impose upon this country the responsibility of taking over and administering the enormous territory subject to the concessions. We must also bear in mind the position of the Company north of the Zambesi.'[21]

The Liberal government which succeeded Salisbury's Unionists in 1892 might have been expected – containing as it did noted 'anti-imperialists' and 'little Englanders' – to be more critical of the Chartered policy. Yet they, too, followed in the parsimony arguments of their predecessors. They were encouraged and influenced by Sir Hercules Robinson, who was now in retirement but still highly active in supporting 'imperialism through colonialism' in South Africa. When the BSA Company was under attack from Exeter Hall, for its methods in the war of 1893, he came strongly to the defence not merely of the Rhodesians but of the policy which had initiated empire by chartered company. 'As far as I can judge the Company has done its work well as regards the opening up of the country', he wrote in an extensive and noted letter to the *Times* (7 November 1893):

It has expended considerably over a million sterling in the undertaking, a sum which it would have been impossible to have extracted from the House of Commons for the purpose. The local managers have worked in full accord with the High Commissioner [Lord Loch] deferring to his views in every respect . . .

I cannot believe that the Company would seek either the extermination of the Matabele or their expulsion beyond Zambesia. But if, unfortunately, the Company's views should be irreconcilable with those of Her Majesty's Government, and the establishment of direct Imperial control over such a vast and distant country as Matabeleland be decided on, I trust the cost of such a policy will be counted beforehand, and that if adopted it will not be sought subsequently to escape from the inevitable consequences. Hitherto annexations and protectorates in South Africa have been decided on only to be followed later on by a perpetual wrangle with the Treasury for the means of maintaining a decent administration.

Robinson's extensive experience of trying to cope with administrative consequences of the Scramble in the 1880s did not allow him to be sanguine as regards creating a 'decent administration' in Rhodesia. He pointed out that the Bechuanaland Protectorate cost £120,000 per annum, though run on a shoe-string budget; and Zambesia could consume at least half a million pounds sterling annually, for a basic administrative infrastructure.

His view was widely canvassed and carried to the cabinet itself. 'If there remain any lingering doubts as to Matabele policy', Harcourt wrote for example to Gladstone that very day,

I wish you would look at a letter in today's *Times* by Sir Hercules Robinson. Oddly enough he places the extra cost of administering Matabeleland at precisely the figure I fixed, of £500,000 per ann[um]., besides having to do all the slaughtering ourselves.[22]

The new high commissioner in South Africa, Lord Loch, watched the violence in Rhodesia with increasing trepidation, and wondered aloud if the Liberal government in London could not exercise some restraining influence on the BSA Company officials.[23] But Whitehall would have none of that.[24] Nor were they prepared to act after the war in supervising the peace settlement. Rhodes wrote haughtily to warn them away from any intervention in the political affairs of Matabeleland: 'The British South Africa Company never asked the British Government for any assistance [in the war]. We have paid expenses, and I claim we should have [control of] settlement of the terms of peace.'[25] Rhodes had his way.[26]

Beyond a preference for cheap empire, the British refusal to move against the chartered company also had larger political reasons which tell us much of the nature of the Victorian initiatives in the Partition of Southern Africa. 'The immediate policy of Her Majesty's Government may be briefly stated as follows', Loch's 'Instructions' as high commissioner noted on the very eve of the implementation of the chartered policy for the interior Partition (November 1889):

They desire to maintain and strengthen firmly relations with the South African Republic and the Orange Free State ... they desire to work in harmony with the Colonial Government of the Cape and Natal, and ... leave to the Cape Ministers full freedom of action in regard to matters for which those ministers are responsible, paying at the same time due regard to the views of the Colonial Government in respect of external affairs affecting the Colony; and lastly, they desire ... the peaceful settlement and good government of the native territories not now under any form of civilised government, to increase the facilities of communication with them, and to encourage the opening up of their hitherto undeveloped resources by the gradual introduction of capital and labour under British control.[27]

It was in that last, but vast, area of imperial responsibility that the BSA Company was to operate, 'under such conditions imposed upon them by the Imperial Government as may be absolutely compatible with the best interests of the native chiefs and their people'. Carefully controlled, it was to act 'in proxy' for the already hard-pressed imperial government:

A strongly constituted British Company has . . . been formed, uniting the interests of all the principal holders of valid concessions in the native territories south of the Zambesi . . . The Company is incorporated for trading and mining purposes in the first instance, and is empowered to assume, subject to the control and super-vision of Her Majesty's Government through the High Commissioner, such administrative functions as, by cessions of territory, or delegation of powers from the native chiefs, may hereafter devolve upon it.[28]

Cancelling the charter because of the misdemeanours of its officials in 'Rhodesia' was thus soon quite out of the question. 'I don't favour the system of administering great districts of country by Chartered Company,' the Liberal secretary of state for colonies commented in 1893 to the high commissioner, 'but I found this Company in existence when I came into office. It is my duty to work honestly with it, and to make it succeed as an administrative arrangement, if I can. I have a personal liking for Rhodes: his boldness and resource attract me.'[29] That faith in Rhodes was cruelly exposed a mere two years later when the scandal of Jameson's Raid sur-rounded the imperial protégé. But before that moment of truth, every effort was made to see that Rhodes and the charter policy were supported in carrying imperial burdens in South Africa. 'Mr Rhodes dined with me on Saturday,' Knutsford wrote to Salisbury, soon after the charter was granted, 'and had some talk with me about South Africa.' Knutsford's assessment of that conversation is interesting.

I think Rhodes may be trusted, but it [is] as yet difficult to say whether his posi-tion as Premier is safe. His opponents will always be able to contend that all he does is done in the interest of the B[ritish]. South Africa Company, but so long as Hofmeyr, who represents the Afrikander party, supports him, he is probably stronger than his opponents.[30]

The British commitment to Rhodes was complete.[31] Lobengula had lost any support from the Imperial Factor he might once have enjoyed.

Now that we have granted a Charter to the South African Company, it is more desirable that we should urge Lo Bengula to acknowledge and assist it. This is the more important for the Queen's former message to Lo Bengula would lead him to view any concession with suspicion, and specially the concession which he granted to Messrs. Rudd, Maguire and Thompson, which really is the conces-sion taken up by the Chartered Company.[32]

Further, when it soon emerged in the early 1890s that the charter, based on that Rudd Concession, did not actually cover the rights to land settle-ment[33] – which had actually already begun on a large scale – the British government stood by Rhodes. Every effort was made to assist the charter company in acquiring rights to settle and develop Central Africa, as against merely exploiting its mineral potential. The British high commissioner, Lord Loch, in some alarm spoke of the 'necessity [which] now exists for acquiring some authority from Lo Bengula, either direct or in some way clearly explicit, by which occupation titles can be given to settlers [,] both for agricultural purposes . . .'[34] In fact, as the high commissioner and the Rhodesians soon discovered, Lobengula had already issued such a 'settlement concession' to a syndicate led by Lippert. Undaunted by this awkward discovery, the British authorities suggested that Rhodes swiftly acquire this concession. In Loch's measured words, 'If the Lippert Concessions are genuine, then it might be well for the [BSA] Company to consider the advisability of buying them, for altho' some are contrary to Rudd's Concessions, others seem to provide for a land settlement, which is much required.'[35] When the broad validity of the Lippert Concessions were established, the high commissioner became even more insistent that the BSA Company buy out the options; such a course appeared to be 'the best solution of a difficult position, for it will enable the Chartered Company to make some land settlements before the next trekking season'.[36] Ultimately, a potential crisis was averted when Lippert sold out to the Rhodesians. The British were as relieved as the charter syndicate.

Even the shrewd, pragmatic Lord Salisbury ultimately believed that the charter policy was the best technique by which to (a) conduct inexpensive administrative empire in tropical Africa, and (b) serve the political purpose of challenging 'Krugerism' in Southern African politics. He told the Lords, in the Uganda debate of February 1895,

I do not think Governments aid our people much when they go to the possession of a new territory . . . See the splendid work Mr Rhodes had done in the southern end of Africa. He has obtained little from any Government in this country, but he has laid the foundation of a splendid Empire, and even the Government of the Transvaal . . . is finding the pressure of English activity all round them so strong that they are slowly giving way.[37]

Milner's cool, analytic mind, had also come to the same conclusion. He deplored the administrative excesses and lapses in Rhodesia; yet, as he pointed out to a sceptical John Mackenzie, in 1889,

Whatever may be the personal sentiments of its managers, the force of circumstances will make the Company British. He must be a pessimist indeed who does not see but surely . . . [that] British influence is once more on the ascendant. . . The Cape might be separatist, and South Africa by itself might be separatist, but a South Africa reaching up to the Zambesi, marching into foreign spheres of influence, and needing the protecting arm of Great Britain against Portuguese or German interference with its own development, will lean more and more on us. I think I see the development in Rhodes himself.[38]

The high Victorian hopes raised by the chartering of the BSA Company as administrative and development agency in Zambesia were to be progressively eroded by events such as the wars with the Shona and Ndebele; and then finally shattered by Rhodes' use of the BSA Company troopers in the invasion of Kruger's state in December 1895 when Dr Jameson's 'Raid' took place.[39] Sir William Harcourt, previously a strong supporter of empire by charter, and 'empire on the cheap', spoke of the latter affair as one of 'disaster and disgrace'.[40] It was epithet which could well apply to the charter policy itself in the era of the Scramble.

That policy had substituted a commercial agency, headed by an expansive capitalist, for responsible trusteeship administration. Little wonder that Rhodes allowed such a concentration of power to go to his head. Ripon soon claimed that he was behaving in South Africa like 'the king' of the region; and Milner argued that the finance imperialist had created his own 'absolute monarchy' at the Cape.[41] Whitehall had rightly been sceptical of Rhodes and his associates when they first approached London for a charter. But the possibilities of empire 'on the cheap', together with a political counterpoise to Krugerism which would bring Afrikanerdom to heel, had caught the imagination of the 'official mind' in a manner which blinded them to the limitations of a Rhodes-based policy.

The British authorities had, in short, come to reason that the great Northern Expansion was necessary to strengthen the Imperial Factor acting through the local agency of Cape 'Colonialism'. A single act therefore appeared to be all that was required to solve the manifold and fundamental problems of *Pax Britannica* in South Africa. By granting a charter to the BSA Company they would assist the Cape in its struggles to regain the economic and political paramountcy on the *veld*; win new political friends and influence among the white settlers of the Cape; develop a political federal grouping of British states against the Afrikaner republics; avoid the necessity of direct British administrative activity in Zambesia; and meet any Portuguese, Belgian or German threat to British interests in Central Africa. The motives for the charter policy were therefore as old as the traditional concepts of British supremacy at 'the Cape'; and as new as the changing economic balance of South Africa, brought about by the highveld gold revolution, and the challenge of Great Power rivalry in the strategy of the 'New Imperialism'.

This, of course, is very much how Rhodes himself had viewed the evolution of the charter policy. He saw it quite clearly as an addendum to his political and economic machinations in South Africa proper; and he justifiably regarded it as a triumph of the agencies of local colonialism, which had now won high favour with the metropolitan Imperial Factor. It was for these 'South African reasons' that he wished the charter's terms to be 'as large as possible, especially with the [boundary] clause and the policy being decided to gradually slide [Rhodesia] into a self-governing state, for the more powerful the Charter, the more likely is [South African] federation'.[42] The British differed from Rhodes only in their lack of enthusiasm in extending territorial advances to help bring this about. Where Rhodes wanted ultimately to secure 'the balance of Africa', British policy-makers were content to secure the balance south of the Zambesi alone. 'What I look to,' Ripon wrote to Rosebery in 1894, putting their long-term policy-aims in a sentence, 'is a sort of federal Union of S[outh] Africa, of British Territory, S[outh] African Republic, and Orange Free State, in which we of course should have the hegemony.'[43]

The British metropolitan imperialists had joined the Scramble for South Africa – and helped to Partition the interior of South-central Africa in favour of the local forces of 'Colonialism' – in the hope that this would set political developments in favour of the Imperial Factor, its interests and peripheral agencies. 'What I am in a hurry to write about today is *Rhodes*, especially with regard to his position in the North', Milner wrote from the perspective of his new high commissioner-ship in Southern Africa (2 June 1897) to the secretary of state. 'He works to making the territory of the BSA C[ompany] into a separate Colony, ultimately self-governed ... The Colony ... he means to unite with the Cape Colony and Natal, and then the three combined will bring peaceful pressure upon the [Afrikaners'] republic to drive them into a S[outh] African federation.'[44] Lord Salisbury thought he detected this happening as early as 1895. He saw the charter policy as challenging the republican Boers so successfully that 'they will be compelled to fall into line and join the great unconscious federation that is growing up'.[45]

Zululand transferred to Natal administration 1887–1904

Variants on the same theme were now to be played out by the Imperial Factor in its relationships with the other African polities of South Africa: having thrown a net of hegemony over these chiefdoms the Imperial Factor steadily moved in the 1890s to see that direct metropolitan trusteeship was replaced by the administration of local colonial authorities. This did not mean that humanitarianism was dropped out of the window in a cynical gesture; but it did mean that, in the final balance, economy had out-weighed trusteeship; and that Whitehall saw incorporation of these remaining independent African groups under local white authority as part and parcel of a general move to encourage the development of a united self-governing 'South African' state. If events in Rhodesia had starkly revealed the new principles of devolved empire operating in the aftermath of the Scrambles for South Africa, then events in South-east Africa – involving Zulu and Natalians – were best to exhibit the techniques for accomplishing this transference of local power.[46] 'All the world wants us to take Zululand, only because it is next door, and lest somebody else should get it', the British colonial secretary wrote to his premier in the midst of the Scrambles for South-east Africa, in language devoid of any concerns of trusteeship, yet singularly pragmatic: 'This passion for annexation, and consequent contempt of economy, is not more to my taste than to yours: but it seems to be the dominant idea of democracy... and I think it will not be a mere passing fashion. Look at America'.[47] In the late 1880s, however, Zululand declined to respond peacefully to the British policies of economy and benign neglect.

Imperial intervention in Zululand during the Partition had created a situation of high instability; the determination to withdraw from those problems now worsened it. By early 1887 the British Resident in the Zulu Reserve, Melmoth Osborn, reported such disorder and impending troubles in Zululand as a whole that the British were forced to reconsider the question of annexation and the responsibilities of trusteeship. Unable to have the Natalians undertake the task, and fearful of humanitarian opinion if the Afrikaners were allowed to implement their own style of administrative policy in Zululand – in 1886 over 40 MPs joined an Exeter Hall campaign to 'save' the Zulu from the New Republicans – the metropolitan government reluctantly took up the administration of Zululand,[48] on a 'temporary' basis. Underlying the annexation was the presumption that the Zulu state and its subjects would eventually pass under colonial control.[49] Until that time, Zululand was placed under the Natal governor, as governor of Zululand, with Melmoth Osborn transposed as Resident Commissioner for all Zululand (1887–93).

The annexation solved little; its administration actually created the conditions for further disorder. The Zulu secured naught for their comfort: the lands which had been lost to the Boers, in the British recognition of their republic in 1886, were now permanently abandoned;[50] the old conflicts between the Usuthu Royal House and their rivals intensified at the hands of the local imperial authorities – Osborn's favouritism for Zibhebhu was blatant; lastly, the imperial policy attempted to control Zululand through magisterial officialdom, so by-passing Dinizulu as head of the Zulu state.

Fearing a revival of Usuthu authority, the imperialists attempted a further resurrection of the divide and rule approach. An excellent case has been made by an African historian for arguing that this was a fundamental error of administrative politics, from which much of the future unrest in Zululand was to rise.[51]

Failure either to conciliate or establish a workable collaborative alliance with Dinizulu certainly meant that, from 1887 onwards, the Zulu always had the choice of an allegiance outside that of the British authority administering the state. The Usuthu were regarded by the imperialists as the legatees of all the political vices of Cetshwayo's rule: it is little wonder therefore that, having been cast in the role of the enemies of imperial and colonial interests, Dinizulu and his supporters finally came to live up to the British expectations. Indeed, Dinizulu had never really expected the British annexation to favour his cause, and he may indeed have regretted it. He appears to have ruled his group after 1887 as he had before the protectorate was declared, by simply ignoring Osborn and his team of magistrates; he also probably continued to use his old alliance with the Afrikaner republicans in the hope of throwing one kind of white intruder against another.[52]

One year after the British annexation of 1887 Zululand fairly seethed with political tension. Osborn's support of Zibhebhu finally tripped the wires of Usuthu discontent – he allowed Zibhebhu to leave the old Reserve area and return to the Black Umfolozo region, at the cost of thousands of Usuthu.[53] Violent disturbances began. The eruptions ended with Dinizulu banished to St Helena, after a stormy trial in Natal, and with Zululand sharply divided between collaborative and hostile chiefs. There was now no chance whatever of governing Zululand through the old Royal House. The Natal governor had rightly commented the year before: 'The House of Shaka is a thing of the past, like water that has been spilt.'[54]

Expansive groups in white Natalian society had watched this progress of events with close interest, and increasing irritation, since the 1879 war and the subsequent British administrative 'settlements' in Zululand. They saw the only 'sound solution to the Zulu problem' – as a settler petition put it (1886) – in the advance of their commercial and agricultural designs through the incorporation of Zululand into Natal.[55] The Zulu would be transformed from warriors into workers, the Natal trade with the interior would increase; the political peace in Zululand would allow an expansion of pastoral and sugar industries from the colony; gold and coal deposits could be properly explored and developed; and this broadening area of Natal's 'co-prosperity zone' would give the colony the kind of rival status to the Cape that it had always craved.[56]

These Natal pressures had hitherto been merely turned aside by the British imperial government. In 1893, however, Natal was granted self-government. The same concerns over Natal's administrative capacity to rule the Zulu, coupled with humanitarian pressures – both in Zululand and England – against settler government of Africans, still applied. But they applied with less force each year after 1893. 'Sooner or later', as even the sympathetic Natal governor Sir W. Hely-Hutchinson (1893–1901) remarked in 1895, 'it will become undesirable to resist the persistent demands of Natal for incorporation'.[57]

The British agreed. They did so for many reasons. Economy, a desire to be rid of the 'Zulu problem', the Natalians' readiness to agree to guarantees for specific Zulu rights, division among humanitarians, the increasing strength of the colony, and a desire to conciliate white Natalian opinion over the loss of territory to the Afrikaners in Zululand and Swaziland, all played their part. But above all they handed Zululand over to the colonial authorities because by the 1890s they saw it as the right decision, both for the cultural development of the Zulu people, and the political strength of the empire. Metropolitan officialdom largely shared the notions of local Natal officialdom that there could be no permanent solution to the political problems of south-east Africa until the Nguni were finally acculturated to the 'civilised' and 'progressive' societies of the white settler. It was only by 'integration' into the white political economy that it was possible to 'convert a savage into a civilised being', or that an African could 'profit by the blessings which a civilised Government gives to him'.[58] G. M. Theal, the colonial historian of Southern Africa, well reflected this Victorian view-point in his summation of events in Zululand from the war of 1879 to the banishment of Dinizulu: 'In this manner the most formidable of the military powers that had their origin in the early years of the nineteenth century was overthrown, to the great gain of not only Natal, which colony was now able to make a great bound forward in prosperity, but of every black man in South Africa.'[59] British statesmen largely accepted the notion of Progress through the civilising influences of the imperial and colonial presence. Political advantages also applied. They saw no lack of humanitarian concern in devolving responsibility for traditional societies in Africa, or the Pacific, onto the local fragments of Victorian England, in the form of the responsible self-governing English settlement colonies. Indeed, the South African expert in the colonial office was even of the opinion that the British colonists 'understand Native management much better than we do'.[60] Set even more broadly, traditional societies benefited from the close association of the white settler: in the inimitable language of Lord Salisbury, traditionalists could never hope to progress if they were shielded from culture-contact, and continued to 'hang back from the movement of the world'.

Zululand was integrated into Natal by phases, between 1897 and 1904. Dinizulu was returned (10 January 1898) as merely an Usuthu chief and as a government *induna*; the authority of the other more than 80 chiefs was to be respected by the Natal administration in civil matters; and there was to be a five year pause before Zululand was 'thrown open' to white entrepreneurs and farmers. The final denouement for the old Zulu state took place after the Anglo-Boer War, when a Land Commission accomplished the last step in the partition of Zululand. Some 3,887,000 acres was set aside for the Zulu, in fragmentary 'Reserves'. The Commission also granted 2,613,000 choice acres in the heart of the old Zulu state to white agencies of expansion and exploitation – for sugar, wattle, cattle and mineral enterprises.[61] 'Zululand' was no more.

The years 1879–1904 had indeed witnessed not so much the reassertion of the Imperial Factor as the triumph of the local settler colonialism of the Afrikaner and the Anglo-Saxon. Dinizulu had attempted to play the politics of Partition by a mixture of diplomacy and defiance. The results were less than satisfactory: his 'allies', the Afrikaners, carved their extensive New Republic out of Zulu pastoral lands, and then joined them to the Transvaal state; his 'foes', the British and Natalians, made agreement with the Afrikaners, and simply Partitioned what they willed without reference to the Zulu people. The Scramble in South-east Africa acquired its belligerent energy from a unique combination of British concern for vital strategic imperial interests at risk, plus the economic concerns of local colonial agencies in African resources.

Imperialism at the point of a gun: Pondoland 1886–94

The pattern of events repeated itself to the south of Zululand. The Mpondo–Cape Agreement of 1886 proved to be only a loaded pause in the local colonial, rather than metropolitan advance, on Pondoland. There was an inevitability in the event which even contemporaries felt: the senior Whitehall colonial official could already speak, at the time of the 1886 Agreement, of that moment 'when the next step – annexation of Pondoland – has to be taken'.[62] Both internal and external factors helped to explain why the Partition came to Pondoland in 1894 in the fashion which it did.[63]

Internally, the Mpondo state suffered severe political crises in the immediate aftermath of the 1886 treaty. Mqikela died (28 October 1887) without a son born to the 'great wife', Masarile, and a succession dispute ensued. The tribal elders appointed Sigcawu (c. 1860–1905) to the chief-tainship, but this was contested by the 'right-hand-son', Mdibanso. After months of dispute, Sigcawu was installed as paramount (13 February 1888).[64] More trouble, however, soon dogged his authority. His father's great adviser, Mhlangaso, declined to adopt a subservient role, and wished indeed to continue as the dominating influence in Mpondo leadership. Sigcawu desired to rule in the personal fashion of his grandfather, Faku, and a smouldering internecine struggle for power began. By 1890 their respective supporters had begun a lengthy civil war, which spilled over into Natal, and sent tremors of unrest through the Cape-administered Transkei Territories. The 'forces of civilisation' – in colonial Natal and the Cape – revived their talk of the necessity for a local imperial advance, in the cause of 'law and order', not to mention 'development'.[65]

Sigcawu also attracted troubles to himself. He encouraged the interest of the adjacent British settler states in his affairs by a dangerous policy of concession-granting. In the short term, this brought him considerable financial advantages: in the long term, it helped bring down the whole uneasy political status quo. Einwald had been allowed to return to Pondo-land in mid-1887, and he brought the 'German factor' back into Mpondo politics. Within a year three distinct German concessionaire groups were at work in the area – that led by Baron von Steinanter having brought much agricultural equipment, and a few settlers, to develop the 40,000 acres they had been granted. Other concessionaires also came to Sigcawu's court, and were rewarded with various 'grants' in return for suitable remunera-tion. J. R. Girling secured an extensive mineral concession; a similar (and conflicting) concession was given to Cooke Bros. Ltd of the Cape; individual Natal traders were given rights to the market in various parts of Pondo-land; and a few white farmers secured parcels of land on the colonial–Mpondo frontiers. Sigcawu was creating, on a small scale, what was already taking place on a large scale in Swaziland.

The political results of these economic concessions was vital. The British discounted the significance of the 'German factor' – and were borne out by the fact that the German government made no move to support the con-cessionaires, while the Mpondo tired of the Germans and expelled them with Mhlangaso's fall from influence. Yet the Cape colony was sufficiently agitated to appoint a Resident Commissioner in Pondoland north of the Mzimvubu. The first strands of the Cape administrative net began to fall about Mpondo politics. Sigcawu did not like it, ignored J. M. Scott as Commissioner, and protested to London: 'I am most anxious to retain the independence of my people relating to the internal affairs of my country.'[66]

He protested too late. The metropolitan government was by now clear in its own mind that the affairs of South-east Africa should be settled by the responsible authority of its local imperial agency, the Cape ministry, and indeed stated categorically in 1892 that it had 'always [been] understood that the responsibility involved in the direction of Pondo affairs was the concern of the Cape government alone'.[67]

Further, the activities of the Natal traders, the German concessionaires, and the Cape Colony's Resident Commissioner, gave an added spur to Natal settler colonialism. Now the possessor of responsible government, eager to secure Zulu lands to the colony, a strong expansionist mood gripped a segment of the Natal political and economic elite. Commercial pressures were particularly important in pressing the new 'independent ministry' to create a 'greater Natal', before the Cape moved to draw Pondoland even more closely into its control.[68] In short: beginning with Sigcawu's unwise concessions, the dynamism for a local rival Scramble for Pondoland, and its resources, was increasingly created. Although Rhodes disclaimed any fears of Natal expansion in pressing for a swift Cape annexation of Pondoland, his disclaimer does not convince: the colony was deeply concerned over its position in Southern Africa, and the Mpondo affair, coming on top of the Transvaal gold discoveries, and the 1893 republican tariff agreements at Charlottetown with Natal, did not augur well for those who saw local politics as basically a struggle between a Cape- or Transvaal-dominated 'South African' federal state. Pondoland did not fall to the forces of Scramble because the Great Powers had designs on an isolated African state. Rather, through its position as interlocking independent territory, between two colonial states, it both fed their sense of rivalry, and also offended their European sensibilities as a 'barbarian' anachronism in an expanding tide of white civilisation. In the apt phrase of the Cape's historian, Dr Saunders, by 1894 'the continued existence of African rule in Pondoland seemed contrary to the spirit of the age'.[69]

This last element, and the pressures of the Cape administrative ideals of paternal trusteeship in the cause of Progress, should not be under-estimated as a factor in the subjection of the Mpondo. Since 1878 the Cape had been increasingly involved in the administrative development of all the Transkei Territories. 'Law and order', 'labour and progress', had expanded with the magistrates; it had been modified in its application as a result of the noted Barry Commission of 1883; but the credo of 'civilisation by administration' still held good into the 1890s. Rhodes placed his own interpretation on the Cape's 'civilising policy', in offering what he took to be a 'native policy' for all Africa in his Glen Grey Act of 1893. A 'benign paternalism', leading to the acculturation of progressive and individualised Africans into Western culture and the market economy, was thought to be the animating direction of Cape policy: law courts, schools, trade institutes, agricultural advisory boards, medical clinics and mission churches were deployed as agencies not merely of social control, but of cultural enlightenment. The Glen Grey Act crystalised much of this Cape posture, with its labour tax – to encourage industrious individualism – and its local councils – to engage the 'progressive' African peasant in his own modernising government.

Pondoland stood as a great rock of resilient traditionalism, paganism and independence, against this Victorian vision of 'Improvement'. Indeed, for the Cape 'improvers' it symbolised all the 'tribal' and 'barbaric' characteristics of African traditional culture. 'Industry, sobriety, and chastity are social virtues unknown to the Pondos', as the Cape Resident in Eastern Pondoland once wrote of this whole question of 'civilisation' vs 'barbarism':

A settled indolence is the bane of this people; it is almost impossible to induce or compel a Pondo to work.

Drunkenness is habitual to all classes and conditions. This confirmed habit of intemperance had tended very greatly to deteriorate the physique of the Pondos. . .

As a result of the late abundant harvest, there has been a vast amount of drinking. Brawls have been frequent. . .

The Pondo code of morals is one of the lowest that can be conceived. Amongst other detestable customs, that of *Intonjane* is very generally practised. Female purity is thereby destroyed at the first signs of budding womenhood. Chastity after puberty is a thing unknown to a Pondo girl . . .

A deplorable case of the very unusual crime of incest has lately occurred on a mission station. A case of poisoning, showing a knowledge of toxicology, almost equal to that of the Borgias, has just been reported to me.

Mission work among the Mpondo – mainly by the Wesleyans – was undertaken on some scale. Yet even here traditionalism apparently remained remarkably resistent to Victorian protestant values:

Unhappily, it cannot be claimed that missionary efforts have produced any marked changes in the lives or conduct of the mass of the people. When, however, we take into consideration the intensely superstitious character of the Pondos, and the tenacity with which they cling to their old barbarous customs, it is not difficult to understand their passive but dogged resistance to Christianity, which is looked upon by them as a destructive innovation of the white man. Against the dead weight of Pondo heathenism the progress of Christianity must, under the circumstances, be necessarily a slow one.[70]

Implicit in this gloomy prognosis of Mpondo society, was the notion that Cape annexation could alone 'throw open' Pondoland to the stimulus of Progress, Improvement and Development.

Administrative pressures to incorporate Pondoland into a uniform Cape system of African government, in the whole Southeast seaboard set of territories, grew ever stronger in the 1890s. The civil war reached a new height of intensity in 1894, and brought a political centre of disorder into the area which was anathema to the administrative mind; Mhlangaso fled to Natal, and began agitating for colonial assistance; and sensational individual instances of Mpondo 'barbarity' were cited, by Cape civil and religious improvers, as a potential threat to the Progress of the rest of the Transkei – the torture of one of Mqikela's widows for witchcraft, for example, being taken as just one such register of Mpondo 'backwardness'. 'At the beginning of 1894,' wrote Theal, 'the colonial authorities regarded the condition of things in Pondoland as such that the country and people must be brought at once under the control of civilised men.'[71]

Rhodes decided to move on Pondoland. He was strongly backed by the Cape administrative corps in the Transkei. Henry Elliot (1826–1912) and Walter Stanford (1850–1933), the senior officials of that service, hastened to implement the annexation. Stanford's *Reminiscences* and private papers give a vivid account of this local colonial expansion. Meetings were held with Sigcawu, and the lesser chiefs, at which the Mpondo were invited to surrender their independence to the Cape authorities. War was the alternative to capitulation. 'So far all is going as smoothly as possible', Stanford wrote to his wife on 27 February 1894. 'The Western people will submit quietly ... doubt is felt regarding my friend Sigcau [sic], but I think he will see that there is no other course for him than to accept the inevitable, with as good a grace as he can.'[72] In his *Diary*, Stanford put the situation even more plainly: 'Sigcau was hemmed in on three sides and behind was the deep sea'.[73] This was pretty well the message spelled out to the beleaguered Sigcawu at the vital meetings in March. Elliot told the paramount chief that

The Government wanted peaceable annexation of Pondoland, but if necessary they would not shrink from war... He had no wish to either coax or intimidate the chief, but he did not want it to be urged hereafter that anything had been kept from Sigcawu on this occasion. Even as he travelled up, the dogs of war were straining at the leash and held back only by the strong arm of the Government.

Sigcawu, in desperate political trouble, tried to temporise with the imperialists. According to Stanford he asked pointedly: 'Were other chiefs under like circumstances dealt with as he was?... What had he done?... What wrong had he committed in the past?' Stanford refused to be drawn from his task:

I replied... His actions since he attained chieftainship had not always been wise, but I well knew there were accusations against him of wrongful conduct which were not true. . . In any case, however, a decision had definitely been taken by the Government. . . Personal feelings he must put aside. . . He must save Pondoland for the people and cattle.

Some Mpondo wished to fight. Sigcawu, however, was aware of the divided nature of the Mpondo state, and of the Cape military forces at his boundary. He accepted subjection bitterly (17 March 1894). As Stanford recorded: 'He said that although it was not clear to him that the Government had sufficient cause against him to justify the action taken, still he had decided to submit himself to the Government. . . The Pondo's submitted without having done the [Cape] Government any wrong.'[74]

Imperialism, at the point of a machine-gun, had proved irresistible; and a minor chief, Bokleni, was actually given a demonstration of a corn field laid low by machine-gun fire to encourage his submission.[75] Rarely had Hilaire Belloc's famous lines –

> Whatever happens we have got
> The Maxim gun, and they have not

– applied so directly to an imperial advance in Africa. The white forces of the periphery had once more extended the Partition of South Africa, according to their own interests; the metropolitan government were quite ready to sit out participation in this 'absurd' local Scramble.

Swaziland and Anglo-Boer relations 1889–1902

The same could not be said of the British concern over the parallel Scramble for Swaziland in the early 1890s; strategic more than humanitarian factors drove them to a close involvement. Yet again however it was an involvement and intervention which kept an eye on the possibility of securing metropolitan interests at the same time as meeting the demands, in land and resources, of the local colonial and Boer frontier agencies of expansion. The result was a pattern of Partition even more complex than that in Rhodesia, Pondoland or Zululand: it involved a greater number and variety of local agencies of private enterprise imperialism; and it was also played out within the larger framework of British relations with the Boers.

At the heart of the Scrambles for Swaziland were two sets of documents – 'the documents that killed us', as Swazi oral tradition maintains[76] – one very 'local', the other more broadly 'regional': there were concessions granted by the Swazi kings to the frontier agents of white expansion; there were also a series of constitutional agreements between British and Boer governments delineating rights to the land in Swaziland. The concession documents indicated how, at ground level, a local creeping Partition was taking place, as the Transvaal borderlands 'expanded' to take in Swazi territory piecemeal; the treaty conventions suggested how British metropolitan authorities were in fact using Swaziland as a 'bargaining counter' with Kruger's republic in the strategic diplomacy of hegemony in the interior of South Africa.

The overall result was a messy and mixed pattern of Partition lasting over the entire decade of the 1890s. The fate of Swaziland was not to be finally settled until after the Anglo-Boer War; the era of the Scramble had left the Swazi state disturbed, its sovereignty eroded and much of its land alienated. Reflecting on the complex and questionable way in which the Scramble dealt with Swaziland, one Christian African newspaper, *Inkanyeso Yase Natal*, commented, at the height of this gradual Partition (19 October 1894) that, 'A good many attempts to rob the Swazis of their country have been made, and the methods which have been adopted . . '. are very mean, and do not give Natives reason to honour the white man.'

The Swazi kingdom had only with extreme difficulty survived the inter-state politics of the earlier Partitions of South Africa.[77] They had early made white alliances to survive; for example with the Afrikaners (July 1846) against the incursions of their fellow African traditionalists, the Zulu of Shaka and Dingane, and the rivalry of the Bapedi of Sekwate. King Mswati (1840–68) thus first began the practice of looking to white groups and agencies as an integral part of Swazi statecraft: as the conditions of survival hardened, so the succeeding kings – Ludovonga (1868–74) and Mbandzeni (1879–89) – increasingly rested Swazi independence on the collaboration of agencies of white expansion. Contemporaneously such an external policy did indeed secure the Swazi state, particularly against Zulu militarism; and it allowed Mswati to devote his political skills to domestic issues, not the least being the unification of the kingdom, and the integration of clans fleeing the *Mfecane* and its aftermath. As a Swazi historian reminds us, it was during Mswati's reign that the society became known as *bakaMswati* – 'the people of Mswati' – or 'Swazis' to the Whites.[78] His achievement was thus considerable. But it was bought at a price. His foreign policy, against aggression, had all the security of feeding the predators.

Swazi indebtedness to its white allies was, therefore, already very substantial by the era of the Scramble. During the Partition it became ruinous for the kingdom Mswati bequeathed. His successor, the seventeen year old Ludovonga, allowed a steady stream of traders and adventurers into Swaziland, including a group of farmers who settled the healthy highlands of the Lubombo area. The kingdom also became a well-known refuge for the more notorious whites escaping the justice of their states.[79] Thus when

Mbandzeni succeeded to the throne – after three years of succession crisis (1872–75) – the situation was far from favourable for the Swazi. He inherited a state over which an undefined Transvaal 'suasion' existed, with white settlers secured both on the sensitive borders adjacent to Cetshwayo's state and within Swaziland; with concessionaires eager to expand their claims, and with Afrikaner frontiersmen restless to transform winter grazing lands across Swazi borders into permanent occupation.[80] It was not without considerable significance that a party of over thirty Boers, with 70 wagons – led by C. J. Joubert – came to represent the Transvaal, and 'oversee' King Mbandzeni's coronation at Nkanini; or that a new Afrikaner–Swazi agreement was signed soon after at Ludzidzini (1 July 1875) which, while speaking of Swazi independence, in fact set limits on it – by recognising all the concessions granted to whites, and by setting out conditions of domestic conduct which could justify Boer interference.[81]

The Swazi king clearly thought that the politics of collaboration would secure his state where other African political communities had fallen to the advance of the whites. He went to considerable lengths to maintain his alliances as a means of securing his state. He assisted both the republican and British governments of the Transvaal in the later 1870s against the Bapedi, on the last occasion even despatching his own age group – the *Indlavela* – to assist the imperialists against Sekhukhune.[82] His policy appeared on the surface to be successful. Swazi intervention against the Bapedi led directly to Sekhukhune's defeat; and the Anglo-Afrikaner Convention of 1881 and 1884 both included clauses recognising the independence of the Swazi. The impression of success was false. In practice, the Boers regarded the Swazi as, in some form, 'subjects' of the Transvaal; the Pretoria and London Conventions did not set out fixed frontiers for Swaziland; while the role of white concessionaires grew without abatement, becoming a near mass invasion during the last years of Mbandzeni's reign.

Were the Swazi aware that they were signing away their land and sovereignty in perpetuity in the concession documents? It seems unlikely. For a start, the king wrongly presumed that the concessions merely granted usufructs of Swazi resources. 'In granting land concessions', as a missionary recorded, 'Mbandzeni had always been under the impression that he had granted the land for the lifetime of the actual petitioner'.[83] It is also apparent that the King and his counsellors never fully grasped the meaning and intent of many of the dozens of concessions thrust before them – some on highly technical subjects, such as one for banking which involved advancing 'money upon property and securities of all kinds, to discount bills, notes and other securities, to deal in exchange and specie ... the issue of, or upon, bonds, debentures, bills of exchange, notes or other obligations or securities . . .'[84] The individual concessionaires were alone aware of the full significance of their documents; the Swazi agreed to the grants very often after a most misleadingly simple explanation of their technical components. 'We hold the feather and sign', as one Swazi elder graphically described the process. 'We take the money, but we do not know what it is for.'[85]

In sum: by the death of Mbandzeni (1889), in Hailey's words, the Swazi 'had "conceded" more than the total area of the country';[86] some areas had been granted in conflicting concessions several times over; and a 'super concession' of 1889 had even, in return for £12,000 annually, granted away all the king's revenues.[87] The range of the concessions was extraordinary, and quite justifies Professor Kuper's description of them as 'a type of economic warfare' against this African state.[88] Everything from land to minerals, banking to farming, printing to oil extraction, tanning to building, photography to pawn-broking, was in fact covered.[89] An informal annexation process was slowly but surely overtaking Swaziland. The Partition which followed, 1890–95, was to be in many ways a formal ratification of this local economic Scramble for Africa.

Even before the end of Mbandzeni's reign, the Swazi found the white intrusion politically so complicating that they turned to the external power of Great Britain to advise them in their desperate predicament. The British, however, declined to become involved in Swazi affairs by the appointment of a resident adviser, as Mbandzeni requested in 1886. Thus in December of that year, the Swazi elders invited the son of Theophilus Shepstone – 'Offy' to his friends, and '*Mhlakuvane*' to the Swazi – to become the personal royal 'adviser'. The real erosion of Swazi authority dated from *Mhlakuvane's* tenure of office. The concessions reached their height; rival white political authority was established; and the Boer connection with the concessionaires was drawn ever more tightly into Transvaal ambitions in South-east Africa.

Offy Shepstone's declared aim on accepting office was to regularise the confusion surrounding the concessions. His work towards that end failed to secure any greater security for the Swazi. An investigation into disputed concessions merely gave greater security to the larger white concession-holders; an attempt to regularise authority over the concessionaires, through a mass meeting, led directly to the creation of a 'White Committee' of 25, which soon exhibited a propensity to independent action, together with a strong Transvaal Afrikaner leaning. Mbandzeni fiercely denied allegations that Shepstone was becoming 'king', in all but name, when he spoke to a mass meeting of concessionaires on 18 May 1887. But if Shepstone was not arbiter of events, then the concession-holders were certainly growing beyond the control of the beleaguered king. Mbandzeni was forced to recognise this unwelcome fact the following year, when he granted the 'White Committee' a charter of administrative authority over all the whites in Swaziland (1 August 1888). The economic struggle for Swazi resources had now shifted to the very question of sovereignty itself.

The king was clearly growing desperate – with good reason. His every move to cope with the intrusion of the whites appeared to tighten the economic and political noose being drawn around Swaziland. A despatch to both the British and Boer governments, setting out the conduct of their subjects and their unhappy effects on Swazi politics, was taken to be an appeal for external intervention and mediation by the metropolitan and local imperialists. In some considerable alarm, the king now stressed that his letters were

only to *report* . . . to the two Governments the preposterous claims made by English and Transvaal subjects. He did not mean . . . to ask for a commission to inquire into the validity or otherwise of grazing licences. The matter is a question of the internal government of the country, that is, himself to decide as king of his country.[90]

Not that the Swazi troubles ended there. The 'White Committee', far from being an aid to the King in controlling the concessionaires, had finally moved to pass a resolution (29 July 1889) in favour of incorporating Swaziland into the Transvaal Republic.[91] Events in Zululand, surrounding the New Republic, appeared to be repeating themselves. Worst of all for the Swazi, the king now contracted jaundice and died (7 October 1889) at the young age of thirty-four. Faced with a political vacuum, and internal struggles between the concessionaires, the British and Boer authorities felt bound to intervene; they simply prepared to Partition Swaziland between them as they saw fit. The Swazi had been reduced to political bystanders in their own country.

Fundamental to what followed was the decision of the British Imperial Factor not to oppose Boer influence in Swaziland. Indeed, to work some solution for the 'Swazi Question' in close co-operation with their local agency of frontier expansion. *Inkanyeso* remarked, on behalf of the Swazi, that the 'illegitimate process by which Swaziland gradually fell into the hands of the Boers, while within the sphere of British influence, by no means reflects credit upon England'.[92]

Why did the British adopt this posture which they themselves found increasingly distasteful? The colonial secretary best set out the reasons in a private letter of late-1887.

We are bound by the Convention of London with the Transvaal Gov[ernmen]t.

to secure the independence of the Swazis, and to do this effectually we must (1) take care to keep up an influence with the Swazi king and not let him think that we take no interest in him ... and (2) we must show a willingness to act with the Transvaal Gov⎡ernmen⎤t. upon any Swazi question, as the peace of S⎡outh⎤. Africa largely depends upon our working cordially with the Gov⎡ernmen⎤t.[93]

In retrospect, it could be suggested that Knutsford's two aims were completely incompatible. However, he hoped to aid the Swazis *and* the Afrikaners with one and the same policy.

We should be very much blamed if we let the Boer influence prevail in Swaziland by inaction on our part when we can justly act, as in the present case ... But I venture to think that friendly co-operation with the Transvaal Gov⎡ernmen⎤t. in matters relating to Swaziland would tend to lessen our difficulties, not only in Swaziland, but Amatongaland, Zululand and elsewhere where we come into contact with the Boers; and would induce them ⎡the Transvaal Government⎤ to put a check upon the marauding Boers who give us so much trouble.[94]

Sir Graham Bower, as imperial secretary to the high commissioner throughout these years (1880–96), provided further elaboration of this policy from the vantage-point of Government House, Cape Town. As he bluntly pointed out, there clearly were problems attached to satisfying Kruger's ambitions in Swaziland, with its ready access to the sea beyond – 'it would have been treason to South Africa to allow the Transvaal to gain access to the sea unless they agreed to surrender their foreign policy into the hands of HM Government' – yet such a possibility had to be faced – 'there were reasons why the dog in the manger policy could not be too rigorously applied'. Namely:

To have shown a feeling of hostility to the Transvaal might have been construed as the indication of an anti-Dutch policy ... Moreover, as the Paramount Power, HM Government stood *in loco parentis* to all South African States and a feeling of hostility to any one of those States would have been taken as a sign of prejudice, that is to say it would have weakened the prestige of the British Government as arbitrator.

Moreover, Swaziland was not contiguous to any British territory. It was in fact quite 'ungetatable'. It would be troublesome and costly to administer and might have involved costly military responsibilities in an unhealthy country.

Finally, we had had painful experience of the political evils resulting from the intervention of ambitious soldiers, backed by firebrand missionaries and a Jingo Press, and there was the strongest reason for sparing the people of South Africa a repetition of all the scandalous episodes of the Warren–Mackenzie expedition and political campaign.[95]

For the metropolitan imperialists, their policy did not mean simply 'handing over' the Swazi to the Afrikaner: they recognised that they 'had incurred certain honourable obligations towards them'.[96] The British hoped to find a *via media* which would meet the ambitions of the Afrikaners and concessionaires yet also secure Swazi rights. The drafting of the First Swazi Convention, of 1890, was to represent an initial attempt at that impossible constitutional balancing act.

The idea of striking political and economic bargains with Kruger's republic for the benefit of 'British Southern Africa', in return for areas of Swaziland, had indeed steadily grown in official thinking with the years as the terms of Great Britain's problems of supremacy in Southern Africa hardened. In 1885, when a Boer *trek* emerged at Walfisch Bay on the western coast, the colonial office had seen the merits of doing nothing, so as to acquire Transvaal good-will. 'This *trek* began in 1877. It shows the futility of our trying to keep the Boers to particular spots in Africa. Starvation, and disease, sufficiently confine the bulk of them to regions already peopled, without one spending money chasing them hither and thither.'[97] Now, in 1889, the colonial secretary could emphatically remark to his premier that Transvaal aid could be acquired in other imperial problem areas if Kruger's frontier Afrikaners were allowed onto 'unclaimed land', and particularly into Swaziland. 'I should be inclined to compromise with them by letting it be known that if they come to terms with Umbandine ... we shall not prevent them from protecting and annexing that country. This will bring them to the sea, which is their chief desire.'[98]

What rated so highly in British policy to justify such concessions? Two specific things: first, the acquisition from the South African Republic of a guarantee not to expand elsewhere in South Africa, notably northwards into 'Zambesia' (the later Rhodesia); second, and perhaps even more important, securing a promise from Kruger to join a pan-South African customs union. Practically this would mean allowing a Cape-owned rail-line into the Witwatersrand, thereby permitting the British colony to partake of some of the fantastic fruits of prosperity now being exclusively enjoyed locally by the goldrich Transvaal.[99]

As set out, the proposed scheme was said to have 'something for everybody'. The British were weary of direct intervention in South African politics; the lessons of Majuba also still stung. The best hope of drawing the local white states into a more viable colonial policy – which would allow a permanent British retreat from coercive imperialism, and place the deep problems of race-relations in local hands – appeared to lie in conciliating, not confronting Afrikanerdom. Such a posture also found the support of the newly-emerging Rhodes–Hofmeyr alliance in Cape politics. Hofmeyr's *Bond* reacted most favourably to such nurturing of Afrikaner interests, over those of African societies; the Cape expansionist groups strongly desired economic stakes in the Transvaal economic bonanza, while Rhodes himself was almost obsessed with keeping Kruger's frontier burghers out of 'Zambesia' while the trans-Limpopo occupation of Mashonaland was being organised. Even the republican Afrikaners were thought to see advantage in the proposals. In return for railway and tariff concessions to the British colonies, Kruger's state would secure a predominant influence in Swaziland and thus be well placed to develop its cherished dream of a 'window to the world' on the coast to the east.

As to the Swazi, the proposals were said to be a compromise between full independence and total subversion by the concessionaires. This may have been true, but it was cold comfort to these British allies to be used as a 'bargaining counter' by the 'Imperial Factor'. In truth, it was the double misfortune of the Swazi state to become enmeshed in the local settler colonialism of the concessionaires, at the same time as being drawn into the larger politics of British imperialism. The main thrust of Victorian imperialism was then to work the problems of South Afrikaner hegemony through Anglo-Afrikaner co-operation, and this inevitably alloted African societies roles of subservience alongside those of the British 'associates' – the white colonial states.

The negotiations over the formal Partition in Swaziland took place in two phases in 1890. The initial talks centred around direct Anglo-Afrikaner diplomacy, and soon broke down; the later negotiations focused on local discussions between Jan Hofmeyr, acting as imperial 'agent', and the Transvaal authorities – which were rather more productive. The very character of these negotiations is historically interesting in relation to the Scramble in Southern Africa. First, it is important to note, as the Swazi have contended in this century, they were not even consulted in this Partition of their state.[100] Second, despite being the pre-eminent world power, the Victorians preferred to deal with the problems of Afrikanerdom through the collaborative agency of the Cape *Bond*, which says much for how they were coming to work their empire on the veld.

The working documents for the negotiations were provided by the Report of Sir Francis de Winton, who had been appointed in 1889 to look into the condition of Swaziland. His Report, based on a close examination of the conditions in the field, was a most political document. It supported much of the Afrikaners' claims to Swaziland, but linked any official recognition of these grants and treaty rights to reciprocal gestures on the part of the Transvaal republicans – to abdicate from ambitions in Central Africa, to the acceptance of a free trade in British colonial goods, and to the entry of Cape

railways into the heart of the Witwatersrand enterprises.[101] Kruger and
the British high commissioner soon met (March 1890) to discuss these
terms. After much haggling, the republicans were given until 18 July to
agree to the terms, or de Winton's joint Anglo-Afrikaner administration in
Swaziland would be removed in favour of a British official. Kruger's
Volksraad happily called the imperialists' bluff; they feared a diminution
of Afrikaner independence in the British terms.[102]

The Imperial Factor now turned to the Cape 'loyal Afrikaners' to assist
them with the republican brethren. Somewhat reluctantly Hofmeyr accepted the role allotted him. 'I went to Pretoria,' he later said, 'because I
thought that I might perhaps be able to prevent a breach of peace.'[103] A
more modern explanation for his actions is provided by the historian of
the *Bond*: 'Hofmeyr's performance in the Swaziland negotiations is intel-
ligible only on the assumption that his conversion was now complete' to the
Rhodes alliance.[104] Under difficult circumstances – Kruger greeted him
with the statement, 'You are a traitor! And you have come up here as a
traitor!'[105] – he secured an agreement. The Transvaal abjured its interests
in Central Africa in favour of joint participation in the government of
Swaziland; and the Cape secured a number of its most prized commercial
ambitions in the republic. It was also agreed that 'Offy' Shepstone was to
represent Swazi interests in that white overlordship.

The British were delighted. 'My dear Mr Hofmeyr,' the colonial secretary
wrote on 4 August, 'I received yesterday on my birthday a most welcome
present in the shape of a telegram ... informing me that the Convention
was signed.'[106] The Transvaal Afrikaners simply used the agreement as a
lever to tighten their control of Swaziland. From Albert Bremer's Hotel –
seat of the new joint government – the republican 'take-over' could be
observed, though nothing was done to stop it. The Transvaal spent a considerable amount of money – over £100,000 – to buy out the major concessions; while the expansionist group in the republic, led by Joubert, who
held concessions in Swaziland, anticipated the moment when complete
control of the region was in their hands. Kruger declared happily in 1892
that 'historically, geographically and administratively Swaziland is ours'.[107]

The British had intended the convention to 'establish a partnership between
Imperial and Colonial interests', as the high commissioner's secretary
frankly stated in his 'Memoirs'.[108] Instead, it had opened the door to yet
greater white Scrambles for Swaziland.[109] Far from settling the condition
of the troubled Swazi state, it had abetted the agencies of frontier expansion. By mid-1892 the Joint-Government was proclaimed a failure by all
concerned. The British colonial secretary hastened its burial by admitt-

ing the necessity to renegotiate the Anglo-Afrikaner agreement on Swaziland.[110]

A second Convention was accordingly devised,[111] at Colesberg in the Cape colony, between Kruger and the British high commissioner in April 1893.[112] The Afrikaners gained the right to acquire from the Swazi an 'Organic Proclamation', which would in practice give the Transvaal effective control over the administration of Swaziland, though not actually incorporate the African state with the republic.[113] The Swazi elders could not believe the terms when they were presented with the document, and they simply refused to sign away their sovereignty. Indeed, they hastily got together a 6-man deputation, and set out for London to protest their rights. They received little but tea and sympathy,[114] and were then packed back to Africa to face their opponents. The British flatly declined to become the trustees of Swaziland against the Afrikaners. The colonial secretary privately defended the terms of the Second Convention, in an unashamed letter to the premier, on the grounds that the British government had

> done the best they could in agreeing that, upon certain conditions, the S[outh] A[frican] Republic administer the government of the whites in Swaziland.
> From the enclosed papers . . . you will see that I thought that this course should have been preferable to a Joint Government, which I felt certain must break down . . .
> The trial of Joint Government has, therefore, been usefully made. But, it has broken down and the anticipated difficulties have been too much for us.[115]

Within the larger canvas of imperial concerns and strategies, the Swazi occupied but a small marginal position.[116] The *uitlander* problem in the Transvaal was beginning to draw attention among British officialdom, and thus it too was now added to those other problems which might be alleviated in Anglo-Afrikaner relations by accepting the republican ambitions in Swaziland. There were obstacles in the way of this policy. At the time of the Second Convention, the British colonial secretary had indeed worried over 'public opinion', more particularly 'humanitarian opinion', in the press and parliament – he recalled how, even in 1890, 'this country and Parliament were not prepared to "hand over", as it was termed, Swaziland to the Transvaal'.[117]

His successor as secretary of state for colonies from 1893, Lord Ripon, a leading Gladstonian and sometime viceroy of India, was however much less worried over 'Exeter Hall'; he considered much humanitarian pressure to have been 'manufactured'.[118] And it was he who turned aside the Swazi Deputation, the protests of the Aborigines' Protection Society, and even the complaints of British commercial interests, to give the Transvalers pretty well what they wanted.[119] 'I am coming to the conclusion that we shall have to let the Boers go in,' he wrote in a highly confidential letter to the foreign secretary (Lord Kimberley) in September 1894, 'maintaining the protection given to the substantial rights of the natives under the Convention of 1893. I greatly dislike the measure – but the only practical alternative that I can see is to run [the] grave risk of a war with the Boers, which I regard as out of the question.'[120] Distasteful or not, this was the basis of the Third Swazi Convention which the British signed with the Transvaal Republicans on 10 December 1894.[121] Swaziland now passed to the Transvaal as a 'Protectorate'. The Boer administration began the following February, despite another Swazi Deputation to London protesting this further Partition without their participation, and in the face of a disillusioned African opinion in educated circles: 'Lord Ripon says that the process of jumping Native territories by encroachment and unlawful concession is well known,' the Zulu newspaper *Inkanyaso* commented, 'but it is one to which Her Majesty's Government was bound not to give way. We regret that this was not realised before the Swazi Nation was delivered up.'[122]

Regrettable or not, the action was in line with the growing tradition of imperial policy in the post-Zulu war and post-Majuba Southern Africa, of conciliating the Afrikaners, and of placing the problems of African administration in the hands of local white agencies of authority.[123] There was a considerable outcry in Great Britain at the action, and Lord Ripon was the centre of a fiery debate.[124] Yet the Swaziland decision should hardly have shocked liberals with a memory: it was also a Liberal cabinet which had 'given away' Zulu lands to the pressures of Afrikaner expansion in the establishment of the New Republic in 1884–85.

In reply to such criticism, Lord Ripon merely pointed to a pragmatic alternative of opposing Afrikaner expansionist ambitions. 'To go to war with the Boers about Swaziland I hold to be out of the question. It would be very costly; it would require a larger force; Rhodes and S[outh]. African opinion would be against us; and I greatly doubt if the cabinet could be got to acquiesce.'[125] So that was that. Indeed, by the logic of the British imperial position in Southern Africa, there might even be political advantage in declining to become involved in the local Scramble for African resources which the Afrikaners and colonials were so eager to pursue. In Ripon's words,

I am . . . reluctantly brought to admit that there is much to be said for letting the Boers go in . . . Swaziland by 'manifest destiny' must ultimately go to the Transvaal . . . if we allow the Boers to go in, we can hold them to the terms of the Convention of 1893, and thus give the Swazi very efficient protection for their substantial rights – and last, but not least, we should have [white] S[outh]. African opinion with us.[126]

The Swazi were far from quiescent through all this. Their protests in London having failed, they gave serious consideration to physical resistance. After some debate they decided against this.[127] In coming to that conclusion the fate of those African political communities who had offered violent confrontation – such as the Zulu and Xhosa – was important. Thus as one authority has put it, 'unwilling to suffer the doom of openly rebellious Bantu nations, the Swazi temporarily submitted'.[128] Remarkably, their submission *was* temporary. After the Anglo-Boer War, Swaziland became a British Protectorate with a consequent renaissance of Swazi traditionalism. The land concessionaires did not depart, however; a mere third of the country was left to the Swazi.[129]

The Partition had left its permanent legacy on the land. Little wonder that the Swazi objected to paying the 'native hut tax' levied by the Transvaal authorities after 1897, regarding it as 'money to keep the white man in the country'.[130] It was small comfort for the Swazi to have the British high commissioner comment that the Imperial government had handed Swaziland over to Afrikaner administration as 'the price which must be paid to avert war between the two white peoples of South Africa'.[131]

Yet that very comment was singularly revealing of the real nature of the politics of Partition in this last phase of the Scramble for South Africa. It was also indicative of the techniques adopted by British imperialism in dealing with the 'South African Question' in the period of the African Scramble. An empire worked through association with self-governing white settlement governments was clearly going to favour colonial interests over African aspirations. Long before the era of decolonisation in Africa more generally, the British had already in South Africa begun a 'transfer of power' – to the settler governments. British statesmen did not necessarily desire to subject African chiefdoms to local white rule; nor did they hold any high hopes concerning the capacity of these colonial authorities to develop administrations of noted humane trusteeship. It was simply because, in the context of the situation, 'empire-by-settler' collaboration was the most pragmatic option for a Great Power concerned for its own interests, and aware of the limits of its authority, in a changing world.

IO
Closing the last frontier: the end of the Scramble 1895

By moving with rather than against the expansive forces of the local settler societies of South Africa, the British authorities had hoped to end the Partition and to do so in a manner which would secure them local allies in protecting their basic interests. They also wished to develop a local empire of devolved authority which might, with careful nurturing, develop into a federal state akin to 'another Canada' — rather than continually relapse into a sub-continental zone of insecurity, conflict and disturbance.

At the heart of this British policy, and its success of failure, was accordingly the *response* of these local white governments to the conciliatory posture of the Imperial Factor. Would the British colonial societies of South Africa carry the administrative burdens passed on to them by Whitehall with due responsibility towards the African inhabitants? Would the republican Boers feel satisfied with the territorial concessions offered to them in Swaziland and Zululand? Would the private enterprise expansionists — such as the Rhodesian and Cape syndicate — accept the status quo as devised by the British administration after the settler occupations of the early 1890s?

The initial answers to all these questions were not at all encouraging for the British. The Imperial Factor accordingly found itself being drawn back into the machinations of the local expansionists when it had quite expected to see an end to the Partition in South Africa. So long as there appeared to be an area outside white control so there appeared to be local agencies ready and eager to work for its incorporation into their particular state.

These ultimate Scrambles to acquire, and to close the last of the frontiers in South Africa, were to be focussed on the only remaining 'open area', a portion of South-east Africa. Two particular contexts were involved, both involving a degree of crisis for Whitehall. The first centred on attempts by the Cape to secure a controlling interest in the rail-line from the Transvaal to Delagoa Bay, as a revival of its earlier tariff and railway strategies against the Kruger state. The origins of this very unwelcome renaissance of Cape economic diplomacy was Portuguese economic crisis, coupled with Rhodesian economic crisis in Zambesia.[1]

The second and further local crisis developed around a resurgence of the old Boer–German 'bogey' in the minds of British statesmen and diplomats concerned with Southern Africa in their perception of the British world role. Having allowed the Transvaal to fulfil to a significant degree its 'manifest destiny' in Swaziland, the Imperial Factor now ironically and unhappily found that such territorial magnanimity had not at all satiated Boer frontier ambitions in South-east Africa. Rather the reverse seemed true: from Swaziland the republicans now began to think anew about their old interests in the strategic harbour of Kosi Bay – on the coast of neighbouring Thongaland – and to offer the Germans yet another opportunity to embarrass the British through connection with republican Afrikanerdom.

The struggle for Delagoa Bay

The British had already steadfastly made plain their dislike of becoming officially involved in private railway investments in foreign countries. Salisbury had indeed elevated his objections into a principle;[2] but it had failed to convert the Cape financial elite which restlessly and relentlessly moved forward its economic strategies against the Transvaal, aiming both to cut into the highveld carrying-trade and also acquire a crucial diplomatic lever against Krugerism.

Rhodes was now superbly placed to move forward these strategies. He had added the Cape premiership (1890) to his financial power – he was head of the amalgamated diamond field giant of 'De Beers', and a dominant figure in 'Goldfields of South Africa Ltd' – and was, further, in his imperial capacity, head of the BSA Company. He was encouraged to combine his official position at the Cape with his private financial desires by the fact of Portuguese economic crisis. It seemed marginally possible that the African possessions of colonial Portugal might be obtainable in an extraordinary intra-imperial financial transaction. At least three interested parties were reported to be concerned in any such possible transaction if it came about – the Transvaal republic, certain German concessionaires and, of course, the Cape expansionist group.

Certainly Rhodes was absolutely determined not to miss out on such an opportunity. He also felt emboldened by a belief that Portugal would necessarily give the Cape 'first option' on the crucial South-east African coastlines involved. It was this possibility that involved the Imperial Factor directly. For not only was Portugal the 'traditional ally' of Great Britain, but in 1875 she had given the British a 'pre-emptive right' to Delagoa Bay,[3] an option confirmed by the Anglo-Portuguese Treaty of 1891 on East African matters.[4]

Undaunted by an initial lack of official British support, Rhodes now bid furiously for the bay. Prompted by this fact, Kruger was led to do likewise; and this local imperial rivalry gradually drew in the interested Great Powers – the Germans and the British. Indeed, it was in these years of the mid 1890s that Anglo-German rivalry again began to develop, as a result of Rhodes–Kruger struggles centred about Delagoa Bay. In retrospect, in 1897, Rhodes stated that his actions in 'fighting' the Afrikaner republicans for the supremacy of South Africa had been largely prompted by the German support for Kruger's regime in South-east Africa.[5] The Germans, on the other hand, explained their activities in support of the Transvaal claims at Delagoa Bay in terms of the *treibereien* of Cecil Rhodes.[6]

The truth was rather different. The Cape colony desired Delagoa Bay for reasons which bore specifically on the local economic balance, and its political consequences. Germany determined to be involved in stopping Delagoa Bay falling to Cape control for reasons which had more to do with the Anglo-German naval rivalry, and international prestige, than with any passion to support Transvaal republicanism. Ultimately, the real struggle for Delagoa Bay was fought out in the respective partisan press journals of the two Great Powers.[7] The British were by no means convinced of the value of supporting the Rhodesian scheme, while German support for Portugal worried Great Britain little. However, German support for the Transvaal – if and when the British ever tried to force Kruger's hand on the political rights of the *uitlanders* – worried the foreign office a great deal.

In the short term, 1894–97, the territorial settlement over the Delagoa Bay area well reflected these facts. German policy was committed to maintaining the status quo in South-east Africa, and no more. Delagoa Bay remained Portuguese, and Kruger's republic was supported against British attempts to influence its economic and political independence. British policy was committed to the maintenance of British paramountcy on the *veld*, a fact which the Imperial Factor felt had little to do with the ownership of a railway line from Delagoa Bay. The royal navy could perform more effectively off the coast in controlling the bay, if necessary, than Rhodes' financial interests could by operating within a Portuguese colony.[8] That was also accomplished. The 1891 Anglo-Portuguese Treaty ceded the vital Gazaland to Portugal, despite Rhodes' protests;[9] and the problems of Anglo-German relations were deemed too serious for Great Britain to oppose the German decision to support Portugal against Rhodes.[10]

This still, however, did not stop the Rhodes–Cape group from working their own policy. They had never professed great faith in accomplishing their imperial views through British imperial governments. The attitude of, and lack of support from, the Salisbury administration over the Delagoa affair merely confirmed that view.[11] Rhodes had already been trying to find his own way to control and neutralise the political advantage gained by Kruger's republic in having a rail-line to Delagoa Bay. In 1890 he had even tried to square Kruger himself, 'on the personal'[12] – Rhodes' favourite phrase when working a bargain – when he had tempted the old Boer leader with the possibility of 'giving' Delagoa Bay to the Boers, in return for Transvaal entry into the Cape–Free State customs union, and a promise not to expand northwards into Zambesia. As reported, the famed 'secret' conversation was said to have run thus:

Rhodes: We must work together. I know that the Republic needs a sea port. You must have Delagoa Bay.

Kruger: How can we work together that way? The port belongs to the Portuguese, and they will never give it up.

Rhodes: We must simply take it.

Kruger: I can't take the property of other people . . . a curse rests upon ill-gotten goods.[13]

Kruger could afford to preach to Rhodes. His own failure to secure the bay from the Portuguese[14] had left him in no doubt that Rhodes would fail as well. Equally, Kruger had no intention of making for difficulties in Portuguese–Transvaal relations when the rail-line got under way. Kruger indeed showed a marked determination to stick by his existing policy. When McMurdo went bankrupt, the Transvaal supported Portugal in confiscating the rail-line and advancing it to the Transvaal frontier.[15] And when Cecil Rhodes attempted to forward his Cape-supported scheme, by trying to buy out the shaky German syndicate working on the line in the Transvaal, Kruger again stood by with financial support.[16]

Rhodes meanwhile, having failed with Kruger 'on the personal', and having failed to pull the British government behind his Cape policy, attempted to put pressure on the Portuguese. His methods were not particularly savoury.[17] He sent agents into South-east Africa with orders to acquire treaty rights to territory from the African rulers, notably at the court of Gungunhana.[18] He also tried, by methods of bluster, to cajole the Portuguese authorities over rights granted in the 1890 Treaty.[19] One of Rhodes' agents, Colonel Willoughby, finally overstepped the mark in forcing his way up the Portuguese end of the Pungwe River.[20] The British premier was *not* amused:

Portugal has never declared the river open. What she has done was to promise last November [1890] that she would give facilities for passing over it . . . If I had contracted to give you a park key that you might go through the park at

Hatfield ... it would not give you the right to kick my park gate down because the key had not come.[21]

Even Rhodes came to recognise the inevitable.[22] He left Portuguese East Africa alone, and concentrated on a new and equally desperate strategy – viz. fomenting revolution in the Transvaal as a means of destroying Kruger's power. The next time Colonel Willoughby was heard of he was riding at Jameson's side in the infamous 'Raid' of 1895.[23]

Before that took place, and partly as a cause of it, the Transvaal's rail-line to Delagoa Bay was completed in October 1894 and opened by Kruger early in 1895. The parsimonious burghers of the *Volksraad* spent over £20,000 in celebrating the realisation of possessing an outlet to the sea through Portuguese and not British territory.[24] Rhodes plunged into unparalleled gloom, particularly as the event coincided with reports from his mining engineers that 'Rhodesia' had little of the gold which had been expected.[25] At the Cape, despite his position as colonial premier, Rhodes indulged in a series of bitter speeches against the Imperial Factor.[26]

In London Lord Salisbury was more philosophic. He had never thought Portugal would yield up the Delagoa Bay,[27] nor for that matter any of the rest of Moçambique. This view had after all been passed on to Rhodes and his Cape associates, by Lord Knutsford as colonial secretary, in an explicit private letter as early as February 1892.

Very confidential   Colonial Office,
                                                       February 4, 1892.

Dear Mr Merriman,

Before the Cabinet this morning I had an opportunity of stating your views to Lord Salisbury. He said the matter, if it arose, would receive the careful consideration of HM's Government, but he added (as I have said to you) that there are no grounds for supposing that Portugal is at all disposed to cede any territory.

                                                       Yours very truly,
                                                       Knutsford.[28]

Salisbury had worked from the premise that the Portuguese 'are a very unreasonable people', with whom he wished to have as little business dealings as possible in his African diplomacy.[29] He warned a consortium of businessmen, who wished to become involved in Moçambique,

From your experience with the Delagoa Bay Railway, you have some knowledge of their [the Portuguese Government's] method of proceeding, and that same transaction indicates that with the best will in the world the power of HM

G[overnment]. to force the Portuguese Government into performing an act of justice is so restricted by the feebleness of that Government, and by the endless subterfuges to which it has recourse, that our inter-position has hitherto been of little practical value. Please therefore do not assume that we can force the Portuguese Government to keep their promises to you.[30]

Salisbury did not doubt that South Africa contained vital British interests, but he took a hard, qualitative approach to each advance in the area. On one occasion he was to cause considerable public consternation, notably at the Cape, when he suggested the limits of responsibility in Southern Africa to an indiscreet private correspondent:

The utility of such colonisation [at the Cape] as facilitating the defence of the Empire is a very material argument in its favour, but not in my judgement an argument of great Parliamentary weight. In their heart of hearts Members of Parliament have made up their minds to abandon South Africa if it ever threatens to cost them any considerable expense again.[31]

The contents of this letter unfortunately became public knowledge, and a very worried Lord Knutsford wrote urgently to his chief on the matter a week later:

I hear in the City there has been a sensation, and Sir C. Mills [Cape agent-general] has thought it right to send an explanatory telegram to the Cape, which I suggested to him. It is all very absurd, but could you say a few words to explain that you were . . . speaking of the heart of hearts of the ordinary members of Parliament and not of that exalted body of H.M[ajesty].'s Ministers.[32]

'Imperial solutions' were to be offered for the local problem of supremacy only when, and where, Salisbury was utterly convinced of their necessity. When it came to the hard facts of formal empire, the extension of British responsibilities and administration in South-east Africa, the Tories were found to be no more enthusiastic than the Liberals.[33] Their very refusal to become involved at Delagoa Bay in support of the Cape colonial expansionists all too clearly pointed at the real imperialists: the Cape–Rhodesian alliance, and its financial supporters.

Gun boats against German diplomacy: the Kosi Bay tangle

The British authorities had managed to avoid becoming drawn into that particular local private-enterprise strategy. They reckoned – correctly – that Rhodes' utility as an agent of British interests in South Africa generally would not be endangered by declining to follow him into conflict with the Portuguese of Moçambique.

But if that problem was relatively easy to side-step then the challenge now almost immediately posed by the Transvaal Boers in trying to develop a 'window on the world' entirely independent of British (or Portuguese) influence, by expanding their holdings down to Kosi Bay, was not to be treated dismissively at all. Some metropolitan authorities were convinced of the solecism that if the Boer state was independently present on the coastline then 'foreign influences' would soon be also present on the Witwatersrand.

The early Swazi Conventions had always been specific on the matter of control of this strategic harbour: Kosi Bay *was* included in the general bargaining. The Third Swaziland Convention, however, had *not* involved Thongaland. The fate of Kosi Bay apparently still lay with the Thonga, and even more with the British as paramount power in South Africa.[34] Certainly the British cabinet was not eager to allow the Transvalers to spill out of Swaziland towards the Thonga coastlines.[35] The prime minister made out a curious case for the dangers of French ambitions in South-east Africa, through an expeditionary force based on Madagascar;[36] the colonial secretary argued a more traditional theme in warning of rumours which spoke of revived Afrikaner–German 'links',[37] and he also claimed to find it significant that Germany was at this time intervening directly in South-west Africa to put down Herero unrest.[38] Combined, these several fears made some British action on the Thongaland coast almost inevitable.[39]

Above all, the old lingering suspicions over Kruger's pro-German sympathies unsettled the British 'official mind', and gnawed at any sense of political insecurity in South Africa now that the Afrikaner republicans had vast gold reserves to back their belligerent foreign policy.[40] 'With wealth and a large horizon came ambitions for territorial extension', a senior British official later recalled of this period.

Access to the sea would have brought the Transvaal nearer to Europe. In touch with Europe. A German ship in a Transvaal Harbour would have created a new international position whilst territorial extension would have made the Transvaal the premier, and probably the dominating state, in South Africa.

For these very reasons, England as Trustee of South Africa, was bound to combat these ambitions. England in this matter was more true to the Afrikaner ideal than either Kruger or his friends. The one wished for a policy which would ultimately call in German influence and authority to the destruction of Afrikanerism. The other sought to protect Afrikanerism, and by Afrikanerism I mean the doctrine that South Africa should work out its own salvation free from outside influences.[41]

The German ambitions may, as ever, have been rather nebulous. Yet their impact is beyond doubt. The British colonial secretary wrote to the Cape high commissioner in late-1894, that

In view of the apparent intention of the German Government to adopt a policy of interference in South Africa, especially as regards Delagoa Bay and the South African Republic, H[er] M[ajesty's] G[overnment] are of the opinion that it would be very undesirable at the present time to modify the terms of Article IV of the London Convention [requiring British approval for Transvaal foreign treaties].[42]

Technically and legally, apart from Article IV, the Transvaal was outside the British sphere of influence. The London Convention had dropped Great Britain's suzerainty over the Afrikaner republic. But that ambiguously worded document did not stop succeeding secretaries of state from claiming in public that the 'suzerainty' was still in operation, even if privately admitting that the British had no hold over the Transvaal. 'You say "we gave up the clause as to suzerainty"', Ripon frankly remarked to Kimberley in the early stages of the Kosi Bay affairs,[43] 'Practically this is probably true, but we never said so to the Transvaal, and saying so to Germany is as good as saying so to Kruger. What we did do in '84 was to say nothing about the suzerainty.' Thus, despite the lack of legal title, and despite the economic growth to maturity of the gold-rich South African Republic, the British imperial authorities continued to think of Kruger's republic as but part of 'British Southern Africa'.[44] The officials in the British colonial office went so far as to suggest that the Boers were still 'British subjects' – the London Convention of 1884 notwithstanding. 'All adult Boers became British subjects in 1877 [when Britain annexed the Transvaal] ... By no Convention were the Boers ever released from this allegiance; and on two occasions the Govt. here [in London] have contemplated, but have shrunk from introducing an Act of Parliament releasing them.'[45] To London, the Afrikaner state *was* in the sphere of British influence and interest. Any foreign intervention or involvement in the Transvaal as seen as being an intrusion into the British 'sphere'. Lord Salisbury, rational in all other matters, gave way to swift temper when foreign involvement in the South African Republic was mentioned: 'Of course Germany has no rights in the affair', he was to comment in 1896 after the Jameson Raid.[46]

Having taken this stand, and having determined to isolate the Afrikaners *within* 'British South Africa', the Salisbury and Rosebery administrations were to undergo a period of considerable strain in the years 1894–97, when German involvement in the area did greatly increase.[47] What interests did Germany have in the Afrikaner republic? 'Over 500 million marks of German capital and ... about 15,000 Germans', according to the German ambassador in London.[48] There was also, of course, a sense in which

Germany played the 'Boer card' for diplomatic advantage.[49] The British were highly sensitive about the region.[50] The foreign secretary, Lord Kimberley, claimed that Germany was doing its 'utmost to trip us up' in South-east Africa.[51]

Certainly, Germany *was* aware of Great Britain's sensitivity over the area. Certainly, too, she also knew how easy it was to make capital of the fact, by rejecting British claims that the Transvaal republic was within a British 'sphere'.[52] Why should the independent Afrikaner state not be independent of the British sphere? became the implicit question in German policy in the mid 1890s. Ultimately, the Germans informed the British they would act upon the belief that, 'except for the limitations set up by the 1884 Treaty, the Transvaal was an independent state and could establish any trade relations it pleased'. The British concept of a Victorian, pan-Southern African sphere – a trading 'Monroe Doctrine' of sorts – was also flatly rejected, on the grounds that it implied 'politically a protectorate' over the Afrikaner state, 'and economically a trade monopoly for [the] Cape Colony and the exclusion of German trade'.[53]

Germany's involvement in the 'independent state' was symbolised, economically, by the rapid inflow of capital – certainly over 300 million marks by 1896[54] – and politically, by greater demonstrations of German support for the Transvaal's independence – notably by the presence of German cruisers at Delagoa Bay, where they faced royal navy warships.[55] The British determined to follow a policy of 'standing up' to the Germans.[56] The British foreign secretary growled that Great Britain was a 'great sea Power, and could speak the strongest word if need be'; and complained bitterly of the direction of German policy. 'Do you observe,' he remarked to the colonial secretary, 'how hostile Germany is about the Transvaal? We shall have trouble with her there, and she will pay us off in European affairs for our resistance to her unwarrantable pretensions in S. Africa.'[57]

The colonial secretary was in fact soon wondering aloud whether the cabinet would stand squarely behind him if he informed Germany 'that the Transvaal is within our sphere of influence, and that they must *keep their hands off*'.[58] A first step towards a firm policy towards Germany, Ripon argued, was British action over Thongaland. This territorial advance

> would probably disturb the mind of the German Kolonials. But again I say that we ought to get all these small matters settled at the same time. The German inclination to take the Transvaal under their protection is a very serious thing . . . and I think therefore we ought to come to some clear conclusion as to how their intrigues are to be met.

The British foreign secretary was eager and ready to support such a policy, and indeed claimed to have been moving towards such a posture in his own diplomacy:

I entirely agree with you [he wrote to Ripon on 25 November 1894] that the German attitude in South-east Africa makes it indispensable that we should put our house in order . . .

As to the Transvaal, I am prepared to tell Germany that they must keep their hands off. You will have observed that I used significant language to Hatzfeld when I told him that in matters concerning the Portuguese colonies we were a great sea power, and would speak the strongest word if need be. The Germans must be made to understand that while we are most anxious to have cordial relations with them, we will stand no bullying.[59]

Delagoa Bay became the new symbolic focus of these British fears about German influence in Southern Africa.[60] The normally pacific Lord Ripon began to share Lord Kimberley's more militaristic spirit. 'I do not suppose you will be inclined to send "two or three ships" to those parts', he wrote to the foreign secretary on 28 September 1894,[61] adding nicely that 'perhaps if a Gun Boat could *accidentally* appear there it might be of use'.

Despite the complications of a divided British Liberal cabinet when it came to conducting Anglo-German relations – 'Harcourt's dread of a strong word, and of Rosebery's hatred of the French, which throws us inevitably on German support'[62] – a firm policy was pursued at Delagoa Bay.[63] The foreign secretary recorded the triumph of his posture in an important letter:

Private   Kimberley House,
                                                                                                      Oct. 19/94

My dear Ripon,

I am very glad we all agreed [in cabinet] that a large ship of war should be sent to Delagoa Bay.

An insolent article, said to be 'inspired', in the '*Cologne Gazette*' against England, declares that Germany will emphatically say 'hands off' to us as regards Delagoa Bay. This I think exactly describes *mutatis mutandis* the policy we must follow. We should intimate to all who want to meddle there that we will not allow it, and if the Germans attempt to interfere I should (if I can have my own way) make them clearly understand that we are determined and able to maintain our supremacy in that part of the world.

As to the Portuguese, although I think it very desirable to keep on good terms with them, I should hold them firmly to their engagement not to cede anything south of the Zambesi to another power. We cannot be dictated to by the Lisbon mob.

                                                                                                      Yours sincerely,
                                                                                                      Kimberley.[64]

The gun boat *H.M.S. Thrush* was duly despatched to South-east Africa.[65]

This was soon followed up by a British Atlantic squadron, which called at Delagoa Bay in early 1895. Clearly and powerfully the British made the point they would accept no second Great Power in the area. The squadron, despatched for the opening of the Delagoa–Transvaal rail-line, conformed to the foreign secretary's dictum that,

It ought if possible to be markedly stronger than the German [squadron], and care must be taken that the arrangements are made by the Admiralty in good time.
We must show the Germans unmistakeably that if they try to play this game, we can play it much more effectively than they can.[66]

This 'diplomacy of bluster' over Southern Africa was, in Berlin, carried to its ultimate extreme. A British representative in Germany was reported to have included the word 'war' in unofficially warning the Germans off the eastern coastline of Southern Africa. The Kaiser could hardly believe his ears: 'War for the sake of a few square miles of niggers and palm trees; war with Queen Victoria's grandson, and England's only friend!'[67]

The British, of course, had no intention of going to war with Germany over the Afrikaners. Yet they were still in deadly earnest in deploying high-profile diplomacy to preserve South Africa in manifest isolation from European interference, as a British 'sphere'. If that also involved territorial advances to maintain the 'cordon' against external influence and the Afrikaner outward ambitions, the imperialists were ready to accept that unwelcome necessity. The fact that the region now involved, Thongaland, was far from empty, and that its inhabitants might have views on their own sovereignty, was naturally only given secondary consideration. Once the three-concerned dance of British–Afrikaner–German strategic politics focused on the land corridor that ran from the Transvaal through Swaziland to Kosi Bay, then the incorporation of the Thonga in British South Africa was only a matter of time.

The last frontier: pre-emptive imperialism in Thongaland

The Thonga had watched the expanding dimension of the Scramble in South Africa closely. Indeed, with the British annexation of Zululand in 1887, and the Afrikaner advance into Swaziland in 1894, the Partition had quite literally come up to their frontiers. The Queen of the Thongas, Zambili, appears to have been uncertain how to deal with the advancing tide of white overlordship. Resistance was out of the question. Yet how to secure Thonga authority? In 1887 she appealed to the Imperial Factor for British protection; in 1890 she repeated the request, but this time to the Portuguese government in Moçambique. Vassal communities of the Royal

House attempted to make their own arrangements: some treated with the British, others entertained Afrikaner agents.[68] The luxury of option was to be swept away by the advance of the New Imperialism in 1895.

British strategists were increasingly concerned over closing the 'gap' which Thongaland represented to their imperial equations.[69] The colonial secretary played a singularly influential role in these events. Ripon was agitated at the prospect of German involvement in 'British South Africa' through Afrikaner machinations; and by late-1894 he was indeed inclined to believe that the Germans harboured an 'inclination to take the Transvaal under their protection'.[70] His opinions were alarmist. Yet a definitive study of the whole Swaziland–Thongaland affair has suggested that this was largely the basis for Ripon's crucial role in British policy.[71] For the colonial secretary – and soon a good majority of the cabinet – to have the Germans 'meddling at Pretoria and Johannesburg would be fatal to our position and our influence in southern Africa'.[72]

The British accordingly moved to evolve a determined two-prong strategy of response. Germany was, in the most diplomatic of language, to be told 'to keep their hands off' both Thongaland and the Transvaal republic.[73] The Imperial Factor regarded Kruger's state as 'a *"point noir"* of no less importance than Egypt'.[74] Secondly, the coastal strip and bay were to be brought under British authority in due course.

The spring for the annexation was triggered not by any Thonga action, however, but rather by the Afrikaner president of the Transvaal.[75] Speaking to the largely German audience in Pretoria, on the occasion of the Kaiser's birthday – the famed *Kaiser Kommers* speech – Kruger became a little too warm and effusive in his eulogy of German–Transvaal links for the observant and sensitive British authorities. Kruger's speech culminated with remarks to the effect that the Transvaal was 'growing up' and, though still young, the Afrikaner republic knew that 'if one nation [i.e. Great Britain] tries to kick us, the other [Germany] will try to stop it'.[76]

The speech had in fact been drafted by Dr Leyds, as secretary of state to Kruger's republic, and Herr Herff, the local German consul at Pretoria, as an attempt to re-interest Germany in the Afrikaner state. Berlin was not so easily drawn into the struggles of Afrikanerdom against Great Britain.[77] But in London Victorian officialdom took alarm. The British ambassador to Berlin was instructed to protest at German 'coquetry'[78] with the Transvaal Afrikaners. Having incorrectly assumed that Germany was behind the *Kaiser Kommers* speech,[79] Great Britain now also incorrectly assumed that Berlin was both unconditionally backing the Transvaal and also encouraging Afrikaner ambitions, in challenging British attempts to 'encircle' the Transvaal.[80] The British foreign secretary of the day, Lord Kimberley, a man of firm views about the need for British supremacy in all of South Africa, determined that the government should make a firm response, if need be.[81] He urged his policy on Lord Ripon in a crucial communique:

Secret   Jan. 13/95

My dear Ripon,

   I entirely agree that it will be better to leave the London Convention alone. Germany is beyond doubt nibbling at the Transvaal, and we ought on no account to relax in the slightest degree any hold which the London convention gives us over the relations of the Transvaal with Foreign Powers. If Germany were to attempt to make any Treaty with the Transvaal we have now the right to veto it, and any attempt to pass us over would justify a remonstrance which she would think twice [of] before she disregarded [it]. If we maintain a firm attitude towards her, we may prevent her doing us any mischief. Writing in strict confidence to you, I may say that if the time comes when Portugal finds it necessary to clear out of her East African possessions, I would insist on all her territory south of the Zambesi falling to our share. Germany might have the rest. Unless we were at the time involved in a great war, we could do as we pleased whatever Germany might wish. She has not, nor is ever likely to have sea power enough to oppose us effectively in that quarter of the world. Meantime, she agrees with us that as regards the possessions of Portugal, including Delagoa Bay, the status quo should be preserved, and this seems to be a fair arrangement for both parties. As to France, Germany will not desire to let her in there any more than we do.

Yours sincerely,
Kimberley.[82]

The colonial secretary agreed with this argument, although he believed that Great Britain's interests could now perhaps be secured best by the use of diplomatic channels rather than the royal navy. Ripon accordingly wrote to Kimberley on the *Kaiser Kommers* speech:

It is not a violent speech, but it ignores the engagements of the Transvaal to us, and is calculated to give a false impression of their position in regard to us . . . it strikes me that we might take advantage of what he [Kruger] said to make a perfectly friendly statement to Germany of the obligation of the Transvaal to us, and of our claim to consider that State [as] within our sphere of influence. I am afraid that if something of this kind is not done, we shall drift into an unpleasant position with Germany.[83]

The British foreign secretary still felt such a response too mild in tone. After the 'Kruger telegram', of early the next year, he was even more adamant in 'standing up' to Germany. Rosebery disagreed.[84] But Kimberley pressed his views on the premier, arguing that the famed telegram to

Kruger[85] was more than a 'merely personal outbreak', as Rosebery had suggested. Rather, in the words of the foreign secretary,

it is part of a settled policy, as was shown unmistakeably in the communications which passed between Hatzfeld and me, and Malet and the Berlin Foreign Office. Moreover, German public opinion has been constantly hostile to us for some time past.

I hope our Gov[ernmen]t. will give the Emperor plainly to understand that we shall offer a firm and uncompromising resistance to his interference in South Africa. I am glad to see that ships are ordered to Delagoa Bay. A display of our naval force may cause the Germans to reflect on their utter impotency to get at us anywhere, if they were to quarrel with us.

An Order-in-Council soon added Thongaland to the responsibilities of the Natal governor. The Thonga had apparently Scrambled successfully for imperial protection. The Zulu newspaper, *Inkanyeso*, certainly took this meaning from the action, in a highly interesting editorial on the politics of Partition in Swaziland and Thongaland (10 May 1895):

Of course it was weakness on the part of the Imperial Government which encouraged the Boers to forget themselves from time to time and to presume too much, and no doubt they hoped to frown down any opposition to their acquiring a long-coveted road to the sea; but happily [in Thongaland] England has promptly stopped any further encroachments within the sphere of British influence . . . We are glad to hear that in this case it is the Natives who are to be considered, and who are to receive British protection – that it is in their interests that the Imperial Government has stopped the encroachment of the Boers who have impertinently disregarded Article 2 of the London Convention of 1884.

In fact, as informed African opinion in South Africa was to discover yet again, the Thonga were taken under imperial authority only in the hope of handing them over to be administered by the local British colonial authorities, in the form of the white settler government of Natal, as loyal agents of the Imperial Factor. Within three years this had indeed been accomplished. In December 1897 Thongaland passed under the 'responsible government' of the Natal colony, in company with Zululand. Whether the Thonga favoured such a course was set aside: a small force, of 25 men, was simply sent to bring about the annexation.[86]

If the occasion of the annexation belonged essentially to 1895, then the British rationale in extending the Partition to Thongaland was as old as the acquisition of St Lucia Bay a decade earlier. There was no 'prestige' to be gained; nor was the area 'regarded as of any commercial value'. Rather, 'the only object of the annexation' as a Whitehall official had remarked on that occasion, 'is to prevent the Germans shaking hands with the

Boers of the South African Republic . . . This can not be prevented as long as any hole is left in the cordon.'[87] That cordon was sealed. The last strategic frontier was annexed and under British control.

With the Thongaland annexation two inter-woven themes in the Partition of South Africa came to a close. The Scramble for the coastlines of Southern Africa was finally at an end. There was simply nothing else to annex: not even a 'gap' to produce a new spasm of rivalry. Europe had taken up every mile of coast, from the boundary of the Belgian Congo on the west, round the Cape to the Portuguese possessions on the east. International cartographers adjusted their maps. It was hard to see how international politics had been changed. The African annexations had been intended to close off the possibilities of friction, not open new European areas of conflict, and this they had largely done.

On the ground, in South Africa, the legacy was, however, all too real. The settler states of Boer and Anglo-Saxon had triumphantly expanded their holdings, and now worked to introduce magisterial authority, white farming and the market economy to their new territorial acquisitions. Only British protectorate areas of Basutoland and Bechuanaland were not under settler administration. Even those states had, of course, been subjected to imperial rule. The Partition had simply, in the space of less than two decades, toppled all non-European authority in South Africa. As a result of the Scramble, 'everywhere the white Government ruled'.[88]

Conclusion:

imperialism
through imperialism

'... as Her Majesty's High Commissioner for South Africa I have, whilst striving to act with equal justice and consideration to the claims and sensibilities of all classes and races, endeavoured at the same time to establish on a broad and secure basis, British authority as the paramount power in South Africa (loud and prolonged cheers).

To effect this I soon saw that a forward policy was indispensable; for if we did not advance, others would. From a very early period of my administration, therefore, I cast longing eyes upon the high healthy plateau to the north of the Cape Colony, which as the gate to the interior of South and Central Africa, seemed to me of infinitely greater importance than the fever-stricken mangrove swamps of the East Coast, the sandy, waterless fringe on the West (hear, hear). I accordingly devoted my best efforts to the acquisition of that territory ...

The true British policy for South Africa seems to me to be what may be termed colonization through Imperialism: in other words, colonial expansion through imperial aid, the Home Government doing what the colonies cannot do for themselves, having constitutionally no authority beyond their borders.

There are three competing influences at work in South Africa. They are Colonialism, Republicanism and Imperialism. As to the last it is a diminishing quantity, there being now no permanent place in the future of the South Africa Factor in the interior ... there remain only the ... competing influences of Colonialism and Republicanism.'

Sir Hercules Robinson, retirement speech, at the Cape Town Commercial Exchange, Monday 29 April 1889.

Conclusion: the empire of sub-imperialism

What had produced the dramatic Scramble for Southern Africa? Is there any simple way of demystifying the complexities of the New Imperialism of the later nineteenth century as expressed in this large-scale regional example?

It is tempting, but essentially misleading, to extract one of the major factors, and give it primacy of role, in the cause of lucidity and understanding – whether it be Great Power rivalry or general geo-politics, overseas investments or economic drives at large, mission societies or the spirit of humanitarianism, officialdom on-the-spot or local colonial societies, capitalist expansionists or social Darwinian theorists. But to stress one narrow element over another, to treat any of these factors in isolation, or to treat expansion separately from its regional context, is clearly unwise and does a severe violence to the historical truth. It may be intellectually less tidy to suggest a pluralistic explanation for the Partition of Southern Africa in the years after 1877, yet at least it avoids the reductionist dangers of a mono-causal thesis, and allows for an explanation which is sensitive to the various actors and societies involved.[1] 'Only the totality of the historical environment can explain a particular course of events,' it has been remarked in the context of another great process of change, 'and this totality, inevitably, is unique to this experience.'[2]

In the case of Southern Africa 'context' and 'environment' were of absolutely vital importance, in several distinct ways. It was the dynamic character of the frontier world of the periphery which had precipitated the coming of a final Partition of resources in the region in the later 1870s and 1880s. And it was the manner in which the forces of the New Imperialism interacted with the existent expansive politics of the local societies which had worked as catalyst in transforming the frontier advances into an international Scramble.

In his noted Cambridge lectures on *The expansion of England*, published in 1883, Professor John Seeley argued that where in a colonial territory the supremacy of an imperial power begins to break down then 'the general law is that a struggle follows between such organised powers as remain in the country, and that the most powerful of these sets up a Government'. In Seeley's acute phrase, this is not so much a new and foreign conquest 'but rather an internal revolution'. His general notion is of value in pointing us towards a general explanation of the Scramble in Southern Africa after 1877 by highlighting the importance of *local* forces and actors in 'bringing on' the geo-political revolution of the next decade.

By the close of the era of Partition, in say 1895, the British still remained the paramount power in South Africa – even if their degree of dominance was not as they had once enjoyed earlier, or as they would ideally have wished. But since 1877 they had been moved to intervene extensively, sometimes it must have seemed incessantly, through expansive actions to counteract the state of frontier South Africa. The British policy-makers were attempting to deal with several major problems posed by the politics of change, and the challenge of disorder, in the region.

First they wished to bring an end to its propensity for disorder, its capacity for inter-group violence, and its tendency towards fissiparous politics. In that sense, South Africa was a problem in 'government' – a problem in bringing stability, law, order and some kind of 'development' to a pluralistic frontier society which obstinately declined to follow modern dictums concerning political or economic progress. The federalist postures of the several British administrations since the early 1870s had, in fact, aimed at precisely this point – of coping with those problems in government, which was also a problem in local authority. And, even after the formal federal initiatives petered out, in the early 1880s, it can be seen that the metropolitan authorities still obstinately, and a little forlornly, clung to the hope of creating some kind of 'South African state' which would knit Anglo-Saxon and Afrikaner polities, so producing a united series of policies to handle the omnipresent questions of race-relations – termed locally, in settler language, 'the native question'.

Next the British wished to restructure the *means* by which control – hegemony and influence – was to be sustained in Southern Africa. Prior to the 1870s they had, necessarily, run their empire through a combination of proconsular agencies and consultative settler councils. From the 1870s the option of 'responsible government', with all its devolutionist administrative possibilities, was increasingly open to policy-makers. A shift began to take place in the working nature of the South African empire, from Whitehall to Cape Town. The trend in the shift of the epicentre of power and responsibility was to be markedly advanced in the years of the Scramble. The Cape was clearly assuming a sub-imperial administrative role, especially 'trans-frontier' over African societies, as agent of the metropolis. It was also doing more than that in the broader inter-state politics of South Africa where it had, in fact, become the spear-head of the British attempts to counteract republican Afrikanerdom. This last role became increasingly important, even before the great gold bonanza in Kruger's republic. It was really from about 1884 that the Cape became a central part of the British attempt to neutralise Boer frontier expansion in the interior, and to act as a base of British interests in a Southern Africa where Germany was now present as a potential imperial rival.

After 1886, and the Witwatersrand mineral revolution on the highveld, the role of the Cape in British Southern African strategies was accordingly heightened yet further. The metropole power stood behind its local colonial agent as the Cape determined to challenge the republican Boers by a combination of tariff policies, territorial expansion and economic enterprise. The 'prize' in this deadly game of inter-state politics was nothing less than hegemony in Southern Africa. It may now appear that the Cape was an inadequate vehicle, both politically and economically, to carry the burdens piled upon it by the Imperial Factor. But in the context of the time, the British rested considerable faith in the capacity of the 'colonial factor' to sustain its essential interests in this crucial imperial region. In the long term, it was argued in Westminster and Whitehall, the forces of modernity emanating from the 'loyal Cape' – with the predominant Anglo-Saxon influence in its politics – would simply overwhelm the unstable Kruger republic. A very high faith was placed in the multiple impact of political encirclement, capital investment, railway development, customs policies and a migrant 'invasion'. A combination of these formal and informal expansionist thrusts by British 'forces', directed at the Transvaal republicans, formed the basis of Salisbury's uncharacteristically optimistic view that an 'unconscious federation' of South African states, based essentially on a Cape leadership, and thus favourable to British interests generally, was in the making.[3]

In short, as the terms of the local inter-state politics hardened – by a combination of economic development and international intervention – so London relied ever more heavily on Cape Town in working the mechanics of empire in the region itself. Whether the loyal servant was not actually in the process of taking over the house was to become a moot question. Certainly the British had invested the Cape leadership with great hopes. And certainly too the colonial agency of the metropolitan power was able to establish initiatives – in the form of expansive actions under the broad banner of British interests – which suggested a degree of autonomy in shaping the local contemporary scene of a singularly striking nature. It was the Cape commercial, mining and farm interests – united behind the

Rhodes–Hofmeyr alliance – which really drew up much of the agenda for the forward actions of the Imperial Factor in South-Central and Central Africa. It was they, too, who were so important to the extension of British sovereignty in the Transkei and Basutoland, not to mention the areas outside German control in South-west Africa.[4]

Hobson may have been quite wrong in arguing, as he did, for a relatively simple lien between certain capitalist classes and the external policy of HM Government.[5] But he was quite right to the extent that in Southern Africa, through the years of the Partition, the metropolitan power *used* local agencies – ranging from the great BSA Company to capitalist-led colonial ministries – in a fashion which suggests a very intimate relationship of indebtedness. It was, of course, a highly complex *two-way* relationship. But there is no gainsaying the fact that while the British government would not place imperial policy at the disposal of individual investors – Salisbury's cogent noted dictum of 1890[6] – it was still all too true that these sub-imperial agents and agencies were often calling the tune when it came to the pattern and pace of Partition.

The British claimed that this was not so; and they depicted the expansive activities of the local colonial agencies in frontier advances in terms of the natural propensity of Anglo-Saxondom working to make itself supreme in competitive contexts overseas. By this logic, imperialism became a concomitant of free enterprise in the New World.[7] But the harsher reality was that the agencies of the metropole were simply more belligerent in their immediate economic hungers – minerals, labour and land – than the Imperial Factor. They were also relentless in expanding the sphere of the Scramble very much beyond the more circumscribed areas of Southern and Central Africa which were deemed crucial to British interests by Whitehall. The success, and the failure, exhibited by this strategy found its composite representative in Rhodes, his politics and his finance.

In sum, the first major rationale for the intervention of the Imperial Factor in the politics of the Southern African Partition – partly by diplomatic strategy, even more through physical expansion and pre-emptive imperialism – had been a response to the inter-state politics of the region as a whole. The British were here acting out a traditional imperial role, albeit in a fashion more dramatic and vigorous than in earlier decades of the century when they attempted to create a colonial context which was loyal, stable and economically self-sufficient – or at least with the promise of these possibilities. In that sense, the expansion of the Scramble years was merely an extension of an existing pattern of Partition. It may have been dramatic when represented on the map, but it was not exceptional. It was an integral part of a cumulative colonial conquest of South Africa dating back to the first arrival of the Dutch in the mid seventeenth century and the British in the opening decade of the nineteenth century.

What was exceptional about the Scramble era was the *scale* of the con-quests, itself a response to the state of Southern Africa's frontier zones, the behaviour of local settler and Boer groups, and the impact of the new German presence on these parochial factors after 1884. Before the inter-national challenge to British interests in Southern Africa, the Imperial Factor already felt deeply threatened by the degree of instability, bordering on internecine explosion, exhibited in the inter-state politics of the region. Frontier wars, African uprisings, the failure of colonial trusteeship rule, the disruption of trade patterns, the slowing of European immigration, the drying up of capital inflows and even the potential collapse of certain of the interior white societies – these were all very real possibilities which the overlord authority was forced to take into account as real contingencies in planning policy. And, within a short time, as a consequence of intervention against the drift of events in South Africa, there was also present nascent Afrikaner nationalism, in conjunction with a new spasm of Boer frontier expansion, to complicate those local politics yet further, thereby directly challenging the imperial notions of hegemony. It was, therefore, a *series* of local crises which had impelled the Imperial Factor to act by intervention in the inter-state politics of South Africa. The British were becoming inextricably enmeshed in these local problems of Southern African politics, and had begun moving forward the frontiers of possession in company with their eager local colonial agents, when Great Power rivalry entered to trans-form an already unfriendly and unresponsive political landscape into one of frightening possibilities for imperial interests.

The Imperial Factor was also, naturally, to be moved by elements intruding on the Southern African context from the *outside* – forces deriva-tive of the world of geo-politics. If the British had initially become expan-sionists in Africa south of the Zambesi for reasons related to 'lateral' inter-state politics in the region, they were also propelled to become Scramb-lers as a result of the 'horizontal' inter-continental relationships of Europe and Africa.

The rise of German *weltpolitik* – paralleled by Portuguese colonial decline – had very considerable meaning for Southern Africa. Because Bismarck chose to launch his first bid for colonies in South-west Africa it meant that an independent variable of great significance had been intro-duced into the general politics of the broad area Cape to Zambesi, and had raised formidable questions in redefining British interests and hegemony. Moreover, the sheer fact that the African Partition was but part of a global Scramble for markets, resources, power and territorial claims 'pegged out for the future', made plain the fact that an area as important to the European Powers as Southern Africa would most likely be drawn into these patterns of world change.[8]

We need not explore the internal metropolitan origins of the New Imperialism to grasp the fundamental significance of that force as it interacted with the existing configuration of power-politics in colonial Southern Africa. Great Power rivalry generally came into the region, and gave new intensity to the local politics of mastery and expansion. Correspondingly, particular political and economic developments in Southern Africa – such as attempts by the republican Boers to make alliance with the Germans, or the gold discoveries of the Transvaal mineral revolution – affected the relations of the Powers themselves as they perceived a changing reality in the immediate conditions and future prospects of the area.

In a subtle and complex manner the local environment accordingly acted as potent catalyst on the New Imperialism itself. Europe would undoubtedly still have been tempted to stake out certain colonial territories in Southern Africa had there been no large-scale existent settler and Boer societies already struggling in and for the region. But the fact that white settlement patterns were so extensive, and so well developed on the landscape, had formidable consequences for the New Imperialism. The white colonial societies agitated the imperialists into frontier advances not planned by the metropole power; and they created the atmosphere of tension, which led to pre-emptive annexations, by playing on the sense of rivalry between the interested Powers. In addition, the delicate balance of highveld politics was made yet more uncertain for the British by the consequences of these new developments. The Boer capacity to endanger British paramountcy was obviously not unconnected to the potential emergence of an Afrikaner–German entente. The Transvaal determination to forge an independent route to the sea, by cutting through the encircling cordon of British territorial possessions, was equally not unconnected with President Kruger's desire to introduce non-British 'influences' into the heart of the Southern African struggles for hegemony.

Why should the British care so deeply about these problems? Simply because the stakes for the British in these series of evolving international and local developments, as they bore on the state of colonial Southern Africa, *were* in fact really enormous – strategic, political and economic interests of the highest order stood at risk. The coming together of both the old inter-state struggles of the locality, and the impact of the New Imperialism, was accordingly dramatic. London and Cape Town acted with a gravity born of long and growing concern over Southern Africa. Where in other parts of the tropical world the British might attempt to delineate their interventions and annexations with a kind of treasury nicety – balancing financial obligation and expansion with a fine hand – here in Southern Africa that kind of contemplative hesitation could be disastrous in its consequences, both to specific interests in this crucial area of Africa, and to broader interests in Asia and the Far East which were dependent on the Cape route. Thus if the Victorian statesmen felt themselves impelled to take part in a general Partition of the undeveloped world because of the quickening impulses of geo-politics and international rivalry, so they were also to be moved in Southern Africa by the exigencies of a highly sensitive, unstable and explosive empire-region.

It was the very nature of those intense local politics of inter-state rivalry for resources and hegemony which also ensured that imperialism did *not* disappear with the final establishment of the 'white governments everywhere' in 1895.

It was true that the territorial Scramble was, to all intents and purposes, concluded: there was hardly an acre to acquire, or a clan to dispossess, short of massive action through military power against the remaining African political communities. Moreover, it was actually highly convenient to leave traditional African tribesmen with land sufficient for subsistence farming: it solved a multitude of problems in labour supplies, unemployment, administration and security. However, the Scramble had left its own restless legacy – in the form of a *continuing* struggle of 're-partition' between white political communities for the very real interests and resources still at stake in late nineteenth and early twentieth century Southern Africa.

It was accordingly not at all paradoxical that the end of the Scramble proper, for territory and occupation, should have become the very prelude for a massive new phase of imperial rivalry and conflict in the region. Hardly had the Thongaland annexation been settled, for example, and the last frontier closed, than Kruger's republic was assaulted by Jameson's raiders; and hardly had the storm which that glaring act created – both the action itself and the official 'cover-up' in committees of so-called enquiry – started to recede into history, than the whole political environment began to smoulder anew. The menace of full-scale war now appeared increasingly likely, between the British and Boer societies. For this conflict involved such fundamental questions as *uitlander* rights and the demands of the mining capitalists; Anglo-German rivalry at Delagoa Bay; Cape–Transvaal commercial-tariff war; *and* fears on the part of the Imperial Factor that the advances of the Scramble had still not brought the region under British 'influence', let alone 'control'. Between 1899–1902 the greatest of all the frontier and colonial wars was fought in South Africa in the name of British strategic and economic interests – in the widest sense – against the highveld regime of Paul Kruger and his Orange Free State allies.[9]

Not that the politics of imperialism was even then finally spent as a force for change and geo-political revolution. After the Anglo-Boer war a major, if forlorn, attempt was made to 'reconstruct' the sociological character of the Boer republican states, to ensure a palpably visible British hegemony, 1902–05.[10] In the failure of that military solution, disguised in humanitarian and scientific language, was born the British acceptance of a united South African state in 1910, to be run by the loyal, collaborationist element among the Anglo-Saxon settlers, and such moderate Afrikaners as would participate.[11] With a kind of iron law of white expansion in South Africa, this British withdrawal of the formal Imperial factor from local politics had little impact on the dynamics of the regional Scramble for power and resources. The act of union left open the possibility of a 'greater South Africa', which would in fact incorporate all the major states of Southern Africa; and in the Smuts–Hertzog era, of 1910–48, areas as widely dispersed as the British protectorates – Basutoland, Bechuanaland and Swaziland – as well as South-west Africa and East Africa all felt the focus of close white-South African interest. These hopes of expansion were largely to fail: Rhodesia declined to join South Africa by narrow referendum result in 1923; the British protectorates were at last, after the Second World War, placed strictly outside any possible transference of power to Pretoria; and East Africa was also to remain outside the South African orbit, despite Smuts' war strategy 1939–45 in tropical Africa. Only South-west Africa moved from mandated territory to South African control.[12] But these very mixed failures to create a greater South Africa well reflected the manner in which the spirit of Scramble had survived the closing of the frontier in 1895, and had indeed been projected well into the twentieth century.

One dominating lesson stood out in accounting for the longevity of white imperial politics, in its various guises, in the Southern Africa post 1895; the reason why the Scramble itself settled little and projected much for the future of imperialism in the region. The Scramble had been a manifestation of a particular combination of local and international forces of white empire which were only partially and temporarily assuaged by a territorial division of Southern Africa into settler, Boer and Imperial spheres of authority. The year 1895 was thus to become no more than a breathing moment as the forces which had conducted the Scramble considered the local situation, and then began to regroup, preparatory to devising, and launching, new expansive political strategies for the future. By its very nature the Scramble had indeed created an unequal power situation, with little 'balance' between the local states; these imbalances accordingly formed the very energising basis for the continuing struggles to win a final hegemony over the veld, its riches, and resources.

Further, the participants in the Scramble still strongly felt the immediate legacy of enmities and rivalries engendered in the decades after 1877: the frontier advances had exacerbated, rather than dissipated, the zeal for progress through expansion of the colonial states. The white settlers of the Cape, for example, were still in fact desperately concerned about the economic balance of the local inter-state system, which did indeed increasingly favour Kruger's republic with its vast riches of the Rand. They nursed severe umbrage at having competed so long, and so hard, for the spoils of frontier expansion only to be faced with the harsh reality of the golden land not merely in the hands of the republican Boers, but a government which enjoyed cutting them off from the prosperity of the commercial well-being which it generated. Moreover, the Cape's metropole power, Great Britain, shared this deepening concern in reading the triumph of anti-British republicanism into the economic power of the Transvaal in the general Southern African state system.[13]

The Afrikaners of the highveld, on the other hand, were determined to have their place in the sun, at last. The Scramble had given them some valuable territory – on their south-western and south-eastern frontiers with Tswana and Zulu – but it had also in fact left them considerably aggrieved. They had been shut out of Zambesia by Rhodes' central African strategy; they sensed the degree to which British expansion, through the Cape, had been an attempt to isolate and surround republicanism on the highveld, they resented the continuing British attempts to qualify Boer independence from without (by frequently raising the controversial matter of the 'suzerainty clause' written into the 1881 convention and omitted from the 1884 Anglo-Boer treaty) and from within (the even more controversial matter of British support for the *uitlander* franchise issue); and the Boers grasped the degree to which they could be pushed around by the might of the Imperial Factor unless they had the arms and the ally of a rival Great Power – such as Imperial Germany. Kruger's republic wished to be genuinely independent of British South Africa. But, by the very nature of the local political environment, that was to be impossible without acquiring the status of premier local state, for the British would not accept such independence at face value. Events were forcing a contest for ultimate hegemony on the veld.[14]

The Scramble for Southern Africa 1877–95 might, then, be said to have left the politics of the region in a state of tense and uneasy equipoise, balanced indeed on the edge of a political precipice. It was only to take

Rhodes' rash actions, in trying to foment a rebellion on the Rand in company with an invasion of Kruger's republic by troopers drawn from his BSA Company forces, for the whole interlinked and fragile inter-state power structure to begin falling apart. Once Rhodes was discredited – Jameson had indeed 'upset the apple cart', as the imperialist sadly admitted – then the whole British strategy, of working empire and influence through the agency of a mixed Cape government of Anglo-Saxon and Afrikaner, had to be abandoned. And once that technique of indirect imperialism had collapsed then there was nothing for it but that the British Imperial Factor frontally face the force of republican Afrikanerdom itself.

In many ways what was happening was a fascinating variant on the Leninist approach to the New Imperialism: in this context imperialism could be seen as a struggle to re-divide the *developed*, or developing world, and not so much a struggle for 'paper conquests' over the tropical areas of the globe.[15] Economic factors did not alone dictate this process, *pace* Hobson and Lenin. But it was the changing economic structure of Southern Africa which created the parameters for the renewed inter-state conflict over interests and resources. The Rand was indeed at the heart of the matter. The decade after 1895 accordingly found the Scramble dead, in the simple geographic sense of a real-estate rush, but also very much alive, in the determination of the old participants to re-divide, re-partition and re-order the status quo.

The origins of the Jameson Raid, and of the Anglo-Boer War, perhaps best testified to this theme. Some highly interesting recent scholarship by a number of authors from quite different intellectual standpoints – Blainey and Kubicek on the Randlords, Trapido and Denoon on the labour needs of the mines, Duminy and Jeeves on the politics of the capitalists, Phimister and Galbraith on Rhodes – has together pointed to the manner in which the Raid actually intimately interlocked with the local Scramble politics, and projected them forward through the harsh rivalry and economic strategies which had been the hallmark of the New Imperialism all along.[16] The Rhodesian group precipitated the assault on the Kruger regime as a result of failing economic fortunes in central Africa and of Rhodes' own determination to make the Cape the leading state in any future united 'South Africa', with him as 'local king' (Milner's later sharp judgement on Rhodes' status in the Cape). The British authorities knowingly allowed the plot against the Transvaal to mature – and even abetted it by kindly providing the territorial staging point in Bechuanaland – because they too wished to see the collapse of Krugerism and the emergence of an imperial-dominated Southern Africa.[17] They had also grown used to working their interests in the region through the collaborative agencies of the local colonies and chartered company. Further, major economic forces within the Transvaal, not least among Rand capitalists such as Beit who had deep-level mining commitments, gave direct financial support to illegal filibustering, out of a deep animus towards the Kruger government, through involvement with Rhodes and in the name of British supremacy.[18] In each case, those parties implicated in the Raid, ranging from Great Power to colony to capitalist, were attempting to secure and to redress interests fundamentally affected by the previous politics of Scramble and Partition.

Jameson's Raid, therefore, was hardly an isolated throwback to Elizabethan brigandage; or a simple moral lapse on the part of the imperial governors, although it was those things too.[19] Rather, the Raid represented, in certainly its seamiest light, the disturbing power of the New Imperialism's continuing role in Southern Africa. The energy, the belligerence, the impatience, the greed, the expansive zeal of the local empire-makers and conquerors, merely took on new forms as this force of the New Imperialism turned away from territorial objectives *per se*, and was, instead, channelled into commercial, diplomatic and subversive strategies for advancing the particular aims of the groups involved.

In turn, of course, the Raid merely heightened inter-state tension in Southern Africa; and it hardened the terms for any peacefully negotiated solution to the problems of resource-sharing, or of political power, in the region generally. The period immediately after 1895, and running right down to 1905, thus witnessed an escalation of the bitter and brittle politics of the previous decades. This was the deepest origins of the Anglo-Boer War. It is quite unhistorical, and incorrect, to label it alone 'Milner's war', or the 'capitalists' war'; or even 'Chamberlain's war'. The war owed its origins undoubtedly to the 'conflict of inter-state interests' in Southern Africa generally, and formed yet another tangible legacy of the Scramble.[20] It represented the final collapse of attempts to divide power and resources in South Africa by diplomacy and politico-geographic adjustment. The Anglo-Boer War became the epitome of the rivalry of the Scramble. At its core was the indivisible question of who was to rule and exploit the resources of Southern Africa.[21]

In that sense, the vital British cabinet memorandum of 6 September 1899 has remained the best insight into the origins of the war, not least because it so well captures the historical dimension of the politics of Scramble and Partition out of which the impasse of that year had finally, almost ineluctably, emerged. 'What is now at stake is the position of Great Britain in South Africa and with it the estimate formed of our power and influence in our Colonies and throughout the world', as Chamberlain wrote vividly in drafting the memorandum:

The Dutch [Afrikaners] in South Africa desire, if it be possible to get rid altogether of the connection with Great Britain, and which to them is not a motherland, and to substitute a United States of South Africa which, they hope, would be, mainly under Dutch influence. . . The existence of a pure Dutch Republic [the Transvaal], floating and flouting successfully, British control and influence, is answerable for all the racial animosities which have been so formidable a factor in the South African situation.

The suspense and tension of the last few years . . . have immensely increased the bitterness of feeling which has always existed more or less since 1881. Everyone, natives included, sees that the issue has been joined, and that it depends upon the action of the British Government now whether the supremacy . . . is finally established and recognized or forever abandoned.

This is, I repeat, the real question at stake. It has been simmering for years, and has now been brought to boiling point by a fortuitous combination of circumstances.[22]

Chamberlain could shape his argument in that fashion for two very practical reasons. He had been a member of the second Gladstone administration in the critical years 1880–85, when the Boer conventions had been negotiated, and when the politics of Scramble and Partition were beginning to reach a crest: the record shows him deeply involved in the South African Question right from this beginning when he was but a lowly minister at the board of trade.[23] Further, and less personally, his cabinet memorandum revealed him reacting not merely to general international pressures on the British as a Great Power, or indeed to jingoistic lobbies in the United Kingdom itself, but rather to that smaller, but intense world, of inter-state politics in Southern Africa itself which he knew so well, and over so many years.[24]

Just why the British Imperial Factor should wish to assert that supremacy, is not set out in any detailed way in Chamberlain's cabinet memorandum. But an understanding of British interests in Southern Africa, as revealed by the politics of the Scramble, suggests all too surely what was at stake by the end of the century. There were traditional, long-standing issues, of South African strategic importance in the British empire – a question which was now actually more important than in earlier years, for the age of *weltpolitik* meant direct German interest in Delagoa Bay and some sort of Boer–Reich connection. There was also the undeniable fact that Southern Africa had become a complex and vital 'interest' in itself to the British as a Great Power. Around the proclaimed need for imperial supremacy in the region, clustered a whole series of critical factors: trade and investment, both growing greatly since the 1880s; commitment to the British settlers and local agencies of influence, which constituted both the means and the rationale for an emigrant settlement-empire in Southern Africa; the 'psychological' issues of power and status raised by the possession of so important, so rich, so strategically placed a zone of the world in the later nineteenth century; and the general issue of the 'pull of Africa', as problems of government, influence and suasion drew the Imperial Factor to ever more extensive counteraction in the face of a palpably destabilised local situation.[25]

The formal Scramble decades after 1877 should therefore be seen as occupying a crucial, but particular place, in the history of the white imperial theme in the evolution of modern Southern Africa. These years stood for that period of heightened and agitated geo-political change and conquest which formed the culmination of two centuries of colonial intrusion into the region. And, they offered the dramatic heights from which a new phase of the contest for Southern Africa could be launched. The Imperial Factor, its allies and agencies, renewed the struggle for hegemony and resources against not the native inhabitants but the highveld Boers, and the Witwatersrand deposits which history and nature had placed in their hands. The Raid and the War (1895–1902) became, simply, exemplars of the New Imperialism by other means.

The politics of Partition in Southern Africa were, accordingly, to become a paradigm of much of the British world predicament in the later nineteenth century. By the end of the era of the Scramble for Africa and Asia, the Victorians could still, in several senses, continue to think of themselves as the paramount power and culture. But that ascendancy was increasingly rooted in a deep *dependency* on the world beyond Europe; and it was a world in which the conditions of trade, power and influence were progressively turning against the British. History was catching up with the Victorians. Expansion in its various forms had meant unparalleled prosperity and power. It had also meant an almost organic attachment to the extra-European regions of the globe. Once those areas and their societies began 'to come back' at the Victorians – often precipitated by a break-down in local authority – then new forces were released, and new situations created, which together were dating back to the heyday of free trade imperialism. Expansion, Partition and Scramble were the evolving metropolitan answer to these overseas problems.

In that sense, too, Southern Africa offered a micro-example of a broader set of developments, a lesson in the importance of the 'periphery' in the extension of Europe overseas, and of the power of dynamic local frontier situations to shape greater international events. Indeed, it provides us with a revealing narrative of how the New Imperialism worked in actuality. Not so much the consequence of a 'stage of capitalism', as a historical development arising out of the state of the overseas periphery. 'Expansion' as a product of frontier dynamics; 'Partition' as a cumulative result of old and new contests for local resources in land, labour and minerals; and 'Scramble' as a consequence of the manner in which the politics of the periphery had galvanised the international rivalry incipient in the New Imperialism. It was simply a demonstration, in fact, of imperialism growing out of imperialism. Or as Schumpeter might have put it much more elegantly, a new twist to the 'ancient truth that the dead always rule the living'.

Notes

1   For a Victorian assessment of the 'South African Question' in 1877, the beginnings of this narrative, see Sir Frederic Rogers' discussion in G. E. Marinden (ed.) *Letters of Frederic, Lord Blachford* (London, 1896), p. 374. A subtle modern perspective on the 'Question' is to be found in Ronald Hyam, *Britain's Imperial Century: a study of empire and expansion, 1815–1914* (London, 1976), ch. 10.

2   Gladstone in the House of Commons, 25 June 1881 and 16 March 1883; *Hansard* (3) CCCLXIII col. 1852 and CCLXXVII col. 720.

3   John Roberts has an excellent summary of the New Imperialism of the later nineteenth century in his *Europe 1880–1945* (London, 1968) pp. 102 ff.

4   J. S. Keltie, *The Partition of Africa* (London, 1895), p. 498.

5   Trevor Lloyd, 'Africa and Hobson's imperialism', *Past and Present*, No. 55, May 1972, p. 143 n. 51.

6   There is a very useful contemporary summary of the regional and demographic figures, as at 1891, in James Bryce, *Impressions of South Africa* (London, 3rd edn, 1900), p. lv.

7   The best critical commentary on the literature of the Partition is still Ronald Hyam's 1963 essay, 'The Partition of Africa; a critique of Robinson and Gallagher', a revised version of which is found in R. Hyam and G. Martin, *Reappraisals in British Imperial History* (London, 1975), pp. 139–66. See also: M. E. Chamberlain, *The Scramble for Africa* (London, 1974), which has a good bibliography; C. J. Lowe, *The reluctant imperialists: British foreign policy 1878–1902* (London, 1967), vol. I, which places the African Scramble in its proper international context; D. C. M. Platt, *Finance, Trade and Politics in British foreign policy* (Oxford, 1969), which is good on economic forces of expansion, esp. pp. 249–61; L. Gann and P. Duignan (eds.) *Colonialism in Africa, 1870–1960* (Cambridge, 1969), ch. 3 of which attempts an overview of the Partition; and Bernard Porter, *The Lions share: a short history of British imperialism 1850–1960* (London, 1975), where an incisive discussion of late-Victorian imperialism is to be found, pp. 129–39.

8   See E. T. Stokes, 'Uneconomic imperialism', a review article in the *Historical Journal*, XVIII, 1975 (2), pp. 409–16.

9   R. J. Lovell, *The struggle for South Africa, 1875–99* (New York, 1934).
10 See Stephen Cooney 'Political demand channels in the process of American and British imperial expansion, 1870–1913', *World Politics*, XXVII, no. 2, Jan. 1975, pp. 227–55, for a broad conceptual discussion.
11 E. A. Walker, *A History of Southern Africa* (first edition 1928; new impression London, 1962), esp. p. 362; and C. W. de Kiewiet, *The Imperial Factor in South Africa* (Cambridge, 1937), esp. pp. 148–245. On the frontier see the notable works of John S. Galbraith, 'The "Turbulent Frontier" as a Factor in British Expansion', *Comparative Studies in Society and History*, vol. 2, 1959–60, pp. 150–68, and W. D. McIntyre, *The Imperial Frontier in the Tropics, 1865–75: A Study of British Colonial Policy in West Africa, Malaya and the South Pacific in the Age of Gladstone and Disraeli* (London, 1967). A recent work has well synthesised the growing acknowledgement of the importance of the frontier zones of the empires: 'Economic involvement on the periphery of empire too often led to political intervention as political instability in areas of trade led local officials to take sides in civil wars or intervene to reestablish conditions conducive to commercial prosperity. Too often officials in Whitehall could do no more than condone actions already undertaken.' C. C. Eldridge, *England's Mission: The Imperial Idea in the Age of Gladstone and Disraeli, 1868–80* (London, 1973), p. 18.
12 Ronald Robinson, John Gallagher with Alice Denny, *Africa and the Victorians; The 'official mind' of imperialism* (London, 1961). Their thesis can also be examined in: 'The Imperialism of Free trade', *Economic History Review*, 2nd ser. vol. VI, no. I. (1953); 'The Partition of Africa', ch. 22 of the *New Cambridge History*, vol. XI (Cambridge, 1962). See also Ronald Robinson, 'Imperial Problems in British Politics, 1880–95', *Cambridge History of the British Empire* (Cambridge, 1959), vol. III, ch. V; 'The Official Mind of Imperialism', *Historians in Tropical Africa* (Salisbury, Rhodesia, 1962), pp. 197–208; and 'Non-European foundations of European imperialism – sketch for a theory of collaboration', in *Studies in the theory of Imperialism*, eds. Roger Owen and Bob Sutcliffe (London, 1972), pp. 117–40. Their critics include: Oliver MacDonagh, 'The Anti-Imperialism of Free Trade', *Economic History Review*, 2nd ser., vol. XIV (1962); A. G. L. Shaw, 'A Revision of the Meaning of Imperialism', *Australian Journal of Politics and History*, VII, (1961); D. C. M. Platt, 'The Imperialism of Free Trade – Some Reservations', *Econ. H. Rev.*, XXI (1968), 'Economic Factors during the "New Imperialism"', *Past and Present* (1968), and 'Further Objections to the "Imperialism of Free Trade", 1830–60', *Econ. H. Rev.*, XXVI, (1973); G. Shepperson, 'Africa, the Victorians and Imperialism', *Revue Belge de Philologie et d'Historie*, XL (1962); Eric Stokes, 'Imperialism and the Scramble for Africa: The new view' (Local Series No. 10, *Historical Association of Rhodesia and Nyasaland*, 1963); and V. G. Kiernan, 'Farewells to Empire: some recent studies of imperialism', *Socialist Register*, 1964. For

a summary of the debate see W. R. Louis, *Imperialism: the Robinson and Gallagher controversy* (1975).

13 See John Hargreaves, *West Africa Partitioned* (London, 1974) vol. 1; also his *Prelude to the Partition of West Africa* (London, 1963) and 'Towards a history of the Partition', *Journal of African History*, I (1960), pp. 97–109; and the excellent account of proconsular initiative in J. A. Benyon, 'The Cape High Commission: another neglected factor in British imperial expansion', *South African Historical Journal*, Nov. 1973, no. 5, pp. 28–40.

14 C. G. W. Schumann, *Structural and Business Cycles in South Africa* (London, 1938), pp. 38, 85, *passim*; S. H. Frankel, *Capital Investment in Africa* (Oxford, 1938), esp. tables 5 and 28; M. H. de Kock, *Selected Subjects in the Economic History of South Africa* (Cape Town, 1924), p. 142 *passim*; D. M. Goodfellow, *A modern economic history of South Africa* (London, 1931), p. 47 *passim*; E. H. D. Arndt, *Banking and the Currency Development in South Africa, 1652–1927* (Cape Town, 1928), p. 235 *passim*; D. Hobart Houghton, *The South African Economy* (Cape Town, 1964), pp. 1–44; Alex Hepple, *South Africa – Social and Economic* (Oxford, 1941), pp. 56–114; D. M. Schreuder, *Gladstone and Kruger; Liberal Government and Colonial Home Rule', 1880–85* (London, 1969), pp. 10–13; W. Schlote, *British Overseas Trade* (Oxford, 1952), esp. tables 18–19; Sheila van der Horst, *Native Labour in South Africa* (London, 1942), pp. 66–85; and J. van der Poel, *Railways and Customs Policies in South Africa, 1885–1910* (London, 1933), ch. 1.

15 D. A. Low, review, in *Journal of Imperial and Commonwealth History*, vol. II, Oct, 1973, p. 110. See also the excellent summary in L. M. Thompson, 'The subjection of the African chiefdoms, 1870–98', *The Oxford History of South Africa* (Oxford, 1971), vol. II, pp. 245–88.

16 Eric Stokes, 'Malawi's Political Systems, 1891–6', in E. Stokes and R. Brown (eds.), *The Zambesian Past* (Manchester, 1967), pp. 353–4.

17 For a spirited account of the 'cultural' manifestations of the New Imperialism see H. Gollwitzer, *Europe in the Age of Imperialism, 1880–1914* (London, 1969).

18 Fieldhouse, *Economics of Empire, 1830–1914*, pp. 63–103.

19 E. J. Hobsbawm's *Age of capital 1848–75* (London, 1975), esp. pp. 48–68 and 135–54 is emphatic on the connections between European industrialisation and the extra-European world of markets, raw materials, capital investment and settlement. J. H. Parry has written definitively on the even earlier *Age of Reconnaisance* (London, 1963); his *Trade and Dominion* (London, 1971) covers the mercantile empires.

20 For a summary of the literature on the significance of 1870–71 in British external policy, see D. M. Schreuder, 'Gladstone as "Troublemaker": Liberal foreign policy and the German annexation of Alsace-Lorraine', *Journal of British Studies*, July 1978.

21 *Africa and the Victorians*, p. 53, passim.

22 Detailed in Schreuder, *Gladstone and Kruger*, esp. pp. 465–76.

23 H. M. Robertson, '150 years of economic contact between white and black', *South African Journal of Economics*, in two parts, 1934–35.

24 For a valuable general discussion of the New Imperialism developing out of existing relations between Europe and Africa see Ronald Robinson (ed.), *Developing the Third World* (Cambridge, 1971), pp. 262–3; and also his comments on the economic dynamic of 'frontiers' in the Introduction to H. Brunschwig, *French colonialism, 1871–1914* (London, 1966), p. viii.

CHAPTER I

1 E. A. Walker, *A history of Southern Africa* (London, 1962), p. 365.

2 See *Parl. Paps.*, LX, C. 1815, and LV, C. 1961; and C. F. Goodfellow, *Great Britain and South African Confederation, 1870–81* (Oxford, 1966).

3 I am much indebted to L. M. Thompson's pioneer essay, 'The subjection of the chiefdoms, 1870–98', *OHSA*, II, pp. 245–86; and also the illuminating narrative in Denoon, *Southern Africa since 1800*, pp. 66–89.

4 Shula Marks, *Reluctant rebellion* (Oxford, 1970), esp. chs. I and II; also D. Morris, *The washing of the spears* (New York, 1964).

5 E. A. Walker (ed.), *Cambridge History of the British empire*, (Cambridge, 1963), VIII, pp. 400–35, 474–91.

6 *OHSA*, II, 246–50; and F. A. van Jaarsveld, *The awakening of Afrikaner nationalism, 1868–81* (Cape Town, 1961).

7 See Shula Marks, 'African and Afrikaner history', a review article, *Journal of African History*, XI, 3, 1970, p. 439 *passim*, for an illuminating discussion of the nineteenth-century frontier.

8 *OHSA*, II, 245–53, is expertly succinct on the forces at work.

9 Summarised in Schreuder, *Gladstone and Kruger*, ch. I.

10 Charles Dilke, *Problems of Greater Britain* (London, 1890), I, p. 500.

11 CO 812/38, pp. 411–13.

12 Schreuder, *Gladstone and Kruger*, p. 15.

13 R. E. Robinson, 'Non-European foundations of European imperialism: sketch for a theory of collaboration', in R. Owen and Bob Sutcliffe (eds.), *Studies in the theory of imperialism* (London, 1972), p. 123.

14 Carnarvon memorandum 1879, quoted de Kiewiet, *Imperial Factor*, p. 69.

15 CO 48/434 (1868); also de Kiewiet, *British colonial policy*, p. 261.

16 Schreuder, *Gladstone and Kruger*, chs. III–IV.

17 Sir Hercules Robinson's retirement speech is summarised in *The Annual Register* (1889), pp. 407–8.

18 Fairfield memorandum, 9 July 1877; CO 48/482.

19 Quoted in D. Hobart Houghton, *The South African economy* (OUP, Cape Town, 1969), p. 10 n. 22.

20 Herbert minute 14 July 1871, CO 48/453; Benyon, 'The high commission and Basutoland', p. 224.

21 Minutes by Bramston, 11 Nov. 1884, CO 179/154.

22 *Cape official handbook, 1886*, pp. 212–13.

23 T. Reunert, 'Diamond mining', in *ibid.*, pp. 177–219.

24 *Ibid.*, p. 320.

25 Anthony Trollope, *South Africa* (London, 1878); quoted from the definitive critical edition by J. H. Davidson (Cape Town, 1973), p. 375.

26 *Ibid.*, p. 368.

27 Port Elizabeth Chamber of Commerce, *Annual Report*, 1875, p. 43.

28 *Idem.*

29 *Ibid.*, 1890. *Report*, p. 6.

30 T. R. H. Davenport, *The Afrikaner Bond* (Oxford, 1966), pp. 80–9.

31 See *DSAB*, I, pp. 126–8; the Brownlee Papers are in the Killie Campbell Library, Durban, Natal; see also, W. T. Brownlee (ed.), *Charles Brownlee: Reminiscences of Kaffir Life and History, with a brief Memoir by Mrs Brownlee* (Lovedale, 1896).

32 See Brownlee's first annual report as Secretary for Native Affairs, 1875, G. 21–75, p. 133.

33 Brownlee to his brother, 6 April [1879]; Brownlee MSS, KCL.

34 Sprigg to Editor, *Grahamstown Journal*, 9 Jan. 1880; quoted in Vanstone, 'Sir Gordon Sprigg', pp. 70–1.

35 Port Elizabeth Chamber of Commerce, *Annual Report 1874*, p. 26.

36 There is no study of Theal, but see M. Babrow, 'George McCall Theal', unpublished MA University of Cape Town.

37 Theal, *History*, x, p. 28.

38 *Ibid.*, p. 96 (my italics).

39 *Ibid.*, XI, pp. 30–1.

40 *Ibid.*, pp. 194–5.

41 *Ibid.*, x, p. 226.

42 *Ibid.*, p. 305.

43 *Ibid.*, p. 172.

44 Schreuder, *Gladstone and Kruger*, pp. 12–98.

45 Brookes and Webb, *History of Natal*, pp. 146–67.

46 Napier to Stanley, 25 July 1842, 'Confidential' J. Bird (ed.), *Annals of Natal, 1485–1845* (Cape Town, 1888: Struik reprint), vol. II, p. 47.

47 Natal Commission Report (1852–53), p. 26. Also David Welsh, *The Roots of Segregation: Native Policy in Colonial Natal 1845–1910* (Cape Town, 1971), p. 33.

48 *NNABB*, 1882, p. 255.

49 *Ibid.*, pp. 50–1.

50 *Ibid.*, p. 102.

51 H. J. Simons, *African Women* (Evanston, 1968), p. 15.

52 Welsh, *Roots of Segregation*, p. 34.

53 *NNABB*, 1888, p. 157.

54 A. F. Hattersley, *An illustrated Social History of South Africa* (Cape Town, 1973), p. 188.

55 Marks, *Reluctant Rebellion*, p. 4.

56 De Kiewiet, *The Imperial Factor*, p. 191.

57 Shepstone in Wolsely to Carnarvon, 14 June 1875. CO 179/177.

58 R. L. Cope, 'Shepstone and Cetshwayo, 1873–9' (PhD, Natal, 1967), p. 16.

59 *NNABB*, 1882, p. 35.

60 *Ibid.*, p. 4.

61 J. Robinson, *Notes on Natal* (1872), p. 130.

62 Musgrave to Kimberley, 6 January 1873. CO 179/111.

63 *NNABB*, 1882, p. 34.

64 *Ibid.*, p. 20.

65 *Ibid.*, p. 4.

66 *NNABB*, 1895, p. 71.

67 Shepstone Memo, 18 November 1878, Shepstone MSS. Also Colenso MSS, KCL.

68 Shepstone to Bulwer, 30 March 1878 (Shepstone MSS, letterbook). Cope, 'Shepstone and Cetshwayo', p. 87.

69 Shula Marks and Anthony Atmore, 'Firearms in Southern Africa: A Survey', *Journal of African History*, XII, 4 (1971), pp. 517–30.

70 *Ibid.*, p. 523.

71 Anthony Atmore and Peter Sanders, 'Sotho arms and ammunition in the nineteenth century', *Journal of African History, ibid.*, pp. 535–44.

72 Marks and Atmore, 'Firearms in Southern Africa', p. 526.

73 *Ibid.*, p. 524.

74 *Natal Mercury*, 13 November 1877. Cope, 'Shepstone and Cetshwayo', p. 87.

75 Sue Miers, 'Notes on the arms trade and government policy in Southern Africa between 1870 and 1890', *Journal of African History*, XII, 4 (1971), pp. 572, 577.

76 *NNABB*, 1885, p. 71.

77 Quoted Marks, *Reluctant Rebellion*, p. 9.

78 Welsh, *Roots of Segregation*, p. 35.

79 *Natal Mercury*, 8 March 1858.

80 Shepstone: 'Tribal distinctions that obtain among them are highly useful in managing them'. Quoted, Welsh, *Roots of segregation*, p. 22.

81 Even the Wolseley Settlement after the Zulu war was to bear the Shepstone imprint in its divided structure of authority. See Brookes and Webb, *History of Natal*, p. 148.

82 Welsh, *Roots of segregation*, p. 211.

83 Bishop Colenso remarked of Shepstone that he was a man whose 'manners are those of a paramount chief', and who 'at heart was but a Zulu chief'. Quoted *ibid*.

84 Welsh, *Roots of Segregation*, is very valuable here, esp. p. 209.

85 *Ibid.*, p. 216 for Shepstone as paternalist imperialist.
86 Simons, *African women*, p. 18 is also most incisive on Shepstone and his politics.
87 Welsh, *Roots of segregation*, p. 211 *passim*.
88 A. 12–'73, Select committee on native affairs, 1873, pp. 133–4 (Cape Government Records, Cape Archives).
89 L. M. Thompson, 'Indian immigration into Natal, 1860–72', *AYB*, 1952, p. 6, has argued that Shepstone had 'failed to civilize', despite a considerable administrative achievement in other areas.
90 C. J. Uys, *in the Era of Shepstone* (Lovedale, 1933), badly needs a replacement.
91 Welsh, *Roots of Segregation*, p. 204.
92 Shepstone to H. Shepstone, 16 August 1870. Shepstone MSS. See also Cope, 'Shepstone and Cetshwayo', pp. 87–92.
93 Shepstone Memo, 28 February 1874. Shepstone MSS, and *ibid.*, p. 15.
94 Brookes and Webb, *History of Natal*, p. 121 and *CHBE*, VIII, pp. 422–3.
95 Benyon, 'High Commission and Basutoland', p. 170 *passim*.
96 Shepstone to Herbert, 30 November 1874. Cope, 'Shepstone and Cetshwayo', p. 92.
97 Martineau, *Life of Frere*, II, p. 305.
98 Min. by Carnarvon, 20 June 1874. CO 179/114, and Cope, 'Shepstone and Cetshwayo', pp. 65–9.
99 See C. F. J. Müller, *Die Britse owerheid en die Groot Trek* (Johannesburg, 1963).
100 Schreuder, *Gladstone and Kruger*, pp. 18–29.
101 Denoon, *Southern Africa since 1800*, pp. 60–5.
102 Quoted Hancock, *Survey of Commonwealth Affairs*, XX, no. ii, part 2, p. 26.
103 S. Trapido, 'The Boer state', unpublished seminar paper, Institute of Commonwealth Studies, London University; and M. Streak, *The Afrikaner as viewed by the English, 1795–1854* (Cape Town, 1974), esp. pp. 211–20.
104 Hancock, *Survey*, II, p. 24.
105 *OHSA*, ii, p. 282, and *DSAB*, ii, p. 556.
106 *Ibid.*, *OHSA*, II, pp. 282–3.
107 Schreuder, *Gladstone and Kruger*, for a discussion of the London Convention, pp. 363–436.
108 J. A. Benyon, 'The Process of Political Incorporation', in W. D. Hammond-Torke (ed.), *The Bantu-Speaking Peoples of Southern Africa* (London, 1974), pp. 367–96.
109 Brookes and Webb, *Natal*, pp. 124–55 and T. O. Ranger, *Revolt in Southern Rhodesia* (London, 1967).
110 J. I. Omer-Cooper, *Zulu Aftermath* (London, 1966).
111 Theal, *History*, X, p. 33.
112 See S. Jones (ed.), *Protest and Hope 1882–1934*, vol. I, of *From Protest to Challenge: A documentary history of African Politics in South Africa* (Stanford, 1972), esp. pp. 3–18.

113 Peter Walshe, *The Rise of African Nationalism in South Africa; The African National Congress, 1912–1952* (California, 1970), pp. 2–29.

114 C. C. Saunders, 'Tile and the Thembu Church: Politics and Independency on the Cape Eastern Frontier in the late nineteenth century', *Journal of African History*, XI, 4 (1970), pp. 553–70.

115 D. D. Jabavu, *The Life of John Tengo Jabavu, Editor of 'Imvo Zabantsundu', 1884–1921* (Lovedale, 1921).

116 E. Roux, *Time Longer than Rope* (Wisconsin, 1966), ch. VII.

117 H. J. and R. E. Simons, *Class and Colour in South Africa, 1850–1950* (London, 1969), p. 110.

118 Roux, *Time Longer than Rope*, p. 61.

119 W. G. Mills, 'The role of the African clergy in the reorientation of Xhosa society to the plural society in the Cape colony, 1850–1915', unpublished PhD, UCLA, 1975. (My thanks to Dr Mills for allowing me to read his thesis.)

120 Roux, *Time Longer than Rope*, pp. 48–9; and *OHSA*, II, p. 428.

121 S. Trapido, 'African Divisional Politics in the Cape Colony, 1884 to 1910', *Journal of African History*, IX, 1 (1968), pp. 61–98.

122 *OHSA*, I, pp. 233–71.

123 Robertson, '150 years economic contact between black and white'; S. D. Neumark, *Economic influences on the South African frontier 1652–1836* (California, 1956); and M. Legassick, 'The frontier in South African historiography', unpublished seminar paper (1970). See also Marks, 'African and Afrikaner history', *JAH*, XI, 3, 1970, p. 439; Hobart Houghton, *South African economy*, pp. 12–15; and *OHSA*, II, pp. 245–53.

124 A. Atmore and S. Marks, 'The Imperial Factor in South Africa in the nineteenth century: towards a reassessment', *Journal of Imperial and Commonwealth History*, vol. 3, October 1974, pp. 105–39.

125 Schreuder, 'The cultural factor in Victorian imperialism; case-study of the civilizing mission', in *ibid.*, May 1976, takes its examples from the administration of the Cape frontier areas, 1870–83.

126 See *Parl. Paps.*, C. 2000, 1878, p. 19: Hon. Cecil Ashley to Sir B. Frere, 19 November 1877. Ashley was the 27 year old private secretary to Sir Bartle Frere as high commissioner, and he had made a tour of the interior in October 1877.

127 Monica Wilson, 'Missionaries: conquerors or servants of God?' *South African Outlook*, vol. 110, no. 1,248, March 1976, p. 41.

128 *Ibid.*, p. 42.

129 Ashley to Frere, *op. cit.*, p. 24.

CHAPTER 2

1 Blachford to Sir H. Taylor, 2 April 1877, in Marinden (ed.), *Letters of Frederic, Lord Blachford op. cit.*, p. 374. See also Goodfellow, *Great Britain and South African confederation*, p. 113; and Marks, *JAH*, X(1) p. 184, for acute assessment of these events as harbinger of Partition.

2   Carnarvon to Barkley, 20 Sept. 1878; de Kiewiet, *Imperial Factor*, p. 110.

3   Frere to Carnarvon, 9 Oct. 1877. *Parl. Paps.*, c. 1961 (1878) pp. 119–20.

4   Shepstone to C. J. Uys, and others, 19 Sept. 1877. *Ibid.*, p. 155.

5   A. Atmore, 'The Moorosi rebellion; Lesotho, 1879', in *Protest and power in Black Africa*, eds. R. Rotberg and A. Mazrui (New York, 1970), pp. 3–35; also CAD records in G. 13-'80, p. 24 *passim*; and Benyon, 'Basutoland and the high commission'.

6   Theal's account in his *History* (vol. x, pp. 52–199) is very much from the perspective of the Cape colonial authorities. Christopher Saunders has shown how that history might be written: 'The Transkeian rebellion of 1880–81, a case-study of Transkeian resistance to White control', *South African Historical Journal* (8) Nov. 1976, pp. 32–9.

7   R. Horwitz, *The political Economy of South Africa* (London, 1967), esp. pp. 1–202.

8   J. A. Benyon, 'The Process of Political Incorporation', in W. D. Hammond-Tooke (ed.), *The Bantu-speaking Peoples of Southern Africa* (London, 1974), p. 387; and Shula Marks (reviewing C. F. Goodfellow, *Great Britain and South African Confederation*) in *Journal of African History*, x (1), 1969, pp. 184–5. There is a sensitive account of these events in C. W. de Kiewiet, *The Imperial Factor* (London, 1937), ch. 7.

9   Quoted Saunders, 'Annexation òf Transkei', p. 247, to which I am most indebted.

10 Quoted in Elliot to Cape Native Affairs Dept., 14 October 1884, in *ibid.*, p. 246.

11 Cape Government Documents: G. 13-'80, p. 181. J. Hemming, Civil Comm. (Queenstown, 1880).

12 G. 17-'78, p. 7. Protest by George Moshwostive.

13 G. 13-'80, p. 49. Comment by Tsita Mofoka.

14 See Cape Blue Book, *ibid.*, p. 40 *passim*.

15 G. 33-'82, p. 50. W. G. Cummings, *Annual Report*, 1882.

16 C. W. de Kiewiet, *Imperial Factor*, pp. 125–309. Dr Atmore has recently made the point that psychological factors, relating to black–white mis-understandings and fears, also strongly influenced the disturbances. In particular, the African fear that 'the white man could destroy a man's very spirit and that of his ancestors, and thereby disrupt the whole moral fabric of the tribe'. Atmore, 'Moorosi's Rebellion', p. 33.

17 Quoted in Saunders, 'Annexation of the Transkei', p. 172, from *Grahams-town Journal*, 15 May 1878.

18 *OHSA*, vol. ii, pp. 253–4.

19 Eric Walker, *A History of Southern Africa* (London, 1959), pp. 369–86; and *OHSA*, ii, pp. 255–84.

20 Stockenstrom quoted in Walker, *History of Southern Africa*, p. 370.

21 Theal, *History*, x, p. 133.

22 *OHSA*, ii, pp. 282–3.

23 G. 43-'79, p. 2. Report of Secretary for Native Affairs for 1878–79.

24 Walker, *History of Southern Africa*, p. 371.

25 G. 43-'79. J. Rose-Innes, R. M. King Williams Town, 7 January 1878.

26 G. 20-'81. R. J. Dick Sp. Magistrate, King Williams Town. 1880.

27 *Grahamstown Journal*, 19 March 1879, quoted in J. Vanstone, 'Sir J. G. Sprigg' (PhD, Queen's University, Kingston, Ontario, 1973), p. 155.

28 G. 13-'80, pp. 43–4.

29 See *ibid.*, for Sprigg's announcement at the *Pitso*.

30 *OHSA*, II, 268–9.

31 G. 20–'81, pp. 13–14. J. M. Austen, R. M. Quthing District.

32 *Ibid.*, p. 138. J. Oxley Oxland, R. M. East Pondoland.

33 G. 33A–'79, p. 4. J. Rose-Innes, R. M. King Williams Town, 7 January 1878.

34 G. 43–'79, p. 7. Charles Brownlee to SNA, *Annual Report*.

35 *Cape Argus*, 5 June 1877.

36 J. Martineau, *The Life and Correspondence of Sir Bartle Frere* (London, 1895), vol. II, p. 233.

37 Frere to Hicks-Beach, 21 March 1880, quoted in Benyon, 'Basutoland and the High Commission', p. 375.

38 Frere to Carnarvon, 7 December 1877. Quoted in *ibid.*, p. 333.

39 Frere to Hicks-Beach, 6 April 1880. Quoted in Saunders, 'Annexation of the Transkei', p. 210.

40 Kimberley to Frere, 18 May 1880. *Parl. Paps.*, c. 2586 (LI, 1880), p. 1.

41 Robert Herbert, 'Future Policy in Zululand and South Africa Generally', 10 March 1879. CO 879/123 (Confidential Prints).

42 Shepstone to C. J. Uys, and others, 19 Sept. 1877. *Parl. Paps.* (1878), c. 1961, p. 155.

43 Shepstone to Bulwer, 20 February and to Barkley, 7 March 1877. Cope, 'Shepstone and Cetshwayo', pp. 158–82.

44 Shepstone to Carnarvon, 31 July 1877, c. 1961 (LV, 1878) p. 63.

45 Brookes and Webb, *History of Natal*, p. 130.

46 Shepstone to Carnarvon, 11 August 1877. *Ibid.*, pp. 70–1.

47 Cited Marks, *Reluctant Rebellion*, p. 96. See also the comment by Dr J. J. Guy: Shepstone believed that an imperial 'invasion would expose the weakness in the structure of the kingdom and many Zulu would desert their despotic tyrant'. 'Firearms in the Zulu kingdom', *Journal of African History*, *op. cit.*,

48 c. 1137 (LIII, 1875), p. 18, Installation of Cetshwayo, 1874.

49 Shepstone to Durnford, 17 September 1877. Shepstone MSS, Letterbook; and Cope, 'Shepstone and Cetshwayo', p. 230.

50 Shepstone to Owen, 14 January 1854; quoted Welsh, *Roots of Segregation*, p. 215.

51 Shepstone to Carnarvon, 5 January 1854. c. 2078 (LVI, 1878), p. 54, and Cope, 'Shepstone and Cetshwayo', pp. 282 ff.

52 Shepstone Memo, 18 November 1878. Colenso MSS, KCL.

53 *Idem.*

54 Guy, 'Firearms in the Zulu Kingdom', p. 566.

55 Frere to Hicks-Beach, 29 January 1879, in Goodfellow, *Great Britain and South African Confederation*, p. 157.

56 Frere to Hicks-Beach, 13 May 1878. C. 2220 (LII, 1878–79), p. 35.

57 Frere to Hicks-Beach, 10 September 1870, CO 48/486. Goodfellow, *Great Britain and South African Confederation*, p. 160.

58 Frere to Hicks-Beach, 12 February 1879. CO 48/489.

59 Guy, 'Firearms in the Zulu Kingdom', pp. 566–7.

60 Dr Guy has suggested: 'The Zulu would perhaps have been better prepared to defend themselves from invasion if Cetshwayo had not decided years before to work for an alliance with the British, in the face of encroachment by the Transvaal Boers on Zululand's northwestern border. But he did not anticipate the *volte-face* British policy took in the late 1870s when it came under the influence of Sir Bartle Frere and Sir Theopilus Shepstone', *ibid.*, p. 565.

61 Cetshwayo, 2 February 1876, quoted Cope, 'Shepstone and Cetshwayo', p. 144.

62 The Zulu had some 8,000 guns but were not trained in a strategy to take maximum advantage of their firepower. Further, in Dr Guy's words, 'Cetshwayo's approach to the war placed the army at a great disadvantage. He realized that even if he won particular engagements, he could not ultimately gain a military victory, and he therefore fought a purely defensive war, hoping for a peaceful settlement.' Guy, 'Firearms in the Zulu Kingdom', p. 565; firearm figures evaluated p. 560.

63 Quoted *ibid.*, p. 565.

64 Denoon, *Southern Africa since 1800*, p. 79.

65 F. E. Colenso, *The Ruin of Zululand* (London, 1884), 2 vols.

66 Brookes and Webb, *History of Natal*, p. 32.

67 See generally, J. Lehman, *All Sir Garnet: A Life of Field Marshall Lord Wolseley, 1833–1913*, (London, 1964); and esp. Wolseley to Hicks-Beach, 3 January 1879. C. 2482 (L, 1880) for Settlement. Also C. 2505, and C. 2584, C. 2586, C. 2655, C. 2676, C. 2695 (LI, 1880).

68 Wolseley to Hicks-Beach, 3 October 1879. C. 2482 (L, 1880), p. 225.

69 *OHSA*, II, p. 265. See also Guy, 'Firearms in the Zulu Kingdom', p. 570, for the political rationale at the base of the Wolseley 'Settlement'.

70 Colenso, *Ruin of Zululand*, II, pp. 10–11.

71 J. Y. Gibson, *The Story of the Zulu* (Pietermaritzburg, 1905), p. 200 *passim*. Also, C. 3616 (XLIX, 1883) and CO 179/141–50.

72 E. K. Krige, *Social Systems of the Zulus* (London, 1936), p. 506; Binns, *Dinuzulu*, p. 180 *passim*; Morris, *Washing of Spears*, p. 598 *passim*; Gibson, *Story of Zulus*, p. 120 *passim*.

73 Marks, *Reluctant Rebellion*, p. 86; Brookes and Webb, *History of Natal*, pp. 147–8.

74 Shepstone to Frere, 4 June 1880. Shepstone MSS, Letterbook.

75 Shepstone Memo, October 1879; quoted Cope, 'Shepstone and Cetshwayo', p. 388.

76 H. Rider Haggard, *Cetywayo and his white neighbours* (London, 1882).

77 Marks, *Reluctant Rebellion*, p. 88.

78 J. J. Guy, 'Mandhlakazi and Usutu' (BA Hons. Thesis, 1966, Natal), p. 20.

79 C. S. Shields, 'The Life of John Dunn' (MA, Unisa, October 1939).

80 Quoted H. B. Steyn, 'Die Britse Beleid Ten Opsigte van Zululand', (MA Thesis, Polchefstroam, 1960), p. 46.

81 Osborn to Wood, 7 October 1881. c. 3182 (XLVII, 1882), p. 139.

82 Shepstone Memo on Zululand, 23 August 1879. Shepstone MSS.

83 Quoted R. L. Cope, 'The British Annexation of Zululand, 1887', (BA Hons. Thesis, Natal, 1959), p. 52.

84 c. 4913 (LXI, 1887), p. 48. Also see Haggard, *Cetywayo and his white neighbours*, p. xxxix.

85 See CO 179/137 on breakdown of order.

86 Quoted in Colenso, *Ruin of Zululand*, I, p. 60.

87 Recorded in Samuelson, *Long, long ago*, p. 103.

88 c. 3182 (LXVI, 1882) for Wood's despatches of 1881.

89 For British reservations about the Wolseley Settlement, see CO Memo, 7 May 1880. CO 879/17, Confidential Print No. 224.

90 Steyn, 'Die Britse Beleid ten opsigte van Zululand', p. 48.

91 See *The Times*, 18 April 1882.

92 Binns, *Dinuzulu*, pp. 189–92.

93 c. 3466 (XLIX, 1883) for details of Cetshwayo's discussions at CO on 7, 15, 17 November 1882.

94 Bulwer to Cetshwayo, August 1882, CO 179/142.

95 Haggard, *Cetywayo and his white neighbours*, p. xviii (second edn).

96 Gibson, *Story of Zulu*, p. 255.

97 Recorded in W. Y. Campbell, *With Cetywayo in the Inkandhla and the Present State of the Zulu Question* (Durban, 1883), p. 11.

98 Binns, *Dinuzulu*, p. 201 *passim* and Morris, *Washing of Spears*, p. 603.

99 Bulwer to Derby (tel.), 5 April 1883. In fact, Bulwer does not appear to have heard of the further defeat until mid-March. CO 179/145.

100 Bulwer to Derby, 5 March 1883, *ibid*.

101 Bulwer to Derby, 5 March 1883. c. 3616 (LXIX, 1883), p. 77 *passim*.

102 Bulwer to Derby (tel.), 5 April 1883. CO 179/145.

103 Bulwer to Derby, 15 May 1883. CO 179/146.

104 Quoted in Robinson to Kimberley, 16 May 1882. c. 3247 (XLCII, 1882), p. 81.

105 Haggard, *Cetywayo and White Neighbours*, p. xxvi.

106 The doctor who certified Cetshwayo's death thought he might have been poisoned. Binns, *Dinuzulu*, p. 210 and Morris, *Washing of Spears*, p. 607.

107 Bulwer to Derby, 12 May 1883, and Ashley Min., 12 June 1883. CO 179/146.

108 Bulwer to Derby, 9 July 1883, *ibid*.

109 Bulwer to Derby (tel.), 27 November 1883. CO 179/148.

110 Bulwer: 'It is impossible to regard without feelings of the greatest pain and concern the ruin that has been brought upon the Chief Usibubu.' CO 179/152.

111 'Inform Sir H. Bulwer definitely that HM Government are unable to adopt any of the courses proposed by him'. Min. by Herbert, 4 December 1883. CO 179/149.

112 CO Mins. of 21 January 1884. CO 179/151; and Bulwer to Derby, 28 April 1884, *ibid.*

113 Derby to Gladstone, 18 December 1883. GP 44142, fos. 25–7.

114 Schreuder, *Gladstone and Kruger*, ch. III.

115 Morcom's description, as lawyer to the Shepstone administration, in Shepstone to Bulwer, 7 Feb. 1877. PRO 6/38; de Kiewiet, *Imperial Factor*, p. 126.

116 Frere to Carnarvon, 5 Feb. 1877, *ibid.*, p. 199.

117 Schreuder, *Gladstone and Kruger*, ch. I.

118 T. R. H. Davenport, *The Afrikaner Bond* (Cape Town, 1966); and J. Hofmeyr (with F. W. Reitz) *The Life of Jan Hendrik Hofmeyr, 'Onze Jan'* (Cape Town, 1913).

119 Quoted in Sheila Paterson, *The Last Trek* (London, 1957), p. 26.

120 In return, S. J. du Toit soon moved to the Transvaal, as Superintendent of Education. See J. D. du Toit, *Ds. S. J. du Toit in Weg en Werk* (Paarl, 1917).

121 *Liverpool Mercury*, 4 March 1881.

122 A. Holmberg, *African tribes and European agencies; colonialism and humanitarianism in British South and East Africa, 1870–95* (1966), for a lucid narrative account, esp. pp. 5–148. See also, Anthony Sillery, *Founding of a Protectorate: Bechuanaland 1885–95* (The Hague, 1966). The classic pioneer study by J. A. I. Agar Hamilton, *The Road to the North, South Africa 1852–86* (London, 1937), may still be read with profit.

123 Derby in the Lords, 1881; *Hansard* (3) CCLXXVII, col. 328.

124 Mackenzie to Chamberlain, 12 April 1885. Mackenzie MSS, Wits. Library.

125 Schreuder, *Gladstone and Kruger*, p. 228 *passim.*

126 *DSAB*, II, pp. 451–2.

127 *Ibid.*, II, 494.

128 *Ibid.*, II, 485, and S. Molema, *Montshiwa, 1814–96* (Cape Town, 1966).

129 *Ibid.*, II, 485.

130 Schreuder, *Gladstone and Kruger*, ch. 7 for London Convention negotiations.

131 'Vindex', *Speeches* (31 January 1888), p. 215.

132 *Cape Times*, 3 November 1897.

133 Scanlen's offer (9 January 1884) in C. 3841 (LCII, 1884), pp. 118–24 and CO 291/26.

134 For a contrary view, Sillery, *Founding a Protectorate*, p. 39.

135 Quoted, *The Times*, 10 January 1889.

136 W. J. Mackenzie, *John Mackenzie* (London, 1902), p. 257, *passim.*

137 Anthony Dachs, 'Missionary Imperialism – the case of Bechuanaland', *Journal of African History*, XIII (4), 1972, pp. 647–58.

138 Memo by F. A. Stanley, 15 July 1885. CO 879/23.

139 *Idem.*

140 Mackenzie to Frere, 10 December 1879. CO 48/498.

141 Mackenzie to Rose-Innes, 10 November 1880. Mackenzie MSS., Wits.

142 Mackenzie to Knutsford, 2 February 1890. *Ibid.*

143 *DSAB*, I, p. 489.

144 CO Mins., 8 August 1884. CO 417/1.

145 Mackenzie, *Life*, pp. 314–15 (8 April 1884).

146 Mackenzie to Warren (?), February 1885. Mackenzie MSS, Wits.

147 Bower 'Memoir', RHL. MSS. Afr. s. 63, fo. 10.

148 Robinson to Mackenzie (tel.), 25, 30 July. c. 4213 (LVII, 1884), pp. 11–13; and CO Mins. of 8 August 1884. CO 417/1.

149 Mackenzie to Dale, 3 August 1884. Mackenzie, *Life*, p. 349.

150 *Idem.*

151 Rhodes added insult to injury by offering Mackenzie a job! *Ibid.*, pp. 357–9.

152 Herbert Min., 31 July 1884. CO 417/1.

153 Rhodes to Robinson, 8 September 1884. c. 4213 (LVII, 1884–85), p. 65.

154 Rhodes to Merriman, 13 January 1885. SAL/MP, 1884/6.

155 Bower to Robinson, 26 August 1884. De Kock, 'Vraagstukke . . .', pp. 163–4.

156 Robinson to Derby, 13 December 1883. CO 179/150.

157 Wood to Kimberley, 30 August and CO Mins. 14 October 1881. CO 179/138; and Bulwer to Kimberley, 8 July 1882. CO 179/141.

158 Bulwer to Derby, 26 April 1883 and H. F. Fynn (Br. Res. with Cetshwayo) to Bulwer, 23 March 1883. c. 3705 (XLIX, 1883), pp. 16–17.

159 Fynn to Bulwer, 22, 26 December 1883; Bulwer to Derby (tel.), 23 February 1884. c. 3864 (LVIII, 1884), p. 312. CO Mins. of 5 and 25 February 1884. CO 179/151.

160 Bulwer to Derby, 3 December 1883, encl. Fynn to Bulwer, 22 December 1883, *ibid.*

161 Bulwer to Derby, 10 March 1884. c. 4037 (LVIII, 1884), p. 64.

162 Bulwer to Derby, (tel.), 10 March 1884. CO 179/145.

163 Bulwer to Derby (tel.), 23 January 1884, and CO Mins. of 29 January 1884. CO 179/151.

164 Bulwer: 'The temptation of obtaining land, concessions of which would be freely promised to them by the Usuthu leaders, in return for their services, is a great temptation, for the rich grazing lands of upper Zululand have very long been a coveted possession in Transvaal eyes.' c. 4191 (LVIII, 1884), p. 8.

165 c. 4191, *ibid.*, pp. 23–56.

166 The Transvaal authorities denied any responsibility for these events. B. Res. (Pretoria) to High Commissioner, 15 May 1884, *ibid.*, p. 34.

167 Min. by Herbert, 5 September on Bulwer to Derby, 5 August 1884. CO 179/153.

168 Robinson to Derby (tel.), 11 May 1884. C. 4037 (LVIII, 1884), p. 91.

169 'Committee of Dinuzulu's Volunteers' to Bulwer, 1 May 1884. C. 4191 (LVIII, 1884), pp. 55–6.

170 Bulwer to Derby (tel.), 28 May 1884. CO 179/152.

171 J. P. Blignaut, 'Die Onstaan en Entwikkeling van die Nieuwe Republiek, 1884–88' (MA Thesis), pp. 22–33; and Bulwer to Derby, 6 May 1884. C. 4191 (LVIII, 1884), p. 21.

172 Bulwer to Derby (tel.), 31 May 1884, and Min. by Derby CO 179/152.

173 C. 4191 (LVIII, 1884), pp. 62–3.

174 Smyth to Hartington, 27 May 1884, *ibid.*, pp. 76–7.

175 *Ibid.*, pp. 100–15.

176 Bulwer to Derby (tel.), 16 June 1884. CO 179/152.

177 Zibhebhu to Bulwer in Bulwer to Derby (tel.), *ibid.*

178 Min. of 5 July 1884, *ibid.*

179 Min. by Fairfield, on Bulwer to Derby (tel.), 30 June 1884, *ibid.*

180 Bulwer to Derby, 3 May 1884. C. 4037 (LVIII, 1884) p. 83; and Robinson to Derby (tel.), 21 May 1884, *ibid.*, p. 118.

181 Blignaut: 'Nieuwe Republiek . . .', pp. 36–79; and Steyn, 'Die Britse Belied ten opsigte van Zululand', pp. 141–64.

182 *Natal Mercury*, 20 May 1884, quoted Blignaut, *ibid.*, p. 44.

183 Min. by Meade, 17 July 1884, on Bulwer to Derby (tel.), 17 July 1884. CO 179/153.

184 *De Volkstem*, 30 May 1884, in Blignaut, 'Nieuwe Republiek . . .', p. 43.

185 Mins by Hemming, Bramston and Derby, 18 June 1884. CO 179/152.

186 Min. by Herbert, 16 August 1884. CO 179/152.

187 British commitment began and ended in the Reserve. Smyth to War Office, in Bulwer to Derby, 27 May 1884. C. 4191 (LVIII; 1884), pp. 62–3.

188 Derby to Bulwer, 19 August 1884, *ibid.*, p. 138.

189 Min. by Ashley, 17 July 1884. CO 179/153.

190 Bulwer to Derby, 16 December 1883, for original of despatch and scored out passage. CO 179/149.

191 Robinson (in London) to Derby, 14 December 1883. C. 179/150.

192 Derby to Bulwer (tel.), 10 May 1884. C. 4037 (LVIII, 1884), p. 117. This was, of course, in line with the cabinet decision of 25 March 1884; see Ramm, II, p. 173.

193 Derby to Bulwer, 17 May 1884. C. 4037 (LVIII, 1884), p. 117.

194 *The Times*, 3 May 1884, and Bulwer to Derby, 2 May 1884. CO 179/152.

195 Min. by Anderson, 7 May 1884. CO 179/152.

196 Gladstone to Derby, 11 June 1884. GP 44547, fo. 72.

197 Kimberley to Chamberlain, 'Private', 25 September 1884. JC 9/1/1/5.

198 Derby to Robinson, 'Private', 25 October 1884. DP x24.

199 Quoted P. Magnus, *Gladstone, a biography* (London, 1954), p. 264.

200 Gladstone to Derby, 11 June 1884. GP 44547, fo. 72 (Copy; my italics).

201 *Idem.*

202 Min. by Bramston, 11 November 1884. CO 179/154.

203 Mins. by Fairfield, July 1885. CO 417/5–6.

204 Min. by Fairfield, 8 July 1885. CO 417/6.

205 Fairfield to Ripon, 'Private', 17 October 1892. Ri.P. 43558, fo. 156.

206 Min. by Bramston, 20 December 1884. CO 179/154.

207 Min. by Fairfield, 23 June 1884. CO 179/155.

208 Note by Antrobus to Derby, 19 November 1884. DP x24.

209 Min. by Fairfield, 8 July 1885. CO 417/5.

210 *Hansard* (3), CCCXVIII, col. 550.

211 Marks, *Reluctant Rebellion*, pp. 90–8; Morris, *Washing of Spears*, pp. 597–608, and Binns, *The Last Zulu King*, p. 140, *passim*; Gibson, *Story of Zulus*, p. 255, *passim*.

212 Marks and Atmore, 'Firearms in Southern Africa', p. 528.

213 Benyon, 'Basutoland and the high commission' *op. cit.*, and L. M. Thompson, *Between two worlds; Moshweshwe of Lesotho* (Oxford, 1976), esp. pp. 311–24.

214 Merriman to Scanlen, 30 July 1882. P. Lewson (ed.), *Selections from the Correspondence of J. X. Merriman* (Cape Town, 1960), vol. 1, p. 109.

215 Quoted in Benyon, 'Basutoland and the high commission', which is excellent on this period. The Sotho side of the story, and their 'victory', is illuminated in Anthony Atmore and Peter Sanders, 'Sotho arms and ammunition in the nineteenth century', *Journal of African History*, XII (4), 1971, pp. 541–2.

216 See Cape Govt. Memo, 30 April 1881, in *Parl. Paps.*, C. 3708 (XLVIII, 1883).

217 Derby to Gladstone, 8 December 1883. Addit. MSS 44142 (Gladstone Papers).

218 Derby to Gladstone, 25 April 1883, *ibid.*

219 G. 66–'83, for details.

220 Davenport, *Afrikaner Bond*, pp. 84–5.

221 *Ibid.*, p. 84.

222 Min. by A. Hemming, 24 July 1884. CO 417/1, quoted Saunders, 'Annexation of Transkei', p. 315.

223 B. N. Pandey, *The Break-up of British India* (London, 1969), p. 18.

224 See Saunders, 'Annexation of Transkei', pp. 284–9.

225 Blachford to Dean Church, 1 January 1877. Marinden (ed.), *Letters of Lord Blachford*, p. 374.

226 Kimberley to Gladstone, 26 July 1871. Addit. Mss 4424, fo. 189.

227 Walker, *History of Southern Africa*, p. 392.

228 Benyon, 'Basutoland and the High Commission', esp. p. 635.

229 Marinden (ed.), *Letters of Blachford*, p. 380.

230 Gladstone to Kimberley, 19 Oct. 1884, 44545 fo. 38; Salisbury to Landsowne, 30 May 1899, quoted Lord Newton, *Lord Lansdowne* (London, 1929), p. 157.

231 Gladstone to Granville, 7 May 1881; Ramm, *Gladstone–Granville*, I, p. 273.
Also Schreuder, *Gladstone and Kruger*, p. 195.

232 Salisbury to Baden Powell, 13 October 1888. SP 379/437.

CHAPTER 3

1 W. O. Aydelotte, *Bismarck and British colonial policy; the problem of South-west Africa, 1883–5* (Philadelphia, 1937); A. J. P. Taylor, *Germany's First Bid for Colonies, 1884–5* (London, 1938); J. H. Esterhuyse, *South-west Africa, 1880–94* (Cape Town, 1968) and H. Bley, *German South-west Africa* (London, 1971). Also: W. O. Henderson, *Studies in German Colonial History* (Chicago, 1962) and M. E. Townsend, *The Rise and Fall of Germany's Colonial Empire* (New York, 1930).

2 H. Pogge von Strandmann, 'The Domestic Origins of Germany's Colonial Expansion under Bismarck', *Past and Present*, February 1969, pp. 140–59. I am also indebted to Dr von Strandmann for passing comment on an earlier draft form of this chapter.

3 Hans-Ulrich Wehler, *Bismarck und der Imperialismus* (Köln/Berlin, 1969), and 'Bismarck's Imperialism, 1862–90', *Past and Present* (1970), vol. 48, pp. 119–55. P. M. Kennedy, 'German Colonial Expansion. Has the "Manipulated Social Imperialism" been ante-dated?', *Past and Present* (1972), vol. 54, pp. 134–41, and 'Bismarck's Imperialism: the Case of Samoa, 1880–90', *Historical Journal*, XV, 2 (1972), pp. 261–83. There is a valuable critical bibliography of works dealing with German imperialism by H. Pogge von Strandmann and Alison Smith in *Britain and Germany in Africa*, eds. P. Gifford and Wm. Roger Louis (Yale, 1967), pp. 709–96.

4 H. A. Turner, 'Bismarck's Colonial Policy – anti-British in origin?', in *Britain and Germany in Africa, op. cit.*, a deeply valuable case-study to which I am much indebted.

5 Frere to Kimberley, 19 July 1880, encl. an article by Ernst von Weber in *Geographische Nachrichter*, on the value of South-west Africa as a potential colony. c. 4190 (LVI, 1884), pp. 1–8.

6 Chargé d'affaires at Berlin to CO, 31 August 1883, *ibid.*, p. 13.

7 Bismarck's lack of interest in colonies was reflected in his reference to them as mere overseas 'maintenance posts' – *Versorgungsposten* – see J. H. Esterhuyse, *South-west Africa*.

8 W. Schuszler, *Lüderitz* (Bremen, 1936), p. 210 *passim*.

9 *DSAB*, vol. II, p. 816.

10 *Ibid.*, vol. I, p. 345.

11 FO to CO, 22 September 1883. c. 4190 (LVI, 1884), p. 15.

12 See R. J. Lovell, *The Struggle for South Africa* (New York, 1934), p. 81; and Granville to Münster, 21 November 1883, in FO to CO, 17 November 1883. c. 4190 (LVI, 1884), p. 24.

13 Aydelotte, *Bismarck and British colonial policy*, p. 30.

14 Turner, 'Bismarck's colonial policy', p. 52.

15 Robinson to Derby, 4 December 1884, giving detailed history of the Cape claims. C. 4265 (LVI, 1884–85), pp. 3–13.

16 C. 4190 (LVI, 1884), pp. 26–8.

17 *Ibid.*, pp. 20–1 (tels.) Derby to Smyth, 22 October 1883, responding to urgent Smyth tel. of 19 October 1883.

18 *Ibid.*, p. 28, Merriman to Smyth, 31 October 1883.

19 *Ibid.*, pp. 26–7, for the Cape map – in Smyth to Derby, 6 November 1883 – setting out Cape claims. See also, Lovell, *Struggle for South Africa*, p. 83.

20 See also Merriman's extensive letter to Smyth, 31 October 1883. C. 4190 (LVI, 1884), pp. 27–8.

21 *Ibid.*, pp. 34–5, CO to Admiralty, 13 December, and reply, 27 December 1883.

22 The Cape weakness was also financial. See Scanlen to Merriman, (from London) 22 November 1883, SAL/MP, 1883/244. Also, P. Lewson (ed.), *Selections from the Correspondence of J. X. Merriman* (Cape Town, 1960), vol. I, p. 142.

23 Scanlen to Merriman, 7 November 1883, SAL/MP, 1883/7. Also see P. M. Laurence, *The Life of John X. Merriman* (London, 1930), p. 85.

24 CO 48/507, Min. of 7 November 1883, and W. J. de Kock, 'Ekstra Territoriale Vraagstukke van die Kaapse Regering, 1872–85', *AYB*, 1948, p. 185.

25 It is interesting that Bismarck early rejected the Cape colony's claim to an informal British 'Monroe Doctrine' over Southern Africa as an 'international abnormality' – '*volkerrechtliche Abnormität*'. Esterhuyse, *South-west Africa*, p. 54.

26 Scanlen to Merriman, 15 November 1883, SAL/MP, 1883/222.

27 Mins. by Fairfield and Branston, 8 October 1883. CO 48/507.

28 All the relevant official tels. for the period are printed in CO 'Confidential Print' No. 274, CO 879/21. See also, C. 4190 (LVI, 1884) pp. 10–11, and J. Spence to Merriman, 23 and 29 October 1883. SAL/MP, 1883/201, 207.

29 Quoted Turner, 'Bismarck's colonial policy', p. 59.

30 Ampthill to Granville, 18 September 1880, in FO to CO, 22 September 1880. C. 4190 (LVI, 1884), pp. 8–9.

31 Walsham to Derby, 31 August 1883. *Ibid.*, p. 13.

32 In FO to CO 22 September 1883. *Ibid.*, p. 15.

33 FO to CO, encl. Münster's request, 10 November 1883. *Ibid.*, p. 24.

34 Granville to Münster, 21 November 1883. *Idem*. Also, Lovell, *Struggle for South Africa*, p. 84.

35 *Idem.*

36 Laurence, *Merriman*, p. 85.

37 Min. by Ashley, 4 December 1883. CO 48/507.

38 Merriman to Smyth, 21 October 1883. C. 4190 (LVI, 1884), pp. 27–8. On De Pass, see *DSAB*, I, pp. 221–2.

39 Scanlen to Merriman, 29 November 1883. SAL/MP 1883/244.

40 Quoted, de Kock, 'Vraagstukke . . .', p. 185.

41 Merriman to Mills, 16 January 1884. *Ibid.*, p. 192 n. 130.

42 Merriman to Mills, 3 January 1884. *Idem.*

43 Münster to Granville, 31 December 1883, in FO to CO, 19 January 1884. C. 4190 (LVI, 1884), pp. 35–7. For Münster's misreading of Bismarck's Memorandum see Lovell, *Struggle for South Africa*, pp. 94–5, 102–7.

44 Derby to Robinson, 29 January 1884, quoted Aydelotte, *Bismarck and British colonial policy*, p. 49. See also CAD/PM, 19, Smyth to Ministers, 4 February 1884.

45 *Cape Hansard* (1889), p. 352.

46 The tactics and attitudes of the Cape politicians are excellently revealed in the Merriman Papers. SAL/MP, 1883/261 (Bechuanaland); 1883/270 (Basutoland); and 1883/244 (Cape financial position).

47 Robinson to Mills, 10 February 1884, encl. (copy) in SAL/MP, 1884/15c.

48 Quoted Turner, 'Bismarck's colonial policy', p. 65.

49 Idem.

50 Derby to Robinson, 4 December 1884. C. 4265 (LVI, 1884), pp. 3–13.

51 Aydelotte, *Bismarck and British Colonial Policy*, p. 86 *passim*. See also, Ampthill correspondence in 'Letters from the Berlin Embassy', ed. P. Knaplund, *Annual Report to the American Historical Association* (1942), II, pp. 329–30.

52 Turner, 'Bismarck's colonial policy', p. 67.

53 Heinrich von Kusserow, 'Fürst Bismarck und die Kolonial-politik', published in the *Deutsche Kolonialzeitung*, 15 (1898), quoted in Turner 'Bismarck's colonial policy', p. 69.

54 For Bismarck's interest in charter-imperialism, see von Strandmann, 'Domestic origins of German colonial expansion', p. 149, n. 35, and Townsend, *Rise and Fall of Germany's Colonial Empire*, p. 125.

55 Turner, 'Bismarck's colonial policy', p. 69.

56 Robinson to Derby, 29 April 1884, encl. German Consul to Cape ministers, 25 April 1884. C. 4190 (LVI, 1884), p. 43. Aydelotte, *Bismarck and British Colonial Policy*, p. 55.

57 Min. by Herbert, May 1884, on FO to CO, 25 April. CO 48/510.

58 Opinion of parliamentary under-secretary of state, Evelyn Ashley, 2 May 1884. *Idem.*

59 Min. by Ashley, 22 May 1884. CO 417/1.

60 *Hansard* (3), CCLXXXVIII, col. 645. Derby in Lords, 19 May 1884.

61 Upington to Robinson (tel.), 29 May 1884, encl. in Robinson to Derby, 4 June 1884. Recd. CO 26 June 1884. C. 4190 (LVI, 1884), p. 49.

62 Robinson to Derby (tel.) 29 May 1884. DP x24.

63 CO to FO, 2 June 1884. C. 4190 (LVI, 1884), p. 44.

64 Granville to Bismarck (copy) encl. in Derby to Robinson, 4 December 1884. C. 4265 (LVI, 1884), pp. 3–13.

65 See Aydelotte, *Bismarck and British Colonial Policy*, p. 75.

66 Ampthill to Granville, 31 May 1884. C. 4190 (LVI, 1884), p. 46.

67 'Letters from the Berlin Embassy', p. 329.

68 Turner, 'Bismarck's colonial policy', p. 72; and Agatha Ramm, *Germany, a political history* (London, 1968), p. 357.

69 See Granville to Derby, 7 June, and protest from Münster, 4 June 1884. C. 4190 (LVI, 1884), p. 48.

70 Not without some justice did Derby comment: 'If Mr Scanlen had been willing to do this [earlier], the Angra Pequena question would have solved itself long ago'. Min. by Derby on Robinson to Derby, 6 June 1884. CO 417/1, D. 57.

71 Granville to Derby, 7 June 1884. C. 4190 (LVI, 1884), p. 48.

72 Derby Min. of 8 June 1884. Quoted Taylor, *Germany's First Bid for Colonies*, p. 39, n. 1.

73 C. 4190 (LVI, 1884), p. 56 *passim*, and Lovell, *Struggle for South Africa*, pp. 95–6. See also Granville to Dilke, 'Private', 24 September 1884. Dilke Papers 43851.

74 FO to CO, 4 July 1884. C. 4190 (LVI, 1884), p. 57.

75 See Dilke 'Memoir', 43938 fo. 181.

76 Dilke Diary (21 June 1884), 43926 fo. 18.

77 Derby to Robinson (tel.), 17 June 1884. C. 4190 (LVI, 1884), p. 47.

78 Wm. R. Louis, 'Great Britain and German Expansion in Africa, 1884–1919', in Gifford and Louis (eds.), *Britain and Germany in Africa*, p. 8.

79 Bismarck's statement encl. in Russell to Granville, 25 June 1884. C. 4190 (LVI, 1884), p. 53.

80 *Cape Hansard* (1884), p. 396, Upington statement of 2 July.

81 Robinson to Derby, 9 July 1884. C. 4190 (LVI, 1884), p. 57.

82 CO to FO, 8 July 1884. *Idem*.

83 C. 4252 (LVII, 1884), pp. 6–7.

84 C. 4265 (LVI, 1884), p. 13.

85 Plessen to FO, 26 August 1884. C. 4262 (LVI, 1884), pp. 8–9.

86 Granville to Ampthill, 12 July 1884. C. 4190 (LVI, 1884), p. 59.

87 Derby to Gladstone, 2 October 1884. GP 44142.

88 Min. by Herbert, 29 August 1884. CO 417/3.

89 Granville to Gladstone, 1 Sept. 1884. Ramm, II, p. 242.

90 Ashley to Derby, 30 August 1884. DP X24.

91 The Cape was allowed to annex the offshore islands as compensation. Robinson to German Consul, 18 August 1884. C. 4262 (LVI, 1884), p. 23.

92 *Pall Mall Gazette*, 20 September 1884. On the other hand, the *Daily Telegraph* gave a 'hearty welcome to ... the Teuton abroad', 22 October 1884.

93 Derby to Granville, 30 January 1885. GrP., PRO 30/29/120. Also see Anglo-German conversations of December 1884. GP. 44629 fo. 148 *passim*.

94 Ampthill to Derby, July 1884. C. 4190 (LVI, 1884), p. 54; and Von

Strandmann, 'Domestic origins of Germany's colonial expansion . . .', p..
149.

95 Bismarck of course lived under few illusions about the value of the colonies.
He referred to South-west Africa as a 'little pot of sand' (*Sandpotjie*).
Esterhuyse, *South-west Africa*, p. 66.

96 Schüszler, *Lüderitz*, p. 212 *passim*.

97 Bismarck quoted in von Strandmann, 'Domestic origin of Germany's colonial
expansion . . .', p. 157.

98 Lovell, *Struggle for South Africa*, p. 78.

99 Min. by Fairfield, 8 August 1885. CO 417/5.

100 Min. by Ashley, 18 April 1885. CO 417/9. On the Cape title to the islands,
see Herbert to Granville, 28 November 1884: 'They have been ours for
years, there is no shadow of a doubt about the title – Bismarck might as well
ask us to refer the question of the title of the Cape Colony itself.' GrP. PRO
30/29/120.

101 Granville to Gladstone, 7 September 1884. Ramm, II, p. 249.

102 'Germany has behaved badly towards us, and we have deserved to lose this
coast.' Herbert Min., 18 August 1884. CO 417/1.

103 Gladstone to Granville, 7 December 1884. Ramm, II, p. 291.

104 Gladstone to Derby, 24 December 1884. GP 44547 fo. 153.

105 Gladstone to Derby, 21 December 1884. *Ibid.*, fo. 151. See also Gladstone to
Granville, 29 January 1885: 'German colonisation will strengthen and not
weaken our hold upon our Colonies; and it will make it very difficult for
them to maintain the domineering tone to which their public origins are too
much inclined.' Ramm, II, p. 329.

106 Min. by Wingfield, on Robinson to Derby (tel.), 18 August 1884. CO 417/1.

107 Derby to Granville, 30 January 1885. Gr.P., PRO 30/29/120.

108 *The Times*, 20 September 1884.

109 'In assenting to their [Germany] taking the coast we have virtually assented
to their expressed intention to consider whether they should annex the
country some distance "in land".' Min. By Herbert, 13 October 1884. CO
417/2.

110 'Germany has told us that she now protects 20 miles inland from the coast
and reserves the question of going further inland. We cannot therefore,
without going into direct collision with Germany . . . annex the Namaqua
and Damara Country . . . But we might let the Cape have the Kalahari
Desert.' Herbert Min., 16 September 1884. CO 417/2.

111 Esterhuyse, *South-west Africa*, pp. 66–7.

112 M. Busch, *Bismarck, Some Secret Pages from his History* (London, 1898), vol.
III, p. 120. See also Lovell, *Struggle for South Africa*, p. 101.

113 See Derby to Robinson, 11 November 1884. c.4252 (LVII, 1884–85), p. 37.

114 Derby to Granville, 28 December 1884. Gr. P., PRO 30/29/120.

115 J. E. Butler, 'The German Factor in Anglo-Transvaal Relations', in Gifford
and Louis (eds.), *Britain and Germany in Africa*, p. 128, and H. Backeberg,

'Die Betrekkinge tussen die Suid-Afrikaanse Republiek en Duitsland tot na die Jameson Inval', *AYB*, 1949. I have relied heavily on both.

116 A mere 2,929 German emigrants went to the Transvaal, 1871–84. Backeberg, 'Betrekkinge . . .', pp. 42–3.

117 *Ibid.*, p. 41, and Butler, 'German Factor . . .', p. 183.

118 Well set out in Lovell, *Struggle for South Africa*, p. 109.

119 Backeberg, 'Betrekkinge . . .', p. 51.

120 Quoted, Butler, 'German Factor . . .', p. 184.

121 Backeberg takes the view that the Germans deliberately used the Transvaal as a pawn in German diplomatic tactics. 'Betrekkinge . . .', p. 48.

122 *Ibid.*, p. 46.

123 *Annual Register* (1884), p. 297.

124 *The Times*, 27 December 1884.

125 D. W. Kruger, *Paul Kruger* (Johannesburg, 1963), 2 vols., II, p. 39.

126 Treaty in FO to CO, 20 May 1885, carefully noted by British officials, 26 November 1885. CO 417/8, 'Foreign'.

127 'These gentlemen appear to have been remarkably well received in Berlin'. CO Minute, 20 June 1884. CO 417/3. Kruger was received as a 'Vreemdeling van distinksie' and clearly associated himself with the Germans: 'I myself am proud of descent from German stock, although I regret being unable to address your Majesty [the Emperor] in the language of my ancestors.' FO Translation of Kruger's speech in Afrikaans-Nederlands; in FO to CO, 20 June 1884. CO 417/3.

128 Min. by Sir P. Anderson, 27 October 1884. FO 84/1814. Quoted in Gifford and Louis (eds.), *Britain and Germany in Africa*, p. 5.

129 Derby to Granville, 28 December 1884. Gr. P., PRO 30/29/120.

130 Min. by Augustus Hemming, on Bulwer to Derby, 19 January 1885. CO 179/156.

131 CO Minutes, 23 January 1884. CO 48/509.

132 *CHBE*, VIII, pp. 522–31.

133 Min. by Herbert, on Admiralty to CO 23 January 1884. CO 48/509. See the *Pall Mall Gazette* for 10 March 1891 which was still regretting that so 'great [a] slice of the [African] map . . . got painted Prussian blue by mistake in 1885'.

CHAPTER 4

1 Min. by Kimberley, 8 June 1882. CO 179/141.

2 Bulwer to Derby, 25 February 1885. C.4587 (LVI, 1884–85), pp. 42–3.

3 Natal telegrams August–September 1884. C.4214 (LVI, 1884–85), pp. 27–8.

4 Min. by Herbert, 4 May 1884. CO 179/153.

5 Bulwer to Derby, 12 January 1884. C.4587 (LVI, 1884–85), pp. 15–16.

6 Min. by Meade, 22 August 1884, CO 179/155.

7 Min. by Herbert, 25 August 1884. *Ibid.*

8   Derby to Robinson, 'Private', 25 October 1884. DP x24.

9   *Idem*.

10 Bulwer to Fairfield, 22 September 1884. CO 179/153.

11 Bulwer had already been termed a 'rather alarmist' pro-consul by the CO officials. Fairfield Min. 1 July, on Bulwer to Derby, 1 June 1885. CO 179/157.

12 Robinson to Derby, 'Private', 25 November 1884, encl. cutting from *Volksblad*. DP x24.

13 Min. by Sir R. Herbert, 20 December 1884. CO 417/2.

14 Gladstone to Granville, 9 December 1884, on German imperial activity in Southern Africa. Ramm, II, p. 293.

15 See H. Rudin, *Germans in the Cameroons, 1884–1915. A case study in Modern Imperialism* (London, 1938), p. 120 *passim*.

16 Lord Derby's phrase, in a letter to Granville of 28 December 1884. Gr. P. PRO 30/29/120.

17 See Derby's angry letter to Gladstone, 2 October 1884. GP 44142, fo. 110.

18 Dilke diary, 22 September 1884. Dilke P. 43926 fo. 31.

19 Kimberley to Chamberlain, 'Private', 25 September 1884 JC 9/1/1/5.

20 See CO reflections, 19 March 1885, and Min. by Sir R. Herbert, 14 November 1884, on Bulwer to Derby, 22 September 1884. CO 179/157.

21 Bulwer to Derby (tel.), 27 August 1884, *ibid*.

22 Blignaut: 'Nieuwe Republiek. . .', pp. 82–3.

23 *Ibid*., p. 84.

24 Min. by Herbert, 29 August 1884. CO 179/157.

25 See Herbert to Derby, 'Private', 1 October 1884. DP x24.

26 *Idem*.

27 Kimberley to Chamberlain, 'Private', 25 September 1884. JC 9/1/1/5.

28 Ashley to Derby, 'Private', 30 August 1884. DP x24.

29 *Idem*.

30 See Lovell, *Struggle for S. Africa*, p. 85.

31 Min. by Herbert, 6 November, on Bulwer to Derby, 22 September 1884. CO 179/153.

32 *Idem*.

33 Herbert to Derby, 'Private', 15 November 1884. DPx24.

34 *Idem*.

35 Min. by Derby, 14 November 1884, on Bulwer to Derby, 22 September 1884. CO 179/153.

36 Min. by Ashley, 14 November 1884, *ibid*.

37 See Sir Donald Currie to Gladstone, 1 October 1884. GP 44488 fo. 1.

38 Transcript of the meeting of 3 November 1884. CO 879/22 No. 299 (Confidential Prints).

39 *Idem*.

40 Hamilton to Currie, 20 November 1884, *ibid*., p. 5.

41 Currie to Gladstone, 21 November 1884. GP 44488 fo. 102.

42 See CO Mins., 21 November 1884. CO 879/22.

43 Comment by Hamilton on back of letter, Currie to Gladstone, 21 November 1884. GP 44488 fo. 102.

44 See GP 44645 fo. 224 (cabinet notes) for meeting of 11:30 a.m., Sat., 22 November 1884.

45 The decision to do 'something' at St Lucia Bay pre-dated the actual cabinet decision. See Memo. for cabinet of 5 December 1884. CO 179–155.

46 Gladstone's cabinet notes, Tuesday, 2 December 1884. GP 44645 fo. 234.

47 Derby took this course as there were no formal cabinets after the meeting of 5 December until 2 January 1885. See GP 44645 fos. 234–5 and GP 44646 fo. 2.

48 Circular to cabinet 4 December 1884, returned to Derby 5 December 1884. DP x24.

49 Northbrook here refers to the basis of the British claims, i.e. the treaty of 1843 with Mpande. See c. 4587 (LVI, 1884–85), p. 2 for a copy of the treaty, dated 5 October 1843.

50 Gladstone to Derby, Note of 5 December 1884, DP x24.

51 Derby to Bulwer (tel.), 8 December 1884. c.4557 (LVI, 1884–85), pp. 1–12.

52 Draft despatch to Bulwer, dated 5 December 1884, including the sentence struck out from final despatch. CO 179/155.

53 CO Mins. of 22 November and 5 December 1884. CO 179/153.

54 Bulwer to Fairfield, 22 September 1884. *Ibid.*

55 CO to Admiralty, 8 December 1884. c. 4587 (LVI, 1884–85), pp. 1–12.

56 *Idem.*

57 Bulwer to Derby (tel.), 21 December 1884, *ibid.*, p. 2.

58 Gladstone to Granville, 9 December 1884, Ramm., II, p. 293.

59 Bulwer to Derby, 8 December 1884, CO 179/154; and C. 4587, *ibid.*, pp. 3–5.

60 *DSAB*, I, p. 415.

61 Bulwer to Derby (tel.), 19 December 1884. CO 179/154.

62 *DSAB*, II, pp. 628–9.

63 C. L. Engelbrecht: 'Dinizulu en Adolf Schiel; belangrike dokumente uit die Jaar 1884', *Die Huisgenoot*, 8 August 1941; M. C. van Zyl, 'Die Uitbreiding van Britse gesag oor die Natalse noordgrensgebeide, 1879–97', *AYB*, 1966, part I; and *DSAB*, II, pp. 628–9.

64 Nagel to CO, 5 December 1885, 179/162. Also, Fitzmaurice, *Granville*, II, p. 369.

65 Min. by Hemming, 31 October, on Bulwer to Derby, 30 September 1884. CO 179/153.

66 Min. by Ashley, 19 December 1884, on Bulwer to Derby (tel.), 19 December 1884. CO 179/154.

67 Min. by Herbert, 20 December 1884, *ibid.*

68 Mins. by Derby and Herbert, 3/4 November 1884. CO 179/153.

69 Min. by Ashley, 19 December 1884, *ibid.*

70 Min. by Derby, 19 December 1884, *ibid.*

71 Memo by Fairfield, 20 December 1884, *ibid.*

72 Min. by Hemming, 20 December 1884, *ibid.*

73 *Idem.*

74 Min. by Derby, 20 December 1884, *ibid.*

75 Bulwer to Derby, 16 December 1884, *ibid.*

76 Min. by Bramston, 16 January 1885, *ibid.*

77 Bulwer to Derby, 30 December 1884, *ibid.*

78 Bulwer to Derby, 'Most Confidential', 3 February 1885 (Recd. in CO 3 March 1885). CO 179/156.

79 Bulwer to Derby, 30 December 1884. CO 179/154.

80 Bulwer to Derby, 2 February 1885. Circulated to Cabinet 7 March 1885. CO 179/156.

81 Bulwer to Derby, 2 February 1884. CO 179/156. Circulated to Cabinet, 7 March 1884.

82 The CO minuted on Bulwer's warning, 'If we allow the Boers to deprive the missionaries of their stations, we shall have no ground for objecting to the interference of Germany – which will be only too glad of the opportunity.' Hemming Min. 26 February 1885. CO 179/156.

83 Min. by Herbert, 16 January 1885. CO 179/154.

84 Min. by Hamilton, 12 January 1885. CO 179/156.

85 Min. by Fairfield, November 1884. CO 417/2.

86 CO Mins., December 1885. CO 179/162.

87 Detailed in CO 879/22.

88 This narrative draws largely from: *OHSA*, II, pp. 278–9; M. Hunter, *Reaction to Conquest*, ch. 1; Stanford, *Reminiscences*, II, p. 25 *passim*; *Precis of Information Concerning Pondoland* (London, 1886); and Saunders, 'Annexation of Transkei', pp. 247–400.

89 *DSAB*, II, p. 499.

90 See G. 92 – '83, *Cape Commission on Pondoland* (1883).

91 *DSAB*, II, p. 499; C. 3855 and C. 4590 (LVI, 1884–85); Stanford, *Reminiscences*, II, pp. 24–6; Saunders, 'Annexation of Transkei', pp. 282–385.

92 See C. 4590 (LVI, 1884).

93 D. Cragg, 'Mdlangaso', in *DSAB*, II, 460.

94 The concession is printed in full in Stanford, *Reminiscences*, II, pp. 43–5; CO 879/22, p. 31 *passim*.; *OHSA*, II, pp. 279–80; and *DSAB*, II, p. 460.

95 Stanford, *Reminiscences*, II, pp. 42–5.

96 *Cape Times*, 27 October 1885.

97 CO 879/22–3, CO 179/162, and CO 417/10; C. 5022 (LXI, 1887).

98 Kimberley to Derby, 28 December 1884. DP x 24.

99 Derby to Granville, 25 December 1884 (copy). DP x 24.

100 Granville to Derby, 26 December 1884, *Ibid.*

101 Derby to Granville, 28 December 1884. Gr. P., PRO 30/29/129.

102　*Idem.*

103　Derby to Gladstone, 26 December 1884. GP 44142 fo. 108.

104　Derby to Gladstone, 27 December 1884, *ibid.* fo. 110.

105　Derby to Gladstone, 26 December 1884, *ibid*, fo. 108.

106　Fitzmaurice, *Granville*, II, p. 371.

107　Derby to Gladstone, 27 December 1884. GP 44142, fo. 108.

108　Chamberlain to Derby, 30 December 1884. DP x 24.

109　Kimberley to Derby, 28 December 1884, *ibid.*

110　Derby to Robinson (tel. in cypher), 20 December 1884. CO 417/2.

111　Gladstone to Queen, 5 January 1885. *LQV* (3), III, p. 592.

112　Granville to Queen, 3 January 1885, *ibid.*, p. 591.

113　Gladstone to Granville, 28 December 1884. Ramm, II, p. 304.

114　Gwynne and Tuckwell, *Dilke*, II, p. 96.

115　Dilke to Derby, 26 February 1885. DP x 24.

116　In FO to CO, 11 February 1885. CO 179/162.

117　Derby to Dilke, 26 February 1885, DP x 24.

118　Dilke to Derby, *ibid.*

119　FO to CO, 11 February 1885, encl. Münster to Granville 4 February 1885. CO 179/162.

120　Herbert Memorandum, 'Confidential', January 1885. CO 48/511.

121　CO 879/22, 'Confidential Prints', No. 293.

122　Lord Crewe, *Lord Rosebery* (London, 1931), vol. I, pp. 234–5.

123　*Grosse Politik*, IV, No. 760 for details.

124　Granville to Gladstone, 4 March 1885. Ramm, II, p. 341.

125　FO Memorandum 'Africa', No. 96. FO 64/1149.

126　Proclamation of 7 May 1885. c. 4442 (LV, 1884–85), No. 3, p. 104.

127　CO 879/23, p. 47 *passim*; and Saunders, 'Annexation of Transkei', pp. 393–5.

128　Stanford, *Reminiscences*, II, ch. 31.

129　Saunders, 'Annexation of Transkei', pp. 399–400.

130　He also lost his son Oscar, who died while being educated abroad. *DSAB*, II, 460.

CHAPTER 5

1　'Vindex', *Speeches*, p. 200.

2　*OHSA*, II, pp. 306–7.

3　D. W. Krüger, *Kruger*, II, pp. 39–60; F. Nathan, *Kruger*, pp. 209–11; and Backeberg, 'Betrekkinge . . .', pp. 46–7.

4　Proclamation of 16 September 1884, in Robinson to Derby (tel.), 17 September 1884. CO 417/2.

5　Herbert min., 4 January 1885 on FO to CO, 2 January 1885. CO 179/162.

6　Robinson to Derby, 'Private', 16 September 1884. DP x 24.

7　*Idem.*

8 c. 4213 (LVII, 1884–85), pp. 53–4 for Cape reactions to Proclamation.

9 Hamilton Diary, 30 September 1884. HD 48636, fo. 134.

10 Robinson to Derby (tel.), 17 September 1884. CO 417/2.

11 Robinson to Derby, 'Private', 16 September 1884. DP x 24.

12 Min. by Herbert, 18 September 1884, on Robinson to Derby (tel.), 17 September 1884. CO 417/2.

13 *Idem.*

14 Derby to Robinson, 19 September 1884. c. 4213 (LVII, 1884–85), pp. 75–6.

15 Robinson to Derby (tel.), 23 September 1884. CO 417/2.

16 Min. by Sir R. Herbert, 18 September 1884. CO 417/2.

17 Robinson to Derby, 'Private', 24 September 1884. DP x 24.

18 Note by Derby on margin of letter, *ibid.*

19 De Kock, 'Vraagstukke . . . ', pp. 241–2.

20 Robinson to Derby, 'Private', 24 September 1884. DP x 24.

21 *Cape Times*, 25 September 1884; and see *Zuid-Afrikaan* and *Die Patriot*, for late-September 1884.

22 I.e. Thomas Fuller (1831–1910) MP for Cape Town 1879–1900.

23 See T. E. Fuller's *Life of Rhodes* (London, 1910), pp. 48–9.

24 Bower 'Memoir', RHL Afr. MSS s. 63, fo. 127.

25 Chamberlain to Derby, 21 September 1884. DP x 24.

26 *Grosse Politik*, IV. p. 83.

27 J. Chamberlain, *Political Memoir* (Ed. C. H. D. Howard), pp. 105–7.

28 *Ibid.*

29 Derby to Gladstone, 16 September 1884. GP 44142, fo. 75.

30 *Idem.*

31 Kimberley to Chamberlain, 'Private', 25 September 1884. JC 9/1/1/5.

32 Derby to Gladstone, 19 September 1884. GP 44142, fo. 77.

33 WO 33/42, No. 971 (6 October 1884). Printed in full in Schreuder, *Gladstone and Kruger*, pp. 504–13.

34 *Idem.*

35 Derby to Gladstone, 23 December 1884. GP 44142, fo. 106.

36 Fuller, *Rhodes*, pp. 48–9.

37 Robinson to Derby, 1 October 1884, 'Private', DP x 24.

38 *Idem.*

39 Min. by Herbert, 29 September 1884. CO 879/22, No. 287.

40 Herbert to Derby, 'Private', 28 September 1884. DP x 24.

41 Derby to Gladstone, 29 September 1884. GP 44142, fo. 77.

42 Derby to Gladstone, 2 October 1884, *ibid.*, fo. 84.

43 CO Memo by Sir R. Herbert (29 September 1884). CO 879/22, No. 287.

44 Derby to Gladstone, 30 September 1884. GP 44142, fo. 79.

45 Garvin, *Chamberlain*, I, 492 *passim.*

46 Cabinet Mins., Monday, 6 October 1884. GP 44645, fo. 179.

47 Chamberlain, *Political Memoir*, p. 105.

48 Hamilton Diary, 6 October 1884. HD 48637, fo. 115.

49 Derby to Robinson (tel.), 7 October 1884. GP 44645, fo. 180.
50 *Hansard* (3), CCXXIII, col. 38.
51 *Ibid.*, col. 985 *passim*.
52 *Daily News*, Editorial, 30 October 1884.
53 Only Harcourt disagreed. Dilke Memoir, 43938, fo. 295.
54 Cabinet notes, 19 November 1884. GP 44645, fo. 220.
55 Sir Charles Warren (1840–1927); Br. imperial soldier, 1857–85;
    Commissioner of London police, 1886.
56 Hamilton Diary, 11 November 1884. HD 48638, fo. 45.
57 Dilke Memoir, 43938, fo. 295; Chamberlain, Political Memoir, p. 107;
    and *Hansard* (3), CCXCIII, col. 1655 (13 November 1884).
58 Quoted A. Ponsonby, *Henry Ponsonby, His Life and Letters* (London, 1942),
    p. 351 (my italics).
59 Herbert to Derby, 'Private', 16 October 1884. DP x 24.
60 Robinson to Derby, 'Private', 15 October 1884, *ibid.*
61 Derby to Gladstone, 21 October 1884. GP 44142, fo. 88.
62 Gladstone to Derby, 27 October 1884. GP 44527 (Letter-book), fo. 129.
63 Ponsonby, *Life*, p. 269.
64 The mission consisted of: Sprigg, J. S. Marais (*Bond* leader in Paarl),
    and R. W. Murray (editor, *Cape Times*).
65 Robinson to Derby, 'Private', 25 November 1884. DP x 24.
66 Robinson to Derby (tel.), 29 November 1884, encl. tel. from Upington,
    same day. See also c. 4275 (LVII, 1884–85) pp. 37–40.
67 Fairfield Min., 26 November 1884. CO 417/2.
68 See *The Times* and *Daily News*, 27 November 1884.
69 Hartington to Derby, 27 November 1884. DP x 24.
70 Fairfield min., 3 December 1884. CO 417/2.
71 *Cape Argus*, 19 November 1884.
72 Robinson to Derby, 10 December 1884. DP x 24.
73 CO to Warren, 10 November 1884. CO 417/3, and c. 4227 (LV, 1884–85),
    pp. 4–5.
74 Hartington to Queen Victoria, 7 November 1884. Devonshire Paps. 340/
    1575.
75 Herbert Min., 6 December 1884. CO 417/3.
76 Fairfield, 9 December 1884, *ibid.*
77 Gladstone to Derby, 'Private', 17 November 1884. GP 44547, fo. 138.
78 Froude to Chamberlain, 13 December 1884. JC 5/32/4.
79 *Ibid.*, from Cape Town.
80 *Ibid.*, p. 69.
81 De Kiewiet, *Imperial Factor*, pp. 324–8.
82 Agar-Hamilton, *Road to the North*, p. 394 *passim*, and Rhodes to Bower,
    19 February 1885. c. 4432 (LVII, 1884–85), p. 52; Rhodes to Merriman,
    21 February 1885, giving his side of the argument. SAL/MP, 1885–79
    Also, W. D. Mackenzie, *Life*, p. 381, *passim*.

83 Warren to Robinson (tel.), 4 March 1885, *ibid.*, p. 72.

84 Gladstone letterbook, 19 March 1885. GP 44547, fo. 187.

85 Gladstone to Childers, 26 January 1885. GP 44547, fo. 168.

86 Gladstone to Derby, 14 March 1885. GP 44547, fo. 185.

87 Agar-Hamilton, *Road to the North*, pp. 394–8.

88 c. 4432 (LVII, 1884–85), pp. 82–3.

89 Warren to Derby (tels.), March 1885. CO 417/4.

90 Robinson to Derby, 'Private', 11 March 1885. DP x 24.

91 *Idem.*

92 GP 48639, fos. 90–1, and GP 44547, fo. 187, 19 March 1885.

93 Derby to Gladstone, 1 April 1885. GP 44142, p. 122.

94 Gladstone to Derby, 14 March 1885. GP 44547, fo. 185.

95 Gladstone to Derby, 17 April 1885. GP 44545, fo. 3 (my italics).

96 Fairfield Min., 24 June 1885. CO 417/5.

97 CO Mins., March 1885. CO 417/4.

98 CO Min. of 18 May 1885. CO 417/8.

99 Fairfield Min., 2 May 1885. CO 417/4.

100 Gladstone to Derby, 17 April 1885. GP 44548, fo. 3.

101 Derby to Robinson (tel.), 28 March 1885. CO 417/4.

102 Fairfield Memo, 24 April 1885. CO 417/4.

103 Cabinet Mins., 16 May 1885. GP 44642, fo. 131.

104 Details of the offer, and a map, are contained in Warren to Robinson, 4 June 1885 (encl. in Robinson to Derby, 14 June), c. 4588 (LVII, 1884–85), p.36.

105 Encl. in Robinson to Derby, *ibid.*

106 Robinson to Stanley (tel.), 7 July 1885, *ibid.*, pp. 31–2.

107 Robinson to Derby, 'Private', 24 March 1885. DP x 24.

108 Fairfield CO Memo, 24 April 1885. CO 417/4.

109 CO Memo on future of Bechuanaland (by Fairfield), 24 June 1885. CO 417/5.

110 Derby to Robinson, 21 March 1885 (tel.), *ibid.*, p. 57.

111 'Vindex', *Speeches*, p. 128.

112 Robinson to Stanley (tel.), 1 July 1885. CO 417/6.

113 Fairfield Min., 13 June 1885. CO 417/9.

114 Fairfield Memo, 24 June 1885. CO 417/5.

115 Stanley to Robinson, 13 August 1885. c. 4588 (LVII, 1884–85), p. 106.

116 CO Min., 8 July 1885, on Cape decision, CO 417/6.

117 The Cape terms are in Robinson to Stanley (tel.), 7 July 1885. c. 4588 (LVII, 1884–85), pp. 31–2.

118 Fairfield Min., 8 July 1885, on Robinson to Stanley, 7 July 1885. CO 417/6.

119 *Idem.*

120 Robinson to Stanley, 15 July 1885. c. 4588 (LVII, 1884–85), p. 116.

121 Stanley to Robinson, 13 August 1885; *ibid.*, pp. 118–19.

122 Memo, printed for Cabt, 15 July 1885. PRO Cab. 37/15/44.

123 Sillery, *Protectorate*, p. 58, and de Kock, *'Vraagstukke'*, p. 165.
124 CO Min., 10 July 1885. CO 417/5.
125 Robinson to Stanley, 30 September 1885. CO 417/7.
126 CO Memo, African No. 301. PRO Cab. 37/15/44.
127 Mills to Merriman, 16 September 1885. SAL/MP, 1885.
128 Min. of 18 July by Fairfield, CO 417/6.
129 Robinson to Derby, 'Private', 8 May 1885. DP x 24.
130 Upington to Herbert, 30 December 1885. CO 417/9.
131 In Robinson to CO, 30 December 1885. CO 417/7.
132 Min. by Herbert, 25 January 1886. CO 417/7.
133 Confidential Prints, Africa No. 320, of 23 May 1886. CO 879/24.
134 Granville Min. of 24 June 1886. CO 417/11.
135 Robinson to Holland, 13 July 1887. CO 417/15.
136 Bramston to Mackenzie, 25 March 1887. Mackenzie MSS, Wits.
137 Mackenzie to Holland (copy), 5 April 1887. *Ibid.*
138 Holland to Mackenzie, 6 April 1887. *Ibid.*
139 Fairfield Min., 13 July 1888. CO 48/516.
140 Chamberlain to Mackenzie, 2 October 1888. Mackenzie MSS, Wits.

CHAPTER 6

1 D. K. Fieldhouse, *Economics and Empire 1830–1914* (London, 1973), p. 362.
2 Denoon, *Southern Africa since 1800*, pp. 74–6, is excellent on this theme.
3 W. MacDonald, *The Romance of the Golden Rand* (Johannesburg, n. d.), p. 26.
4 G. S. Preller, *Argonauts of the Rand* (Pretoria, 1835), pp. 76–84, 140–67.
5 Robinson to Herbert, 30 December 1885. CO 417/7.
6 O. Fletcher, *The Gold Mines of Southern Africa* (London, 1936), p. 114.
7 See de Kiewiet, *A History of South Africa*, p. 118.
8 A. Briggs, *Victorian Cities* (London, 1964), ch. 3 'Manchester'.
9 K. F. Bellairs, *The Witwatersrand Goldfields; a trip to Johannesburg and back* (London, 1889), p. 34.
10 W. J. Breytenbach, *Migratory Labour Arrangement in Southern Africa* (Pretoria, 1972), p. 10 *passim*. Also, L. V. Praagh (ed.), *The Transvaal and its mines* (Johannesburg, 1906), p. 516.
11 Leo Katzen, *Gold and the South African Economy* (Cape Town, 1964), p. 65.
12 *OHSA*, II, pp. 113–27.
13 Katzen, *Gold and the South African Economy*, pp. 64–73.
14 Bellairs, *The Witwatersrand Goldfields*, p. 34.
15 Sheila van der Horst, *Native labour in South Africa* (London, 1942), p. 136; and Alan Jeeves, 'The control of migratory labour on the South African gold mines in the era of Kruger and Milner', *Journal of Southern African Studies*, vol. 2, Oct. 1975, pp. 3–29.

16 F. H. Hatch and J. A. Chalmers, *The Goldmines of the Rand* (London, 1895), p. 254.

17 In 1896 some 64,012 African labourers earned £48 per head per year, compared to £302 per head for 9,375 white workers per year. White wages amounted to £3,029,069; African wages to £2,999,308. Source: *Report of the State Mining Engineer for the year 1896*, p. 5.

18 *Ibid.*, p. 129.

19 Mins. of May 1891. CO 417/89.

20 Bellairs, *Witwatersrand Goldfields*, p. 36.

21 PM to Governor, 4 February 1886. CAD/GH. 15/11.

22 Annual revenues of Transvaal in February 1884 were £188,000; by 1886 the state was reputed to be near bankruptcy, failing to raise a loan of £5,000. See Schumann, *Business Cycles*, p. 53, and Walker, *History of Southern Africa*, p. 407.

23 *Gold output of the Witwatersrand mines, notional figures of investment and return on capital 1887–97* (values in pounds sterling)

	Gold amount (fine oz.)	Value	Investment	Dividends
1887	19,000	81,000		
1888	171,000	729,000		
1889	306,000	1,300,000		
1890	408,000	1,735,000		
1891	601,000	2,556,000	40,000,000	1,000,000
1892	1,011,000	4,297,000		
1893	1,221,000	5,187,000		
1894	1,639,000	6,963,000		
1895	1,845,000	7,840,000		
1896	1,851,000	7,864,000	55,358,000	1,694,000
1897	2,491,000	10,583,000	63,188,000	3,001,000

Source: Goodfellow, *Economic History*, pp. 174–6.

24 Schumann, *Business Cycles*, p. 52.

25 *Idem.*

26 Goodfellow, *Economic History*, pp. 21–2.

27 M. Nathan, *Paul Kruger* (Durban, 1944), pp. 300–1.

28 Rhodes to Scanlen, 3 September 1882. NAR/RP, Rh/1/1/1 fo. 443.

29 Herbert Min., 31 July 1884. CO 417/1.

30 Fairfield Min., *ibid.* (my italics).

31 All Rhodes speeches from 'Vindex'.

32 *Ibid.*, p. 137.

33 L. Michell, *The Life of the Rt. Hon. Cecil John Rhodes* (London, 1910), 2 vols., 1, pp. 93–5.

34 J. G. Lockhart and C. M. Woodhouse, *Rhodes* (London, 1963), p. 80.

35 Michell, *Rhodes*, I, pp. 93–5.
36 *Ibid.*, I, p. 95.
37 *Ibid.*, II, p. 168.
38 B. Williams, *Rhodes* (London, 1921), pp. 62–3.
39 Davenport, *Afrikaner Bond*, p. 128.
40 'Vindex', *Speeches*, pp. 274–5.
41 Quoted Robinson and Gallagher, *Africa and the Victorians*, p. 218.
42 Van Winter, *Kruger's Hollanders*, vol. II, p. 114, and J. van der Poel, *Railway and Customs Policies in South Africa, 1885–1910* (London, 1933), p. 40, *passim.*
43 Kruger, *Kruger*, vol. II, p. 119.
44 Goodfellow, *Economic History*, p. 87.

45 *Tonnage carried by 'rival' Cape lines to interior, 1886–94 (in 000 tons)*

	Cape Western Line	Midland (PE) Line	Eastern (EL) Line
1886	141	106	64
1887	146	131	81
1888	165	163	85
1889	203	227	111
1890	217	279	121
1891	239	296	136
1892	255	277	157
1893	299	267	224
1894	296	279	257

Source: Goodfellow, *ibid.*, p. 88.

46 For example: Cape Town to Johannesburg (via Mafeking): 957 miles
Cape Town to Johannesburg (via Bloemfontein): 1,011 miles
Port Elizabeth to Johannesburg: 712 miles
East London to Johannesburg: 665 miles
Durban to Johannesburg: 482 miles
Delagoa Bay to Johannesburg: 394 miles

Source: Lovell, *Struggle for South Africa*, p. 128, n. 21.

47 Natal invested even more heavily in railways to the Rand; e.g. (in £000s):

	Public debt	Railway debt
1881	1,631	1,204
1885	3,762	2,594
1890	3,060	3,650
1895	8,054	6,117

Source: Goodfellow, *Economic History*, p. 88.

48 *The profitability of Cape/Natal railways; return on investment 1886–95 (per £100)*

	Cape	Natal
1886	£2.16.11	£ 5.10.0
1887	4. 3. 1	9.12.0
1888	4.17.10	12.10.0
1889	5.15. 1	17.16.0
1890	5.15.10	16.12.0
1891	4.13. 4	12.12.0
1892	4.14. 8	9. 2.0
1893	4.16.11	6.16.0
1894	5. 6. 5	7.12.0
1895	7. 9. 0	8.10.0

Source: Goodfellow, *ibid.*, p. 89.

49 See D. W. Kruger, *Kruger*, II, pp. 138–42.
50 Marais, *Fall of Kruger's Republic*, pp. 34–40, and van der Poel, *Railway and Customs*, p. 59.
51 *Life of Hofmeyr*, p. 348, *passim*.
52 Walker, *History of Southern Africa*, p. 408. Indeed, the OFS was favourably disposed to a customs union with the Cape at this time. Details in H. Comm. to Ministers, 26 October 1887. CAD/PM/246, Min. 380 and enclosures.
53 The Cape–OFS customs agreement of 1889 is to be found together with the working documents for its negotiation, in CAD/PM/246, Min. 128 *passim*. A printed version of the Cape–OFS correspondence on the matter is in CAD/PM/248, part III.
54 The Natal rail-line reached the Rand in 1895. Brookes and de B. Webb, *History of Natal*, chs. 16–20. For Cape reactions to Natal–Transvaal relations, see CAD/PM/246 mins. of 1889.
55 P. Natham, *Kruger*, p. 279.
56 The McMurdo Rail contract was signed on 14 December 1883. See contract encl. in FO to CO, 1 January 1884. CO 291/26 'Foreign'.
57 See Marais, *Fall of Kruger's Republic*, ch. 2 for Transvaal 'Concessions policy' generally, and van Winter, *Kruger's Hollanders*, I, p. 150 *passim*, for McMurdo Concession.
58 Van der Poel, *Railway and Customs*, pp. 58–71.
59 Lockhart and Woodhouse, *Rhodes*, pp. 106–22.
60 Salisbury to Castledown, 11 October 1890. SP 412/484.
61 *Africa and the Victorians*, p. 219.
62 See Salisbury to Castledown, 16 May 1888. SP 378/436.
63 Min. by Sir Robert Herbert, 7 May 1889. CO 417/31 (my italics).
64 Min. by Edward Fairfield, 2 November 1889. CO 417/33.
65 Marais, *Fall of Kruger's Republic*, p. 33.
66 Salisbury to Castledown, 16 August 1888. SP 378/436.

67 Salisbury to Castledown, 11 October 1890. SP 412/484.
68 Van der Poel, *Railway and Customs*, ch. 4, pp. 48–71.
69 'Vindex', *Speeches*, pp. 339–40 (6 Jan. 1894).
70 *Ibid.*, p. 224.
71 Rhodes to W. T. Stead, 19 Aug. 1891. Stead Papers, fo. 18.
72 *Cape Assembly Debates*, 1894, p. 362.
73 *Ibid.*, pp. 367, 418.
74 *Ibid.*, p. 363.
75 *Ibid.*, p. 419.
76 'Vindex', *Speeches*, p. 213 (28 Sept. 1888).
77 Salisbury in Lords, 10 July 1890. *Hansard* (4) CCCXLVI, col. 1256.
78 Rhodes to Shippard, 14 August 1888. NAR/RP, Rh 1/1/1 fo. 666.
79 See A. K. Cairncross, *Home and foreign investment* (Cambridge, 1953), p. 185.
80 See Rhodes speech of 28 Sept. 1888 in 'Vindex', *Speeches*, p. 224. As early as 1885 Rhodes was in fact raising alarms about alien influences in Central Africa: 'The only thing we have now to work for is that the Germans shall not take Matabeleland'. NAR/RH, Rh 1/1/1 fo. 663. is also useful.
81 R. Taylor, *Lord Salisbury* (London, 1975), p. 177.

CHAPTER 7

1 Rhodes' speech of 28 Sept. 1888. 'Vindex', *Speeches*, p. 226.
2 H. A. C. Cairns, *Prelude to Imperialism* (London, 1965), ch. IX.
3 *DSAB*, II, pp. 662–3.
4 Holland to Robinson, 5 May, 1 June (tels.) 1887 for initial one-year appointment of Moffat. CO 417/14 and 147/18.
5 Sillery, *Founding a Protectorate*, chs. IV–VIII.
6 Shippard to Moffat, 26 December 1887. NAR/MP, Mo. 1/1/4, fo. 180.
7 Shippard to Moffat, 13 February 1888. *Ibid.*, fo. 195.
8 Rhodes to Shippard, 1 August 1888. NAR/RP, Rh. 1/1/1, fo. 666.
9 Rhodes to Shippard, 14 August. *Ibid.*
10 For example, Rhodes to Newton, (?) August 1888. *Ibid.*, fo. 412.
11 See Sillery, *Protectorate*, p. 99.
12 Moffat to Miss E. Unwin, 28 April 1889. NAR/MP, Mo. 1/1/6, fo. 2546.
13 Quoted in R. Moffat, *John Moffat* (London, 1921), p. 221.
14 Moffat to Miss E. Unwin, 6 October 1889. NAR/MP, Mo. 1/1/6, fo. 256.
15 Moffat to Miss E. Unwin, 24 October 1890 (from Matabeleland). *Ibid.*, fo. 259.
16 See Moffat to Coghlan, 10 October 1914. *Ibid.*
17 This *was* within his instructions, 3 August 1887. CO 417/15.
18 Moffat's tour began in September; he was at Lobengula's court in February 1888. See Moffat to Shippard, Reports, September 1887 to

February 1888, encl. in Robinson to Holland, same dates. CO 417/16–19, and NAR/MP, Mo. 1/1/5/1.

19 The Treaty is printed in full in c. 5524 (LXXIX, 1888), p. 868. See also, Williams, *Rhodes*, p. 121; and H. M. Hole, *The Making of Rhodesia* (London, 1926), p. 54.

20 Rhodes to Shippard, 14 April 1888, from Kimberley. NAR/RP, Rh. 1/1/1, fo. 666.

21 Min. by Fairfield, 10 November 1887, on Robinson to Holland, 19 October 1887. CO 417/6. Also, Sillery, *Protectorate*, p. 100.

22 Previously Sir Henry Holland; he had gratefully accepted a title from Salisbury to escape the rigors of life in the Commons: 'Smith [p. sec.] informed me several times . . . that you did not feel it possible to go on in the House of Commons on account of the extreme fatigues and this morning he informs me you wish to join our Assembly where no such inconvenience is to be apprehended. The Queen has approved the idea. I hope you will keep the Colonies in your conduct of which has obtained universal approbation.' SP. 42 (copy).

23 CO Mins. of 26–7 March 1888. CO 417/19.

24 CO to FO, 29 March 1888. CO 879/29.

25 The limits of Robinson's enthusiasm for the imperial advance into Zambesia – *before* Rhodes began his work on him – are well illustrated in a Shippard letter reporting the high commissioner's opinions: 'His Excellency, the High Commissioner, is extremely anxious that you [Moffat] should not force the pace with Lo Bengula, and he seems to fear that I have been urging you to go too fast . . . Sir H. R[obinson]. plainly says that in the present temper of the [British] Cabinet a request from Lo Bengula for a Protectorate would be completely thrown away – positively and finally declined. H.M.G. has refused to extend the Protectorate to the Zambesi at present on account of possible boundary disputes and they have told the Transvaal Gov[ernment]t. that they claim no Protectorate beyond 29° 20′ E. longitude.' Shippard to Moffat, 19 September 1887. NAR/MP, Mo. 1/1/4, fo. 173.

26 Conversation recalled by Rhodes, in speech of 29 November 1892. 'Vindex', *Speeches*, pp. 337–8.

27 Moffat to Shippard, 12 December 1887, encl. in Robinson to Knutsford. CO 879/29, p. 3; and printed in c. 5918 (LI, 1890), p. 3; encl. in Kruger to Robinson, 29 August 1888.

28 Lockhart and Woodhouse, *Rhodes*, pp. 137–9.

29 Shippard's account of the meeting can be found in his article, 'Bechuana land', *British Africa*, in 'British Empire Series' (1899), vol. II; also cited in Sillery, *Protectorate*, p. 100, n. 33.

30 'Vindex', *Speeches*, pp. 338–9.

31 Official British approval of Moffat's action was not despatched for several months, until 25 April 1888. See Robinson to Shippard, 17 May, encl.

Knutsford to Robinson, 25 April 1888. NAR/MP, Mo. 1/1/4, fo. 200.

32 Bower, 'Memoir', MSS Afr. RHL, Oxford.

33 Robinson to Knutsford (tel.), 2 April 1888. CO 879/29, p. 15.

34 CO to FO, 7 April 1888, *ibid.*, p. 16. Knutsford was now (23 May) of the opinion that it might well be best 'to accept the Zambesi River as the southern boundary of the Portuguese sphere of influence'.

35 FO to CO, 23 July 1888, *ibid.*, p. 50.

36 FO to CO, 20 April 1888, *ibid.*, p. 18.

37 CO to FO, 7 April, *ibid.*, p. 16.

38 Knutsford to Mackenzie, 9 December 1888. Mackenzie MSS, Wits.

39 Knutsford Min., 28 September 1888, on Robinson to Knutsford, 29 August 1888. CO 417/22.

40 Africa (South) No. 439, Confidential Print. CO 879/33.

41 *Ibid.*, pp. 2–3.

42 *Idem.*

43 Salisbury Min. (n.d.), probably July 1888. FO 84/1924.

44 In FO to CO, 9 February 1889. CO 879/29, p. 92 (my italics).

45 Min. by Meade (n.d.) cited in Sillery, *Protectorate*, p. 103.

46 Robinson to Holland, 'Private', 7 March 1888. CO 417/19.

47 Robinson to Knutsford, 8 August 1888. CO 879/29, p. 59.

48 CO to FO, 28 August 1888, encl. Glasgow Chamber of Commerce to FO, *ibid.*, p. 160.

49 FO to CO, 7 May 1888, *ibid.*, p. 27.

50 CO to Treasury, 29 January 1890, reporting a deficit of £86,000 for 1890–91.

51 Rhodes in Cape Assembly, 23 July 1888. 'Vindex', *Speeches*, p. 201.

52 The fact that Bechuanaland joined the Cape–OFS Customs Union in 1890–91 hardly altered the position. CAD/PM/246, pt II.

53 Mills to Merriman, 12 November 1888. SAL/MP/888/153.

54 Robinson to Knutsford, 17 October 1888. c. 5918 (LI, 1890), p. 26.

55 *Idem.*

56 Knutsford to Salisbury, 4 October 1888. SP Letter 156.

57 Supported by Joseph Chamberlain: see Chamberlain to Knutsford, 31 January 1889–SP Letter 189.

58 W. D. Mackenzie, *Life*, p. 429 *passim*.

59 Knutsford to Salisbury, 4 October 1888. SP Letter 156.

60 Knutsford to Robinson, 19 November 1888. CO 879/30, No. 369, p. 141.

61 Robinson to Knutsford, 17 October 1888. c. 5918 (LI, 1890), p. 26.

62 Salisbury to Knutsford, 12 October 1888. SP c. 64.

63 Knutsford to Sprigg, 9 February 1889. SP Letter 190.

64 Knutsford to Salisbury, 6 December 1888. SP Letter 177.

65 Knutsford to Sprigg (tel.), 9 February 1889 (copy). SP Letter 190.

66 Sprigg to Knutsford (tel.), 9 February 1889. SP Doc. 190, (Knutsford file).

67 Knutsford to Salisbury, 6 December 1888. SP Letter 177.

68 See above, ch. 6.

69 For the Rhodes pressures on Sprigg to commit the Cape to a vigorous rail advance, see Rhodes–Sprigg correspondence of October 1889, in NAR/RP, Rh. 1/1/1, fo. 336.

70 Described at length in the Cape governor's despatches for early 1890. CO 879/32, No. 392, p. 34 *passim*.

71 Historian, and former private sec. to Sir C. W. Dilke.

72 Salisbury to Knutsford, 21 April 1888. SP (Copy) C. 50.

73 Robinson to Knutsford, 2 May 1888, CO 879/29, p. 30.

74 FO to CO, 7 May 1888. CO 879/29, p. 30.

75 Robinson to Knutsford, 5 December 1888, encl. Portuguese declaration in *Cape Argus, ibid.*, 83.

76 CO to FO, 2 December 1887. FO 403/108.

77 Rhodes cited in Lockhart and Woodhouse, *Rhodes*, p. 165.

78 See the valuable studies by J. Duffy, *Portuguese Africa* (Cambridge, Mass., 1959), p. 214 *passim*; E. Axelson, *Portugal and the Scramble for Africa* (Johannesburg, 1967), pp. 137–200; and P. R. Warhurst, *Anglo-Portuguese Relations*, p. 23 *passim*.

79 Salisbury to H. S. Cross, MP, 16 October 1890. SP 414/488.

80 Admirably described in *Africa and the Victorians*, p. 225, *passim*.

81 Cecil, *Salisbury*, IV, pp. 240–78.

82 CO to FO, 23 May 1888. FO 403/108.

83 FO to CO, 20 June. CO 879/29, p. 37.

84 Knutsford to Salisbury, 15 October 1888. SP Letter 161.

85 Knutsford to Robinson, 28 June 1888. CO 879/29, p. 138. Also Cecil, *Salisbury*, IV, 268.

86 Duffy, *Portuguese Africa*, p. 215; Axelson, *Scramble*, p. 137, *passim*.

87 Salisbury to Sir D. Currie, 9 March 1891. SP 420/500.

88 Salisbury to Knutsford, 27 April 1889, repudiating Johnston's work. SP B 72.

89 See C. 5904 (LI, 1890), pp. 150–2.

90 H. H. Johnston, *The Story of My Life*, p. 226 *passim*.

91 *Ibid.*, p. 231.

92 Hanna, *Rhodesia and Nyasaland*, pp. 141–7, and p. 173 *passim*.

93 Johnston to Lister, 5 April 1889. FO 84/1969. 'I cannot bear the idea of our making the Zambesi a hard and fast limit to British enterprise in Southern Africa.'

94 See H. H. Johnston, 'British Policy in Africa' (anon. article) in *The Times*, 22 August 1888.

95 *Story of My Life*, pp. 236–7, for Johnston's account of the discussion.

96 Salisbury Min., 26 April 1889, fully quoted in E. Axelson, *Portugal and the Scramble for Africa*, pp. 198–9.

97 Salisbury to Knutsford, 27 April 1889. SP B.72.

98 Robinson to Knutsford, 8 August 1888, on the need to keep open all central Africa up to the Tanganyika Lakes. CO 879/29, p. 59.

99 Knutsford to Salisbury, 27 April 1889. SP Letter 200.

100 Knutsford to Salisbury, 1 May 1889. SP Letter 202.

101 Full details in CO 417/34 for 1889–90; and Warhurst, *Anglo-Portuguese Relations*, pp. 48–77.

102 c. 5918 (LI, 1890), p. 115.

103 Robinson to Knutsford, 7 December 1888. CO 879/30, No. 369, p. 143.

104 For Grobler Treaty of July 1887, see Kruger to Robinson, 29 August 1888, and in Robinson to Knutsford, 12 September 1888, *ibid.*, p. 3. Treaty on pp. 5–6.

105 Robinson to Knutsford, 'Private', 24 December 1888. CO 417/27.

106 See Sillery, *Protectorate*, ch. IX, 'The Grobler Affair', for a concise analysis of the evidence.

107 Robinson to Knutsford, 3 October 1888. c. 5918 (LI, 1890), p. 17.

108 Robinson to Knutsford, 19 December 1888. CO 879/30, No. 869, p. 229.

109 *Idem.*

110 Knutsford to Robinson, 31 January 1889. c. 5918 (LI, 1890), p. 157. See also CO 879/30, No. 369, p. 288.

111 Knutsford to Salisbury, 28 January 1890. SP Letter 188.

112 *Idem.*

113 See Knutsford to Salisbury, 18 May 1880, for a further elaboration of the idea – SP Letter 268 – and Knutsford to Loch (tel.) 'secret', 15 April 1890 – SP Doc. 282 (copy). 'It was left to Rhodes' private enterprise to relieve the captive government.' *Africa and the Victorians*, p. 234.

114 Newton to Moffat, 26 August 1888, 'Private, from Cape Town'. NAR/MP, Mo. 1/1/4, fo. 229. (Newton's italics).

115 *Idem.*

116 Signed at Bulawayo on 30 October 1888. The original Rudd Concession is with the BSA Company. A photocopy, and a copy in Rudd's hand, are in the NAR, Salisbury, reference NAR/RuP, Ru. 2/2/1 and Ru. 2/2/2. Lobengula's copy also still exists – NAR/LP, Lo. 1/2/2. A facsimile print is in Hole, *Making of Rhodesia*, p. 74. For an account of the Rudd trek to Bulawayo, see his Diary (August 1887 – October 1888), NAR/RuP, Ru. 2/3/1-1, and printed in *Gold and Gospel in Mashonaland*, pp. 149–218, Oppenheimer Series, no. 4.

117 Maguire to Newton, 27 October 1888. NAR/NP, NE 1/1/10.

118 Robinson to the *Times*, 7 November 1893.

119 *Idem.*

120 Richard Brown, 'Aspects of the Scramble for Matabeleland', in E. Stokes and R. Brown (eds.), *The Zambesian Past* (Manchester, 1966), pp. 63–93. See also his paper, 'The External relations of the Ndebele kingdom in the pre-partition era', in *African Societies in Southern Africa*; *Historical Studies*, ed. Leonard Thompson (London, 1969), pp. 259–81.

121 Cairns, *Prelude to Imperialism*, p. 116.

122 Brown, 'The Scramble in Matabeleland', p. 68.

123 *Ibid.*, p. 70.

124   *Ibid.*, p. 25.
125   A. J. Wills, *An Introduction to the History of Central Africa* (Oxford, 1964), pp. 132–4.
126   Moffat to Shippard, 31 August 1888. NAR/MO, 1/1/5/1.
127   Moffat to Shippard, 28 September 1888. *Ibid.*, 1/1/5/2.
128   See Stanlake Samkange, *Origins of Rhodesia* (London, 1968), pp. 68–86.
129   Brown, 'Scramble for Matabeleland', pp. 80–2, is excellent on this.
130   Rhodes to Rudd, 10 September 1888. NAR/Ru, 2/1/1 (Letter rearranged).
131   Quoted Brown, 'Scramble in Matabeleland', p. 69.
132   Quoted Wills, *History of Central Africa*, p. 135.
133   Quoted Cairns, *Prelude to Imperialism*, p. 24.
134   Quoted Brown, 'Scramble in Matabeleland', pp. 68–9.
135   Elliot to Thompson, 19 February 1890, quoted Holmberg, *African Tribes and European Agencies*, p. 216.
136   Moffat to Shippard, 1 August 1889 (in Smyth to Knutsford). CO 417/32.
137   See Mackenzie to Chamberlain, 21 October 1895. Mackenzie MSS, Wits.
138   Rhodes to Shippard, 3 September 1889. NAR/RP, Rh. 1/1/1, fo. 666.
139   Queen Victoria to Lobengula, 10 September 1890. CO 879/32, no. 392, p.321.
140   *The Times*, 29 March 1889, and *Pall Mall Gazette*, 1 May 1889.
141   Rhodes quoted in Helm to Thompson, 11 August 1890; Holmberg, *African Tribes and European Agencies*, p. 216.
142   Rhodes to Rudd, 10 January 1888. NAR/NP, NE 1/1/10.

CHAPTER 8

1   J. S. Galbraith has provided two scholarly reappraisals of Rhodes and the central African expansion, to which I am considerably indebted: 'Cecil Rhodes and his "Cosmic Dreams" – A Reassessment', in the *Journal of Imperial and Commonwealth History*', vol. 1, January 1973, pp. 173–89; and 'Origins of the British South African Company', in *Perspectives on Empire*, eds. John Flint and G. Williams (London, 1973), pp. 148–71. See also his extended study of the period, *Crown and Charter: the early years of the BSA Company* (UCLA, 1974).
2   James Rose-Innes, *Autobiography* (Oxford, 1948), p. 87.
3   John Flint's new life of *Rhodes* (London, 1975) offers some recent thoughts on refining the analysis.
4   I. R. Phimister, 'Rhodes, Rhodesia and the Rand', *Journal of Southern African Studies*, Vol. 1, No. 1, Oct. 1974, pp. 74–90.
5   Milner to Asquith, 18 Nov. 1897. C. Headlam (ed.), *The Milner Papers* (London, 1931), vol. 1, p. 178.
6   Knutsford to Loch, 4 November 1889, 'Instructions' as high commissioner. CO 879/31.

7   Coined at the time for the 1880–81 Anglo-Transvaal War. Schreuder, *Gladstone and Kruger*, pp. 126–8.

8   See Sir H. Robinson (Speech, 27 April 1889): printed in full CO 879/31, No. 380.

9   Knutsford to Salisbury, 1 May 1889, SP Letters 202.

10 E.g. FO to CO, 27 May 1889, agreeing to examine the Rhodesian proposal carefully, CO 879/30, No. 376, p. 77. See also, C. 5918 (LI, 1890), p. 194.

11 Expertly set out in Galbraith, 'Origins of the BSA Company', pp. 151–4.

12 Draft Agreement, Lobengula–Gifford, Maund MSS. A 77, fo. 25, Wits.

13 Memo of Maund–Lobengula meeting (copy), 24 November 1884; Maund MSS A 77, fo. 23, Wits.

14 Lobengula to Queen Victoria, 24 November 1888 (copy), *ibid.*, fo. 24.

15 Cawston to Knutsford, 30 May 1888, *ibid.*, fo. 18.

16 Maund MSS A 77, fo. 22, Wits.

17 For example, Gifford to Maund, 28 March 1889, *ibid.*, fo. 31.

18 Galbraith, 'Cecil Rhodes . . .', p. 177.

19 Rhodes to Cawston, 5 October 1889. NAR/RP, RL 1/1/1.

20 CO879/31, No. 380 (speech of 27 April 1889).

21 Robinson to Knutsford, 18 March 1889. CO 879/30, No. 372, pp. 36–8.

22 *Ibid.*; see also C. 5918 (LI, 1890), p. 171.

23 Robinson interview with *Cape Times* (3 November 1897, p. 2(b)).

24 Robinson to Knutsford, 'Confidential', 21 July 1887. CO 879/30.

25 *Idem.*

26 *Idem.* (my italics).

27 Robinson to Knutsford, 17 October 1888, *ibid.*

28 Robinson to Knutsford, 18 March 1889. CO 879/30, p. 36. Also see C. 5918 (LI, 1890), p. 171.

29 Wingfield to Cawston, 14 May 1888. Maund MSS A 77, fo. 17, Wits.

30 Knutsford to Robinson, 'Confidential', 20 August 1888. CO 879/30.

31 Hofmeyr, *Life of Hofmeyr*, p. 356.

32 Knutsford to Robinson (tel.), 17 December 1888. CO 879/30, p. 178, and C. 5918 (LI, 1890), p. 129.

33 Robinson to Knutsford (tel.), 18 December 1888. CO 879/30.

34 CO 879/10, p. 178.

35 Rudd to Thompson (n.d.), in Lockhart and Woodhouse, *Rhodes*, p. 147.

36 Rhodes to Rudd, 17 December 1888. NAR/RuP, Ru 2/1, fo. 18. See also Knutsford Min. on the firearms in the concession. CO 417/30 (19 April 1890).

37 Bower 'Memoir', MSS Afr, RHL, fos. 171–2.

38 Rhodes to Shippard (?) August 1888. NAR/RP, Rh. 1/3/1.

39 Galbraith, 'Origins of the BSA Company', p. 163.

40 Gifford to Maund, 24 May 1889. Maund MSS A. 77, fo. 3, Wits.

41 Robinson to Knutsford, 4 February 1889. CO 879/30.

42 Gifford to Cawston, 13 March 1889. Quoted Galbraith, 'Origins of BSA Company', p. 165.

43 See his letter to Cawston, 5 October 1889. NAR/RP, Rh. 1/1/4.

44 Brown, 'Aspects of the Scramble for Matabeleland', p. 85. See also Samkange, *Origins of Rhodesia*, pp. 123–36.

45 Knutsford to Salisbury, 22 February 1888. SP Letter 193.

46 Queen Victoria to Lobengula, 26 March 1889, encl. in Knutsford to Robinson. c. 5918 (LI, 1890), p. 162.

47 Rhodes to Maund, 7 September 1889. NAR/MaP, Ma. 23/1/1.

48 See, for example, BSA Co. to Maund, 17 May 1889. NAR/CT 1/13/8.

49 Rhodes to Maund, 26 September 1889. NAR/MaP, Ma. 23/1/1.

50 Maund to Directors, Exploring Co., 11 June 1890. Maund MSS A. 77, fo. 46, Wits.

51 Rhodes to Cawston, 5 October 1889. NAR/RP, Rh. 1/1/4.

52 Mackenzie to Chamberlain, 8 July 1891. Mackenzie, *Life*, p. 457.

53 Mackenzie to CO, 1 August 1889. CO 879/30, p. 109 (No. 372).

54 Mackenzie to Knutsford, 10 July 1891. Mackenzie, *Life*, p. 453.

55 Quoted, *ibid.*, p. 455.

56 Mackenzie to CO, 24 January 1890. CO 879/32, pp. 4–5.

57 *Idem.*

58 Knutsford to Salisbury, 12 January 1889. SP Letter 183.

59 CO to Mackenzie, 13 August 1889. CO 879/30, p. 115.

60 Herbert to Mackenzie, 13 August 1889. Mackenzie MSS, Wits.

61 Lobengula to Queen Victoria, 23 April 1889. c. 5918 (LI, 1890), p. 201.

62 Quoted Lockhart and Woodhouse, *Rhodes*, p. 195.

63 Chamberlain to Grey (n.d.), 1889. Quoted Williams, *Rhodes*, p. 136.

64 Quoted Oliver, *Johnston*, pp. 154–5.

65 Knutsford to Salisbury, 12 January 1889. SP Letter 202.

66 See C. C. O'Brien, *Parnell and his Party, 1880–90* (Oxford, 1957), p. 266.

67 The Rhodes–Parnell correspondence, of June 1888, is printed in full, in 'Vindex', Appendix IV, pp. 839–59.

68 Knutsford to Salisbury, 12 January 1889, SP Letter 202.

69 Knutsford to Salisbury, 22 August 1890. SP Letter 304.

70 Salisbury to Knutsford, 10 January 1889. SP c. 70.

71 *Ibid.* SP B. 90.

72 For example Knutsford to Salisbury, 22 January 1889. SP Letter 186.

73 Knutsford to Salisbury, 12 January 1889. SP Letter 202. Also see Robinson and Gallagher, *Africa and the Victorians*, pp. 235–6.

74 Knutsford to Salisbury, 31 May 1889. SP Letter 208.

75 Min. by E. Fairfield, 8 January 1889. CO 417/27.

76 CO Mins., 10 January 1889 on Rhodes–Robinson–Shippard relationship – *ibid.* – on Robinson to Knutsford, 10 January 1889.

77 Min. by E. Fairfield, on Robinson to Knutsford, 6 January 1889, *ibid.*

78 I am much indebted to Dr A. Sillery for drawing my attention to the

Daily Chronicle article. It is also cited in his study of the Bechuanaland *Protectorate*, pp. 134–5.

79   Min. by Fairfield, 1 November 1893. CO 417/109. See also Sillery, *ibid.*, p. 135, n. 43.

80   Min. by Bramston, 10 November 1893, *ibid.*, p. 136, n. 44.

81   For Hofmeyr's ownership of BSA Co. shares, see Van der Poel, *Railway and Customs Policies*, pp. 170–6.

82   Rose-Innes, *Autobiography*, p. 87.

83   *Idem.* See also Davenport, *Afrikaner Bond*, pp. 132–4.

84   John Moffat to Shippard, encl. in Smyth to Knutsford, 10 April 1889. c. 5918 (LI, 1890), p. 217.

85   Grey to Mackenzie, 11 July 1889. Mackenzie MSS, Wits., and Mackenzie, *Life*, p. 435.

86   Comment by Cawston (in London), recorded in Mackenzie, *Life*, p. 433.

87   *The Times*, 15 October 1889; the BSA Company would 'be able to draw into their nets most of what is worth having in Central Africa'. Quoted *CHBE*, III, p. 168.

88   Knutsford to Salisbury, 12 January 1889. SP Letter 183.

89   *Idem.*

90   Knutsford to Salisbury, 1 May 1889, *ibid.*

91   Quoted, Lockhart and Woodhouse, *Rhodes*, p. 20.

92   *Idem.*

93   See, for examples, Knutsford Min. 5 March 1889 on the merits of the charter system – CO 417/28 – and Knutsford to Salisbury celebrating the grant of the charter to the BSA Co. consortium. SP Letter 254.

94   Milner to Mackenzie, 20 June 1889. Mackenzie MSS.

95   Knutsford Min., 5 March 1889. CO 417/30.

96   Robinson to Knutsford, 27 February 1889, *ibid.*

97   Knutsford Min., 6 March 1889, *ibid.*

98   CO Mins., 7 May 1889, *ibid.*

99   Gifford to CO, 30 April 1889, c. 5918 (LI, 1890), p. 189 *passim.*

100   Rhodes, *et al.*, to CO, 30 April 1889. CO 879/30, p. 66 (No. 372).

101   Knutsford to Salisbury, 1 May 1889. SP Letter 202.

102   Herbert Min., 7 May 1889. CO 417/31.

103   CO to FO, 16 May 1889. CO 879/30, p. 71 (No. 372).

104   *Ibid.*, see also c. 5918 (LI, 1890), p. 192.

105   Gifford to CO, 19 June 1889. CO 879/30, pp. 87–92.

106   See c. 5918 (LI, 1890), p. 192.

107   FO to CO, 27 May 1889. CO 879/30, pp. 87–92.

108   CO to Rhodes, 20 June 1889. c. 5918 (LI, 1890), p. 207.

109   Rhodes to CO (encl. Maguire letter), 21 June 1889. CO 879/30, p. 93.

110   *Ibid.*, also c. 5918 (LI, 1890), pp. 207–8.

111   Knutsford to Ponsonby, 11 July 1889. *LQV*, p. 512.

112   FO to CO, 27 May 1889. CO 879/30, p. 77.

113   Rhodes to CO, 1 June 1889, *ibid.*, p. 79.
114   CO to FO, 4 June 1889. C. 5918 (LI, 1890), p. 195.
115   CO to Rhodes, 14 June 1889. CO 879/30, p. 86.
116   *Ibid.*, 28 June 1889, p. 95.
117   Salisbury was later to speak in the City of the chartered companies as those 'great associations . . . for the purpose of pushing forward the civilisation of Africa' (9 November 1889). See *CHBE*, III, 168.
118   CO to FO, 28 June 1889, *ibid.*, 97; see also C. 5918 (LI, 1890), p. 210.
119   Min. by Sir R. Herbert, 8 July 1889. CO 417/36.
120   *Idem.*
121   FO Min. 11 July 1889. FO 84/1999.
122   Salisbury to Lakes Co., 8 July 1889, *Ibid.*
123   Currie to Herbert, 10 July, 'Private', 1889, *ibid.*
124   CO to Exploring Company, 10 July 1889. CO 879/30, No. 371, pp. 103–4.
125   Herbert to Currie, 'Private', 9 July 1889. FO 84/1999.
126   FO Min., on the Rhodes visit, 11 July 1889, *ibid.*
127   *Idem.*
128   See Rhodes–Herbert correspondence of July–Aug. 1889. CO 417/37.
129   Draft of Charter for Crown Lawyers and Council, 27 July 1889, *ibid.*
130   Final draft, 29 August 1889. FO 84/2002.
131   FO to CO, 13 August 1889. CO 417/37.
132   FO to CO, 20 August 1889. FO 84/2002.
133   See CO to Gifford, 22 October 1889. CO 879/30, No. 372, p. 223.
134   Knutsford to Loch, 14 November 1889, *ibid.*, p. 156. The charter as forwarded to Loch, in C. 5918 (LI, 1890), pp. 635–40.
135   *Idem.*
136   Knutsford to Lobengula, 15 November 1889. CO 879/30, p. 233. See also Knutsford to Lobengula, 10 September 1890. NAR/MP, Mo. 1/1/4, fo. 411B.
137   Duke of Abercorn to Lord Knutsford, 6 November 1889, encl. draft of CO to Lobengula. CO 417/37.
138   *Ibid.*, with Knutsford's corrections. Printed in C. 5918 (LI, 1890), p. 233.
139   Loch to Lobengula, 2 April 1891. NAR/MOP, Mo. 1/1/4, fo. 510.
140   Mackenzie to CO, 1 August 1889. CO 879/30, p. 109.
141   Knutsford Min., 28 August 1889. CO 417/32.
142   Min., and sketch by Fairfield, 8 November 1889. CO 317/37.
143   Milner to Asquith, 18 November 1897. C. Headlam, (ed.), *The Milner Papers*; *South Africa, 1897–8* (London, 1931), i, p. 178.

CHAPTER 9

1   Ripon to Asquith, 29 December 1897. Quoted Saunders, 'Annexation of the Transkei', p. 314.
2   See *OHSA*, II, pp. 278–81.

3 Galbraith, *Crown and charter* (*op. cit.*), pp. 128–53, 255–309.

4 *Ibid.*, p. 153. Also, Bryce, *Impressions of South Africa* (1900), ch. 17.

5 Reported in Jameson to Harris, 1 November 1889. Brown, 'Aspects of the Scramble in the Matabeleland', p. 87.

6 Harris to Hepburn, 17 January 1890. NAR/CT, 2/11/1. Also Brown, *ibid.*, pp. 89–90.

7 Jameson to Harris, 17 July 1893. RHL MSS Afr. s. 228.

8 Jameson to brother (Sam), 4 October 1893. NAR/JP, Ja. 1/1, fo. 109.

9 Grey to (?), 15 October 1893. NAR/GP, Gr. 1/1/1, fo. 1.

10 Fairfield Min., 4 January 1889. CO 417/38.

11 Ripon to Gladstone, 4 November 1893. GP 44287, fos. 172–4.

12 Milner to Chamberlain, 1 December 1897. *Milner Papers*, I, p. 141.

13 Fairfield Min., 27 September 1892. CO 417/80.

14 Best set out in Galbraith, 'Origins of the BSA Company', pp. 166–71.

15 *Truth*, 23 April 1891.

16 'Memd. on Origins of Operations of the British South Africa Company'. CO 879/34, Confidential Print No. 439.

17 *Ibid.*, pp. 9–10.

18 *Ibid.*, p. 10.

19 *Ibid.*, p. 11. A/80. CO 366/92.

20 *Idem.*

21 *Idem.*

22 Harcourt to Gladstone (copy), 7 November 1893. GP 44203, fos. 126–7.

23 CO 879/38, Confidential Print No. 439, pp. 29–31.

24 Rhodes need not have feared. The cabinet, led by Gladstone, dreaded the prospect of a Matabeleland 'protectorate'. See Ripon to Loch, 'Confidential', 10 November 1893. RP 43562, fo. 46.

25 BSA Co. to CO encl. Rhodes to BSA Co., 2 November 1893. CO 417/110.

26 Ripon desired that the BSA Co. only be given control of Matabeleland once they had 'turned Mashonaland to best account'. Ripon to Meade, 'Private', 8 October 1893. Ri. P. 43557, fo. 72.

27 'Instructions' to Loch, 4 November 1889. CO 879/31, p. 2.

28 *Idem.*

29 Ripon to Loch, 'Private', 27 October 1893 (copy), Ri. P. 43526, fo. 31.

30 Knutsford to Salisbury, 2 March 1891. SP Letter 340.

31 Knutsford to Queen Victoria, 13 November 1889. *LQV*, p. 533.

32 Knutsford to Salisbury, 9 November 1889. SP Letter 254.

33 Lippert Concession, NAR/LP, Lo 1/2/5.

34 Loch to Moffat, 20 June 1891. NAR/MoP, Mo. 1/1/4, fo. 525.

35 Loch to Moffat, 4 August 1889, *ibid.*, fo. 530.

36 Loch to Moffat, 12 September 1891, *ibid.*, 'Confidential', fo. 545.

37 *Hansard* (4), xxx, col. 701, 14 February 1895.

38 Milner to Mackenzie (n.d.), 1889, in Mackenzie, *Life*, p. 433.

39 For an expert and comprehensive account, J. E. Butler, *The Liberal Party and the Jameson Raid* (Oxford, 1968).

40 Harcourt to Chamberlain, 12 June 1897. JC 5/38/108, cited in Butler, *ibid.*, p. 2.

41 Ripon to Rosebery, 12 May 1894. Ri. P. 43526, fo. 110.

42 Rhodes to Hawksely, 25 May 1889. NAR/RP, Rh. 1/1/1, fo. 340.

43 Ripon to Rosebery, 5 September 1894 (copy). Ri. P. 43516, fos. 148–9.

44 Milner to Selborne, 2 June 1897. *Milner Papers*, I, pp. 105–6.

45 *Hansard* (4), xxx, col. 701 (14 February 1895).

46 Brookes and Webb, *History of Natal*, pp. 146–88; and Marks, *Reluctant Rebellion*, pp. 104–7.

47 Derby to Granville, 1 April 1885. GP 44142 fo. 122.

48 See Proclamation, 14 May 1887. Havelock to Holland. C. 5143 (LXI, 1887), p. 50.

49 *Ibid.*, p. 782.

50 FO to CO, 28 August 1885, CO 179/162. Havelock to Stanhope, 22 October, 2/27 November 1886, C. 4980 (LXI, 1887), pp. 301, 36–7. The New Republic's independence ended in 1888, when it was absorbed by the Transvaal, being returned to Natal in 1902. C. 5331 (LXXV, 1888), p. 35 for treaty of 'union' with Transvaal of 19 September 1887.

51 Marks, *Reluctant Rebellion*, pp. 91–116.

52 *OHSA*, II, 261–7; Marks, *Reluctant Rebellion*, pp. 92–3; Binns, *Dinuzulu*, p. 117 *passim*; Morris, *Washing of the Spears*, p. 609 *passim*.

53 Marks, *Reluctant Rebellion*, p. 93.

54 Gibson, *Story of the Zulu*, p. 276.

55 Binns, *Dinuzulu*, pp. 92–3.

56 Marks, *Reluctant Rebellion*, pp. 102–3; Brookes and Webb, *History of Natal*, pp. 181–8; Robinson and Gallagher, *Africa and the Victorians*, pp. 215–17.

57 Quoted Marks, *Reluctant Rebellion*, p. 109.

58 *NNABB*, 1895, p. 71; and 1896, p. 68.

59 Theal, *History of South Africa*, XI, p. 28.

60 Min. by Fairfield, July 1885. CO 417/6.

61 Brookes and Webb, *History of Natal*, p. 186.

62 Min. by Herbert, 13 December 1886. CO 417/12. Saunders, 'Annexation of the Transkei', p. 401.

63 Theal, *History of South Africa*, X, 218–23; *OHSA*, II, pp. 271–81; Saunders, 'Annexation of Transkei', pp. 401–33; and Stanford MSS, University of Cape Town Library, Cape Town.

64 *DSAB*, I, 722–3.

65 Theal, *History of South Africa*, p. 230.

66 Sigcawu to Knutsford, 13 November 1888. CO 417/26. Also Saunders, 'Annexation of Transkei', p. 408.

67 Knutsford to Loch, 4 February 1892. CO 417/68.

68 Loch to Knutsford, 28 November 1893. CO 417/154.

69 Saunders, 'Annexation of the Transkei', p. 428.
70 Rev. Oxley-Oxland to Sec. of Native Affairs, 1 January 1880. G. 13-'80, p. 162.
71 Theal, *History of South Africa*, x, 220.
72 Stanford to wife, 27 February 1884. Stanford MSS F(s) 8.
73 Stanford, 'Diary of Annexation of Pondoland', F(s), p. 13.
74 Stanford, *Reminiscences*, II, pp. 155, 157.
75 Saunders, 'Annexation of the Transkei', p. 430, n. 4.
76 H. Kuper, *African Aristocracy* (London, 1947), p. 24. Also B. A. Marwick, *The Swazi* (London, 1966), pp. 1–5.
77 *OHSA*, II, p. 275 *passim*.
78 J. S. M. Matsebula, *A History of Swaziland* (Johannesburg, 1972), p. 22.
79 *Ibid.*, p. 25.
80 *OHSA*, II, pp. 275–6.
81 Matsebula, *History of Swaziland*, p. 29.
82 *Ibid.*, p. 32.
83 Rev. C. C. Watts quoted in *ibid.*, p. 38.
84 Kuper, *African Aristocracy*, p. 25.
85 *Idem.*
86 Lord Hailey, *African Survey* (Oxford, 1938), p. 729.
87 *OHSA*, II, 276.
88 Kuper, *African Aristocracy*, p. 24.
89 *Ibid.*, p. 25; and N. G. Garson's excellent dissertation, 'The Swaziland Question and a Road to the Sea, 1887–95', *AYB*, 1947, p. 349.
90 Mbandzeni to Natal governor, 16 April 1888. Quoted Matsebula, *History of Swaziland*, p. 46.
91 *Ibid.*, p. 47.
92 *Inkanyeso*, 10 May 1885.
93 Knutsford to Salisbury, 21 December 1887, SP Letter 103 (Knutsford file).
94 *Idem.*
95 Bower MSS, 'Memoir', fos. 174–6.
96 *Idem.*
97 Fairfield Min., 8 July 1885; on Robinson to Derby, 17 June 1885. CO 417/5.
98 Knutsford to Salisbury, 28 January 1889. SP Letters file (Knutsford).
99 Hailey, *Native Administration in the British African Territories* (London, 1953), pt V, pp. 366–7.
100 For an excellent summary of the 'bargain' and the Transvaal terms, see C. 6200 (LII, 1890), p. 135 *passim*. For Hofmeyr's working documents in negotiating the Convention, see SAL/HP, vol. 10, notes, letters and Agreement.
101 See Garson, 'The Swaziland Question', p. 320 *passim*; also *OHSA*, II, 275–8, and Davenport, *Afrikaner Bond*, ch. 8.
102 Matsebula, *History of Swaziland*, p. 72.
103 Hofmeyr, *Hofmeyr*, p. 406.

104 Davenport, *Afrikaner Bond*, p. 129.

105 Davenport, *Afrikaner Bond*, p. 355 (n. for p. 130).

106 Hofmeyr, *Hofmeyr*, p. 404.

107 Matsebula, *History of Swaziland*, p. 72.

108 Bower MS, 'Memoir', fos. 176–7.

109 See Garson, 'Swaziland Question', p. 321, *passim*.

110 Knutsford was himself not altogether convinced of the rectitude of handing the Swazi over to the Transvaal and, on 18 March 1890, remarked to Salisbury that he thought he did not think 'that any part of Swaziland should become [the] territory of [the] S. African Republic', as 'only strips of land along the railway are desired'. See Knutsford to Salisbury, 18 March 1890. SP Letter 268 (Knutsford file). The idea had also been toyed with, and dropped by Salisbury and Knutsford, in 1891; see SP. Letter 370, 371 (Knutsford file) for correspondence of September 1891.

111 British terms for a new Convention are in Ripon to Loch, 1 December 1892. Ri.P. 43561, fos. 26–31.

112 Knutsford to Salisbury, 15 November 1893. SP Letter 424 (Knutsford file).

113 The permanent under-secretary at the CO, Sir Robert Herbert, spoke of the Swazi 'independence' in the Convention as being regarded in a 'Pickwickian sense'. Quoted in Fairfield to Ripon, 17 October 1892. Ri.P. 43538 fo. 159.

114 See Ripon to Kimberley (copy), 15 May 1894, stressing the need to come to an agreement with the Transvaal – Ri.P. 43526 fo. 190 – and see also Garson, 'Swaziland Question', p. 417 *passim*.

115 Knutsford to Salisbury, 15 November 1893. SP Letter 424 (Knutsford file).

116 Ripon was far more concerned over the latent dangers of the position on the spot. In particular, he dreaded that disorder in Swaziland would provide the Transvaal with a ready excuse to intervene in the cause of peace. See Ripon to Kimberley (copy), 26 August 1894. Ri.P. 43526 fo. 209.

117 Knutsford to Salisbury, 15 November 1893. SP Letter 424 (Knutsford file).

118 Ripon to Rosebury, 4 September 1894, in Wolf, *Ripon*, ii, p. 224.

119 Ripon to Kimberley (copy), 15 March 1895. Ri.P. 43527 fo. 48.

120 Ripon to Kimberley (copy), 4 September 1894. Ri.P. 43526 fo. 217.

121 See c. 7611 (LXII, 1895), p. 25 *passim*, and esp. pp. 93–6.

122 *Inkanyeso*, 10 May 1895.

123 Ripon to Kimberley (copy), 16 May 1894. Ri.P. 43526 fos. 188–9.

124 Ripon to Roseberry, 'Private' (Copy), 4 September 1894, Ri.P. 43526 fos. 218–21. See also c. 7611 (LXII, 1895), pp. 17–21. Ripon–Loch correspondence; Wolf, *Ripon*, ii, pp. 222–6, and Ripon to Loch, 'Private' (copy), tel. in cypher, 16 June 1893, Ri.P. 43561 fo. 179.

125 Ripon to Rosebery, 4 September 1894. Ri.P. 43526 fos. 218–21; see also Ripon to Loch, 'Private', 30 May 1894; *ibid*. fo. 134.

126 *Ibid*. In agreeing to allow the Transvaal into Swaziland it is interesting that Lord Kimberley, an advocate of the firm policy of British supremacy in

South Africa, should *support* Ripon. See Kimberley to Ripon ('Private'),
6 September 1894. Ri.P. 43526 fo. 222.

127   Matsebula, *History of Swaziland*, p. 77.
128   Kuper, *African Aristocracy*, p. 28.
129   *OHSA*, II, p. 278.
130   Kuper, *African Aristocracy*, p. 28.
131   Loch quoted in Matsebula, *History of Swaziland*, p. 77.

CHAPTER 10

1   These struggles for Delagoa Bay, 1890–95, are superbly narrated in P. R.
Warhurst, *Anglo-Portuguese Relations in South-Central Africa* (London,
1962), see esp. chs. 1–4.
2   Salisbury to Castledown, 11 October 1890. SP 412/484.
3   See Marais, *Fall of Kruger's Republic*, p. 47.
4   Van der Poel, *Railway and Customs*, pp. 53–4.
5   See Rhodes' statement of 16 February 1897 before Jameson Raid Enquiry:
Butler, *Jameson Raid*, p. 179, and van der Poel, *Jameson Raid*, p. 157 *passim*.
6   See Marais, *Fall of Kruger's Republic*, p. 48; and *Grosse Politik*, XI, 5–7.
7   Butler, 'German Factor . . .', p. 192.
8   Williams, *Rhodes*, p. 198 *passim*.
9   Lovell, *Struggle for South Africa*, p. 222.
10   For German support of Portugal, see Marais, *Fall of Kruger's Republic*, pp.
47–8; and van Winter, *Kruger's Hollanders*, II, 230 *passim*.
11   For Rhodes' attitude to the Salisbury policy, the royal charter and the
Anglo-German Agreement of 1890, see Warhurst, *Anglo-Portuguese Relations*,
p. 100. *passim*.
12   Here Rhodes was not alone: the British Foreign Office seriously considered
offering Paul Kruger a GCMG in 1895, to acquire his assistance in settling
outstanding difficulties, notably re: Swaziland, and the *uitlanders*. See
Ripon–Kimberley correspondence of June 1895, in Ri.P. 43527 fo. 56
passim.
13   Nathan, *Kruger*, p. 291; and Warhurst, *Anglo-Portuguese Relations*, pp. 114–
15 for an alternate version.
14   Van Winter, *Kruger's Hollanders*, II, pp. 230–9.
15   Van der Poel, *Railway and Customs*, pp. 35–45.
16   Van der Poel, *ibid.*, pp. 81–2; Lockhart and Woodhouse, *Rhodes*, ch. 14; and
Warhurst, *op. cit.*, ch. 4.
17   See Fairfield's indictment of Rhodes' methods, in Fairfield to Ripon, 'Private',
16 October 1894. Ri.P. 43558 fos. 187–99.
18   Van der Poel, *Railway and Customs*, p. 54.
19   Expertly described in Warhurst, *Anglo-Portuguese Relations*, ch. III.
20   *Ibid.*, pp. 56–72 for graphic description of the affair.
21   Salisbury to Granby, 23 May 1891. Cecil, *Salisbury*, IV, p. 274.

22 On Portugal's refusal to sell the area, see Warhurst, *Anglo-Portuguese Relations*, pp. 118–19.

23 Lockhart and Woodhouse, *Rhodes*, p. 311 *passim*.

24 Van der Poel, *Railway and Customs*, p. 81.

25 Lockhart and Woodhouse, *Rhodes*, pp. 292–3. Hays Hammond was the engineer.

26 'Vindex', *Speeches*, pp. 226–7, 244–5, 272–3.

27 Warhurst, *Anglo-Portuguese Relations*, p. 46.

28 Knutsford to Merriman, 4 February 1892. SAL/MP 1892, and Lewson, *Merriman Correspondence*, II, 87.

29 Salisbury to H. Shepherd Cross, MP, 16 October 1890. SP 414/488.

30 Salisbury to Castledown, 11 October 1890. SP 412/484.

31 Salisbury to Arnold White, 15 February 1887. SP Letters, fo. 348.

32 Knutsford to Salisbury, 23 February 1887. SP Letter 23.

33 See Knutsford to Merriman, 'Private', 17 February 1892. SAL/MP 1892/73, and Lewson, *Merriman Correspondence*, II, 91–2.

34 Garson, 'Swaziland Question', p. 350 *passim*.

35 Ripon to Kimberley, 30 January 1895. Ri.P. 43727 fo. 32.

36 See Walker, *A History of Southern Africa*, p. 444.

37 Marais, *Fall of Kruger's Republic*, pp. 46–50, for an excellent summary of German ambitions.

38 Ripon to Rosebery, 7 June 1893. Ri.P. 43516 fo. 90; see also Wolf, *Ripon*, II, p. 231 *passim*.

39 The annexation is detailed in C, 7780 (LXXI, 1895), p. 25 *passim*. See also Ri.P. 43561, fos. 167–91.

40 See *The Times*, 30 April 1895, and the *Annual Register* (1895), p. 359.

41 Bower Memoir, Bower Papers, Afr. MSS. RHL, fos. 160–1.

42 Ripon to Loch, 7 November 1894, encl. in CO to FO, 7 December 1894, in Warhurst, *Anglo-Portuguese Relations*, pp. 131–2.

43 Ripon to Kimberley, 15 February 1895; Wolf, *Ripon*, II, p. 228; and Ri.P. 43527, fo. 32.

44 Ripon said as much in 1894; *ibid.*, II, pp. 232–4.

45 Fairfield to Ripon, 25 June, 1894. Ri.P. 43558, fos. 192–3.

46 Salisbury to Chamberlain, 'Private', 30 December 1895–JC 5/67 – cited by Louis, in Gifford and Louis, *Britain and Germany in Africa*, p. 24.

47 See Marais, *Fall of Kruger's Republic*, pp. 46–52.

48 Hatzfeld to Salisbury, early 1896, *ibid.*, p. 48.

49 See P. J. van Winter, *Onder Kruger's Hollanders* (2 vols., 1937–39), II, p. 236 *passim*.

50 Warhurst, *Anglo-Portuguese Relations*, p. 130 *passim*.

51 Kimberley to Ripon, 13 June 1895. Ri.P. 43527, fo. 54.

52 This is well set out in J. van der Poel, *The Jameson Raid* (London, 1951), p. 157 *passim*.

53   Memorandum by German foreign secretary, 1 February 1895; cited in
      Butler, 'German Factor', p. 194.
54   Figure cited in Lovell, *Struggle for S. Africa*, p. 347.
55   Great Britain soon complained of this German naval presence. Wolf, *Ripon*,
      II, p. 233. See also, Kimberley to Ripon, 14 January 1895, on matching the
      German naval strength. Ri.P. 43527, fo. 8.
56   This came as a considerable surprise to British officialdom in South Africa;
      they had long since become convinced that Great Britain's reluctant
      imperialism would passively let the Germans into the region when a trial of
      strength arrived. See, for example, Shippard to Moffat, 19 September 1887:
      'There is a general impression in Cape Town that Germany will obtain
      Delagoa Bay from Portugal and that the Transvaal will accept German
      protection in order to secure that harbour while at the same time Germany
      will secure Mashonaland, and Matabeleland . . . The prospect is very dis-
      heartening but we seem powerless to improve it. England appears to have no
      policy whatever in South Africa and only to be anxious to shirk responsibility
      and avoid expense'. NAR/MP, Mo 1/1/4, fos. 173–5.
57   Kimberley to Ripon, 31 December 1895. Ri.P. 43527, fos. 76–7.
58   Ripon to Kimberley, 25 November 1894. Ri.P. 43526, fo. 251 (my italics).
59   Kimberley to Ripon, 25 November 1894, *ibid.*, fos. 253–5.
60   In the late 1880s fears had also been raised over German interest in Delagoa
      Bay. The Cape agent-general, Sir Charles Mills, was convinced of the
      dangers of allowing Germany to move on the bay. Mills correspondence in
      Merriman Papers of September 1887 – November 1889, with Merriman
      and Robinson. SAL/MP, 1887–70, 1888/153, 1889–43.
61   Ripon to Kimberley, 'Confidential', 28 September 1894. Ri.P. 43526, fos.
      227–8 (my italics).
62   Ripon's opinion, cited in Wolf, *Ripon*, II, p. 231.
63   For the wider implications of this policy, see Warhurst, *Anglo-Portuguese
      Relations*, pp. 110–27.
64   Kimberley to Ripon, 19 October 1894. Ri.P. 43526, fo. 238.
65   Kimberley to Ripon, 'Private', 1 October 1894, reporting the sailing of the
      vessel, *ibid.*, fo. 236.
66   Kimberley to Ripon, 14 January 1895. Ri.P. 43527, fos. 8–9. Ripon agreed
      with Kimberley's argument. See Ripon to Kimberley, 15 January 1895, *ibid.*,
      fo. 10.
67   Kaiser's account of a conversation with Col. Swaine – *Grosse Politik*, XI,
      no. 2579 – cited in Lovell, *Struggle for S. Africa*, p. 354.
68   Brookes and Webb, *History of Natal*, pp. 187–8.
69   Lord Kimberley was extremely influential in pushing a hard line policy
      on the cabinet, and especially on Ripon. Kimberley greatly suspected
      German ambitions. See Kimberley to Ripon, 14 January 1895. Ri.P.
      43527, fo. 8.
70   See Ripon to Kimberley, 25 November 1894. Ri.P. 43526, fo. 250.

71 See Garson's valuable study, 'Swaziland Question', esp. p. 391 for his assessment of Ripon's motives.

72 Ripon to Kimberley, 25 November 1894. Ri.P. 43526 fo. 251.

73 See Kimberley to Ripon, 25 November 1894, *ibid.*

74 FO opinion of February 1895, cited in *Africa and the Victorians*, p. 420.

75 The Transvaal view is contained in W. J. Leyds, *The Transvaal Surrounded* (1919), p. 470 *passim.*

76 See *CHBE*, VIII, p. 541.

77 Butler, 'German factor . . .', pp. 192–3; also Langer, *Diplomacy of Imperialism*, p. 221.

78 The protest was made on 26 January 1895. See Butler, 'German factor . . .', p. 193.

79 *Ibid.*, citing denial of Marschal, German foreign ministry, on 1 February 1895.

80 Backeberg, 'Betrekkinge . . .', pp. 231–4.

81 In fairness to Kimberley, it should be noted that while he wished to be very firm with Germany in Southern Africa, he was eager to find a conciliatory agreement on all other areas of Anglo-German friction in Africa. See esp. Kimberley to Ripon, 23 March 1894. Ri.P. 43526, fo. 179.

82 Kimberley to Ripon, 13 January 1895. Ri.P. 43527, fo. 6 (my italics).

83 Ripon to Kimberley (copy), 30 January 1895. Ri.P. 43527, fo. 32.

84 Rosebery to Ripon, 'Secret', 5 January 1896. Ri.P. 43516, fo. 228.

85 From the Kaiser to Kruger, congratulating him on repulsing Jameson and his Raiders on 3 January 1896. See Langer, *Diplomacy of Imperialism*, p. 237; Marais, *Fall of Kruger's Republic*, p. 198 *passim*; and Grenville, *Lord Salisbury and Foreign Policy*, pp. 102–7.

86 Brookes and Webb, *History of Natal*, p. 188; and *OHSA*, II, p. 277. See also, Kimberley to Ripon, 8 January 1896. Ri.P. 43527, fos. 81–3, and C. 7780 (LXXI, 1895), p. 40 *passim*. The area was incorporated into Natal in 1897.

87 Min. by Fairfield, 20 December 1884 on Bulwer to Derby (tel.), 19 December 1884. CO 179/154.

88 Brookes and Webb, *History of Natal*, p. 188.

CONCLUSION

1 A similar thesis has, of course, already been advanced by Robinson and Gallagher in a revision of their original statement: *NCMH*, vol. XI, p. 593.

2 M. W. Flinn, *Origins of the industrial revolution* (London, 1966), pp. 103–4.

3 R. Taylor, *Lord Salisbury* (London, 1975), p. 177; and Salisbury in the Lords, on 'our capital that will rule' the South Africa of the future. *Hansard* (4), XXX, cols. 700–1.

4 Salisbury was also emphatic on the significance of British emigrants in the expansion of a free trade empire: 'I do not think Governments aid our people much when they go to the possession of a new territory – our people bring

with them such a power of initiative such an extraordinary courage and resource in the solving of new difficulties, that if they are pitted against an equal number – I care not what race it is, or what part of the world it is – and if you keep politics and negotiation off them, in a few years it will be our people that wil̸l be masters.' *Ibid.*

5   J. A. Hobson, *Imperialism: a study* (London, 1902), pp. 66–7.

6   Salisbury to Castledown 11 October 1890. SP 412/484.

7   Salisbury: 'We incur some little ridicule and no little discontent from our foreign friends for our peculiar action. They prefer to do anything officially – by action of bureaux, by order of the Sovereign of the State – but we have conducted almost all our enterprises in Africa through the agency of three great ⌈chartered⌉ companies.' Speech at Glasgow, reported in *The Times*, 21 May 1891.

8   Despite their reluctance to indulge in Scrambles for the world, it is clear that British statesmen *did* still worry greatly over the fact that the undeveloped portions of the globe could be locked up against Victorian England by other Great Powers, notably Powers who favoured protection in tariff policies. As Salisbury himself firmly stated, 'It is our business . . . to make smooth the paths of British commerce, British enterprise, the application of British capital, at a time when other paths, other outlets for commercial energies of our race are being gradually closed . . . by the enormous growth which the doctrines of Protection are obtaining . . . and ⌈which⌉ operate to the exclusion of British commerce wherever their power extends.' Salisbury in the Lords, 14 February 1895. *Hansard* (4), xxx, cols. 698–9. Also Cecil, *Salisbury*, IV, pp. 228–9.

9   See J. S. Marais, *The fall of Kruger's republic* (Oxford, 1961); J. Butler, *The Liberal party and the Jameson Raid* (*op. cit.*); and R. H. Wilde, 'Joseph Chamberlain and the South African Republic 1895–99' (*Archive Year Book for South Africa*, 1956). Also see J. A. S. Grenville, *Lord Salisbury & foreign policy* (London, 1964), p. 236 *passim.*

10   D. Denoon, *A grand illusion; the failure of imperial policy in the Transvaal colony during the period of reconstruction 1900–5* (London, 1973).

11   R. Hyam and G. Martin, *Reappraisals in British imperial history* (London, 1975), pp. 167–200.

12   R. Hyam, *The Failure of South African Expansion 1908–48* (London, 1972).

13   *OHSA*, II, pp. 301–13.

14   There is an admirable summary in N. G. Garson, 'British imperialism & the coming of the Anglo-Boer War', *South Africa Journal of Economics* xxx (1962).

15   See E. T. Stokes, 'Late nineteenth century colonial expansion and the attack on the theory of economic expansion: a case of mistaken identity?' *Historical Journal*, XII, 2 (1969).

16   See: G. Blainey, 'Lost causes of the Jameson Raid', *Economic History Review* (2nd ser.), XVIII, 1965; R. Kubicek, 'The Randlords in 1895: a reassessment',

Journal of British Studies, XI, 2 (1972); S. Trapido, 'South Africa in a comparative study of industrialisation', *Journal of Development Studies*, VII (1971); D. Denoon, *Southern Africa since 1800* (London, 1972) ch. 10; A. H. Duminy, *The capitalists and the outbreak of the Anglo-Boer War* (Durban, 1977); A Jeeves, 'The Rand capitalists and the coming of the South African War, 1896–9' (Paper presented to the Canadian Historical Association); I. R. Phimister, 'Rhodes, Rhodesia and the Rand', *Journal of Southern African Studies*, I, 1 (Oct. 1974); and J. S. Galbraith, *Crown and Charter: the early years of the British South Africa Company op. cit.*

17 Richard Shannon, *The crisis of imperialism* (London, 1974), pp. 323–37; and R. R. James, *The British Revolution; British politics, 1880–1939* (London, 1976), vol. I, pp. 167–95.

18 I am fully aware of the limitations of the Blainey thesis; in particular the difficulties of discriminating between 'deep level' capitalists and 'outcrop' capitalists. But it still seems to me striking that a financier like Beit, with widely spaced Rand investments, and with very close Rhodesian connections, should have 'invested' so heavily in the Raid.

19. R. C. K. Ensor provides a critical moral evaluation of Chamberlain's imperialism in his *England, 1870–1914* (Oxford, 1934), pp. 245–63.

20 Hyam, *Britain's imperial century*, p. 306.

21 Porter, *The Lion's Share* pp. 167–8.

22 PRO CAB 37/50, no. 70, 6 Sept. 1899: partially printed in K. Bourne, *The foreign policy of Victorian England, 1830—1902* (Oxford, 1970), pp. 460–1.

23 See Schreuder, *Gladstone and Kruger*, on Chamberlain and South Africa in the 1880s, pp. 29–31, 92–4, 324–6, 363, 428 *passim*.

24 Robinson and Gallagher, *Africa & the Victorians*, p. 429 *passim*.

25 Hyam, *Britain's imperial century*, pp. 293–318.

Select recommended bibliography

Full references to all footnotes are given above in the Notes to each chapter. In addition, those Notes included the basic texts introducing the major themes of this study, and they are cited at the opening of each chapter. The main manuscript sources used in this book, together with the published documentation, are listed in full at the front of this volume. This select recommended bibliography is accordingly designed to serve a different purpose: it indicates those works of general significance which a student of the Partition might pursue as either further reading, or as a major source for developing an understanding of particular aspects of the Scramble for Southern Africa. It also notes those studies which place a different interpretative or ideological interpretation on events than offered in this work of re-appraisal and conspectus.

I BASIC WORKING BIBLIOGRAPHIES

There are good general bibliographies of published source material on Southern African history in the nineteenth century in T. R. H. Davenport, *South Africa – a modern history* (1977); *The Oxford History of South Africa*, Monica Wilson and Leonard Thompson (eds.), 2 vols. (1966, 1969) which divide at 1870; C. F. J. Müller (ed.), *500 Years – a history of South Africa* (1969); and *The Cambridge History of the British Empire*, vol. VIII, Eric Walker (ed.) (1963), with a long bibliographic chapter by A. Taylor Milne and A. Lloyd, which includes British parliamentary papers in an annotated list. Leonard Thompson has published a useful guide to South African historical literature in R. W. Winks (ed.), *The historiography of the British Empire-Commonwealth* (1966) pp. 212–36, as well as a select bibliography of scholarly articles on *Southern African History before 1900* (1971), with R. Elphick and I. Jarrick; and D. M. Schreuder has offered a survey of the literature as at 1969 in 'History on the veld – towards a new dawn?' in *African Affairs* (April 1969).

The character of South African history was much debated with the publication of *The Oxford History of South Africa* in the later 1960s. See especially A. Atmore and N. Westlake, 'A liberal dilemma: a critique of the Oxford History of South Africa', in *Race*, XIV, 2 (1972), pp. 107–36; Shula Marks, 'Liberalism, social realities and South African history', *Journal of Commonwealth Political Studies*, x, (Nov. 1972), pp. 243–9; and B. S. Kantor and H. F. Kenny, 'The poverty of neo-marxism: the case of South Africa', *Journal of Southern African Studies*, Vol. 3, No. 1, 1976.

2 THE SCRAMBLE IN HISTORY: GENERAL SOURCES

Probably the earliest history of the Scramble was the almost contemporary work of J. S. Keltie, whose *Partition of Africa* was published in 1895. More recently it has been treated analytically in D. K. Fieldhouse, *Economics and Empire, 1815–1914* (1973) and D. C. M. Platt, *Finance, trade and politics in British foreign policy, 1815–1914* (1968). For Southern Africa, the early works of significance are: G. M. Theal, *History of South Africa* (1919), vols. IX and X; and Eric Walker, *A History of South Africa* (1962; 1st edn. 1928). The pioneer analysis of the Scramble year is to be found in R.I. Lovell, *The struggle for South Africa* (1934), which has a strong materialistic–deterministic bias: and in the pre-War work of C. W. de Kiewiet, which first established the degree to which the Scramble was here also a struggle for human resources – notably in *The imperial factor in South Africa: a study in politics and economics* (1937).

Several recent studies have provided valuable general perspectives, from very different ideological bases, of the period of the Partition in Southern African history. Donald Denoon's lively *Southern Africa since 1800* (1972) is excellent in posing challenging new views about the motivation and character of the Scramble; T. R. H. Davenport has provided the best overall perspective of the Partition in his *South Africa – a modern history* (*op. cit.*), section III, pp. 97–172; Leonard Thompson has written two concise and luminous chapters on the age of imperialism in late-nineteenth century South Africa in the *Oxford History*, vol. II, where he incisively captures the meaning of the Scramble for the peoples of the region; and John Benyon has accomplished a triumph of compression and analysis in his study of 'The process of political incorporation' for the tribesmen, up to 1910, in W. D. Hammond Tooke (ed.), *The Bantu-speaking peoples of Southern Africa* (1974) pp. 367–96.

A special issue of the *Journal of Imperial and Commonwealth History* (no. III, Oct. 1974) contained important articles on the Partition of Africa. Two are of notable use here: Alan Sanderson has given us an excellent critical assessment of the general literature for the whole continent; and Anthony Atmore and Shula Marks have written a revisionist essay, of great vitality and power, which is indispensible for further examination of the Scramble on the veld – 'The imperial factor in South Africa in the nineteenth century: towards a reassessment', pp. 106–39, and which has been of great value to me.

The drama and impact of the politics of African partition south of the Zambesi is still first best approached through the celebrated, and controversial study, by Ronald Robinson and Jack Gallagher, *Africa and the Victorians: the official mind of imperialism* (1961). There is a most useful commentary on the debate set in motion by the Cambridge historians in W. R. Louis, *Imperialism: the Robinson–Gallagher controversy* (1976), which has an extensive bibliography. The most trenchant single criticism of the Robinson–Gallagher controversy is still Ronald Hyam's essay, 'The Partition of Africa', a revised version of which has been published in R. Hyam and Ged Martin, *Reappraisals in British imperial history* (1975).

N. G. Garson's review article on 'British imperialism and the coming of the Anglo-Boer War', in the *South African Journal of Economics* (1962), is of great value in discussing British interests generally in the region; and John Benyon's study of 'The Cape high Commission: another neglected factor in British imperial expansion', *South African Historical Journal*, 5 (1973), pp. 28–40, provides an inside account of the 'sub-imperial' forces of empire developed by the local British settlement societies.

3 FRONTIER AND PARTITION

The period of the 1870s and 1880s was clearly crucial for bringing-on a full-scale Scramble for Southern Africa. Two works revise the shrewd initial ideas of de Kiewiet: C. F. Goodfellow, *Great Britain and South African confederation, 1871–84* (1961) is a first-rate analysis of a critical period for British policy and concludes with a challenging psycho-historical view of imperialism; and D. M. Schreuder, *Gladstone and Kruger: Liberal Government and colonial 'home rule', 1880–85* (1969) which offers a new interpretative view of the inter-play of British imperialism and Afrikaner nationalism.

For a more general study towards understanding the forces of instability on the South African frontier see: C. C. Saunders (ed.), *Beyond the Cape frontier* (1974); I. D. MacCrone, *Race attitudes in South Africa*, esp. part I (1937); W. B. Campbell, *The South African frontier, 1865–85*, *Archives Year Book for South African History* (1959); S. D. Neumark, *Economic influences on the South African frontier, 1652–1836* (1957); J. S. Galbraith, *Reluctant empire: British policy on the South African frontier, 1834–54* (1963); W. M. MacMillan, *Bantu, Boer and Briton* (2nd edn. 1963); H. M. Robertson, '150 Years of economic contact between black and white', *South African Journal of Economics* II, (1934) and III (1935); Martin Legassick, 'The Frontier tradition in South Africa', a revision of MacCrone, in *London University Seminar Papers, South Africa*, no. 12 (1970–71); Sir Keith Hancock, 'Trek', in *Economic History Review*, x (1958); H. J. and R. E. Simons, *Class and Colour in South Africa, 1850–1950* (1969), esp. pp. 11–72; Richard Elphick, *Kraal and Castle: Khoikhoi and the founding of white South Africa* (1977); and D. M. Schreuder, 'The cultural factor in Victorian imperialism – a case study in the "civilizing mission"', on the Cape frontier 1870–84, in *The Journal of Imperial and Commonwealth History*, IV, no. 3 (May, 1976), pp. 283–317; and Leonard Thompson, on the comparative character of South Africa as a colonial region of settlement – frontier in Louis Hartz' innovative and controversial work, *The Founding of new societies* (1964), pp. 178–218. Christopher Saunders' important thesis on 'The annexation of the Transkei', is now published in the *AYB*.

4 EXPANSION BY REGION

Although the Scramble for Southern Africa was a cumulative, and total experience for the whole region, it is perhaps most easily understood in its regional components. First-rate maps of this expansion can be found in T. R. H. Davenport and Keith Hunt, *The right to the land* (1974).

Cape expansion can be best traced in Saunders, *Beyond the Cape Frontier* (*op. cit.*) and J. A. Benyon, 'The Cape high commission . . .' (*op. cit.*); Anthony Atmore, 'Moorosi's rebellion' in colonial Basutoland, in Robert Rotberg and A. A. Mazrui, *Protest and Power in Black Africa* (1970); J. A. I. Agar Hamilton, *The Road to the North* (1937), into south-central Africa; A Sillery, *Founding a Protectorate* (Botswana) (1965); A Holmberg, *African tribes and European agencies* (1966) part I; and Anthony Dachs, 'Missionary imperialism: the case of Bechuanaland', *Journal of African History*, XIII (4) 1972, pp. 647–58; Leonard Thompson, *Survival in two worlds . . . 1786–1870* (1975) a classic study of Moshweshwe of Lesotho; T. R. H. Davenport, *The Afrikaner Bond* (1966), chapters 5–8 on Bechuanaland and the Transkei; Colin Bundy, 'The emergence and decline of a South African peasantry', *African Affairs*, vol. 71 (Oct. 1972) pp. 369–88; Ruth Edgecombe, 'The Glen Grey Act: local origins of an abortive "Bill for Africa"', in J. A. Benyon et al. (eds.), *Studies in Local History: essays in honour of Winifred A. Maxwell* (1976), pp. 89–98; and for those who can manage Afrikaans, W. J. de Kock has written a learned and very well documented account of Cape expansionism – *Ekstra-territoriale vraagstukke van die Kaapse regereing, 1872–85, Archives Year Book for South African History* (1948), vol. I.

The impact of the South-west African Question on Cape/British policy in the 1880s can be traced in a number of works: W. O. Aydelotte's pioneer study is still the place to begin – *Bismarck and British colonial policy: the problem of South-west Africa, 1883–5* (1937). A. J. P. Taylor has, not so surprisingly, written the most controversial account in his *Germany's First Bid for Colonies, 1884–5* (1938), and which has been persuasively rebutted by H. A. Turner, 'Bismarck's colonial policy – anti-British in origin?', in P. Gifford and W. R. Louis (eds.), *Britain and Germany in Africa* (1967). Good local accounts of the Angra Pequena affair will be found in: J. H. Esterhuyse, *South-west Africa, 1880–94* (1968) and H. Bley, *German South-west Africa* (1971). The international dimension of German overseas expansion is best approached through the work of Hans-Ulrich Wehler, *Bismarck und der Imperialismus* (Koln/Berlin, 1969), and his 'Bismarck's Imperialism, 1862–90', in *Past and Present* (1970), vol. 48, pp. 119–55; together with the trenchant criticism of that view in Paul Kennedy, 'German colonial expansion: has the "manipulated social imperialism" been ante-dated?', *Past and Present* (1972), vol. 54, pp. 134–41, and 'Bismarck's imperialism: the case of Samao, 1880–90', *Historical Journal*, XV (1972), pp. 261–83. Also valuable are W. O. Henderson, *Studies in German colonial history* (1962), M. E. Chamberlain, *The rise and fall of Germany's colonial empire* (1930), H. Pogge von Strandmann, 'The domestic origins of Germany's colonial expansion under Bismarck', *Past and Present* (Feb. 1969), pp. 140–59, and W. R. Louis, 'Great Britain and German expansion in Africa, 1884–1919', in

Gifford ·and Louis (eds.), *Britain and Germany in Africa (op. cit.)*. There is a valuable bibliography of the subject, as at 1967, by Alison Smith and H. Pogge von Strandmann, in Gifford and Louis (eds.), *ibid.*

Natal–Zulu relations were notably tangled and only recently have they been partially untangled. Edgar Brookes and Colin de B. Webb have written a general *History of Natal* (1965) which is clear on narrative; and Webb has provided a useful reassessment of the critical early 1880s in 'Great Britain and the Zulu people, 1879–87', in L. M. Thompson (ed.), *African societies in Southern Africa* (1969), pp. 302–24. The best account of Zulu history is to be found in a remarkable chapter of background synthesis in Shula Marks, *Reluctant rebellion: the 1906–8 disturbances in Natal* (1970). There is an outstanding analysis of the Shepstone era in Natal in David Welsh, *The roots of segregation: Native policy in colonial Natal, 1845–1910* (1971); and R. L. Cope has written a most incisive account of 'Shepstone, the Zulu and the annexation of the Transvaal', in *The South African Historical Journal*, 4 (1972), pp. 45–63. Henry Slater has opened up a new dimension of the·issue of white expansion in south-east Africa, in his 'Land, labour and capital in Natal . . . 1860–1948', *Journal of African History*, XVI (1975), pp. 257–83. There is a first-rate, popular account of the fall of the Zulu kingdom in Donald Morris, *The washing of the spears* (1964).

Transvaal expansion is much less studied. The major work is by N. G. Garson, *The Swaziland question and a road to the sea, 1887–95*, in *The Archives Year Book for South African History* (1957) vol. II, which is broader in its treatment than the title suggests. See also: M. C. Van Zyl, 'States and colonies in South Africa, 1854–1902', In Muller, *500 Years* (1969), pp. 259–88; C. T. Gordon, *The growth of Boer opposition to Kruger* (1970); Jeffrey Butler, 'The German factor in Anglo-Transvaal relations', in Gifford and Louis, *Britain and Germany in Africa (op. cit.)*, pp. 179–214; J. S. M. Matsebula, *A History of Swaziland* (1972); J. A. I. Agar Hamilton, *The native policy of the Voortrekkers* (1928); K. W. Smith, 'The fall of the BaPedi of the north-east Transvaal', *Journal of African History*, x, 2 (1969), pp. 237–52; C. J. Uys, *In the era of Shepstone* (1933); H. Kuper, *An African aristocracy* (The Swazi) (1947); D. M. Schreuder, *Gladstone and Kruger, (op. cit.)*; There is an intriguing 'contemporary account' of this theme in John Nixon, *The complete story of the Transvaal* (1885; reprinted 1972). A very different emphasis is given in the important new work of Stanley Trapido, 'Landlord and tenant in a colonial economy: the Transvaal, 1880–1910', *Journal of Southern African Studies*, vol. 5 (Oct. 1978) no. 1, published after completion of this study.

The massive chartered company thrust in south-central Africa has attracted a great deal of attention. Much of this new work has been drawn together in J. S. Galbraith, *Crown and charter; the early years of the British South African company* (1974), which has an extensive bibliography. But see also: P. Mason, *The birth of a dilemma; the conquest and settlement of Rhodesia* (1958); S. Samkange, *The origins of Rhodesia* (1968), A. J. Wills, *An introduction to the history of Central Africa* (1964) which is much more than an introduction. Robin Palmer has written definitively on *Land and racial domination in Rhodesia* (1977), with a most comprehensive bibliography of Rhodesian history. The collected volume of essays edited by Eric Stokes and Richard Brown, *The Zambesia Past* (1966) has much to say on the politics of the Partition. T. O. Ranger has written a noted account of African reactions to the white conquest in his *Revolt in Southern Rhodesia* (1967). Challenging new research by younger scholars is also of much interest: John M. Mackenzie, 'African labour in the Chartered company period', *Rhodesian History* (1970) pp. 43–58; J. R. D. Cobbing, 'Lobengula, Jameson and the occupation of Mashonaland', *Rhodesian History*, 4 (1973), pp. 39–56; P. Stigger, 'Volunteers and the profit motive in the Anglo-Ndebele war of 1893', *Rhodesian History*, 2 (1971), pp. 11–23; and a debate between Mackenzie and Charles van Onselen in *The Journal of Southern African Studies* (April and October 1975).

Critical commentary on the role of Rhodes in the period of high empire can be found in the new biography by John Flint (1976), in the work of Galbraith (*op. cit.*), and in I. R. Phimister, 'Rhodes, Rhodesia and the Rand', *Journal of Southern African Studies*, 1 (Oct. 1974).

The inter-relationship between British imperialism and Portuguese colonialism, as it affected the Partition in Central Africa, is superbly set out in the model monograph by P. R. Warhurst, *Anglo-Portuguese relations in south-central Africa, 1890–1900* (1962). See also, Lord Blake, *Rhodesia* (1977), J. Duffy, *Portuguese Africa* (1959) and *Portugal in Africa* (1961).

5 THE ADMINISTRATIVE POLITICS OF CONQUEST AND EXPLOITATION

The process by which the conquered African lands and societies were incorporated into the political and economic function of the colonies and republics of white settlement in the region is a subject of growing interest and attention. The best introduction to the theme is the shrewd, incisive account in Jack Simons, *African Women* (1968), pt. 1 of which expertly surveys the 'races policies' of colonial South African governments, both British and Boer. Edgar Brookes has chronicled the rise of those policies in his *White rule in South Africa* (revised edition 1975). Excellent work by David Welsh has shown what might be accomplished in this field: 'The cultural dimension of apartheid', *African Affairs*, vol. 71 (Jan. 1972), no. 282, pp. 35–53; and Martin Legassick has emphasised the British imperial factor in the emergence of segregationist practices, in an important seminar paper, 'The making of South African "native policy", 1903–23: the origins of segregation', *London University Seminar Papers* (15 Feb. 1972). T. R. H. Davenport's *The origins of urban segregation*, an 'occasional paper' for the Rhodes University Institute of Social and Economic Research, also expertly outlines nineteenth-century developments.

Political economy and colonialism is now a subject of fiercest contention in a voluminous and often acerbic literature. Readers here must hazard finding their own way. Leading views include: Ralph Horwitz, *The political economy of South Africa* (1967); D. Hobart Houghton, *The South African economy* (1973); and Sheila van der Horst, *Native labour in South Africa* (1942). See also useful articles of interpretation, in composite volumes, such as Richard Harris (ed.), *The political economy of Africa* (1975) with a notable article by M. Legassick; Adrian Leftwich, *South Africa: economic growth and political change* (1974) which contains N. Bromberger's answer to neo-marxian arguments; and H. Adam (ed.), *South Africa: sociological perspectives* (1971), which has P. van den Bergh on race segregation in historical dimension (pp. 37–49). Harold Wolpe has provided perhaps the best 'radical' interpretation of events in his 'Capitalism, and cheap labour in South Africa, from segregation to apartheid', *Economy and society*, I (1972), pp. 425–66; the most substantial non-marxian reply can be found in the thoughtful paper by David Yudelman, 'Industrialism, race relations and change in South Africa – an ideological and academic debate', *African Affairs*, vol. 74, no. 294 (Jan. 1975), pp. 82–96. Alan Jeeves has provided an important synoptic account of 'The control of migratory labour on the South African mines in the era of Kruger and Milner', in the *Journal of Southern African Studies*, II (Oct. 1975), pp. 3–29. The last word has not been said on the subject.

Much less recent scholarly effort has been expanded on understanding the 'non-modern' forces in South African history, not least Afrikaner politics. Four recent works have shown how significant is this lacuna: Herman Gilliomee, 'The development of the Afrikaner's self-concept', in H. W. van der Merwe (ed.), *Looking at the Afrikaner Today* (1975), pp. 1–39; Dunbar Moodie, *The rise of Afrikanerdom: power, apartheid and the Afrikaner civil religion* (1975); T. R. H. Davenport, 'Paul Kruger', *Encyclopedia Britannica* (1970 edn.) XIII, pp. 496–7; and D. W. Kruger, *Paul Kruger*, 2 vols. in Afrikaans (1961–2).

White settler politics could also stand revision, as is shown by the possibilities raised in J. L. MacCracken, *The Cape parliament, 1854–1910* (1967); and A. Keppel-Jones, 'A case of minority rule: the Cape colony, 1854–98', in *Canadian Historical Association Papers* (1966), pp. 98–114.

There is a pioneer and limited *Historical geography of South Africa* by N. C. Pollock and L. S. Agnew (1963), but it stands alone. There is no good genre of regional or provincial histories; and most major institutions of the colonial period are not written about, with the exception of Albie Sachs' account of the legal profession in his *Justice in South Africa* (1973), esp. pp. 17–122. Sheila van der Poel's *Railway and customs policies in South Africa* (1933) has remained a lonely pioneer work in a critical aspect of the growth of colonial South Africa. Bala Pillay's *British Indians in the Transvaal . . . 1885–1906* (1976), has filled an important gap in historiography. The innovative and important study of *The roots of rural poverty* (1977), Palmer & Parsons (eds.), should be read along with the penetrating critique by T. O. Ranger, 'Reflections on Peasant Research in Central and Southern Africa', *Journal of Southern African Studies* (5), I (Oct. 1978), both published since J finished this reappraisal.

6 TOWARDS THE CRISIS OF IMPERIALISM IN SOUTH AFRICA 1899–1902

If the Scramble decades established the triumph of the white man 1875–95, it was left to the decade immediately following to settle the unresolved issue of which whitemen were to be the masters of the region and its resources. Here, again, the literature is rather voluminous. Recent works, with good bibliographies or references, include: Jeffrey Butler, *The Liberal Party and the Jameson Raid* (1968), which excellently covers the high politics of empire; G. H. Le May, *British supremacy in South Africa, 1897–1907* (1965), which is concise and lively; J. S. Marais, *The fall of Kruger's republic* (1961), which will always be a point of reference; and R. H. Wilde, *Joseph Chamberlain and the South African Republic, 1895–99*, Archives Year Book of South African History (1956), which is capacious. Recent revisionist work of real importance is contained in Donald Denoon, *A grand illusion: the failure of Imperial policy in the Transvaal during the period of reconstruction, 1900–5* (1973), and A. A. Mawby's questioning of that view, in 'Capital, government and politics in the Transvaal 1900–7', *Historical Journal*, XVII (1974), pp. 387–415.

The best account of J. A. Hobson and imperialism can be found in Bernard Porter, *Critics of empire* (1968) and Peter Clarke, *Liberals and Social Democrats* (Cambridge, 1978), while essays of reappraisal by A. H. Duminy throw open the whole question of the origins of the South African war: *Sir Alfred Milner and the outbreak of the Anglo-Boer War* (1976), and *The capitalists and the outbreak of the Anglo-Boer War* (1977). A new book of importance is announced by R. V. Kubicek: *Economic imperialism in theory and practice – the case of the South African gold mining finance, 1886–1914* (1979). The early history of frontier South Africa will be much better understood with the publication of the collected work, *The shaping of South African society, 1652–1820* (Cape Town, 1979) edited by Richard Elphick and Hermann Gilliomee.

A finely balanced and acute account of this general period of crisis in empire and South African politics at the turn of the century is to be found in chapter 10 of Ronald Hyam's *Britain's Imperial century, 1815–1914* (1976); and the growing debate over interpreting the colonial history of South Africa is appraised and summarised in the critical historiographical 'essay' by H. M. Wright, *The burden of the present: liberal-radical controversy over South African history* (1977), which has a detailed bibliography.

Index